Royal Commission for the Paris Exhibition

Reports on the Paris Universal Exhibition

1867

Royal Commission for the Paris Exhibition

Reports on the Paris Universal Exhibition
1867

ISBN/EAN: 9783337150006

Printed in Europe, USA, Canada, Australia, Japan

Cover: Foto ©Andreas Hilbeck / pixelio.de

More available books at **www.hansebooks.com**

REPORTS

ON THE

PARIS UNIVERSAL EXHIBITION,

1867.

VOL. III.

CONTAINING REPORTS ON

COTTON, WOOLLEN, WORSTED, SILK, AND OTHER FABRICS.

CLOTHING AND SMALL WARE MANUFACTURES.

EDUCATIONAL APPLIANCES; DWELLINGS FOR THE POOR, CONSTRUCTED ON SANITARY PRINCIPLES AND AT SMALL COST, AND ARTICLES EXHIBITED WITH THE SPECIAL OBJECT OF IMPROVING THE PHYSICAL AND MORAL CONDITION OF THE PEOPLE.

Presented to both Houses of Parliament by Command of Her Majesty.

LONDON:

PRINTED BY GEORGE E. EYRE AND WILLIAM SPOTTISWOODE,
PRINTERS TO THE QUEEN'S MOST EXCELLENT MAJESTY.
FOR HER MAJESTY'S STATIONERY OFFICE.

20400.

1868.

REPORTS

PARIS UNIVERSAL EXHIBITION, 1867.

VOL. III.

CONTAINING REPORTS ON

The Reports on the Paris Exhibition will be printed in Six Volumes.

Volume I. will contain the General Report, with Tables of Statistics, &c.; Volumes II., III., IV., V. will contain the Reports on the various Classes; and Volume VI. the Returns relative to the New Order of Reward.

Presented to both Houses of Parliament by Command of Her Majesty.

LONDON:

PRINTED BY GEORGE E. EYRE AND WILLIAM SPOTTISWOODE,

PRINTERS TO THE QUEEN'S MOST EXCELLENT MAJESTY.

FOR HER MAJESTY'S STATIONERY OFFICE.

20400.

1868.

CONTENTS.

INTRODUCTION.

THE following Reports on the various Classes in the Paris Exhibition, 1867, were prepared for the Science and Art Department in accordance with the directions of the Lords of the Committee of Council on Education, and must not be confounded with the International Jury Reports to be issued by the French Government, which are quite distinct.

The scope and object of these Reports will be gathered from the following extracts from the letter to the gentlemen who were requested to prepare them, and who in many cases were not connected with the International Jury :—

"The Lord President of the Council, following the precedent of the Paris Exhibition of 1855, is desirous of obtaining a series of Reports on the objects exhibited in the Paris Exhibition of this year. . . ."

"The special object of this Report is to direct the attention of British visitors, manufacturers, and others, to the useful novelties exhibited by various nations on the present occasion, to which it appears desirable their attention should be called. It is not intended to be an exhaustive Report upon the class, which it is presumed will be made by the International Juries for the Imperial Commission. The British Report should have special reference to the objects exhibited by the British Colonies and by Foreign countries, rather than those exhibited by the United Kingdom, although the latter should not be overlooked."

"It is desirable that the Report should be as short as may be consistent with the nature of the subject, and it is absolutely necessary that it should be published during the Exhibition. It will therefore be indispensable that if the Report be undertaken by you, the manuscript should be delivered before the 15th of June at latest, and as much earlier as may be possible, to Captain Donnelly, R.E., the Secretary to the British Juries, who will afford all necessary information in Paris, and will act as Editor to the Reports."

"It is probable that the Exhibition will be sufficiently arranged to enable an examination of the Class to be commenced about the 15th April."

With the view of rendering these Reports useful to the public while the Exhibition lasted it was determined to publish them in a newspaper as quickly as possible. Arrangements having been made with the manager of the *Illustrated London News,* who undertook to produce them free of all cost to the Science and Art Department with a certain amount of illustration, the publication commenced on the 6th July 1867, and continued till the 7th December. By that time about two-thirds of the Reports had been published. These have been revised by the authors, and with the unpublished ones are complete in these volumes.

In arranging the Reports the order of the French classification has not been implicitly followed. The amount of matter rendering the division into four volumes desirable, those Reports were brought together in each volume which appeared most allied to one another, an arrangement dictated as much by what seemed likely to be to the convenience of purchasers of single volumes as by any idea of a scientific classification.

REPORTS.

REPORT for the MANCHESTER CHAMBER of COMMERCE on COTTON GOODS.—(Class 27.)—By J. O. MURRAY, Esq., Paris.

BEFORE entering on the detailed review of cotton goods in the French Exhibition, which is the special subject of this Report and which must be mainly interesting as comparing our own with foreign, especially with French cotton manufactures, it may be well to understand a little more of the mutual commercial relations between France and England than is usually known, and to look a little carefully into the results of the Treaty of which we have had now, in six years, time and data to form a judgment. When Cobden undertook that great work there were no very distinct data on which to go. An exaggerated and almost lunatic conception of the outrageous cheapness of English goods prevailed in France, and was appealed to and taken advantage of by the French monopolist manufacturers. Among English merchants and manufacturers an almost equally crazy if somewhat less exaggerated idea prevailed that, if duties similar to and if possible less than those in the States could be obtained, an immense market would open at their doors. The latter forgot that the French, though living under a system of strict prohibition of English goods generally, yet managed to be quite sufficiently clad and housed with their own manufactures—in this totally unlike the States, Italy, Spain, &c. The former, in their excited selfishness, shut their eyes to all facts and reasons, and blindly shouted for heavy duties. I don't think the only simple and business-like data on which a correct judgment could have been formed in regard to the real position, an independent and correctly priced sampling of the manufactures of both countries, was ever properly made and authoritatively appealed to ; or the wild alarms of the French and the quiet confidence of the English would have been considerably modified, and more reasonable duties, at all events as regards cottons, would have been provided for ere this date in the Treaty. My own impression, on pricing French calicoes, six months before the treaty, was that certain classes were actually cheaper than similar descriptions by our first and largest makers; and on sending over a few hundred pieces of greys to Manchester, they, to the surprise of every one in the trade, sold readily at a profit, and were the precursors of the large importations of French calicoes which have followed since.

Amid our annual flourishes of trumpets over the increasing greatness of our French trade, we seldom look even roughly into its component elements and their relative importance. I will take some figures on the subject from French government statistics, as they give the actual consumption of our imports, and the export of their own products and manufactures; whereas our Board of Trade tables give, as exported to France, all that is shipped for French ports, much of which is only in transit for Germany, Switzerland, and Spain; and as imports from France much which, though coming from French ports, is not of French origin at all. In 1865 (the tables for 1866 are not yet out), the total imports into France from England were $29\frac{1}{2}$ millions, of which $25\frac{1}{2}$ went into consumption; the exports from France into England were 53 millions, of which over 40 were French products and manufactures. We see, then, which of the two countries is the greatest producer and exporter; and an analysis of the relative amounts will still further show how differently from what was expected the Treaty has developed trade. Of the $25\frac{1}{2}$ millions of English imports no less than 18 are raw materials ($\frac{2}{3}$ foreign produce, $\frac{1}{3}$ coal) paying an average duty of $\frac{1}{2}$ per cent., except coal which pays $5\frac{1}{2}$ per cent.; four millions are half raw materials, of which over a quarter is yarn, paying $5\frac{1}{2}$ per cent. duty, and nearly half colonial produce, paying 30 per cent. duty, except cigars (a government monopoly), the duty on which is $1\frac{1}{2}$ per cent.; and of the $25\frac{1}{2}$ millions sterling not 3 millions are British manufactures, which paid an average duty of 10 per cent. from $27\frac{1}{2}$ per cent. on potteries and glass, 20 on cutlery, 16 on timber, 13 on cottons, to $7\frac{1}{2}$ on metal works, and 1 per cent. on silks. But of the 40 millions sterling of French products imported into England, 6 only are raw materials and 12 half raw, all home produce, while no less than 21 millions are manufactures imported duty free, against the 3 millions of ours, admitted grudgingly into France under heavy duties. And not only is there this great disparity in the amounts of manufactures exchanged, but all the rest of the French exports are French products, while nearly all the rest of ours are foreign or colonial produce. That is, while nearly all our exports to France are the results of foreign labour on which we have merely the profits of an exchange, raw materials which our industry has not touched further than is involved in transport and bill broking, their exports to us are nearly all, 40 millions out of 53, the results of home labour, the products of French industry, whose successive profits in each successive operation are entirely concentrated in French hands.

Now, without enlarging on this great disparity of positions or thinking for a moment of reversing or narrowing that free-trade policy which we have recognised as logically just, and which in this case enables France to send us in 21 millions of her manufactures while she shuts out all but 3 millions of ours, I think we may at least say that the position thus revealed by the figures of the French government itself, as made to French industry by the Treaty of Commerce, is not one which can be honourably maintained, at all events towards us. The plea that French industry could not stand before ours without a strong protection is utterly falsified by the facts. An industry which exports 21,000,000*l*., against 3,000,000*l*. imported, is not in the delicate and imperfect position so loudly pretended by the protectionist manufacturers. To continue to import into our markets without duty, and without even a prejudice, and yet to shut out our cottons by duties of 10, 20, and 30 per cent., which are prohibitions rather than duties, would be to take a mean and unmanly advantage of our adoption of a large and noble principle. Whatever the unlimited selfishness of the monopolist leaders may be shameless enough to utter, the nation and the government cannot honourably continue such duties, so purely inimical and so evidently unnecessary. Besides, the cotton duties have remained, since the beginning of the treaty, unchanged, while those on woollen cloths, Bradford goods, carpets, &c., have been reduced from 15 to 10 per cent., a reduction which has, in some of these goods, served to maintain, with great difficulty, a comparatively feeble trade ; and the absence of which reduction, as regards cotton, maintains an almost absolute prohibition.

But we will not content ourselves with the merely general figures quoted above—we will analyse these totals, at least, as far as regards textile manufactures, and see the details of each sort imported and exported. These I give in French figures, that is in millions of francs, since, as regards the small import of manufactures, we cannot descend into details, if we maintain as a unit of calculation that pleasant round sum, a million of pounds.

LEADING MANUFACTURES EXPORTED FROM FRANCE TO ALL
PARTS, NATIONAL PRODUCTS ONLY.

—	1860.	1861.	1862.	1863.	1864.	1865.
Silks - - -	454·8	333·3	363·5	370·3	408·2	428·5
Woollens - -	229·3	188·0	221·7	293·6	355·9	302·8
Cottons - -	69·6	56·4	63·3	88·2	93·7	93·5
Linens - - -	15·4	14·9	14·7	19·0	24·5	25·2
Yarns—Cot., wool. lin.	12·6	9·2	17·3	43·7	43·1	35·4
Dresses, mercery, umbrellas, furniture, all more or less the above manufactures made up.	202·0	172·7	235.3	242·0	305·2	326·0
	983·7	774·5	915·8	1056·8	1230·6	1211·4

LEADING MANUFACTURES IMPORTED INTO FRANCE FROM ALL
PARTS FOR HOME CONSUMPTION.

—	1860,	1861.	1862.	1863.	1864.	1865.
Silks - - -	3·9	4·1	4·5	4·6	7.1	11·2
Woollen and wor. threads.	7·4	26·5	47·7	39·2	37·7	43·5
Cottons - -	0·8	9·4	14·3	8·7	9·5	10·5
Linens - - -	11·6	13·9	13·5	12·5	14·3	13·4
Yarns—Cot., wool. lin.	4·7	11·6	26·0	25·5	23·9	34·2
Dresses, mercery, &c. nil, or nearly so.	—	—	—	—	—	—
	28·4	65·5	106·0	90·5	92·5	112·8

In order to show the effect of the treaty, I have begun
with the year previous to its coming into force, but a good
deal of the small imports of 1860 is already due to it. The
insignificance of the imports as compared to the exports is
remarkable, the total imports being only a tenth part of the
exports. Of these exports the great bulk always comes to
England, and the rest goes to markets in which they
compete successfully with our goods. Even in cotton goods
there is hardly an article of which the French do not send
us in much more than they take. In gray and bleached
calicoes, while they take from us for 19 millions of francs,

they send us in for nearly 22 millions; in prints they take 620,000 francs, and send us for 3 millions; in dyed goods they take 160,000 francs, and send us for over 1 million; in muslins they take 350,000, and send us over 1 million; in hosiery they take 57,000, and send for half a million; and so with several other smaller articles. And yet, while sending these comparatively large quantities into our markets, without duty and without question, they still maintain against our goods heavy inimical duties and all the force of strongly prejudiced opinions. Surely these facts entirely confute the false impressions on which the French government, influenced by the selfish fears of the manufacturers, was induced to impose these almost prohibitive duties; and though the manufacturers will no doubt be as selfish as ever, and will repeat as boldly as ever the old protectionist fallacies, the irrefragable evidence of facts has made a new position, on which the government may safely take its stand for a change of duties more in accordance with the entire freedom and friendliness exhibited on our side.

FRANCE.

The splendid display of the French cotton trades takes the lead in this class, and in fulness of representation and excellence of arrangement, is a great contrast with the British display. The simple, united, and effective mode in which each branch, and the whole trade together, is arranged in a succession of six large connected courts, all open so that a general impressive view may be had of all, and yet each distinct and marked by its own character, cannot fail to produce on hundreds of thousands of visitors from all lands a conviction that they see before them the great producing centre of the world, beside which our English exhibition sinks into insignificance. There is no branch absent, and if the plain goods want perhaps in general attractiveness, the splendour of large portions of the dress and furniture draws the attention and admiration of crowds. In place of our 30 exhibitors, there are here 210, besides two general district exhibitions, and a dozen exhibitors under Algeria. It is impossible, therefore, to go into detail, and a few general discriminations must suffice. If we begin with the Rouen Court, in which the heavy yarn and calico trades are represented, and take with it the Alsace Court alongside, where the lighter calicoes are shown, it will be noticed that in their yarns and in their grey calicoes the French makers still employ, for similar numbers and weights, more superior cotton and less low cotton or waste than we do, and give their yarns more twist, thus reducing the production, and in this respect, as well as in cost of raw material, enhancing the cost of the manufactured article. Among the 80 exhibitors of yarns, representing the 6,250,000 spindles of the French cotton trade, we have some, in low numbers especially, whose samples closely resemble our ordinary makes; but the average is cleaner, harder, and finer in material. This produces a cloth generally in all weights harder in feel, purer in appearance, and, doubtless, in so far superior to similar counts and weights of English make. Indeed, there are some grey calicoes, representing makes of shirtings and linings generally sold, and military-contract cloths (with a blue line up the piece), so fine in material, even when heavy in style, that we have nothing in current production to match them. In regard to price, so far as I have been able to obtain prices and make comparisons, there does not seem to be more difference than would be accounted for by this difference in material and make. The French market, doubtless, demands this superior article, or the French manufacturer would not continue to make on this system; but it seems as unnecessary as it is dog-in-the-manger-like to shut out by heavy duties the inferior article from such consumption as it might find, in order to maintain a style of make from which the French manufacturers seem indisposed to change. The superior article would, doubtless, find, as it seems to have found since the Treaty called the attention of English merchants to it, an increasing demand abroad to balance any diminution of consumption at home. For, now that the French manufacturers, whose attention and ambition were excited by the English superiority in 1855, have laid down new machinery, with all the modern improvements in almost every mill in France, the difference of position is almost abolished, and their 200,000 to 300,000 looms can produce almost, if not entirely, as well and as cheaply as ours. Indeed, while exporting nearly 38,000,000f. worth of their own calicoes, they do not take 2,000,000f. of foreign calico; showing, surely, a strong enough position. The French bleached calico still appears almost universally with a hard, gritty finish, which is partly in the nature of the cloth and partly in the nature of the finish, as may be remarked in the samples of their leading bleachers, Gros Roman and Co., Metzdorff and Davillier; and the market seems to prefer this to any variety of ours, though some improvements in it are noticeable of late years, and one of these bleachers shows several attempts at varied finishes, still far behind ours. The two principal dyers, Cronier, of Rouen, and Haeffely, of Mulhouse, show very interesting and skilful sets of sample pieces. In some small details of treatment, as in making up, they are behind us; in varieties of finish they do not need to come up to us; but in the styles of work, either dyeing, printing, or finishing, required by their market, they turn out as well and quite as cheaply as we can, and have no real need of the heavy protection they have established against us of nearly 1½d. on the pound of English dyed cloth, in addition to the duty on the undyed cloth. Indeed, so little need have they of protection, that one of them, who gets through 600,000 pieces a year, I am told, is yet so unable to cope with his work that he keeps regularly three months' work before him—a singular inconvenience to merchants in times of such irregularity of prices. I may also add that, while the customs acknowledge for 241,600f. of dyed cottons imported, they give the exports at 14,000,000f. more; so that the imports are a mere inconsiderable fraction; and this does not include the yarns and cloths exported after free admission for dyeing. In printed calicoes and muslins it is hardly necessary to quote statistics in order to show an equality in many respects and a superiority in some, which all the skill of our great printers cannot dispute. That there should be for only 22 millions of francs exported (against less than one million imported), only shows the baneful influence of protection, the material on which they work being protected by a heavy duty, which hinders the extension of their foreign trade. It is true they are allowed to receive free of duty, to print in bond, three millions worth of foreign cottons, which they re-export worth four millions and a half; but this is a lame and round-about way of doing a foreign trade. And yet the most liberal and one of the most considerable of the French printers, M. Jean Dollfus, who ranks himself among freetraders, would fain have had the Treaty give his trade a protection equal to a doubling of the duty on grey calicoes. Surely, no one can imagine that the magnificent displays in the Rouen and Mulhouse courts really require any such crutches to sustain them. In the heavier prints, for the use of the million, shown in the Rouen court, there is much resemblance, of course, to the great productions of the Manchester district. Putting aside a noticeable difference of tone in the colours and a preference of blue whites to clear whites, demanded by the taste of their market, there is nothing in the work of the Rouen printers to distinguish it from similar work in Lancashire. Some styles there may be which have not yet

MR. MURRAY ON COTTON GOODS.

Dyed fabrics.

Printed calicoes and muslins.

Heavier prints.

Mr.
Murray
on Cotton
Goods.

reached us, and some clever applications of practical ingenuity in individual instances, which Manchester printers
will quickly distinguish; but similar things would have
been remarkable in the work of the English printers had it
been exhibited. The muslins and lighter prints, however,
in the Mulhouse court decidedly surpass in splendour anything England produces. I do not say could produce, if it
suited English printers to determine to do so. And yet I
doubt much if it lies sufficiently in our modes of thought
to produce these gay and fanciful and changeful elegancies.
In any case, the large cost and the small return, the difficulty and uncertainty and risk, would rise before the eyes
of the English printer, shutting out their beauty and their
richness, and sadly disturbing his pride in their splendid
work and artistic style. But no such doubts hold the hands
of the Koechlins, Thierry-Miegs, Dollfus-Miegs, Schlumber-
gers, Steinbach Koechlins, Gros Romans, and others, whose
dazzling displays of printed muslins, reps, muslins de
laine, and other tissues, in dresses, furnitures, and shawls,
seem to concentrate all the taste and talent and disregard
of cost which the most spendthrift humours of imperial
Babylon could desire. The colours may be pigment, artificial, unsolid, evanescent; but the general effect is rich and
elegant, and charming. And who among the light and easy
class which will wear them looks beyond these superficial but
all-sufficient graces, or thinks of counting costs of production in relation to extent of sales? This wonderful display,
unsurpassable in its kind, does great honour to the enterprise of the French printers in the direction of *hautes
nouveautés*. Crossing to the Tarare court, we find ourselves among a display almost as magnificent of embroidered
curtains, of white and coloured muslins (plain and embroidered), of grenadines and tarlatans, gauzes and tulles.
The well-managed effects in the curtains of various muslins
worked on the tulle foundation among the embroidery, the
bold and soft contrasts, the skilful and elegant designs, are
well exemplified in Mr. Ruffier Leutner's display, and
carried even to excess in Messrs. Meunier's remarkable
pieces. The defect of the display in this court generally
is that the articles shown are mostly got up expen-
sively and especially for exhibition, and the ordinary
articles of current sale are hardly represented. And yet
with all their effort and all their protection the Tarare
makers are quite equalled if not surpassed by the unprotected Swiss. In the excellent show of plain muslins there
is no sign of a trade lagging behind or needing protection
from superior energies abroad.

Superiority
of French
muslins
and lighter
prints.

The next court, that of St. Quentin, cannot be said, in its mousselines brochées nor in its guipures, to be equal to Glasgow and Nottingham, nor, in its quiltings, to be quite equal to Manchester; but in neither the first nor the last article is it far from parity. In quiltings decided progress has been made since 1855. The next court—that of Flers and Roanne, opposite the Rouen court—completes the French cotton display, and contains articles in many respects peculiarly French, the blouse cloths so largely worn by the working classes and the toiles de Vichy. What is remarkable in the blouse is its excellence of material and of make, and it is a pity that the dye is not better and faster. We have no cotton stuff for the million at all resembling it in real goodness of quality. A stuff for the million with us somehow goes down rapidly in price and quality to a mere mockery and sham; but the million in France is not to be deluded into such false economy. These coutils for shirts, trousers, and blouses, as well as those for stays and mattresses, of which a full and varied assortment is here laid out, have an industrial centre of their own at Flers, in Normandy, where three hundred manufacturers employ some 14,000 looms and 28,000 hands in the production of 200,000 to 250,000 pieces annually, of the value of 25,000,000*l*. to 30,000,000*l*. The prices in 48 in. vary from 8*d*. to 2*s*. 6*d*. a yard. The toiles de Vichy, whose centre is Roanne, in the middle of France, are a sort of gingham, but as superior for women's wear to our nearly extinct and always miserable gingham as the blouse-cloth for men's wear is to its nearest similar with us, the cotton stripe and check. The fustian trade, to judge by the only two exhibitors, does not seem to be as flourishing as these other branches. One exhibitor, from Amiens, professing to make from patriotic motives, evidently expects the consumer's patriotism to shut his eyes to the mediocrity of the stuff exhibited; and another from Ourscamp, Oise, shows a very fair and well-made article, but would probably appeal to patriotism also in regard to price. In fact, velveteens, moles, and cords, as working-class costume, do not accord with the national habits, firmly and universally fixed as they are in favour of the blouse cloth; so that fustians have but a partial and unimportant consumption, and no great impulse is given to their production, beyond a sort of greedy little jealousy to make, and be protected, that is, subsidised in making, whatever English makers produce. Among the exhibitions in the Rouen court is one of coloured cotton reps for furnitures, in lively coloured stripes of good effect, which

Blouse cloths.

Toiles de Vichy.

Fustian.

Coloured cotton reps.

is an article unattempted, I think, in England, and yet one of sufficient consumption in warm countries to merit some attention.

UNITED KINGDOM.

Great
Britain.

The exhibition of British cotton goods is chiefly remark-able, as to its contents, for the absence of many important or essential departments, and, as to its arrangement, for the absence of the practical common sense one is accustomed to expect in connection with that large and active manufac-

Arrange-
ment of the
Cotton
court.
ture. The Cotton court should have been arranged upon a simple and systematic plan, by which those products requir-ing to be hung would be draped against its sides or outer walls, while those most fitly shown in pieces, on tables, would occupy the centre of the court, thus leaving it open throughout to the eye, with an impressive effect and a distinct relationship of parts. In place of this we have an entire absence of any general constructive idea and a domi-nance of mere individualisms, each stretching as high and as wide as possible, without regard to his neighbour, or even to any special suitability to his own requirements. Thus we have a trade display without any unity beyond what is in-volved in mere juxtaposition, and without proper effect as a whole. The quilts, which occupy a large space, and would have hung well around the court, with the dimities, figured furnitures, and coloured stuffs, are hung in the middle, obstructing the view, and not sufficiently seen themselves; while white calicoes, tapes, yarns, and other quite unsuitable articles form the walls of the court—though, in fact, there is no court at all, but a muddle of cases of all sorts, heights, and shapes, without any attempt at plan or classification. To make matters worse, all the cases are glazed—the refrac-tion and reflections of the glass rendering it often impossible to see the goods, and the glass preventing all examination by touch. It seems hardly comprehensible that practical business men should incur trouble and expense to send their goods so far, in order to shut them up from the examination they were sent to invite. As for any damage they might receive from dust or fingering, it would cost less to re-bleach them than to case them in glass. As it is, the greater part of the British cotton display is mute and useless to a practical visitor, and quite unattractive to the general public. It is not so in the French calico courts, where all the goods are entirely open—the whitest calicoes and the finest muslins—and where unity of arrangement has been firmly and effec-

tively carried out. It was not so when Manchester last exhibited in Paris, in 1855, when pieces of all sorts lay open on the tables, and when a calico court, simply but systematically arranged, showed that plain goods *could* be made to attract a large share of public interest, notwithstanding preconceived ideas of some authorities who had thought otherwise.

MR. MURRAY ON COTTON GOODS.

The absences which are remarkable include, unfortunately, most of the leading branches of the trade; and it would be impossible to make any discriminating remarks on this class without referring to them. The Scotch manufacturers entirely abstain, and thus several of the lighter branches of the trade are quite unrepresented. There are no plain or printed muslins, no embroidered muslins, no Jacquard muslin curtains, no muslin linings, no ginghams, no handkerchiefs; and we are thus deprived of means of comparison with many of the products of Mulhouse, of St. Quentin, and Tarare, as well as of Switzerland, Belgium, and Prussia. Even from Manchester, whence the only exhibitors come, most of the leading branches have failed to appear. Yarns, with one exception, are conspicuously absent; not only is there no complete range of numbers and sorts, but this immense article of production, of which we export over 10,000,000*l.* worth in the year, is as completely unrepresented as if we did not know it. The still more important article of calico, of which we export for 23,000,000*l.*, is, except in one branch—best-class shirtings, which is triply or quadruply represented — equally absent and ignored. Another immense branch, that of prints, which spreads for more than 16,000,000*l.* of its products over the world, has also refrained from appearing. Except the article of sewing-thread, which is well represented, of which we export for 750,000*l.* sterling, and the one branch of calicoes just mentioned, the Manchester exhibition consists of a few minor branches—in most cases imperfectly represented—which do not sum up altogether a million in our exports.*

Incompleteness of the exhibition.

This remarkable absence—remarkable especially when compared with the crowds of exhibitors in the French and other cotton industries--is the result partly of a general indifference to exhibitions as business speculations, and partly of a special indifference to exhibiting in a market which sends into England, without a shadow of duties, 21,000,000*l.* of French manufactures, while shutting out by a

---

* These statistics are taken from the Board of Trade Reports for 1865, the last published; and those in relation to French goods from the French Customs Reports for the same year.

MR.
MURRAY
ON COTTON
GOODS.

Yarns.

Sewing
cottons.

Calicoes.

hostile tariff, erroneously called a free trade treaty, all but 3,000,000*l.* of British manufactures.

In yarns, as already mentioned, there is no consecutive display. A single and remarkable example of fine numbers, from 160 to 410, is shown by Messrs. Henry Bazley and Co., Ancoats ; but of common and coarse numbers there are no specimens at all, one or two fancy sorts alone appearing; samples for union woollens, by Mr. J. M. Johnson, Mirfield; and dyed samples by Messrs. J. Townshend and Son, of Coventry. But of sewing cottons we have half a dozen remarkable displays—Messrs. J. Brook and Brothers, of Huddersfield ; Walter Evans and Co., of Derby ; Clark and Co., and J. and P. Coates, of Paisley ; E. Ashworth and Son, Dickens and Co., and J. and E. Waters, of Manchester, all exhibit carefully-arranged assortments, the case of the last-mentioned house being a large and elaborate imitation of the Albert monument in Manchester, and one of the leading attractions in the vestibule of the Exhibition. In grey and bleached calicoes we have a single example of first-class heavy shirtings and sheetings in a range shown by Messrs. S. Radcliffe and Sons ; and three full representations of bleached shirtings of the best and finest sorts by Messrs. Crewdson and Worthington ; Horrockses, Miller, and Co ; and J. Hawkins and Son. These I have no doubt maintain the wide and well-founded reputations of those houses ; but, being under glass, and in many cases so placed that no details whatever of the cloths can be seen, while no examination can be made of their peculiarities in finish, in feel, and in structure, the drapers, shirtmakers, or wholesale dealers who might have been led to try and to adopt some of the sorts in their trades, are precluded from making any acquaintance with them. The most prominent and attractive displays in the Manchester cotton space are the quilt and quilting cases. Messrs. Barlow and Jones have made, perhaps, a mistake in composing the principal part of their exhibition with quilts, evidently made expressly for show, and of too costly a sort for large or general sale ; while Messrs. Johnson and Fildes have evidently taken fair ordinary specimens of current sale from their usual production ; but both displays are good, and highly creditable, and in quiltings also, of which they show a varied and excellent assortment, maintain a position which is quite unequalled in the French, Belgian, German, or other exhibitions. The styles of pattern in the quilts—neat grounds, and symmetrical objects, well balanced, and contrasting well with the grounds and with each other—are a decided progress from the sprawling, ill-concerted, and ineffective styles prevailing some years ago, and seem, besides, to work up much better in the cloth. Of this article we export over 50,000*l.* Some well executed bed quilts are also shown by Messrs. W. M. Christy and Son in terry patterns ; but the most important part of their display is their well-known towels and bath cloths, in cotton and linen terry ; a make, the original of which may be seen in the Turkish kiosk, in the park, and in the Ottoman exhibition, in many beautiful samples of similar towels, as well as in hangings and couch coverings. In this article Messrs. W. H. Glover and Co. also make a varied and successful show. In fustians, a large branch which exports over a quarter of a million sterling, we have no ranges of the commoner sorts, but of the better sorts we have a few excellent examples. Messrs. Kesselmeyer and Mellodew show admirable specimens (under glass unfortunately) of that superior make and silk-looking finish, by the introduction of which some dozen years ago they raised the character of cotton velvets and velveteens, and astonished those most familiar with the manufacture. Messrs. Langworthy also show what, as far as can be judged through glass, are equally remarkable specimens of similar goods, accompanied by a beautiful range of cords of different sizes, and by a first-rate collection of cotton drills, making altogether one of the most noteworthy displays in this class in the exhibition. The equally important and interesting exhibition of Sir E. Armitage and Sons, consisting of sail-cloths, tent-cloths, and other heavy cottons, as well as light negro trouserings, &c., would also attract deserved attention more largely if they were not shut in from examination. The large article of home and foreign trade, checks and stripes for shirtings and trouserings, is otherwise quite unrepresented. The dimities and figured furniture cottons of Messrs. Martin and Johnson are interesting, but do not seem to be different from what they have been for many years back. The great branch of prints, as I have said, is completely absent. And another important branch in which, I think, we equal and excel all competitors—dyed cottons—is also almost entirely absent. One department, most successfully pursued by several Scotch and English dyers, that of beetled imitation-silk finish, is well represented by Messrs. Barlow. Their specimens are invariably taken at first for silk, even by practical cotton merchants, and deserve decidedly favourable remark. An important branch of production, which besides extensive consumption at home supplies 320,000*l.* worth abroad, that of small wares, is but slightly represented by Messrs. Waters in the base of their fine specimen of bobbin-architecture ; and by Messrs. Cash, of Coventry, who show cotton frillings and edgings.

Fustians.

MR.
MURRAY
ON COTTON
GOODS.

India

and other
countries.

Continuing our tour onwards beyond the English exhibition, we may trace out the cotton manufactures of the other countries in their order as they follow each other along the Galerie de Vêtements. India has but a small display in Class 27, but interesting as far as it goes—coloured striped tablecovers, and furniture stuffs in cotton reps, damasks, fancy towels, bedcovers, calicoes, fine spot and stripe muslins, and muslins embroidered in cotton, gold, silver, and beetle wings, from Agra central prison, and from Bengal and Bombay. The other hand-made goods also exhibited by Malta, close by ; and, a little further on, by the Central and South American Republics ; and in the machine gallery by Brazil, consist chiefly of coarse but strong stripes and checks, ginghams and calicoes for native wear ; the checks are open and thin, as required by the climate ; coarse, and with less appearance than our power-loom similars ; more roughly made, but more genuine and better wear. If, as I am told, there is a desire in Manchester to bring machine-made goods as near as possible to hand-made in their peculiar qualities, these specimens deserve attention as including good examples of articles of large consumption, made in native looms to suit exactly local requirements. There are among them also samples of nankins, capital calicoes in the natural light brown of this sort of cotton, a shade which has been fashionable lately, and is thus much better obtained than by any dyeing, and which constitutes an article that our cotton trade might do well to take up a little, though possibly our power-looms might not turn it out so well.

UNITED STATES.

United
States.

The United States have not sent any contributions to this class, except a case from the Clark Thread Company, similar in contents to that of Messrs. Clark, of Paisley.

TURKEY.

Turkey.

In Turkey we have, in the catalogue, the extraordinary number of 203 exhibitors of cotton goods, but, except a few specimens of yarns, I do not find any evidence of their existence. A good many nicely-made and fringed terry towels, the originals of the productions of Messrs. Christy and Glover in Manchester, are shown in another class. But I have looked in vain several times for the shirtings, sheetings, sail and tent cloths, aladjas, tenfis, abanis, manissas &c. temptingly announced, and promising to gratify a natural curiosity concerning the peculiar taste and habits in regard to cotton goods of the varied tribes of the Ottoman empire. Let us hope they will yet appear, with the additions which are being still daily and slowly produced in many parts of this immense Exhibition. Egypt and Tunis are equally insignificant in this class—a few bits of plain and dyed calicoes are shown; the colours, when on separate scraps, looking very dirty and dull, products of the simplest and most aboriginal dyeing ; but when combined and contrasted they come up much more richly and agreeably. Greece also shows nothing remarkable : a few coarse yarns, cotton plush, and stripes and checks.

PERSIA.

Persia, which is not mentioned in the catalogue, has lately opened out a rich display of goods, among which are printed cotton furnitures of excellent styles, simple and quiet, but rich and novel. There is much to be learned among these Oriental designs, the growth of the traditional talents of ages.

ROUMANIA.

Roumania, also not in the catalogue, sends a few specimens of hand-made cottons, in dresses and furnitures; a mixed stripe of plush and coloured reps on a couch is worth noting.

ITALY.

Italy has forty-seven exhibitors, chiefly in the Italian annexe in the park, who show calicoes machine-made, though more like hand-made than the French and English domestics and printers usually ; ginghams, stripes and checks, and blouse cloths, having the solid qualities of the French similars; heavy quiltings and fancy cottons, coarse but stout and genuine ; well-made reps for furniture ; Turkey-red yarns and cloths, all evidencing considerable activity and enterprize.

RUSSIA.

Russia has twenty-one exhibitors (chiefly printers) of whom it may be said that the displays of Zindel, of Hubner, of Konschine, of Zimine, and other Moscow printers, are as good in styles and execution, both in ordinary and in Turkey-red work, as any in the Exhibition, and are really very varied and extensive ; while the calicoes and fancy cottons, and stripes and checks are evidently fair and good work.

SWEDEN AND NORWAY.

Even Sweden and Norway take very fair positions. The Rosenlund Mill (E. D. Lundstroem) shows yarns, from No. 2 to 100, as well as calicoes, dyed goods, and sail-cloths ;

Mr.
Murray
on Cotton
Goods. Ch. Hill, E. W. Bley, and others show calicoes as fine in material as the French; several other spinners show very good grey, bleached, and dyed yarns; and the Nydalen Company, at Christiana, make a fair display of yarns, twines, calicoes, sail-cloths, and checks.

SPAIN AND PORTUGAL.

Portugal.

Spain.

Portugal shows nothing remarkable. There are eight exhibitors of common prints, calicoes, dyed goods, bedticks, raised twills, stripes—evidently a small and not advanced trade. But Spain, with fourteen exhibitors, makes a considerable and decidedly creditable display, showing that, whatever may be the decadence of the country generally, there is spirit and energy at Barcelona. Ferrer, Achon, Paul, Juncadella, and other printers, send work as good as any of Manchester or Rouen, the only thing remarkable being that the samples show nothing distinctively Spanish, but the styles and execution might have been just as well shown from England or France. In quiltings and cotton damasks Bauvier Brothers make a varied and respectable display, but are behind in finish. Grey and bleached, plain and fancy calicoes are freely shown by other makers.

As regards the prints shown by Spain, by Russia, and by Italy, it is evident enough that the designs are French, and the rollers, in all probability, from Manchester, as well as the foremen and directors; so that there is very little really national about them except the mere underling labour. It is a kind of hothouse forcing of productions neither indigenous nor natural, at a foolish and miscalculated cost of national outlay and protection; and a great pity it is that there are not national statesmen capable of seeing that the same labour employed in indigenous products, under home capital and direction, would be more profitable, and would require no artificial and costly sustaining.

How long will it be ere these statesmen attain the common sense to see that the nation suffices for itself far more rationally and profitably when the peasant clothes himself by an exchange of his hemp or olive oil, than when he spends twice the capital and labour to make his own clothes in a mill sustained by national protection?

SWITZERLAND.

Switzerland.

The Swiss Turkey-red room is the finest practical display in the Exhibition of prints and grey and dyed cottons. Switzerland has 49 exhibitors in Class 27, chiefly from Zurich and St. Gall. The show of Turkey-red prints is so splendid as to be at first quite confusing. The exhibitions of Rieter-Ziegler and Co. and of Tschudy and Co. are unsurpassable; while those of Egg, Ziegler, and Co. Jenny and Co., Luschinger and Co., L. Meyer, Fruhler Brothers, Kubli ; Barth ; Jenny, and Co. ; Schiesser, Sulzer, Wiedenkeller, Deutch Brothers, come not far behind. A conjunction of favourable circumstances, plenty of pure water, cheap labour, and steady, determined industry, have given the Swiss evidently the lead of the world in this branch. As an element of their success, too, must be remarked the beautiful grey muslins and prints produced by the Swiss calico manufacturers, eight of whom exhibit, and in their special articles decidedly surpass similar French goods. With all the disadvantages of position and natural circumstances of which the French cotton manufacturers complain with such persistent whinings, and on which they base their claims for protection, the Swiss boldly and successfully face the world unprotected. What disadvantages has the Rouen or Alsatian manufacturer that the Swiss does not labour under still more? And yet he quietly and determinedly sets himself to balance them by such advantages as he can create without any plundering of the national exchequer, or any shutting out of foreign competition. The Swiss show of woven coloured cottons is equally extensive and remarkable ; and their display of muslins and sewed muslin curtains from St. Gall, arranged with great taste in the beautiful Swiss salon and along the passage, is not surpassed, nor indeed equalled, by all the efforts of Tarare.

AUSTRIA.

Austria has thirty-six exhibitors of cotton goods, quite up to the mark in general, and showing as fair an average as our own would do. The yarns and calicoes are clean, even, and well made, as far as can be judged under glass. The Bohemian printers, from Prague and neighbourhood, Messrs. Dormizer, Leitenberger, Przibram, Porges, and others, show good, creditable work. Richter, also, of Bohemia, shows good velvets and velveteens. Graumann, of Vienna, very fair quiltings and plush. It is plain that, as far as capabilities of good marketable productions are concerned, there are few branches of the cotton trade in which the Austrian manufacturers are not already far enough advanced to hold their own against foreign competition without any, or with only a very moderate protection indeed, in the long discussed tariff.

WIRTEMBERG.

The Wirtemberg Cotton court, with eleven exhibitors, consists chiefly of an excellent display of ticks, drills, and

MR. MURRAY ON COTTON GOODS.

Excellence of the Swiss exhibits.

Austria.

Wirtemberg.

MR.
MURRAY
ON COTTON
GOODS.

ginghams, well worth the attention of our manufacturers. The cotton coatings and trowserings of Schoop & Co., of Biberach, are remarkably good, as well as their ginghams ; and capital specimens of similar goods appear in the assortments of Gutmann, Ottenheiner, Kaufmann, and Elsass. Messrs. Staub show well-made plain and fancy greys, and Mr. Faber, of Stuttgart, good quilts and quiltings, with jacquard furnitures of a neat make, worth noting.

BADEN.

Baden.

Baden has only one cotton contribution, a remarkably excellent display of printed muslins and de-laine shawls, by Messrs. Koechlin, Baumgartner, and Co., which seems, however, to belong as much to Paris and Mulhouse as to Loerrach.

PRUSSIA AND NORTH GERMANY.

Prussia and North Germany.

In the important exhibition from Prussia and the North German Confederation, the bulk of the display comes from those active Rhine-Prussian provinces which take so largely of our Lancashire yarns, through Rotterdam. As might be expected, but little prominence is given to native spinnings, though a few sewing cottons and calicoes are shown. Almost the entire exhibition is devoted to cotton clothing, imitating wool ; and an imposing collection of this article is displayed, well worthy the attention of our cotton districts. Messrs. Wolff and Co., of Gladbach, and the Gladbach Cotton Company. show an excellent and varied assortment of dyed and printed swandowns, and other low fustians for linings, &c. a branch in which Rhenish Prussia has long equalled or excelled our own makers. Prices, from 6d. to 15d. a yard in 25 inches wide. But the most remarkable productions are the useful and economical cloths, of mixed wool and cotton, or all cotton, of which Messrs. Bornefeld, Ax, and Frowein, Zartmann and Co., Nacken, Boetterling, H. Ax, and a dozen others, from Gladbach and Rheydt, show an extensive and capital assortment, chiefly from 9d. to 1s. a yard. Mr. Mitscherlich, of Eilenbourg, shows a fair variety of quiltings and other white figured cottons. The Power-Loom Company of Linden make a fair show of cords, and a rather imposing display of velvets and velveteens, not quite up to the mark in dyeing ; but decidedly noteworthy as the best Continental example of these goods, approaching nearest to Manchester in general excellence. Messrs. Liebermann, of Berlin, and three or four other printers, show work of the Rouen character, but not generally remarkable. From Saxony, Chemnitz only sends one representative, Mr. Hauschild, whose specimens of excellent yarns and threads are noteworthy ; and those of Heydenreich, and of Hoeffer, alongside, are also remarkable. The principal display from Saxony consists of some good hand and machine embroidery, as well as curtains—which, however, hardly come up to Glasgow productions—shown by Messrs. Jahn, Boehler, Schnorr, Mammen, and others, from Plauen. Some good drills, also, are exposed by Mr. Herzog.

BELGIUM.

The last, but by no means the least, of the cotton industries in our tour is that of Belgium. This wonderful little country, whose splendid energies and indomitable national spirit place it on a par in industrial importance with the first countries of the world, and far beyond many of much greater superficial extent, takes, of course, a leading place in this branch, and sends sixty-nine exhibitors from Ghent, Renaix, Tournai, Courtrai, &c. Their cotton court is well planned, architecturally; but the different branches are not as well classed, nor the individual displays, in many cases, as well laid out as might have been. In yarns and calicoes we have about ten exhibitors, rather scattered about, among whom Messrs. De Bast, Desmet Brothers, and Rosseel and Co., all of Ghent, are remarkable. In quilts and quiltings and dimities there are four or five exhibitors, among whom Messrs. Lousbergs and Brac-Vercruysse, of Ghent, are noticeable, and represent well a class of goods which, as well as Belgian calicoes, have entered successfully into competition with our own goods, both in our own and in the French market. But if there be occasionally some advantage in their heavy Marseilles quilts, our other quilts and quiltings are certainly superior in make, finish, and appearance. Only one printer—the Stalle Company—shows a variety of plain work of the Rouen sort, and of ordinary style and execution. There are half a dozen or more makers of cotton blankets from Termonde, remarkable for excellence and cheapness. But the greatest strength of the cotton trade seems put into the display of drills and imitation woollen clothing. About half of the cotton court and half of the exhibitors are devoted to varieties of these mixed or all cotton coatings and trowserings, similar, though with many differences, to the Gladbach and Wirtemberg goods, and constituting, on the whole, a branch of cotton manufacture evidently more important and more developed on the Continent than with us, and which does not seem to have been checked by the cotton crisis or beaten by low woollens, as similar goods have been to some extent with us. The prices, where given, seem often remarkably low, and the styles and makes are very varied. It is not easy to distinguish among so many ; but Messrs. Hemptinne, Joniaux, Rubay, and Desimpel, Masquelie, Dujardin, Saffre and Graveline, Duchatelet, Gilson, and Bossut, Lienart, Asou, may be mentioned as good representatives of this manufacture, which, were it as largely developed with us, and as important for home consumption and for export as it is with the Continental manufacturers, would certainly excite their emulative efforts. In a separate court Messrs. Van der Smissen Bros. show a remarkable case of yarns and sewing or crochet cottons, plain, dyed, and fancy, in great variety.

NETHERLANDS.

I should add that three or four Netherlands exhibitors show a peculiar article, specially for their colonial market, quite singular and characteristic. Mr. Wilson limits his display to a single article, an imitation of the Japanese Batick, remarkable in execution and interesting by its dissimilarity to anything else in the cotton trade. Messrs. Salomonson and Dyk show a greater variety of articles, including Baticks, and all marked by peculiarities of style, suited to their special markets, and worthy the notice of our foreign merchants.

CONCLUSION.

Few practical and reflective observers will glance, even as hurriedly as we have thus done, round these competitive displays of industrial ability in cotton manufacture without feeling that, however long and largely England may retain the leadership, anything like an exclusive empire or undisputed sway in the cotton trade is no longer possible. The superior education of Continental workmen in certain branches, or the better position of foreign merchants in regard to certain articles, already reduces us to a secondary position in some respects. If in all countries as excellent a system of public education and as independent a spirit prevailed as in Switzerland, our position would soon be menaced in many more directions. These exhibitions of the rapidly-developing powers of so many rival centres of production must quicken our efforts—by education, by political development, by co-operative interest, by every means in our power —to bring every latent energy of our population to bear in maintaining our position. While we are hovering round the question of national education, and hesitating over the petty interests of parties in regard to it, the industrial sceptre is imperceptibly slipping away from us ; and, with practical obtuseness, we shall refuse to see it till the fact is accomplished, and it is too late to mend.

Another important point brought prominently into relief by this Exhibition is the universal adoption by every European country of the cotton trade as a branch of national industry. I don't know that there is one European nation without an attempt to establish it, and several other countries, as the United States, Canada, Brazil, adopt it more or less largely and successfully. Now it is very evident that they cannot all be equally endowed naturally for its profitable working, possessing rich coal fields and iron beds, extensive and easy sea communication, great facilities of internal transport, and large centres of population. To take the European countries only, which have doubtless been led into the attempt by the wonderful example of England; if some in certain branches have natural advantages which enable them to maintain a more or less successful competition with England, as Belgium, France, Switzerland, Rhenish Prussia, and Saxony; the others, Spain, Portugal, Italy, Germany, Austria, Turkey, and Russia, have none or almost none of these natural advantages, and their attempt at a national cotton industry is entirely a forced, unnatural, and miscalculated effort. It is not a national industry but only a national burden, based upon entirely false ideas. And even in those countries better qualified to work certain branches of the cotton trade, the existence of protection shows their acknowledged inferiority to England, and the necessity for a forced contribution from the nation generally in order to maintain a relatively small portion in an industry which openly proclaims that it would otherwise be unable to exist.

As this system is a national loss to the countries thus subsidized for its support, so is it also a loss to England, whose goods would otherwise be used by those countries thus driven into the consumption of dearer home-made goods. But it is a double loss to those countries whose cotton industries work upon a national tax, for not only are they paying home manufacturers a full price and a useless extra duty, but they are precluding themselves from paying the English manufacturer a cheaper price and exchanging at the same time a real and natural home product with a profit. For evidently if commerce, which is simply exchange, were not thus impeded and driven into false and wasteful channels, real national products, yielding a natural profit and developing national wealth, would be allowed freely to exchange themselves for all foreign articles, in place of maintaining artificial industries, which are not national and never can be, and are a charge in place of a source of wealth to the nation.

Now as protection is only ignorance of true commercial principles, it is not only the interest of England, as the greatest manufacturing and commercial nation, but her duty, as the most enlightened nation on commercial subjects, to make continuous efforts for the removal of this ignorance. And surely no more useful, more necessary, or, viewed in its higher bearings as uniting national interests and tending towards international friendliness, no more noble mission could be given to England's foreign representatives than that of actively taking and making every means to correct these false views, and disseminating those truer and friendlier principles which are also more secure and profitable for all.

It is, it seems to me, to the Chambers of Commerce and Manufactures of England we must chiefly look for initiating and maintaining such a spirit and purpose among our diplomatic and consular agents; and that these Chambers may have due and undeniable influence, a large and enlightened support must be given them by the merchants and manufacturers of the districts they represent, a support not yet sufficiently given, through an ignorant and selfish indifference, which will if continued soon meet its own punishment through the continuance among foreign or rival nations of that progress in many directions of which this Exhibition gives marked evidence.

MEDALS.

The above was written before the awards were known, and I confess it did not seem to me of much importance to know or notice them in the review with which I was entrusted. That a medal may be of some importance to a shopkeeper, or to a worker and exhibitor in any branch of industry in which his individuality stands really apart and can thus be brought into greater prominence, is readily admissible. But in great and complicated industries like the cotton trade, where so many successive hands are employed to attain a final result, and where progress is so much the product of a general movement in which the influence of a single firm or individual is little appreciable, it is scarcely possible that any awards hurriedly made by a jury, often more curiously than suitably constituted, can have any real or practical signification. A little special expenditure, a little special care will produce articles likely enough to attract attention and admiration in an exhibition, though of little or no use in the actual market; as the medal also is itself found to be, for no buyer will pay a penny a piece more for a printing cloth or a shirting because the firm producing them have obtained a lot of medals. Nor do the medals, even taken in the aggregate, serve in any way to indicate the actual position of the different countries in the cotton trade. Thus we find that, out of 26 gold medals awarded, France, which has already seven leading manufacturers, " hors concours," through being on the jury, has 15, and all the rest of the world put together only 11; Britain having five, Switzerland and Belgium two each, Austria and Prussia one each. Of silver medals France has 75, and the rest of the world 62 ; namely, Switzerland 13, Austria and Prussia 12 each, Belgium seven, Prussia six, Britain five, Saxony, Holland, and United States two each, and Spain one. And in bronze medals the case is about the same. Now no one can pretend to find in these awards any evidence of the relative positions of the different countries in cotton manufacture. France takes the lead, quite out of sight of all competitors ; but if this be the opinion of French cotton lords acting as jurymen, we know how as legislators, or as competitors in view of a commercial treaty, they groan and lament about their distance behind England, which no improvements in machinery and no growth of years ever enables them to diminish. Nor is the way in which the medals are awarded likely to be satisfactory even to those who get them. Thus France, wanting 15 of the 26 gold medals, chiefly for those printers whose costly and splendid products are admirable in an exhibition but very limited in their adaptation to the world's needs, could give only one medal to the half dozen British sewing cotton manufacturers, (grouped together for economy of award and condemned to internecine war over the single bone thrown to so many ;) whose one medal, however, represents a production of far more importance in the world's commerce than that of the 15 French medallists. And the only English printer exhibiting, whose work was certainly quite equal in its kind to any of the similar French work, was graciously awarded a " Mention honorable ! " Thus also, the two leading French dyers, exhibiting a fair but nowise remarkable set of products, get a silver medal each, and one of them an extra bronze medal as well ; but the only English dyer, who exhibited quite as remarkable a set of ordinary products, and a very remarkable set of samples of silk finish, so admirable as to be always taken even by practical men for silk mixtures, of which the French dyers showed and could show nothing, was condemned to a mere bronze medal.

Without then needlessly multiplying instances, it can hardly be contested that such awards, in such industries as those connected with the cotton trade, can have little or no practical value or signification, whether taken individually or nationally, and had better be left out of future exhibitions, or at least may be left out of any critical review of such industries. It is also in part the discovery of this uselessness of medals by those manufacturers whose products would add interest to such exhibitions, and whose importance places them above medal-hunting, and in part this perhaps inevitable but at all events certain confusion in their award, which has influenced such manufacturers so largely in abstaining from the display of their products.

REPORT on LINEN THREAD, and FABRICS of LINEN and HEMP.—(Class 28.)—By JOHN STEVELLY, Esq.

WE find in the Paris Exhibition of 1867 the great number of 621 exhibitors in this class, without counting the Belfast trophy, which does not appear in the catalogue; and, although Scotland, England, and America are unrepresented, we have still a show of linens which would have been believed impossible in 1851 or 1855. This Exhibition confirms what we already know by experience—that Great Britain, although doubtless the largest manufacturer of linen goods in the world, has been hitherto by no means a great consumer.

The cotton famine has now forced many to use linen who previously used cotton; and these, I hope, we have secured as permanent customers for our linen manufactures. Such a crisis was not needed to induce the consumption of linens on the continent, where a cotton blouse or a cotton shirt has long been a mark of exceptional poverty.

It is certainly singularly easy to find anything in the Paris Exhibition, and to compare it with similar products of the same or of other countries. This simplicity of arrangement has doubtless been achieved at a great expense of general effect; but, in a practical point of view, its advantages are immense. To find the linens we enter the building by the Porte d'Jéna, and, after passing the circle devoted to machinery and the smaller one given up to raw materials, we come to the large circular gallery going round the entire building, and headed "Group 4.—Vêtements," which comprises all articles worn, either completed or having gone through some manufacturing process. In this group are included not only yarns and brown and white linens, but also the made-up articles. General arrangement of the exhibition.

Commencing our circuit of this gallery on our left hand, we come to France, whose linen manufactures we shall first consider, not only because we are at present the guests of France, but also on account of their importance. Then follow Holland, Belgium, Prussia, and the Northern States of Germany and Austria; and passing through several countries of minor importance as linen manufacturers, including our own colonies, we come to Ireland, almost at the point at which we started. I say Ireland advisedly, for the absence of Dundee, Dunfermline, Barnsley, and a Ireland.

host of other places celebrated for their linens, leaves a woeful want in the British Class 28 as it appears in the Champ de Mars. The unrepresented members of our trade urge their expense, labour, and loss of time at former exhibitions, and the small appreciable advantages which they derived therefrom, as an unanswerable argument against their exhibiting. I believe this however to be a mistake. Even in an economical point of view, it is certainly the cheapest and most telling advertisement An exhibition of the ordinary tissues, however fine, can scarcely be made attractive to the multitude, and this department is, accordingly, almost forsaken for the French jewellery, the Prussian guns, the German toys, and the English and Bohemian glass ; but we must remember that it is these grim bales which mainly contribute to those annual tables of commercial statistics whose enormous totals our mind can scarcely grasp, while, judged by the same standard, the show things sink into utter insignificance,

The French portions of the linen exhibition.

France has not underrated the importance of exhibiting a complete series of her linen manufactures, but, in common with Belgium and Prussia, she has devoted to it the largest space allotted to any one industry. Certainly the linens exhibited by France have nothing in common with our makes or consistent with our ideas of what she would find most profitable ; we must, however, study these French manufactures as they are, and try to imitate them if we wish France to become to any extent our customer. In a

Statistics of the linen trade in France.

remarkable report to the Belfast Chamber of Commerce by the deputations sent by it to the Paris Exhibition of 1855, for which I am indebted, along with many valuable statistical tables, to Mr. M'Ilwrath (*see note* A.), secretary of the linen-trade committee, it is estimated that the annual consumption of linens in France amounts to 250,000,000 yards. Without accepting completly those figures, which I have no means of verifying, it is yet certain that the consumption of linen goods is greater in France than in any other country in the world. France had at work on 1 Jan. 1866, 226 mills, containing 705,350 spindles, and had going, in the Department du Nord alone, 4,305 power-looms, which latter number has been since so largely increased that the present number of power-looms working in France cannot be estimated at less than 8,000. In addition to the proceeds of these powerful means of production, she imported, in 1866, 3,800,000 lbs. weight of yarn and 3,500,000 lbs. of linen 2,800,000 lbs. of which are brown. These few figures give in a small space all the importance of her linen consumption.

Of the above large amount of brown linens we must not fall under the delusion that we sell the principal part. We contribute 200,000 lbs. only, while our intelligent neighbours of Belgium supply 2,500,000 lbs. The Belgians, it is true, are aided by cheap labour; but we have, on the other hand, our immense development of power-looms. What we have neglected to acquire is the experience which the Belgians possess both in producing the goods demanded by the French trade and in adapting themselves to the fancy tariffs of the French custom-house. In the present report I should wish to draw special attention to those particular classes of goods which appear to me the most important for our manufacturers to become acquainted with, and which it would be most easy for them to make their own; so that, in case of a sudden suspension of purchases on the part of a large customer, such as America, or of the reduction or the abolition of the present French tariff, they might be able to avail themselves in some measure of the outlet which France affords them.

Allow me to say a word on the subject of the French duties. The present French Government carried in 1860 a comparatively liberal measure in spite of a formidable opposition. A tariff on the principle of a 15 per cent. maximum rate was far from a radical measure; but at that time the intelligent Minister, now the Minister of State, held out the hope that, if the powerful band of manufacturers who opposed any change were neither ruined nor seriously affected by the modification of the tariff the further reduction of the duty would be limited only by the fiscal wants of the country.

During the seven years of the new régime the spindles have increased from 400,000 to 700,000. The power-looms have taken a firm place in the country. The exports of linen yarn and thread have increased from a nominal quantity to 4,000,000 lbs., and the export of linen has reached the enormous amount of 9,000,000 lbs. The sudden general demand for linen might diminish the value of these facts, were it not that precisely the same results have followed in the cases of the cotton and the woollen trades. The French Government has partly recognised these results, first, in the treaty with Belgium, when certain duties were modified, especially on low plain goods and drills; and, secondly, in the beginning of this year, when 20 per cent. reduction was made on the finest class of linen in the special Austrian treaty. Under these circumstances I believe that the time has arrived when it would be most important to

Mr.
Stevelly
on Linen
Thread,
&c.

French
duties.

urge on the French Government to abolish protective duties which the French manufacturers no longer require, or, at all events, to place them at the lowest per-centage which they believe the financial arrangements of the country would justify. A 5 per cent. maximum rate would in all probability greatly increase the revenue. In making such a representation I would especially call attention to the case of heavy makes of coarse linens, and to drills, which

are both virtually excluded, and also to the importance to the French manufacturers of having extended to them the beneficial effects of article 40 in the Belgian law on entrepôts, which allows to be taken out of bond, duty free, yarns destined for the manufacture of linens for export. This would allow the French manufacturers to compete on terms of equality with other nations in the markets of the world.

I hope the reporter of Class 43, to whom this more properly belongs, will excuse my making a few remarks on the important subject of the "raw material." At the beginning of the present century, during the wars of the Empire, owing to the want of labour, the growth of flax was small in France, each household only growing what it required for its own use. Little or none could be exported. In 1822 we find, however, some 35,000 acres under flax, but in 1845 the area falls to 11,000 acres in consequence of the slowness of the French in following the lead given by England and Ireland in adapting machinery to spinning flax. At this time our sales of yarns to France reached in one year the large amount, for the period, of 11,000 tons. It was now clear that hand-spinning was doomed, and with the erection of mills we find the culture of flax gradually increasing. In 1864, in the Department du Nord alone, there were 45,000 acres devoted to flax ; and in 1866 we may safely assume that France had at least 60,000 acres under the same crop, besides importing 31,000 tons of flax, principally from Belgium and Russia, 7,000 tons of hemp, and 17,000 tons of jute. The exportations during the same period reach in the aggregate, exclusive of flax straw, 7,400 tons. Notwithstanding these figures, the supply of flax was so evidently inadequate that a few enterprising spinners and

merchants of Lille formed, a few years ago, a company for the culture of flax in the colony of Algeria, where the plant was remarked to grow abundantly in a wild state. The success of this speculation is worthy of notice, for last year, three years after their modest commencement, they sold 1,000 tons of flax fibre. We find exhibited, not only by several spinners, but by the "Compagnie de la Culture du

Lin et Coton d'Algérie," besides exceptional samples spun into yarns, numbering from 100 to 300, a good quantity of medium flax, suitable for spinning wefts, forty to seventy, of good colour, resembling in many respects those better marks of Russian flax which of late years have become so scarce. They have great facilities for the weeding and pulling of flax in Algeria in the large native population who do this kind of work well, cheaply, and quickly. The water for steeping is good, and the scutching-machines used are the best that can be had. As the crop is gathered in May, the produce can be early in the market. The seed also deserves notice; for the grain originally imported from Riga has so much improved after its third year in Algeria that, when tried with freshly imported Riga seed, it gives flax not only 10 in. longer, but with a finer fibre. Trials of this seed, under official surveillance, have been made both in France and Belgium with the like result.

MR. STEVELLY ON LINEN THREAD, &c.

Messrs. Droulers et Agache (117) give us examples of this flax spun; and they exhibit likewise an extensive range of well-spun yarns, extending from 10 to 300, shown so as to make the difference between the qualities of flax grown in different districts easily appreciable. Messrs. Le Blan Frères (64 and 120) have also a very creditable collection of yarns. The principal honours of the French department, must, however, be reserved for Messrs. Wallaert Frères (13), both as spinners and manufacturers, who exhibit a collection of family linens and sheetings, all power-loom goods, which certainly show considerable progress, although closely followed by the large manufacturers of Armentières, Messrs. Beghin Duflos, Victor Pouchain, and Mathieu Delangre (9, 10, and 11).

Notice of some remarkable French flax spinners and manufacturers.

Normandy was the cradle of household linens, under the name of " cretonnes;" and these Norman combinations are more or less those copied at Lille. Foremost among the large houses of Normandy are the old house of Laniel (93), the first to employ power-looms in France, and still ready to adopt every improvement; M. Fournet and Messrs. P. Marie et Cie., both of Lisieux, who have seen nearly all their smaller neighbours disappear in the unequal struggle between hand and power looms. Even they, with their powerful organisation, have to contend with the high rate of wages, or rather with the difficulty of finding skilled labour in a region so far removed from the present centre of the linen trade. In these goods, whether they be from Lille or from Normandy, the base in the same. The lower sets are 42 in. wide, the finer 36 in., and a little is made 32 in.

French household linens and the yarn employed in their manufacture.

3.   C

The yarns are well boiled, and we get some idea of the qualities employed by examining the samples exhibited by Messrs. Méry, Samson, Rattray, et Cie. (51), an establishment founded by Messrs. Duffin, of Belfast, and making yarns specially for these goods in 25-40 line.

In these we find a quality of stuff employed in the spinning which would go with us to at least 20 numbers higher, while the prices range from 14s. to 12s. per bundle.— (*See note* B.)

The setting of the cloth is as follows :—

9¾ threads in 5 millimetres or 55 porters - -	{ 16 warp, 20 weft.
13 ,, ,, 60 ,, - -	{ 28 warp, 40 weft.
15½ ,, ,, 67 ,, - -	{ 40 warp, 55 weft.
18 ,, ,, 87 ,, - -	{ 60 warp, 80 weft.
22½ ,, ,, 102 ,, - -	{ 90 warp, 120 weft.
32 ,, ,, 136 ,, - -	{ 130 warp, 160 weft.

Messrs. Jongley-Hovelacque, Caron Cardon, et Cie., and Messrs. Duhamel Frères, respectively 5 and 71 in the catalogue, give us all the types of cloth used in the naval and military services, both of which, as well as the hospitals, prisons, and other public departments, unlike our own, have always employed linen in preference to cotton. These types have a special interest for our manufacturers at present, from the fact that, in the last adjudication of a linen contract, the French military authorities, contrary to their invariable rule since 1840, left out the clause in the conditions requiring the contractor to guarantee that the goods are *bonâ fide* of French manufacture. Of this return to a liberal spirit we cannot speak too highly, and we accept it as a good omen for the future.

Messrs. J. Scrive et Fils (67) and a number of others show samples of blouse linens, blue, slate, and drab, in all variety of shades. These cloths are generally made 41 inches to 42 inches wide, although a small portion are in 55 inches; but for our purpose we can study such goods more profitably in Belgium, where the manufacturers, without neglecting the preference given in France to heavy linens, have at the same time kept the French tariff in view. The heavy linens made of dry spun yarn, although forming an important part of the French consumption, have

less interest for us than the preceding descriptions ; still
we cannot pass over the exhibitions of Messrs. Dickson et
Cie. and of the " Société Linière du Finisterre," from their
well-known position in the trade of France.   Besides the
goods they sell for shirts and sheets in the agricultural
districts, they are the principal linen contractors for the
navy ; and their sailcloth competes with the best marks of
Dundee in every market.   Nothing could more thoroughly
prove the absurdity of their being still "protected" by a
15 per cent. duty in France.

The trade in hempen fabrics is largely represented in the
Exhibition.   The peasants use both these and the low linen
goods for sheetings and shirtings, and both, after being
steeped in a preparation of sulphate of copper, to make them
waterproof, serve to make those cart-covers with which
every railway waggon, waggon and cart in France is provided.   Important hemp-mills are placed in the localities
where they grow the largest quantity of the fibre which they
employ.   The wonderful hemp of the valley of the Loire,
the best in the world, is nearly monopolised by the Angers
spinners (46, 37, and 76), and they certainly know how to
make the most of it, whether in shoe-thread, fishing-tackle,
or cloth.   In this part of the trade they have no competitor.   The hemp of the Sarthe would be insufficient for the
quality of hempen cloth made by Barry, jeune, et Cie., and
Messrs. Cornilleau aîné, et Cie., of the Mans, whose reputation as power-loom manufacturers is well sustained in the
Exhibition.   The hemp of Picardy is much used in the
north of France, although no house represents it exclusively ;
and we must mention, in connection with this subject, the
exhibition of Messrs. Hambis et Cie., Ligugé (Vienne).

Passing quickly over the jute yarns (represented by the
Nos. 24, 26, and 55, the latter formerly the director of the
large house of Cohen et Cie.), we come to the sacking and
hessians of Messrs. Saint Frères, and Messrs. Drummond,
Baxter et Cie., both large houses and both spinners as well as
weavers, Messrs. Saint alone producing over 70,000 yards of
cloth a day.   Messrs. Devailly Frères, of Amiens, exhibit the
novelty in this department—a sack woven without seams.

We find eight exhibitors of fancy drills under the Nos.
101 to 106 and 110 to 112 of the official catalogue.   Two
districts appear to monopolise this trade—Roubaix, in the
immediate neighbourhood of Lille ; and Laval, in the May-
enne.   In both the arrangements of colour are tasteful, and
the goods are well made and cheap.   Fancy drills, either in
the piece or in made-up articles of clothing, form a large

MR.
STEVELLY
ON LINEN
THREAD,
&C.

item in the linen exports of France. Let me specially draw attention to (105) Messrs. Parent et Danchin, who show very nice fancy drills, 24 in. wide, linen warp and jute weft, at $7\frac{1}{2}d.$ to $11d.$, a new and very useful combination.

Cholet district and its manufactures.

In the Cholet district (represented by the Nos. 1–4 and 86–90) the trade in light linens and in linen handkerchiefs gives employment to about 20,000 looms. There they make also checked Madras handkerchiefs, the colours dyed in the yarns. For these they have an outlet not only in France, but in the remoter districts of Italy, Germany, and Spain, where snuff-taking still lingers. This class of goods is, I believe, unknown to our manufacturers.

The "batiste" of Cambrai.

Cambrai is also an important centre for the finer handkerchiefs, and for fine linens. The wages are higher than in the Cholet district, and the weavers are singularly intelligent. Eight manufacturers give a proof of this in a very varied exhibition. The three of those first on the list, Messrs. Vinchon et Basquin, M. Bricont-Molet, and M. Bertrand-Milcent, show a beautiful series of " batistes," which are made from hand-spun yarn, and to which the town of Cambrai has given its name, and also of more ordinary fabrics. If one had an opportunity of visiting M. Bertrand-Milcent's important power-loom factory, of comparing his goods and prices with ours, and of asking his opinion as to the danger of English competition, I think his answer would settle for ever the question of the necessity of maintaining a duty for the protection of this class of goods in France.

Linen thread of Lille.

The thread of Lille, which is exhibited by eighteen of the principal makers (27 to 45), including such names as Descamps, Humbert Frères, Crespel, and Verstraete, shows what good dyeing and finishing can do for cheap thread. I think, however, that in this case low prices and a convenient way of balling sewing-thread have more to do with their success than the intrinsic value of the article they make.

Yarn bleaching.

The yarn bleaching of Messrs. Vandewynckele (128) deserves notice both for colour and for the roundness of the thread. Although not falling under the class on which I am reporting, I may be permitted to mention here the new system of bleaching yarn of Messrs. Jarrason, and A. Bastaert, of Lille, which has been adopted by several large manufacturers in France. I hope we shall have the valuable opinion of Dr. Hoffman, the reporter of Classes 44 and 45, upon this invention, and also upon the attempt which has been made by Messrs. Tessie du Motay and C. R. Maréchal to substitute or the action of the sun in bleaching that of a preparation of the permanganate of soda or potash.

The progress which has been made during the last 10 years in the damask trade in France is most remarkable, and the dazzling show of French damasks in the Exhibition, and the number and importance of the exhibitors, show that damask goods are now fast taking their proper place with the consumers, and replacing the plain linens and low diapers which were formerly in almost universal use as table linen. The show of everyday damasks of Messrs. J. Casse et Fils (12) is very creditable, without considering their two chef-d'œuvres, which it would require the more authorised pen of an art-critic to discuss ; as also are those of Messrs. Deneux Frères (96), Messrs. Danset Frères (14), who need fear no competitor in their ordinary sorts, and M. J. Joanard, of Paris (92), whose designs are very beautiful, and so varied that every taste may be satisfied except that of the admirer of geometrical patterns, of which I do not see a single example.

MR. STEVELLY ON LINEN THREAD, &C.

Damasks in France.

An honourable mention is due to Mr. Turquet, of Senlis, who has devoted himself to bleaching and finishing damask goods. Those in this Exhibition are nearly all bleached by him and do him great credit, although his name does not appear in the catalogue.

Algeria has nothing worthy of note in Class 28. The few wretched examples of native manufacture are most un-interesting. I sought in vain for something analogous to the " Algerian stripes," made at one time largely in Belfast, of which the Arabs make the unique article of clothing worn in the tents during the hot weather. The interest in this country is more in its flax, to which I have already alluded. It is singular that, during the plague of locusts which devastated Algeria last year, while every other green thing was devoured, the flax plant was generously spared.

Algerian exhibition.

Holland being our customer for 250,000*l.* worth of yarn yearly, I cannot speak evil of her linen manufactures ; but, as I cannot praise them, I have no other course than to proceed to the next country on our circuit.

Holland.

Belgium shows much in common with the Lille district. The separation of French Flanders is of comparatively recent date ; and the foundation of the linen manufacture in this part of the Continent is attributed to certain barbarous tribes from the region of the Caspian Sea, who are said to have settled in this district some 300 years before the Christian era. Whether there may be truth in this legend or not, it is certain that Flanders linen can be traced back to a very early period. At the time of the first invasion of Gaul by the Romans these northern people wore the

Belgium is early noted in history for its linens.

MR.
STEVELLY
ON LINEN
THREAD,
&c.

"sagum," or blouse, which is still the national dress. Belgium offers many advantages for the development of the linen trade. The climate is very suitable to the growth of flax, which is accordingly of excellent quality; the water for steeping it is well suited to the purpose, and abundant; and a great amount of care and skill is employed in its cultivation and preparation. The inhabitants are naturally industrious, and are well trained by centuries of traditions; and the Belgian flax has always been esteemed the best in the world. The quality has, however, of late years been below the average, from the desire of the farmers to produce the greatest possible quantity on a given surface, which could only be effected at the expense of the quality by the employment of guano and artificial manures, whose effect is no longer doubtful. The growth of flax has by no means increased in the same ratio as the prices. In 1840 we find the production estimated at 21,000 tons; while in 1864, with the prices trebled, the quantity grown is estimated at 25,000 tons. The larger proportion of the finer descriptions finds its way to Belfast and England, the middle sorts and the coarse flax are bought by the Lille spinners, or go to supply the 250,000 spindles which turn in Belgium itself. The total exportation of grey yarn is to an amount of about 600,000*l.*, and of bleached yarn and thread about 400,000*l.*, making in round numbers a total of 1,000,000*l.* Of this nearly half is sold to the neighbouring Prussian State, and the remainder is divided between Holland, France, and Switzerland. The exportation of linen from Belgium reached in 1864 the imposing amount of 1,600,000*l.* France heads the list of customers by taking 440,000*l.* worth; Holland buys nearly as much, while the wonderful little island of Cuba absorbs 185,000*l.* Prussia and Switzerland take 100,000*l.* each; and, although the Hanse Towns figure for over 160,000*l.*, a large portion of that sum must no doubt be attributed to Russia, as she only received directly for 70*l.* The remaining 175,000*l.* are distributed over the globe. These results are really surprising in a country with a population of four millions and a half.

Amongst the most remarkable of the Belgian manufacturers is the well-known name of M. Rey Aîné, of Brussels, who, after a long life devoted to this trade, finds himself, as he tells us, at the head of 750 power-looms, and nearly double the number of handlooms, employing some 4,000 workers, and producing over 11,000,000 yards of linen annually, embracing nearly every class of goods. I propose drawing attention to the most remarkable varieties of

Growth of flax in Belgium.

Linen yarn exported from Belgium.

Belgian exports in linens.

A remarkable Belgian manufacturer.

Belgian linens only, and to those manufacturers who appear to me to succeed best in their specialties.

Amongst these I class shirting as the most important; and the combined exhibition of Courtrai and Roulers gives us ample means of judging both of their merits and of their defects. Among the latter I would class an inferior bleach, and perhaps a somewhat smaller quantity of weft, than we are accustomed to, and an overboiling of the yarn, which renders it soft and gives it a tendency to form small lumps in the after processes. The yarns are, however, excellent, the cloth is well woven, and the prices are moderate, as may be judged by the quotations of more than one of the exhibitors. Taking the excellent example of M. Van Acker (16), or M. Parmentier (51), we find the following quotations for 4–4 light medium linens, by the number of threads in the warp :—(*See note B.*)

Threads in Warp.	Per Metre, Fr.	Per Yard.
3,400	1·90	1*s.* 4¾*d.*
3,800	2·10	1*s.* 6½*d.*
4,200	2·40	1*s.* 9*d.*
4,600	2·80	2*s.* 0½*d.*
5,000	3·25	2*s.* 4½*d.*
5,600	4·75	3*s.* 5½*d.*
5,800	5·25	3*s.* 10*d.*
6,400	6·50	4*s.* 9½*d.*
7,000	8·50	6*s.* 2½*d.*

And I consider these lower figures a valuable indication of the cheap rate at which they can work. Of course, above 5,600 these are only Exhibition goods. In the sheetings exhibited by the same houses and in those of M. Dathes (8) and M. Denys (9) we have examples of goods used largely on the Continent, especially in Spain, Italy, and Germany, which are little made with us. They command a large sale, for they are of good material, and lighter and cheaper than goods of the same class of British make. Many houses exhibit blouse linens, of which the sale is very important ; it will be sufficient to mention M. Tant-Verlinde and Messrs. Van Damme Frères, of Boulers (55 and 57), M. Parmentier, of Iseghem (51), and M. H. Van Bradander (375), of the Belgian catalogue. I consider M. Parmentier one of the most successful of the Belgian manufacturers. He has adapted his goods with the greatest intelligence and success to the countries with which he deals, whether in the strong makes for Switzerland and Germany or in the lighter makes for France. The immense sale of these goods naturally draws our attention particularly to them, and, seeing them, a manufacturer will have little difficulty in imagining that Belfast, paying the same duties for their entrance into France, cannot sell a single piece, and, after many trials, has fairly given up the attempt as hopeless. The whole of the trade is thus left in the hands of Belgium, whose sales are estimated by millions yearly in this one article, the range being $10^{\circ\circ}$ to $18^{\circ\circ}$, and nine-tenths of the sales in the three middle numbers, 13, 14, and 15. The difficulty in attaining an object of the greatest importance often lies in the very simplicity of the means required; the most trifling element neglected spoils all. Let me lay down a few rules on which all are agreed. Brown, width 44 in. full, avoid streaked yarns, as every shade will not only show after the cloth is dyed, but will be emphasised by the indigo; light blue coloured yarns are very much preferred, as they dye best; gold-yellow colour passes, but Irish flax is considered unsuitable, from the variety of shades. I fancy that could be obviated by sorting to colour as well as to quality. It should be well understood that the question of colour is one of the very first importance. The yarn should be well boiled.

Settings vary, but the following may be taken as the average :—

	12	13	14	15
Count by 5 millimetres				
Warp „ „	40	45	50	55
Weft „ „	65	70	80	85
Price per metre approx., fr.	1·20	1·30	1·45	1·60
Price per yard	$10\frac{1}{2}d.$	$11\frac{1}{2}d.$	$12\frac{3}{4}d.$	$14d.$

Two shots over square of weft at least: some make four shots, but with fine weft like the above that is easy. Some quantity is also made in yarns coloured with pounded slate. The Belgians had this assimilated to brown linens in their Treaty, and we enjoy the benefit of this clause. In any case the goods must be well picked and cleaned, especially for dyeing purposes. There is another important point; the calculation of cost must be based upon a large quantity, and not upon a few samples, otherwise the manufacturer is disappointed and tires of working at a loss, abandoning an enterprise which might probably have succeeded if commenced on a scale of a certain importance. Some makes of these goods are much stronger; and this Exhibition affords, as I have already stated, a very valuable opportunity of studying them in every variety. Their study is much facilitated by the very general habit amongst the exhibitors, as men conscious of their strength, of giving us widths, prices, counts of threads, and numbers of yarns.

The cheap labour in Belgium is doubtless a difficult element to contend with; but sooner or later it must follow the general advance. Although the goods produced by our power-looms are now more costly, their price is diminishing day by day by new inventions and by the improving skill of the weavers; and they are at all times more regular. All these considerations should encourage us to emulation.

The Belgium drill, of which, however, we have but few examples in the Exhibition, are remarkably good value. We have an opportunity of judging of them in the samples of Messrs. Cornille-Bartholomeus et Bartholomeus Frères, and one or two others.

Hessians figure very creditably. M. Van Robaeys (20), who shows 30-in. wide sacking, at $4\frac{1}{2}d.$, and made-up sacks, 30 in. by 40 in., at $9\frac{3}{4}d.$, is not exorbitant; while Veranneman et Sœur (61), who quote 40 in. Hessians at $5\frac{1}{2}d.$, are, perhaps, even cheaper. A step higher in manufacture, M. William Wilford, of Tamise, whose name indicates his nationality, shows as good a collection of sailcloth as if his manufactory had been at Dundee.

One word here in praise of the intelligence of the Belgian spinners who have struck out for themselves a new path which, so far, no English spinner has disputed with them— making a class of yarn which is almost unknown to our manufacturers, and which has contributed greatly to the success of theirs, especially in the manufacture of cloth for dyeing. The samples exhibited by the Société de la Lys and the Société Linière Gantoise perfectly justify the competition which exists for their produce and explain their enormous and well-sustained profits, as well as their very high prices:—(*See note* B.)

> 1st quality, 40 to 100, at about 10s. 0d.
> 2nd ditto   „   „   9s. 6d.
> 40 to 70, in Russian flax „   7s. 0d.

M. Simon-Boucher, of Tournai (74), speaks of the success he has had in his wet-spinning by allowing the fibre to remain a much longer time than has been customary in the water; he also exhibits some fine samples of spun hemp. Sample of hand-spun yarns ranging from 200 to 1,600, exhibited by M. Devos, remind us of the past, and afford a striking example of the perfection of hand labour compared with that of the most perfect machines. The blind, aided by their fine sense of touch, succeed best in this delicate manipulation.

The Belgian handkerchiefs are but poor; and the damasks, of which there are several exhibitors—the best, perhaps, Messrs. Noel Frères, of Alost (69), and M. Brandt (2)—are indifferent in pattern and detestable in bleach.

Damasks, &c.

Thread trade in Belgium.

I have in vain searched the Exhibition for an explanation of the fact that in 1864 Belgium exported 300,000*l.* worth of linen thread, while England in 1866 exported only for 510,800*l.*, and France for 100,000*l.*

The samples of Messrs Ch. de Coq and Co., of Lokeren, and Messrs. Declercq et d'Huyvetter, of Iseghem, which appear to be the best of their kind, only add to my embarrassment.

From France and Belgium we have much to learn; I have therefore thought myself justified in studying their productions somewhat in detail. In dealing with the remaining countries we can afford to be comparatively brief.

Prussia and the northern States of Germany.

Prussia and the northern States of Germany, however, still present important fields of manufacture, of which the nearest home is Bielefeldt, whose linens are well known, not only in Germany and Russia, but also in France and Italy. The celebrity of this region for fine linens dates from the time of hand-spun yarns. Of this we have many proofs even in this Exhibition. Above 21^{00} these linens are admirable; below that number I think their prices must shut them out from every market where an old and honourable connection does not weigh in their favour. Of these fine linens we can have no better example than those of F. G. Kroenig, whose existence dates from the year 1763;

Bielefeldt fine linens.

and of Bertelsmann and Son (20). The sale of this very fine linen is of course limited. Here they push it by turning it into shirt fronts by the aid of sewing-machines. Herr Westermann (3) and Herr Heidsieck (4) give us some good

Damasks.

examples of well-executed damask, which appears, however, to be an accidental article of manufacture in this country, entirely devoted to plain fine linen. Side by side with these fine goods and this old-fashioned trading, we find

Flax spinning in Westphalia.

modern industry represented by several large flax-spinners and power-loom manufacturers, such as the Bielefeldt Company (28), the Ravensberg Company (34), the Vorwörts Company (29), Herr Mevissen (35), Herren Schoeller, Mevisson, and Bückler, of Düren (36), and the Viersen Spin-

Viersen Spinning Company.

ning Company (37), who average 15,000 spindles each, and many of them have large power-loom factories. These establishments, put up recently on our own models, only interest us as a pupil's success must always interest his teacher.

Passing north from Bieldfeldt, we reach Osnabrück, where we find that the old-fashioned manufacture of that name is still a reality. The Hanoverian market officers who measured and sealed only a part of their cloth last year, state that the value of the linen which passed through their hands amounted to 170,000*l.* In this neighbourhood Herr Aschrot, of Cassel (42), is certainly the most remarkable manufacturer. He appears to make every kind of goods, from white shirtings to Hessians, at 4*d.* a yard, including dowlas, russians, and many other familiar names. I particularly noticed a hessian made nine yards wide on a five yard wide loom by the system of doubling, long since applied to silk,

Leaving Hanover, we come to the classic land of damasks, Saxony, which, however, leaves its reputation in the hands of but few exhibitors. Herr Joseph Meyer, of Dresden (57), besides his special piece, Rembrandt and his Wife, gives us many cloths excellent both in design and bleach; and Herr Proelss (58) is a manufacturer above the average. The 2,000 looms of Herr Fraenkel, of Neustadt (44), enable him, with his ordinary goods, to make, perhaps, the best show of damasks from the district; at all events, they justify his success as a manufacturer, for he commenced in 1855 with two looms, and gradually extended his trade to its present importance. The exhibition of the above-named Dresden houses is no doubt creditable; but I should have liked to have seen more numerous samples from Zittau and its neighbourhood, where damask manufacturers are plentiful, to have compared their goods with those of France, and thus to have been enabled to judge what portion of the old and wide-spread reputation of Saxon damasks is real and how much is kept up through tradition.

H. Waentig and Co., of Zittau, show an excellent collection of fancy drills, both linen and mixtures, for which they have a sale of 30,000 pieces yearly; and in plain power-loom goods Herren Kaemelo, Erben, and Co., of Gross Schöneau, makes a very saleable article 8*d.* to 1*s.* 6*d.* a yard. Herr C. T. Matthes (56) and Herr Neumann, of Eylau (60), have an excellent display of " listadoes," used like those we make ourselves, for negro clothing in the West Indies. In Germany they have given a much greater variety to these goods, and have thus secured a larger share in the trade than we have done in Ireland.

Nos. 45 to 50 form the collective exhibition of Lauban, and are almost entirely devoted to linen handkerchiefs. These goods are perfectly got up—weaving, bleaching, and finishing. Many manufacturers employ 300 or 400 looms,

MR. STEVELLY ON LINEN THREAD, &c.

Osnabrück.

Saxon damasks.

Drills and listadoes made in Zittau or its neighbourhood.

Lauban and its linen handkerchiefs.

MR.
STEVELLY
ON LINEN
THREAD,
&c.
—
and the manufacture of these goods fully justifies the favour in which they are held by all, and especially by their Russian neighbours.

In the Russian trade, Irish linen handkerchiefs have always found them the most formidable competitors.

Silesian
manufac-
turers of
note.
We are also favoured with an exhibition of the products of the " Kramsta," one of the largest houses in Germany, if not in the world. The mill, it is true, has only 17,000 spindles on flax, and the power-looms are only 500 in number on linen goods; but, between their linen and cotton manufactures, they give employment to 10,000 persons, and are buyers of 420,000 bundles of English yarn yearly. Erdmannsdorf (68), the King of Prussia's model flax-mill, is a large concern, on which nothing has been spared to put it on the best footing. Some 4,000 persons are employed, and they give us a good idea of their makes in drills, diapers, and family linens.

" Hanse
Towns " in
statistical
tables.
Before leaving Prussia, I must express my regret that the exportation from England for this country, as for many others, appears under the head of " Hanse Towns." This prevents us from knowing exactly what sum we sell to each country, I think our trade with the Silesian part of Prussia is improving under the present tariff, although a wide margin is still left for reduction.

Prussian
duties levied
on linen
and yarn.

			£
On grey yarn the duty per ton is about	-		6
On bleached yarn	„	„	- 12
On grey linen	„	„	- 12
On white linen	„	„	- 30

On fine yarns this is not perhaps enormous; but on the yarns for the Saxon drills and damasks it is very heavy, and something might perhaps be done towards having it reduced.

Austria.
The linen
trade in
Bohemia.
Leaving here the order of the catalogue, which separates Prussia from her late adversary by the kingdom of Wirtemburg, it will be simpler to cross the Austrian frontier. Here a close resemblance to what we have seen in Prussian Silesia points clearly to the common origin of the manufactures of both sides of the mountains. In this industrious and thriving country the standard of living is low, and the present rate of wages reminds one of the scale in Ireland fifteen years ago. The war of last year fell heavily on the inhabitants of this district, and nearly every village, known before only for its linens — Trautenau, Nachod. Hermannseifen, Rumburg, and many others—has now given its name to a battle. As it has turned out the war has

proved only an episode, and the number of mills built or now building will, no doubt, in a few years, make a great change in the linen industry in this patriarchal country, for which nature has done so much. The great manufacture, both of this district and of Moravia, is fine linen, and the principal peculiarity of the manufacture is the common use of bleached yarns ; these they handle in a very superior way, otherwise their weaving them at all would be impossible, as they use daily, yarn as fine as 180 in the weft. The Exhibition is wanting both in a series of manufactured goods and in samples of the yarn ; still a poorer show of linen than that of Austria might be redeemed by the goods of Herran Rayman and Regenhart (25), as their quality places them first of their kind amongst the Continental exhibitors. The variety is not great—a tablecloth made for the Emperor of Austria, with a few plainer damasks, a range of linen handkerchiefs, and some fine light linens, but every one must be struck by the perfection of bleach of these latter. A. Küfferle and Co., a Vienna house, who have their manufactory at Frievaldau, a village in Silesia, amply prove that the art of making good damasks and cheap handkerchiefs, with a bleach only to be found elsewhere in Ireland, has taken deep root in the country.

Wirtemburg has in Herr A. F. Lang a manufacturer of more than ordinary merit. He shows excellent reproductions of our own light linens, made both by power and by hand labour. We must regret however that his "bleubeuren bleiche," however great its name in Germany, has not yet attained our standard. The damasks of Herr Faber, of Stutgard, and the fancy drills of Herr Kissel are very excellent.

Switzerland, the next country in the list, has also cheap labour; but I could only find in her exhibition the fancy drills of M. Schoop-Vonderwahl, worthy of notice. Spain, by poor samples of manufacture, shows the effect of a long continued system of protection.

Spain is by far our largest customer for yarn, her purchases amounting in 1866 to three quarters of a million sterling in value ; but her manufacturers are not sufficiently excited by competition from without to make any figure in the world's show.

Portugal buys nearly all its linens from England, amounting in value to about 50,000*l.* a year. The climate does not seem to suit the manufacture of anything except the very coarsest towelling, hessians, sailcloth, and such coarse fabrics.

MR. STEVELLY ON LINEN THREAD, &c.

Wirtemberg.

Switzerland.

Spain.

Portugal.

MR.
STEVELLY
ON LINEN
THREAD,
&c.

Greece.
Sweden.

Russia.

In Greece I could see no signs of the exhibition announced in the catalogue.

Sweden shows us some damasks and plain linens, made apparently a century ago; but the sailcloth of Messrs. W. Gibson and Sons might have come from Dundee to Paris.

Russia is certainly advancing. She employs good materials, and makes an excellent article both in yarn and cloth. Both the Baltic and the Sammerfors Companies (12 and 15 respectively) give excellent samples; the former in yarns, the latter both in yarns and linens, fine and coarse. The native manufacturers in white shirtings, hessians, &c., present some interest; but perhaps the most important exhibitor is the Russian Government, which shows the types of linen employed in its naval and military services, giving the weight, width, and price of every article.

The Italian
section.

In the Italian section I was struck with the quantity of embroidered towels, of which many were at one time made in Ireland. The Italian linen manufactures may have held a high rank in past ages; they certainly have but little in common with the present, although I could name several honourable exceptions.

Turkey.

Turkey has thirty-seven exhibitors, but their collective productions would go into a carpet-bag. The primitive appearance of these goods is their principal merit.

United
States.

The United States do not even put in an appearance. They are too intelligent not to feel that, even with their natural advantages and Saxon industry, their protective system prevents their competing on an equal footing with European nations, and they are too proud to figure by the side of Spain or Italy.

Great
Britain.
Statistics
of its linen
trade.

During the last few years the linen trade of great Britain has made a prodigious stride. The declared value of linen manufactures, exclusive of yarn, exported from the United Kingdom during the 11 months ending Nov. 30, 1861, was 3,592,157*l.*; for the same period of the year 1862, 4,585,170*l.*; of 1863, 5,806,522*l.*; of 1864, 7,505,226*l.*; of 1865, 8,244,118*l.*; and of 1866, 8,885,595*l.* This extraordinary development, I need not say, has been mainly due to the unnatural stimulus of the cotton famine. It is greatly to be regretted that Barnsley, Dundee, Dunfermline, and the other minor centres of the linen manufacture of England and Scotland are unrepresented; in their absence, however, the credit of the British trade is fully sustained by the unrivalled exhibition of linen goods from Belfast. Crowded into this small court we have every article which.

can be made from flax, each unsurpassed of its kind, from nail-bags made of scutchers tow to the finest linens and damasks.

[MR. STEVELLY ON LINEN THREAD, &C.

Belfast.

In the Exhibition of 1867 the manufacturers of linen and yarn of the north of Ireland have received four gold medals and one silver medal, an amount of honour higher than has been awarded to any other district or to any other industry.

Lest anyone unacquainted with the machinery employed in the distribution of these prizes should ascribe any portion of that success to partiality on the part of the judges, it is right to state that of the eight members of the linen jury only one was an Englishman; and it is said that he, with laudable delicacy, allowed his colleagues to decide upon the merits of his countrymen. Belfast may now certainly be said to have fully established her position as the metropolis of the linen trade.

The extraordinary advance of this industry, and the enormous importance which it has now acquired, may be gathered from the following figures :—In Belfast and within a radius of seven miles, the value of the spinning-mills, including buildings, steam-engines, and machinery, is estimated at 2,700,000*l.*, and the power-looms at 300,000*l.* The imports of flax seed, flax, tow, linen yarn, and thread to this district amounted for the year 1866 to 2,117,500*l.*; and the exports for the same period to 7,150,000*l.*

The progress of the Irish trade.

The most striking among the gold medallists is undoubtedly the Belfast "trophy," or collective exhibition, to which 30 of the leading firms of the Belfast district are contributors, and which forms a small museum of the products of the trade. It contains samples of power-loom warps, first, second, and third qualities, from fine to coarse, with the wefts to suit; strong and light linen warps, with fine wefts up to 300; and the different qualities of tows.

The Belfast trophy.

The prices of all these are seen by reference to the Belfast linen trade circular, better than by any price-list. Perhaps the power-loom linens may be found the most interesting item. They are in all descriptions, 7°° to 20°°, narrow and wide, from lawns to strong makes. In fineness and regularity in weaving these goods are not only unequalled but unattempted elsewhere, and yet nothing in the case is made specially for the Exhibition—a thousand pieces of each could be produced of exactly the same quality on the shortest notice.

In fine fronting linens and lawns Belfast has kept up its old reputation ; and cambric and linen handkerchiefs, white, printed, sewn, or embroidered, are shown in every form.

Irish exhibitors and their goods.

The damasks are also in great variety; but, unfortunately, the small space prevents their being seen to advantage; even those selected for the most prominent place, and made for crowned heads, are exhibited rather for the bleach, and only a judge can appreciate the perfection of the execution.

The one peculiarity of all the Irish exhibitions, which strikes every passer by, is their splendid bleach. This seems natural to the country, and for perfect colour, unaltered strength of the tissues, and cheapness of production, forms a wonderful contrast to the foreign courts.

In the Belfast court we have such a multitude of goods for different purposes, and for the use of different nations, that it is hopeless to attempt to notice all, though each is of vast importance as an article of trade. We have linens for American clothing; drills equal in quality to any made at Barnsley, and produced in Belfast at a much cheaper rate; towelling, sheeting, tailors' and shoemakers' thread; the goods sold in South America and the West Indian markets, from the listadoes for the clothing of the negroes to the creas, or the plutillas, silesias, estopillas, and grano di oras, half hidden in their rich ornaments; and printed linen cambric dresses, an article hitherto almost unknown, which has found many admirers among the foreign ladies. These types are to be found repeated more or less fully in all the Irish exhibitions, except, perhaps, in that of Mr. John S. Brown (3), who has won his medal through the special merits of his damasks. Mr. W. Girdwood, of Belfast (9), gives the only examples of linens printed in anything like variety. Mr. Girdwood's skill as a printer is too well known to require praise, and the samples which he has shown are neither better nor worse than his everyday work. He deserves double credit for the beauty of the linens which he has selected for the purposes of his art.

The honours accorded to Belfast must be accepted as addressed more to the trade generally than to individuals, else we could scarcely explain the distributive justice which adjudges a silver medal only to the unsurpassed exhibition of Messrs. Matier and Co. (13); and Mr. Ainsworth's threads, I cannot but think, with due respect to a decision which is now irrevocable, deserved something more than a mere "honourable mention." The linen trade of Great Britain cannot but be gratified by the generous award of the international jury.

NOTE A.—I am likewise indebted to Mr. V. Vinelle, Secretary of the Lille Committee "du Journal Circulaire du Marché Linière," for many interesting statistics and papers relating to the French linen trade.

Many of the figures and facts which I advance with reference to Belgium and Prussia, will be found in the official catalogues of those countries.

NOTE B.—To render quotations of prices comprehensible to English readers, it is necessary to bear in mind that at the time this report was written the common weft yarns of Belfast were selling, Nos. 60 to 100, above 6s. per bundle 38 inch wide. Light power-loom linens 10d. per yard, and 17^{00} light medium linen at 16d. brown.

REPORT on the WORSTED TRADE.—(Class 29 and parts of Class 43 and Class 56.) — By the DEPUTATION of the BRADFORD CHAMBER of COMMERCE.

FOLLOWING the example of 1855, the Council appointed Messrs. Venimore Godwin, Charles Stead, Alfred Illingworth, and George Motley Waud as a deputation to report on such portions of the Paris Exhibition of 1867 as might concern the worsted trade of this district in its various departments.

The deputation met in Paris on June 5, and proceeded to examine the wools in group 5, Class 43 ; the tops, yarns, and worsted fabrics in group 4, Class 29 ; and the worsted machinery in group 6, Class 56. They have to express their acknowledgments to the various gentlemen to whom they had occasion to apply for information, especially to M. Larsonnier, Member of the Chamber of Commerce of Paris, and President of Class 29, group 4.

WOOL.

The collection of wool from almost all parts of the world under one roof rendered two facts very striking. The one, the absence of any adequate substitute for English deep grown wools ; the other, the slow rate of improvement in those wools of foreign growth which are used in aid of the lower qualities of English combing wool. As to the first of these points, your deputation found reason to believe that however largely inferior foreign wools—such as Algerian, Persian, Chilian, Montevideo, Turkish, and other wools of the Levant—may be used for combing purposes in the Bradford trade, they are utilised by French manufacturers comparatively to a much greater extent.

With regard to the second point, your deputation examined with much interest various samples of alpaca, mohair, and foreign deep grown wools, and endeavoured to estimate their increase and improvement, questions to which the Wool Supply Committee of the Bradford Chamber of Commerce has directed so much attention.

The Acclimatisation Society of Victoria shows the progress made in the production of alpaca wool since the first results of the importation of alpacas into that colony, which were exhibited in 1862. It is clear that alpaca wool can be grown in Australia, but there is hardly sufficient evidence

D 2

that the experiment has been worked out to the extent necessary to decide whether the true alpaca character can be not only produced but retained and perpetuated. The growth of mohair appears to have been more generally attempted. Mohair is shown from Victoria, from the Cape, from the United States of America, and from the Banda Oriental; and there is evidence of the efforts which continue to be made to naturalise English long wool in our colonies—as shown, for instance, in the case of Mr. J. H. Angus, of Collingrove, South Australia. In all these instances a wool of serviceable character is produced; but, however successful the first clips appear, the great difficulty seems to be the tendency to deteriorate, and to obviate this will apparently require much effort and some time. But, on the other hand, there is ample evidence of a capability of improvement in the native wools of many countries, which have length enough but want regularity of staple. And it would seem that, from the improvement of the wools of various countries, apart from the naturalisation of new types, we have reason to look for such a supply as will in course of time materially supplement the home growth of the lower classes of English wool. For instance, while on the one hand the splendid show of merino combing from Venezuela and Uruguay gives promise of a large addition to the Australian class of wool, in the other direction the native long wool shown by the Argentine Republic only requires to be improved from a bad-bred to a true-bred wool to become of great value to the Bradford trade.

Your deputation could not fail to notice the marked extension in the use of Australian wool in French goods, and that not only for weft but also for warp. Very beautiful specimens of its use for both purposes were shown by the colony of Victoria in the shape of poplins and merinos, manufactured by Messrs. Siebert, Ledouz, and Co.; and in shawls and printed goods, by Messrs. Larsonnier frères, and Chenest. The report prefixed to class 29, group 4, in the French catalogue, states that the importation of Australian wool into France, which in 1855 was not large, had risen in 1865 to 50,000,000 lbs., or probably upwards of 140,000 bags; and the importation of wool from other countries in the same year amounted to 110,000,000 lbs. The report of the deputation from this chamber, in 1855, went very carefully into the varieties of French wool, and their adaptation to the production of French goods. But it is very evident that the French no longer rely upon their home-grown wool to the extent they did, and are indebted to the Australian colonies and River Plate wools for the greater part of the increase in their production of fine goods. The same remarks apply to Germany, though to a less extent. The Australian and New Zealand colonies may well feel proud of the magnificent wools they show in this Exhibition and of the extent to which they are produced; for without them the manufacturers of England, France, and Germany would be in a very different position.

MACHINERY.

In machinery, group 6, Class 56, but little is exhibited *Machinery.* that is novel or superior to that which is already in use in the Bradford Trade, and exhibited by Messrs. G. Hattersley and Son; Mr. G. Hodgson, Messrs. Keighley and Co., Messrs. Leeming and Son, Messrs. J. and S. Smith, and Messrs. Sowdon and Stephenson, and for which a gold medal has been received by Mr. Hodgson and Messrs. Leeming and Son; and silver medals by Messrs. G. Hattersley and Sons, J. Keighley and Co., and J. and S. Smith.

For general purposes the best looms are, beyond com- *Looms.* parison, those by the well-known makers of this district, the demand for which for exportation continues from every foreign country competing in the production of worsted goods. In frames, the French appear to introduce the throstle to a limited extent, but still draw on what is known as the French system, and spin chiefly on the mule.

TOPS AND YARNS.

Tops and yarns are exhibited in large quantities (especially *Tops and* by France) of every description except alpaca, which the *yarns.* French do not as yet succeed in spinning. In Roubaix, mohair has been recently spun to a very small extent, and considerable progress has been made in spinning the coarse wools on the mule and the better numbers on English throstle frames. But though the Roubaix spinners are evidently paying great attention to the spinning of long wool, they have not yet attained the Bradford standard. France, however, preserves the same superiority in the spinning of fine yarns for all wool goods which England shows in yarns for mixed fabrics, and is closely followed in this respect by Germany. Amongst other cases of yarn might be noticed the fine warp of wool and silk shown by P. Dufourmantel and Co., the exquisitely beautiful yarns, 360s., shown by Seydouz, Siebert, and Co., the moucheté yarns, beaded yarns, yarns with a thread of cotton twisted

REPORT ON
THE
WORSTED
TRADE.
and broken in it, yarns with threads of different colours in an opposite twist on a white roving, and a variety of gold and silver thread yarns shown by various French houses, as also a large assortment of twisted yarns from Verviers and Rheims. Nor, on account of its relation to this district, can notice be omitted of the very beautiful case of silk waste products shown in Class 31 from Halifax by Messrs. Lister and Co.

WOVEN FABRICS.

Wool and
mixed
fabrics.

In all wool and mixed fabrics there is much in the Exhibition of 1867 which is interesting to Bradford. England is represented in Class 29 by Messrs. James Akroyd and Son, Messrs. C. F. Taylor and Co., Messrs. Mitchell and Shepherd, Messrs. Middleton, Answorth, and Co., and one or two others in addition to the Bradford collective exhibition. Perhaps the first thing that fixes the attention is the little effort at

England.
display which England makes, within very little compass, and in cases not so handsome as we understood were ordered. Bradford shows a very complete range of the market goods upon which the trade of the district rests, and from the manner in which they are shown, less regard has evidently been had to the eye of the casual observer than to facility for examination and comparison as a matter of

France.
business. By France, however, just as in 1862, no effort has been spared either in taste of arrangement or profuseness of display; one hundred and ninety-five, or, curiously enough, exactly the same number of exhibitors as in 1862, being catalogued in Class 29, including the collective displays of Rheims, Roubaix, and Tourcoing, the whole being shown with ample space in very handsome cases. In these France clearly maintains her long-established superiority in the finer all-wool plain goods, and this not by the introduction of any special novelty since 1862, but by the cheapness and beauty of the fabrics produced in merinoes, reps, poplins, &c. And it is also equally evident that in mixed Bradford goods, France, though not perhaps approaching us more nearly than she did in some few things that were shown in 1862, yet has made an approach much more general and on a vastly larger scale. On this point, however, it may be said first, that these woven fabrics are exceedingly similar in colouring and design to those of this district: and, secondly, that there is no means of applying the final test of prices, inasmuch as no prices are given that are of any avail in making a comparison. But it must at

the same time be recognised that Roubaix, the Bradford of France, has displayed great energy and skill in competing with goods admitted under the commercial treaty. Indeed, we are informed on good authority that Roubaix has increased her machinery fivefold since 1862. Her success proves in the most striking manner both the advantage of a wholesome competitive stimulus, and her ability to hold her own in her own market without the adventitous aid of a protective duty of 10 per cent. It is difficult to select for remark from so many cases, but we especially noticed the following :—Sautret Pousinet, double merinoes; Bossuat, beaded stuffs ; Durand, fancies; Moreau, fabrics of Angora rabbits' wool ; Sellier Delaforge, mixed fabrics ; Larsonnier frères and Chenest, very splendid prints, both in large and small patterns; Chatteau, fancies ; Pin Byart, ditto ; Louis Cordonnier, ditto ; Delfosses frères, ditto ; Leclerq Dupin, heavy Órleans and Alpaca ; and in one class of mixed goods, hand made from fine organdzine, silk warp, and mohair weft, with a swivel figure, some very beautiful goods, which Bradford does not attempt to make, were shown in several cases. The report in the French catalogue states that the number of hand-looms employed on worsted goods in France continues to be about the same that it was, and is even yet considerably greater than the number of power-looms, but that the increase of the trade may be measured by the extent to which power-looms have been introduced. That the wages of combing and spinning are generally higher than they were, and that whereas the exports of woollen and worsted goods together were about six millions and a half sterling in 1855, the exports of worsted goods alone exceeded eleven millions sterling in 1865.

The coloured checks and shawls of Austria, Prussia, and Saxony, and the damasks of Austria, show to great advantage ; and with them are exhibited cases of very good fine merinos and some mixed worsted fabrics. An excellent case is shown from Belgium by the Société Anonyme of Loth-les-Bruxelles. The goods shown from Carlsvik in Sweden fully maintain the high position they took in 1862, and are shown in cases combining effective display with great facilities for examination. In Russia, judging from the goods shown, and the number of exhibitors, there is evidence of great skill and progress, and of a considerable extension of the trade having take place. In addition to the cases of Messrs. Armand, of Moscow, and Schepeler, of Riga, which were so interesting in 1862, there are now very admirable collections of goods from Messrs. Bordine, Messrs. Bontiguine, Messrs. Elaguine, Messrs. Mikhailoff, Messrs. Schrader, and others, of Moscow ; Mr. Krouche, of Warsaw ; Schneidemann, of Riga, &c. In these cases a general range of all wool and mixed fabrics may be found, comprising counterparts both of the merinos and poplins of France, and of the cotton warp goods of Bradford, both plain and fancy. In one of these cases, that of Boutiguine, we saw also a very nice range of small China figures. It only remains under this head to notice that Spain, which made no show of these goods in 1862, has bought our looms, and is importing our yarns in addition to spinning herself, and now shows from Barcelona very excellent copies of our Bradford makes.

DYEING AND FINISHING.

Dyeing and finishing. With regard to dyeing and finishing, although the French, from the fact of their using no oil in the manufacture of their merinoes, are enabled to produce their very light colours beautifully bright and clear ; yet we have not seen any superiority in the darker colours of all wool goods over the case shown by Messrs. Ripley and Sons, of Bradford. There is something, however, in the finish of French all-wool goods which adds very greatly to their elasticity and handle. As to the dye and finish of mixed fabrics, the same observations apply as the manufacture of these goods ; and there is nothing in the Exhibition superior in these respects to the dye and finish of the goods shown by the Bradford Chamber of Commerce.

GENERAL REMARKS.

Conclusion. Perhaps we may be allowed in conclusion to state the general impression which we received from the Exhibition of 1867 as to the character and progress of the competition which Bradford has to sustain. As has already been mentioned, the exports of yarns and worsted goods from France amounted in 1865 to upwards of 11,000,000l., sterling, and of England to upwards of 18,000,000l. sterling, the spindles in each country being nearly equal in number. It would be extraordinary if in two trades of such magnitude and long standing, each country had not its special excellence. The superiority of France in fine all-wool plain goods can no longer be attributed to the drawback, as that has ceased ; nor entirely to the hand-loom, as they are largely made by power ; nor can it now be supposed as it was in 1855, that the superiority is owing to the use of French-grown wools, as Australian is used for both weft and warp. Something is, no doubt, due to the adaptation of the French system of drawing to spinning by the mule-jenny, and to the circumstance that the English yarns for all-wool goods generally are spun down too much, by which they are said to be rendered less fit for the purpose, and at the same time dearer. Whatever the cause may be, it is a fact that the price of fine all-wool dress goods has been much cheapened, and their importation into this country increased since 1861. Rheims alone has nearly doubled its production of all-wool merinos since 1862, and the all-wool reps and poplins which have been made in other parts of France have secured a remarkable hold on the English market. It cannot, therefore, but be matter of regret that this portion of the trade should be left to our opponents, with so little effort on the part of Bradford to compete, especially seeing the facility with which the growth of wool required is extended, and that the best wool for the purpose comes from our own colonies, and is sold in our own ports.

With regard, however, to mixed fabrics, it is evident that the superiority rests with England, but that they can be made not only in Roubaix, but in Sweden and Russia, and where we should perhaps least expect it, in Spain; and the bearing of this fact is in no way altered by the circumstance of their being made to a great extent on English looms. As to the maintenance of our superiority, therefore, in these goods, it becomes a question, in the first place, of progress in manufacturing skill and taste, and, in the next place, of value. That a brisk trade, such as prevailed in Bradford from 1862 to 1866, wonderfully lessens the motive to improve in either style or fabric, or, in fact, to introduce any novelty, and that a difficult trade operates in a contrary direction is evidently as much felt at Roubaix as at Bradford. The fair view, therefore, to take is that before the commercial treaty Roubaix fell behind from want of competition, and has since been fetching up arrears as a matter of necessity. But we have not discovered anything in the Exhibition to indicate a probability of our being likely to be distanced in mixed Bradford goods as a matter of skill and taste. As a question of value, we have had no means of comparing prices; but on this point the maintenance of a protective duty speaks for itself, and in this respect there need be little fear of a competition that labours under the disadvantage of being overlaid by a protective duty.

REPORT ON
THE
WORSTED
TRADE.

Effect of
the French
Commercial
Treaty.
We annex tables showing the effect of the French Commercial Treaty in very largely extending the worsted trade of that country, and showing that it has led to a large, though not rapidly increasing, importation of Bradford yarn and goods into France, and at the same time to an increased exportation of French worsted goods to England and other countries; the effect being thus a mutual benefit to the manufacturers as well as to the consumers of both France and England. Is it not a fair inference from these facts that it would be a still further benefit to both countries if the remaining 10 per cent. were out of their way? and would not the same result follow from a reduction in the prohibitory tariff of other countries? For instance, the Russian catalogue states that Russia has already twenty-two mills engaged solely in combing and spinning worsted yarn, and imports, in addition, so large a quantity of yarn at a low duty as to employ together 117 mills in weaving worsted yarn, the goods produced being of the annual value of a million and a half sterling. Is it not evident, from the results of the French treaty, that a country with such a trade established as Russia has, and with such skill as she displays at this Exhibition, can need, even for purposes of protection, no such duty as an average of nearly 70 per cent., and that such a duty must equally injure both her customers and her producers.

TABLE No. 1.

Exports of yarn and worsted goods from Great Britain to France.

The English Board of Trade returns comprise goods in transitu. The French official returns of imports from this country exclude goods in transitu, and are as follows:—

YARN.

—	Alpaca.			Mohair.			Other Yarn.			Totals.		
	£	s.	d.	£	s.	d.	£	s.	d.	£	s.	d.
1861	4,066	19	0	226,384	0	0	24,236	19	3	254,687	18	3
1862	538	16	0	197,290	1	7	259,036	17	5	456,865	15	0
1863	119	9	6	173,914	0	0	381,444	11	2	555,478	0	7
1864	—			204,226	17	5	364,570	15	0	568,797	12	5
1865	—			262,681	8	8	271,306	19	3	533,988	7	11
1866	—			280,081	15	0	274,799	12	0	554,881	7	0

WORSTED AND MIXED GOODS FOR THE SAME YEARS
1861–6.

Merinos.	Other All-wool Goods.	Mixed Goods.	Alpacas.	Totals.
£ s. d.	£ s. d.	£ s. d.	£ s. d.	£ s. d.
—	52,004 14 4	486,920 12 8	1,186 17 5	540,112 4 5
176 10 0	27,764 6 4	1,095,557 0 0	68,367 1 7	1,191,864 17 11
2,769 11 3	19,259 4 0	735,770 5 6	45,718 17 5	803,517 18 2
—	16,851 18 5	734,064 7 11	80,387 4 10	831,303 11 2
6 10 0	18,643 3 2	822,210 0 0	159,153 17 5	1,000,013 10 7
—	16,326 15 10	1,081,973 15 10	34,201 11 10	1,132,502 3 6

TABLE No. 2.

Imports of worsted and mixed goods from France into Great Britain. There are comparatively no imports of yarn.

The French official returns comprise goods in transitu to the United States and other countries; they do not therefore show the imports for home consumption in this country, but serve to indicate the stimulus given to French manufactures by the commercial treaty, and are as under :—

—	Merinos.	Other All-wool Goods.	Mixed Worsted Goods.	Totals.
	£ s. d.	£ s. d.	£ s. d.	£ s. d.
1861	466,015 4 0	752,209 12 9	431,069 0 9	1,649,313 17 6
1862	823,704 8 0	609,261 12 9	946,638 0 0	2,379,604 0 9
1863	1,209,236 2 6	783,628 18 4	1,057,801 3 11	3,050,666 4 9
1864	1,079,694 17 6	1,065,081 16 9	1,236,461 19 0	3,381,238 13 3
1865	1,443,987 0 0	486,528 13 7	947,666 4 9	2,878,152 18 4
1866	1,291,719 12 0	928,822 12 0	1,501,985 11 1	3,722,527 15 1

The British returns of goods from France do not comprise goods in transitu; but here a difficulty arises from the classification of so many different articles under the head of woollen manufactures. Omitting, however, four items— viz., carpets and rugs, shawls, scarfs and handkerchiefs, cloths and hosiery—there remain only two items, stuffs and unenumerated articles, and it is obvious that these run into each other, because it will be observed that sometimes one item is larger, sometimes the other; but whenever one is larger the other is less. Probably, therefore, no very serious error will be committed if they are taken unitedly to represent either the absolute or otherwise the proportionate amount of goods of Class 29, or Bradford goods imported from France into Great Britain, and are as follows:—

—	Stuffs.	Unenumerated.	Totals.
1861	£474,196	£180,177	£654,373
1862	544,794	315,889	860,683
1863	341,980	832,970	1,174,950
1864	462,289	609,366	1,071,655
1865	250,886	807,228	1,058,114
1866	not yet published by the Board of Trade.		

REPORT on CARDED WOOL AND WOOLLEN FABRICS.— (Class 30.)—By THOMAS NUSSEY, Esq.

EVERY exhibition gives evidence that with increased population woollen manufacture becomes more and more extended, and more universally adopted for the clothing of both sexes. The increased supply of wool given us by our colonial possessions and the using of second-hand material enable us to meet the great demand with reasonable prices, which are within the grasp of all classes. And we must not forget how much we owe to the application of ever-improving machinery both for manufacturing and finishing, together with the taste for fabrics of a soft and pliable character which so much supersedes the old style of hard milled cloth, and is so much more quickly produced. But in writing a report of woollen manufacture in connection with the Paris Exhibition of 1867 our purpose is not to give an exhaustive history of woollens, nor to show how it flourished in the low countries in early times, nor yet to relate how England has progressed in her woollen manufactures since the Duke of Alva, in 1570, drove over a large number of Flemish refugees, who settled especially in Yorkshire, but to collect in a condensed form what we have considered as the most powerful indications of general improvement, and to compare the productions of one country with another, hoping create an honest rivalry, and thus to benefit the world at large.

The insatiable thirst for novelty has been one means of causing a great impetus to the trade, bringing out new materials and introducing improved mixtures and new and beautiful dyes. The removal of trade restrictions, thus opening new markets, has also brought rapid progress, and no doubt has quickened inventive power which otherwise must have laid dormant.

We shall now proceed to enumerate the different countries represented in this department of the Exhibition, beginning first with France.

FRANCE

shows a most varied and superior description of woollens, and has a collection in every respect worthy of so great a country. She still maintains her position in twist and fancy goods, and in all fancy styles where the minutest

Mr. Nussey
on Carded
Wool, &c. attention to spinning and twisting is required; her system
certainly excels ours, which a slight observation will at
once detect.

The figured coatings in silk are beautifully spun and made;
also the witneys, sable furs, and Moscow beavers. She
stands unrivalled for her remarkable productions in velvet
piles and naps, especially adapted for ladies' mantles, they
have such a beautiful softness imparted to them by the
adoption of M. de Montagnac's invention, which is now so
generally used. No doubt this perfection has been the
means of woollens becoming a favourite wear for ladies, and
thus extending this branch of the trade; the astrakans and
fancy rugs are very superior, are well made, and display
great taste.

Amongst the novelties is velvet cloth interspersed with
glass, opaque, steel and gold beads, and brass shavings; also
cloths made from felted yarns, which are commended as
being soft, light, and elastic, and at little cost.

The fancy trouserings are in great variety, in quiet good
styles of the newest patterns, and are the very best exhibited. In superfine cloths we must say that we have seen
France to greater advantage in former exhibitions; there
is no improvement in the finish, and French manufacturers
can scarcely be said to hold their position in this class of
goods. The low fabrics exhibited in Class 91 are remarkably
dear, and do not compare with the same description of
woollens in the Huddersfield, Dewsbury, and Batley departments. The military cloths are well made, good in colour,
and should not be overlooked.

HOLLAND

Holland.

nas a worthy exhibition of blankets and woollen coverlets;
they are thick and soft. There are also some good specimens
in fancy coatings, meltons, and broadcloths.

BELGIUM.

Belgium.

We find some excellent exhibits in plain and medium
cloths, which compare closely with Yorkshire. In superfine
cloths she is not so successful, but in heavy overcoatings,
as reversible beavers, Moscows, Sataras, deer and doe skins,
and other ribbed cloths, she ranks the highest. The figured
and worsted coatings are very commendable, more especially
the dice patterns. A good deal of shoddy is thrown upon
the backs of the heavy coatings, whereby a cheap and
serviceable article is produced, and by which Belgium has
been enabled greatly to increase her trade. England must

be alive lest in this class of goods she is beaten out of neutral markets.

The fancy trouserings have well-developed patterns, and the same excellence of spinning and twisting is as observable here as in the French department. There is a good display of military cloths, of excellent dye, and well manufactured; the meltons, generally, are not so good; they handle hard, and are not well mixed.

AUSTRIA.

This department is not so imposing as the one she had in the London Exhibition of 1862; but the fabrics that are displayed are of general excellence. The trouserings are beautiful both in texture and colour, the shades most delicate, and the patterns are unlike those of any other country, and in remarkably good taste. There is also a good collection of coatings, in which silk is combined with wool, and which have a very neat appearance. The heavy coatings in various makes, such as lambskins and tufted and velvet mantle cloths, are equally successful, are beautifully made and finished, and deserve great praise. The prices, however, run high.

The dyes, for brightness of colour with cleanliness, stand pre-eminent; they cannot be excelled. This is particularly observable in her military cloths; the scarlets, blues, orange, rose, green, and white possess richness and distinctness not equalled by any other country. The finish of the superfine cloths is not good, and is scarcely adapted to the present taste.

PRUSSIA,

which includes the Northern States of Germany, Silesia, and the kingdom of Saxony, manufactures a great variety of woollen fabrics, and has an increasing foreign trade. The principal seats of manufacture are Aix-la-Chapelle, Düren, Leppen, and Hückerswagen. They exhibit an assortment of reversible and sable beavers, tricots, Moscow beavers, and witneys, all of which are excellent, taking the medium prices into consideration.

The superfine cloths are of considerable merit; the finish approaches the nearest to that of England, and the dyes generally are very good, especially the blacks and blues. We notice that the hardness which has been characteristic of the German make is partially lost, and they have attained that softness and elasticity which has for so many years been approved of in the London market. They sustain their

MR. NUSSEY ON CARDED WOOL, &c. reputation for deeskins, and have some good specimens of coatings, but nothing specially upon which to remark. The trouserings are well made, but the style and patterns bad ; they are large and staring.

Görlitz, Silesia, and Liegnitz have a large exhibit of goods made for the Levant and Persian markets ; also billiard and low military cloths in good colours. This class of manufacture forms a considerable branch of their trade, and ranks amongst the cheapest and best makes of the kind exhibited. The display that Saxony has is of a good general character ; the cloths are well made, but we cannot say the same of the finish ; it is too glazey, not a wrought face, and shows too much the effects of the hot press. The plain and fancy flannels, shawls, and woollen materials for underclothing are all commendable, are in great variety, and form an interesting portion of this department.

BAVARIA AND WIRTEMBERG

Bavaria and Wirtemberg. forward a varied assortment, but it is not of much interest. Their best productions are blankets and rugs.

SWITZERLAND.

Switzerland. In this collection we noticed nothing of special importance ; and the goods are hung too high for general observation.

PORTUGAL

Portugal. exhibits some fair specimens of black and military cloths, also fancy coatings and trouserings of merit.

SWEDEN,

Sweden. a primitive but useful assortment of woollen fabrics of all descriptions. A double lambskin, beautifully made, is worthy of notice.

DENMARK

Denmark. exhibits a few coarse woollens, adapted for military use.

RUSSIA

Russia. has a very creditable display. The broadcloths and fancy coatings are well made and good ; the treble overcoatings are among the best exhibited, and vie closely with some of the older manufacturing countries ; there are several descriptions of fabrics peculiarly her own; and Russia's improvement and advance in woollens is considerable.

ITALY

shows a good variety of woollens. The fancy coatings and trouserings are in neat styles, and well made. There is a choice assortment of blankets, coverlets, rugs, and military cloths, also of plain satin and billiard cloths.

TURKEY

exhibits a moderate collection of woollens, chiefly adapted for her own consumption, manufactured from wool and camel's hair mixed. The colours are quite of an Oriental cast.

GREAT BRITAIN,

as a whole, exhibits the best superfine cloths. The west of England has long had a reputation for her superiority in this class of woollens, also for kerseymeres, doeskins, and beavers, and she still maintains her position. She has some advantage in the purity of the water, which greatly assists her in the dyes of scarlet and colours suitable for billiard and livery cloths. The medley cloths are very good; the quiet, neat styles of the coatings denote excellent taste. There is nothing of this class of manufacture superior in the Exhibition or more deserving of praise.

Huddersfield and its vicinity is one of the most important seats of the woollen manufacture, and exhibits, both for make and design, a varied and excellent assortment of trouserings, coatings, vestings, mohairs, Bedford cords, velvet piles, rugs in imitation of skins, and novelties in ladies' mantles. These productions, with their reasonable prices, are unequalled, and bear evidence that the manufacturers are alive to every improvement. Huddersfield is unrepresented by her best makers of broadcloths, Devon beavers, and doeskins, a fact to be regretted, as she holds a good position in this class of fabrics.

Leeds and the neighbourhood, although the oldest and most important district in England for woollens, has, unfortunately, contributed so little to the Paris Exhibition that strangers interested in this manufacture can have no idea, from what they see, of the large, varied, and extensive trade carried on in this part of Yorkshire ; and, this report being confined to goods that are to be found exhibited, Leeds has scarcely done herself justice in allowing such a leading manufacture to be thus overlooked. There are simply a few broadcloths, beavers, meltons, and fancies; they are well done, the meltons especially so.

3.   E

The cotton-warp cloths exhibited by Morley are unequalled for general excellence in make, finish, and cheapness; her display does her much credit; they are all well made, well finished, and handsome goods, at low prices.

Batley and Dewsbury know no rival for their productions in heavy goods, as reversible beavers, witneys, furs, pilots, cheviots, fancy rugs, and low army cloths. The fabrics produced in these districts are chiefly made in cotton warps; the difficulties formerly experienced in dyeing the warps have been overcome, and such perfection in this has been now attained that none but an experienced eye can detect any difference between them and those made entirely of wool. The exceeding lowness of price, combined with excellence, may easily account for the large and flourishing trade which these towns continue to enjoy. These, with the Morley exhibits, will, it is to be hoped, help to remove Continental prejudice with respect to cotton warps; they certainly are very superior to the low goods made from all wool exhibited by other countries; indeed, Morley, Batley, and Dewsbury do more towards clothing the million in woollens than any other part of the globe.

Heckmondwike has a good assortment of blankets, rugs, and carpets.

Scotland is represented by only a few manufacturers, but these exhibit a varied collection of trouserings, shawls, and fabrics of a soft and beautiful character. Their rank in the woollen trade is high, and their trade extensive, so that it is to be regretted that the position they hold is not better sustained here.

Ireland has some good specimens of tweeds, trouserings, and friezes equal to any shown in this particular class. Having done so well, it is difficult to see why she should not greatly extend this manufacture. Her want of coal is certainly an obstacle, but this has not prevented her linen manufacturers from making steady progress, and equal energy and skill would, if applied, no doubt result in considerable advancement in the manufacture of woollens.

Before closing this report, it may be desirable to institute a comparison between this and preceding exhibitions, with a view to giving some idea of the progress of the woollen manufacture generally. It will be readily understood that this manufacture does not afford much scope for artistic design; nevertheless, it gives opportunity for the exhibition of taste or skill in the assortment of colour, in texture, and in finish. It is evident that any improvement in this manufacture cannot be of so striking a character as in some other branches. One of the most marked and striking improvements is in cloths for ladies' mantles. The French have paid great attention to the manufacture of articles for this purpose. The Germans also, as we have previously stated, have shown some excellent goods of this kind. The Huddersfield manufacturers have also exhibited goods of great beauty. The variety of patterns is very great, and as compared with former exhibitions there is a great improvement visible in every respect, whether in design, colouring, or make.

In fine plain cloths no great change is apparent, nor can Cloths. much be expected, as this manufacture has long attained a great degree of perfection. The fine cloths are exceedingly good, and those of the west of England are, beyond doubt, the best exhibited, and are better than have ever been shown before. The Prussian cloths are the next in point of merit, and very good samples are shown by Belgium. In medium low cloths the Belgians are the best. Leeds, the centre of this trade in England, only exhibits two or three specimens; but judging from these, Leeds would, had she contributed more largely in this article, have held a decidedly good position in them. For some years past there have been made in the Leeds district, especially in the village of Morley, large quantities of plain and coloured cloths, with cotton instead of woollen warps. By this means a very handsome and useful cloth can be made at a very low price, and the exhibition of them is very good. They were extensively exhibited by Leeds at the Exhibition of 1862, and the improvement in the manufacture of this kind of cloth since that date is manifest.

In heavy coatings there is not much change so far as respects the make of the cloth, but the styles are generally much neater and in better taste, and France, Belgium, Austria, Prussia, Russia, and Great Britain each make a very good show of them; some from Austria and Russia are remarkably stout and heavy. A class of goods of this description is shown from Dewsbury and Batley, near Leeds, which merits notice. They are of cotton warp, and with the wool is used a portion more or less considerable of shoddy. Much objection is taken to the use of shoddy in cloths, but when judiciously and moderately used the cloth is nearly as good as if made from all wool, whilst much cheaper, and with a better appearance, and thereby brought within the means of classes who could not otherwise afford to buy it. In this branch none of the goods exhibited by other countries at all approach those made in Yorkshire, especially if the cost is taken into consideration.

In fancy trouserings there is a decided improvement in all respects since 1862. The goods generally are better made, and the designs in better taste. In fine qualities the French and Belgians excel, and the goods give evidence of great care and attention to every detail in the manufacture. The spinning is admirable, as is also the twisting, and it is evident that every minute point is strictly attended to The consequence is that they show a greater degree of perfection in the manufacture than any other. Each point may in itself be of little importance, but when combined they make a very perceptible difference in the result. The attention of British manufacturers should be given to this subject. It is probable that this minute care may to some extent increase the labour, and therefore the cost, and it, no doubt, does so; but this, if not too great, is not of such material consequence in fine goods. There is nothing to prevent the British manufacturers equalling the French and Belgians in this respect as in any other; but unless more attention is given to these details, Great Britain will have difficulty in maintaining her position as a manufacturer of fine trouserings.

Felted yarns. Attention has been drawn to the use of felted yarns by the French manufacturers. This is a comparatively new feature in the woollen trade, and excellent use has been made of it in the manufacture of cloths for ladies' mantles. So far as we know it is not used in Britain, but it is desirable that her manufacturers should examine into its merits.

In dealing with any great branch of manufacture it is natural that attention should more particularly be given to those productions which show the most beauty and evidence the greatest skill; but there are others which, having less pretension to either of these qualities, are still of great importance; and these are the fabrics made for the million. In these lowness of price is of paramount importance; and they will not, therefore, bear any unnecessary expense in the manufacture. By utilising material which was formerly cast away as waste great progress has of late years been made in the production of cheap cloths. No country exhibits articles of this description which will bear comparison with those from England.

Technical education. There can be no doubt that the French, Belgian, and Prussian manufacturers are greatly indebted for their progress in this and many other industries to the very superior technical education which their manufacturers and workmen obtain, by means of the schools instituted for special instruction, not only in design, but in everything which has any relation to each particular manufacture. Without education we cannot expect to have skilled workmen of the highest class, and to a fair general education must be added a special training under good masters in every branch of trade. The adoption of similar schools in Britain will before long become a necessity, and the sooner they are established the better.

In most European States the tariffs have within a few years been revised, and the duties on goods generally reduced. This has introduced into such countries a foreign competition which did not previously exist. It has acted as a stimulus to their manufacturers, and has produced a considerable effect. With our present fiscal system the British manufacturer cannot further be subjected to a similar stimulus to force him to press forward in the course of progressive improvement; but, if he wishes to maintain his position, he must spontaneously avail himself of every improvement adopted by others ; and in a careful examination of the goods exhibited here by other countries he will find many things which will give him valuable hints for his guidance.

REPORT on CARDED WOOL, WOOLLEN YARNS, AND WOOLLEN FABRICS.—(Class 30.)—By GEORGE LEACH, Esq.

CARDED WOOL, though occupying a prominent place in the classification of the British catalogue of Class 30, does not appear to have been introduced into the Exhibition as an object of competition for reward. It rarely forms a marketable commodity, except in the shape of carded waste, shoddy, or extract wool (a product obtained by the chemical separation or reclamation of wool from rags containing cotton and wool).

The term itself, "carded wool," however, embraces the whole of Class 30, and the writer, rather than attempt the compilation of an abridged catalogue, proposes to consider the whole class as one general subject, in the exhibits of which the product of carded wool, of necessity, constitutes the germ of the excellences or defects there to be met with.

At the time of inspection only one specimen of carded wool was to be found accompanying the cloth which it composed. This, though interesting, was yet so single and limited in quantity as to admit of no comparison, where comparison is so very desirable ; nor does it merit any special remark, beyond being suggestive for future exhibitions ; for nothing could be more instructive to the uninitiated, and certainly nothing more useful or interesting to the practical manufacturer, than that some of the leading descriptions of goods in this great branch of industry should be accompanied by a complete arrangement of the material, in the various stages of manufacture, out of which the finished fabric itself is ultimately produced.

In this case, first of all in importance would be carded wool, for it is very remarkable that not only is this process carried on in the principal centres of the woollen trade by machinery of very varied and different construction, but where there is a similarity of machine according to the fashion or habit which has become generally practised in the respective districts, so the modes of working or regulating these machines are also equally different. In fact, so opposite are the "notions" (and the term is used advisedly in contradistinction to the word "principle") of the various workmen in carding wool, that it becomes a most important question to consider which are right and which wrong. To explain, however, more fully, it may be said that a fore-

Marginal notes:
"Carded wool."

Diversity in method of working woollen carding machines.

MR. LEACH ON CARDED WOOL, &C.

man or skilled workman from the Leeds district would utterly fail in his management of a certain given " blend " of wool if he were to take charge of the same upon Belgian, French, or even West of England cards and carding machines, whilst, *vice versâ,* the French workman would be equally perplexed and as little successful with the same wool upon corresponding apparatus common to the Yorkshire district. Thus, in reviewing the exhibits in Class 30, it becomes necessary to consider how far this important operation has been instrumental in producing the distinctive features observable in both carded wool, yarn, and cloth. It cannot be contradicted that deficient machinery or management, in the preceding as well as the succeeding processes, may defeat the result good carding would otherwise produce ; but there is no other stage in which an error or deficiency may not more easily be detected and remedied.

Carded wool in process.

But now to the examination of the matter of carded wool itself, to find which we must proceed to the department of machinery in motion ; and by preference, and in the order of merit, first to that exhibited by Belgium.

Superiority and carding of Buenos Ayres wool in Belgium.

Here we find an admirable specimen of carded wool, undyed, in " sliver," produced by Celestin Martin, of Verviers, and, though the product of " greasy," " burry," " Buenos Ayres " wool, is highly commendable for " cleanness," " clearness," and freedom from " nibs," " bits," or extraneous matter. Fortunately for our practical British manufacturer (and it is to be hoped also for many of our most intelligent and *unprejudiced* artisans who may visit the Exhibition), M. Martin not only shows such good results, but also the whole process by which they are attained.

Limited area of card employed.

Upon three comparatively narrow and small diameter single-cylinder machines M. Martin produces an effect which would tax the efforts of many of our Yorkshire foremen to perform upon *six* cylinders (besides " breasts ") and *three times* the surface of " cards."

Economical results in Belgium.

The " condensed sliver " is like a smoothly drawn wire for evenness, and the regularity with which the fibres are laid is certain to ensure a correspondingly regular yarn. The oil used for lubricating the wool is " oleine " (a fine class of Price's patent cloth oil), distributed by machinery, whilst, in one and the same process, the wool is passing through and being prepared or opened in the " brisoir," or " plucker." The importance of the equal lubrication of every lock of wool before being presented to the action of the carding machine cannot be overvalued ; and the infinitesimal division of the liquid, resembling spray, which M. Martin diffuses amidst his uncarded locks of willowed wool, cannot fail to considerably diminish the work the cards have subsequently to perform and contribute towards that faultless specimen of carded wool of which this enterprising spinner and machinist may justly be proud. And yet, as an element of cheapness of production, it is questionable whether the weight of 120 lb. per day of sliver (from a 44 in. wide machine of so limited card area), of the length obtained and with the same excellent properties, is approached or excelled in all Britain.

It would be very interesting if, during the Exhibition, M. Martin would upon the same machines produce for inspection of future visitors examples of carded wool, dyed in the wool, and also mixtures of colours; yet we have sufficient evidence of the ability of these clever Belgian carders and spinners in the exhibits of yarns and cloths to prove how thoroughly they are experienced in this important art.

There are other specimens of carded wool, in sliver and yarn, in process of being spun, in the French department; but though both these and the machinery, as examples, are very creditable, and deserving attention, the production of M. Martin is so perfect, and the completeness of his arrangements leave so little to be desired, that we must allow the catalogue to indicate and mention by name the other exhibitors, and pass on to the English department.

Here, alas! we see a crowded space, and yet a lamentable void.

Our most extensive and incomparable machinists, Platt Brothers & Co., draw their supply of carded wool in the " condensed sliver," from ————, their clients in Belgium! with which to illustrate the working of their self-acting mule. Want of space prevented their showing a complete process and assortment of machines for carding. We are consequently debarred the satisfaction of seeing the production of carded wool upon our most modern models of machinery. Mr. Ferabee, in connection with Mr. John Tatham, of Rochdale, shows wool in the carded and condensed sliver, fed by an admirable and much required " bat feeding machine ;" but, since he, too, receives his supplies of half-carded and oiled wool from a distance (West of England), and a strong draught of wind in that portion of the building disturbs the light and fleecy feed his apparatus so perfectly and ingeniously produces, it would be unfair to compare his carded wool with any other. The same may be said of that of Mr. Lister, of Dursley.

MR. LEACH
ON CARDED
WOOL, &c.

For the sake of instituting a fair comparison, whether the conclusions were either for or against (and in the event of the former being established, for the further encouragement and satisfaction of our own manufacturers ; and in case of the latter, as an instigation to increased emulation and effort), it is much to be regretted that the British had not an equally complete assortment of machinery to enter into fair rivalry and competition with the continental manufacturers in the production of carded wool.

Carded
woollen
yarns.

Proceeding to the examination of "carded woollen yarns" we find Belgium, as in carded wool, the chief exhibitor.

The quantity and quality of yarns exposed in galerie 4 form a suitable introduction to the court where the finished fabrics are exhibited, and prove the importance with which the Belgians regard this branch of their thriving commerce. Nor can it escape attention and comparison that whilst our spinners of hosiery and flannel yarns in two or three isolated instances are the only British exhibitors who have deemed it advisable to bring their productions before the eye of the world the Belgians, the Prussians and Austrians, and the French (in one special novelty) have not merely shown a spirit of emulation in this division of Class 30, but have had the pride and ingenuity to render their display not merely useful and interesting, but attractive and ornamental.

Successful
competition
of carded
woollen
yarns by
foreigner
in Britain.

In paragraph 5 of the general introduction to the British catalogue upon Class 30 is given a list of amounts of woollen and worsted yarns imported into the United Kingdom during the years 1861–5. In 1864 the amount of 4,654,000 lbs. figured as an item of competition against our British spinners, and although there is no means of obtaining reliable or authentic statistical information, yet from the knowledge we have of the extensive and intimate connexion which numerous Belgian, German, and French spinners have for years maintained in Scotland, and the fact of the large carrying trade in yarns which has existed between the ports of Antwerp and Hull and other ports, it may be safely concluded that by far the largest proportion of this considerable importation consisted of carded woollen and angola yarns successfully and profitably produced by our Belgian competitors.

For further corroboration of this conclusion, we may read the advertisements in the Prussian catalogue, and notice those well-filled and well-arranged cases of M. Bouvoisin Fils, Henri Lieutenant, Peltzer et Fils, Henry Leusch, Hauzeur Gérard Fils, Xhoffray et Laoureux (formerly Xhoffray Bruls), all familiar names in the Glasgow and Paisley yarn markets. Let us also inspect the important collections brought together by the Prussians and the Austrians, especially those by G. Pastor, of Aix-la-Chapelle ; Facilides und Wiede, of Plauen, Saxony ; and Teuber Jos. and Söhne, of Brünn; and then, surely, we must be impressed with the great spirit of enterprise and superior intelligence abroad which has enabled these foreign spinners to prosecute so undesirable a competition in our very midst.

There will be found among the exhibits by the above- mentioned firms specimens of almost marvellous carding and spinning, both as regards quality, character, and length ; and in some cases tickets being attached to the samples of yarns upon which are denoted, in English, the descriptions and qualities in English hanks (worsted count), clearly prove the nationality of the customers whose notice and interest these yarns were intended to invite.

In addition, however, to this, the lengths are generally given in metres per kilogramme, whether the exhibits are French, Belgian, or German ; and it is much to be wished that, instead of the dozen different denominations (in fact, varying almost with every locality) by which in Britain the lengths of yarn are understood, we, like our neighours, had one common standard.

Is an explanation asked of the reason of the excellence of these yarns, the reader is referred to remarks upon carded wool. The early adoption of " condensers " and the careful system of feeding the intermediate " carders " practised abroad have also contributed to this result.

Special attention must be called to an exhibit of yarn composed of " shoddy " or " mungo " and wool, by Leidenfrost, Eduard, and Söhne, of Brünn, in the Austrian department. Not that there is noteworthy merit in the yarn itself beyond affording evidence of attention being bestowed upon an article which hitherto has almost remained exclusively the specialty of certain of our Yorkshire districts. But unless vigilance be exercised who can predict how short an interval may intervene between the present imagined security of position and that period when the Austrian spinners of shoddy may, like the Belgians, challenge us with and maintain a successful competition in our own market ?

Of novelties in yarns, those produced by the inventive genius and indomitable perseverance of F. Vouillon, of Louviers, most claim attention. Instead of being spun in the ordinary manner, these yarns are "felted."

In the French division of Class 30 (No. 36, French catalogue) will be found exhibits of this new process, in both yarn,
and woven, and finished fabrics. A still better display of
felted cloth is exhibited in a case in Class 29, by Sabran et
Jessé, near which also is a more complete assortment of
" felted " yarn. It is not within the province of this report
to describe the now successful machinery by which these
yarns (without the means of a spindle) are produced; it
may however be briefly stated, that attached to a condenser is an apparatus which receives the frail sliver, and by
means of heat and friction transforms it into a weavable
yarn or thread.

What, however, is of further importance in the economy
of the woollen manufacture is the small space this machine
occupies—not exceeding that of a single-cylinder carder.

In this process lies a principle the importance of which it
is impossible to foresee. It is not supposed that it will
supersede spinning, but it is highly probable that "felted
yarns" may be introduced with singular advantage into
numerous descriptions of woollen fabrics—such, for instance,
as ladies' mantles, cloakings, coverlets, wrappers, or any
other class where warmth and lightness are required. In
the London Exhibition of 1862 it was shown that felted
yarns, and union cloth made therefrom, containing 60 per
cent. of shoddy, could be produced by this process.

The chief characteristics of this yarn are its extreme
lightness compared with its bulk, and also that the finer fibres
are worked up and laid on the exterior of the thread. The
wool, in fact, is united in a more regular mass without
the internal hard-twisted "core" of fibres necessary for the
adhesion of a yarn spun in the ordinary way. It is also
remarkably round and even, and although it is doubtful
whether the same length of yarn, or even equal strength,
may be obtained as by spinning, yet it possesses sufficient
tenacity to admit of being woven into a fabric to which can
be imparted any required strength in the subsequent
ordinary "fulling-machines, or stocks."

The same inventor's samples of so-called " *moucheté* " yarns
receive some attention. These are formed by small lengths
of "slivers" of a contrasting colour, or mixture, being detached at equal distances and twisted with the yarn forming
the foundation; but these yarns, like the introduction of
"pearls," "beads," "brass or metal shavings or turnings,"
and also yarns with "twisted knobs or knots" ("gezwirnte
noppen") found in the Prussian department, involve no
important principle of manufacture, but, like many other

vagaries of fashion, will pass away without remembrance or regret.

" Carded woollen fabrics " form the most numerous exhibits in this class; it is consequently impossible within the limits of this report to do more than point out generally those objects which are either most meritorious or require consideration on the part of the practical manufacturer or the trade. Undoubtedly, the chief advantage conferred by these international exhibitions is the opportunity they afford, not so much for self-laudation, or even satisfaction, as for the examination of those products wherein our competitors, either at home or abroad, approach or surpass us in excellence. It is further desirable, as proposed at the commencement of our investigation of this class, to endeavour to trace effect to cause, or, in other words, to discover, if practicable, the reason of either our superiority or defeat; and as in such an intricate subject much difference of opinion must exist, the writer of this report ventures his own with all deference to that of others.

First in importance, and that also which affords the greatest opportunity for comparison, is that staple article of our woollen trade, plain black cloth. Taking the highest quality first, it is a pleasurable duty to have to report that in the whole Exhibition there are no specimens possessing such general and surpassing excellence as the " superfine wool-dyed black and blue broads " from Stroud. It is difficult to determine which cloth in the collection of Class 30 contains the finest quality of wool; nor is this a matter of much importance, nor deserving of special praise; but, without doubt, to the practised touch no cloth is so soft and so mellow as this. The richest dye, most evenly-dressed face—bright and fresh, yet with a complete absence of that "baked" and lustrous glare (so cheaply obtained on the Continent by " decatting " with high-pressure steam)— elasticity of texture : all these qualities are combined in the happiest, most apparent, and successful manner. In short, this is " broadcloth " *par excellence.*

The Continental makers also show some wonderful examples of fine cloth; but, though Bischoff, of Aix-la-Chapelle; Grossmann and Söhne, of Bichofswerda (Saxony); Schœller, of Düren; Schœller Gebrüder, of Brün; Simonis, of Verviers; Chatten, of Disen, and others from Sedan, are well forward in the race, the palm must be given to the exhibitors from Stroud, who have so worthily maintained the prestige of their district, and thus saved our national reputation as the first and best makers of " superfine broadcloth."

Mr. Leach on Carded Wool, &c.

Absence of exhibits from Yorkshire.

Old "Billey" process in England.

Cloths with cotton warp. Excellent and superior English exhibits.

Cheap clothing from England.

Fancy woollens.

Of medium qualities (plain cloths), so little is exhibited from the Yorkshire district, that not only is there no opportunity of comparing foreign exhibits with our own, but the stranger and those uninformed might acquire the idea that our trade in this article had completely died out. It may be observed, however, that there are frequent indications amongst the Continental exhibits of an increasing taste for a quieter, less glossy style of finish, and that there are some admirable examples of very excellently made plain cloths in both piece and wool dyes.

In competing for this, really the most important and most universal branch of the woollen cloth trade, those of our manufacturers who adhere to the old "Billey" process may with profit bestow a consideration upon the example long set them abroad of adopting the "condenser" entirely.

Plain union cloths, although not largely exhibited, are worthily represented by Morley manufacturers. Class 91, in Group X, was searched in vain to find anything worthy of comparison with these goods; and it is to be hoped that the wonderful perfection and the extreme and surprising cheapness of these fabrics will attract the attention of our French neighbours interested in this class, obtain from them a due appreciation of their merits, and thus stimulate a demand for these cloths amongst that large portion of the population of France hitherto clad in the "less viewly blouse."

In heavy goods for winter clothing of better qualities, especially in "Moscow beavers" and reversibles, the necessities of the Continental climate, together with a complete mastery over their art in working pure wool, have enabled the Prussians and Belgians to outstrip all rivals and imitators. To be convinced of this, we need only inspect the productions of J. B. Schoeller, of Düren (Prussia), and A. and F. Drèze, of Dison (Belgium).

If we wish, however, to judge whence to draw supplies of warm, heavy, cheap clothing for the million or for army use, we need only turn to the exhibits of the Batley Chamber of Commerce, and we shall again at once be convinced that for goods requiring mixtures of "artificial wool," "shoddy," "mungo," "extract," &c., in order to reduce the cost, and still affording a substantial and wearable article, England stands without a rival.

The same may be said in reference to flannels, blankets, and soft-spun woollens; not omitting the mention of railway rugs and horse clothing.

Of "fancy woollen fabrics" there is an enormous and most varied display. A most heterogeneous mass; and, as leaves on every tree differ in shape or substance, so does the result of "fancy" here bewilder with its multiplicity. To make *one sweeping comment*, and insist that this particular country or district displays the best taste, would be as ill-considered as it would be unfair. Peculiarity of climate, customs, and education must naturally influence this ; so that, without equal experience and complete exemption from patriotic prejudices (which is next to an impossibility), it is undesirable to pass judgment or come to any conclusion on this subject.

Weight, strength, quality, substance, closeness or fineness of texture, and length of spinning, may all be measured and compared ; and we regret to say that, judging from what is exhibited *in the building only*, we must concede to our foreign competitors the preponderance of merit. *Foreign excellence.*

In the particular class requiring fine spinning the race is very even between the French, Belgians, and Germans ; but, for examples, may be specially mentioned goods by Auspitz, Max Bum, and Latzko, of Brünn ; also by Hulin et Paquin, of Sedan ; Simonis, of Verviers, and Schœller, of Düren. Here there must be the very perfection of carding and spinning before such goods can be produced. Our Scotch, Huddersfield, and West of England manufactures are well represented by excellent specimens ; but here the West shows indications of more careful carding and spinning.

An exhibit of well made cheap tweeds, in good colourings, from Cork is a praiseworthy contribution from Ireland. *Irish tweeds.*

In mantle cloths or articles for women's clothing France makes the best display, exhibits the greatest novelties and most costly qualities. Austria has also some attractive specimens. In this department there is a great prevalence of "velvet pile" or plushed face, which, in articles composed of vicuna or mohair wool, imparts a peculiar softness. This process of "plushing" or velveting seems thoroughly to be understood by the French, and is largely introduced into trouserings.

Holland exhibits superior blankets, and very fair black cloths ; but since we have passed in review the productions of those countries from which we may derive interest or information, we must pass over those of Russia and the remaining German States, Denmark, and Spain without further comment.

This report on Class 30 cannot be concluded without a candid admission that (judging from the actual specimens in the Exhibition, and from the general impressions formed), our Continental competitors offer much for our consideration ; and especially do we note numerous proofs of a superiority *Superiority of system of carding pure wool on the Continent.*

in the process of carding. Let it, however, be well understood that the foregoing remark applies more especially to the treatment of pure wool only in the north of England (even to the exception of the West of England, where a system of carding is carried on almost identical with that of our foreign competitors) ; but, whilst we have the satisfaction of knowing that our home and Yorkshire manufacturers possess the "knack" of dealing with those blends of wool and shoddy, and extensive though the scope is for our manufacture of "woollen fabrics" of inferior or medium qualities, is it not a desirable subject for study and ambition to obtain and secure a fair share of the enormous demand there is abroad for the finer descriptions of goods ?

Many warnings are undoubtedly given to us in this World's Fair. Let us take heed, therefore, that though we are fortunate in producing beyond present rivalry the cheaper articles of clothing, we are not overtaken in our "luck" and experience, or outstripped on the very ground upon which it is evident we have lost so much of our trade in fine goods. If an enumeration of these causes be requested, we suggest the following questions which occur now to those who visit this Exhibition of 1867 :—Who first turned their attention to more careful wool scouring and washing ? Who retained truth in their carding-engines by reason of not unduly extending their width, to gain quantity at the expense of quality ? Who have adopted first iron or other non-expanding or warping covers for cylinders or doffers ? Who have adopted improved fixings of these machines whilst our "overlookers" have been "tapping," or rapping their worker shaft ends to make them bed in their clumsy, loose, ill-fitting bearings ? Who further adopted the "condenser" when the blood of our "pieceners'" fingers was lubricating the clumsy over lap-joints of the "cardings" in our antiquated slobbing process ? Who were spinning away upon Platt's self-actor mules, ten years or more ago, whilst we were hesitating and ordering "handmules"? and, lastly, though not the least, who invented and adopted the "milling machine"? This is not a flattering picture to draw. Not many years ago these were "newfangled notions." What are they now? and is there not reason to profit by past experience?

Our woollen trade is, undoubtedly, not keeping pace with our rivals', and the sooner we know it, discover the reason, and act accordingly, the better. But, whilst the foregoing remarks imply a reflection upon our sagacity as *master manufacturers* and employers of labour, the subject would be incomplete without also inquiring whether the character or quality of the labour itself has or has not impeded the progress of the trade. We have the most enduring, able-bodied workpeople, and it would be a libel to deny them the possession of the virtue of industry, and though their labour is *nominally dearer* than on the Continent, it is very questionable whether their physical energy or effort would not, under an improved condition of mental culture, counterbalance the disparity. Unfortunately, however, at present their prejudices are as strong as their sinews, and since the knowledge of the art they perform is acquired and practised, more by rote or habit and faith, than by conviction, or an intelligent appreciation of either science or its principles, much unnecessary toil is undergone, much experience repeated which would otherwise be avoided. As a body, our operatives abhor innovations, and their reluctance to accept either improved system or machinery is incredible, and yet do they inherit a deeply rooted belief that our woollen trade is in advance, and that we have nothing to learn from foreigners. The trade is also fettered by clumsy denominations or definitions of weights, lengths, and measures, and we are delayed and inconvenienced by ugly and tedious arithmetic, whilst our competitors, in the main, have universal and decimalised standard measures.

In this we cannot help ourselves; but it behoves our Chambers of Commerce, if they have any vigour or influence and are not merely conducted as pleasing hobbies, or those who can and must help us—our Imperial Government—to be on the alert and change these things, that we may be spared the loss and disgrace of occupying the second place in this the most universal, as it is the most important, branch of industry which has for its object the clothing of mankind.

REPORT on SILK MANUFACTURES, SHAWLS, LACE and EMBROIDERY, HOSIERY, CLOTHING for both SEXES, and DRESS in different COUNTRIES.—(Classes, 31, 32, 33, 34, 35, and 92.)—By Professor LEONE LEVI, LL.D.

PROF. LEONE LEVI, LL.D., ON SILK MANUFAC-TURES, &c.

IT is not without reason that high expectations have been formed of the Universal Exhibition of 1867. Conspicuous for her position in the very heart of Europe, sumptuous in her palaces and galleries, and rich in every mark of high civilisation, Paris, the great metropolis of art and fashion, is supremely fitted for the holding of great international exhibitions, which are at once high festivals of industry and great tournaments of industrial nations. We might have expected, from the intelligence which distinguishes our neighbours, that when, for the fourth time, invitations were issued to the industrial world to come forth to the great arena of peaceful competition, a newer and fresher vigour would be imparted to the undertaking, and that, together with the purely industrial elements, much would be done to further the artistic and intellectual, the economic and moral, interests of mankind; but, more especially, it was natural to anticipate from a nation so renowned for her skill in the art of display that, both in the collective view presented of human industry and in every department and section of the same, the general arrangement would manifest, not only a perfect unity of design, but that high regard to order and ornamentation which render such displays scenes of great brilliancy and beauty, and constitute them magnificent schools of public taste, highly instructive and interesting even to the most cursory visitors. Nor have we been disappointed in such expectations. The tenth group, consisting of objects exhibited with a view to ameliorate the physical and moral condition of the people, is a decided addition to previous exhibitions. The systematic collocation of all articles belonging to each class in continuous circular lines, without losing the distribution by countries, is a novelty ; and though, in respect of scenic effect, the exhibition may seem somewhat defective, great is the facility thereby afforded for comparing the relative advance of each country in any distinct branch of industry.

Paris and Universal Exhibitions.

At such exhibitions, and in this especially, do we see that, if art and taste can do much to commend those articles which are principally adapted for use and comfort, and whose merits

The art of display.

F 2

PROF.
LEONE
LEVI,
LL.D., ON
SILK
MANUFAC-
TURES, &c.
___
chiefly consist in their cheapness and adaptability to the varied wants of mankind, still more do they accomplish in imparting grace and attractiveness to articles of luxury and finery. The more precious the jewel, the greater the need of the finest setting to bring out all its brilliancy and beauty. The richness of the material, the brilliancy of colour, and the splendid design, seem to acquire a fresh and surprising charm when the objects are exhibited with exquisite taste and with high regard to artistic effect, as we have seen them along the courts and avenues of the great Industrial Palace, side by side, with the choicest products in every branch of human industry. In this respect, indeed, Paris itself is a great school. Visit those emporiums of rarities at the Boulevards and the Palais Royal. See how elegantly are they arranged! What care and what precision are exhibited in the minutest details! Is it too much to say that articles so displayed not only more readily arrest the passers-by, but succeed in commanding a higher price than their intrinsic value would otherwise realize?

Classes in the group "Vêtements" reported upon. The classes upon which I have been desired to report form a part of the fourth group, "Vêtements," comprising tissues and objects worn on the person. The articles included in them are varied and attractive. First, is silk in all its beauty; next, shawls, from the splendid cashmere to the finest lace; next, hosiery in all its branches; after this, embroidery, with gold and silver, and trimming of every possible description; and then, articles of clothing for both sexes, in combination with the specimens of the popular costumes of different countries, which meet us at every corner of the Exhibition. A careful examination of such articles is indeed most suggestive; and, if I am not mistaken, they present some aspects of manufacturing industry which bring out very prominently the relative aptitude of the manufacturing countries of Europe to supply the great wants of mankind in all articles of clothing.

British supremacy in articles of clothing. Taken as a whole, clothing is just the department in which Britain has long claimed to possess a decided supremacy. It is not a vain assumption to say that, by the invention of mechanical contrivances and the discovery of the great motor steam power, the British manufacturer was enabled not only to multiply the production of textile materials to an almost unlimited extent, and to leave handwork of every description far behind, but to outstep the manufacturing industry of every country. The cotton of India and America, the wool of Africa, the silk of China and Italy, crossed mountains and oceans to undergo, in our shores, the mechanical processes of the spindle and the loom; and, by their cheapness and excellence, British goods became adapted to the wants of nations of every race and clime, and of low and high civilisation, to the decided benefit of the whole human family. For a time the British manufacturer enjoyed an almost exclusive monopoly of such powers; and, so long as other countries were ignorant of such inventions, and, either suffering from internal discords or involved in the ravages of war, had neither the power nor the will to enter into the path of industry, Britain had no competition to meet. But the world does not stand still. With a long period of peace Europe has learned the value of the peaceful arts. Inventions spread. The seeds of ancient industry sown amidst happier times, but long neglected, have been nurtured and made more prolific. Art and design have been rendered auxiliaries to labour; and, whilst it seemed the special province of Britain to attend to the production of what is adapted to the masses, France and other nations gave themselves more especially to provide for the opulent and higher classes of society. Nor did it end there. The boundaries of national industry are, however, not marked by compact or understanding; and just as Britain is capable of producing and does produce works of the highest art, so France and Germany are showing their power to produce what is cheap and useful.

For the study of the silk manufacture no moment could be more opportune. For years past we have seen how much the disease in the silkworm has impaired the productiveness of some of the oldest silk-manufacturing countries. In France the injury resulting from it has been so great that it is even now seriously contemplated to adopt, as regards this disease, the same remedies as in the case of the cattle plague. On the other hand, the silks of China, Japan, India, and Siam have come largely into use, and have effected a complete revolution in the imports of the raw material. Then, again, the treaty of commerce between Great Britain and France of 1860-1, which put an end to the last shred of protection in the United Kingdom and greatly liberalised the tariff of France, now may be said to bear proper fruit; and it becomes interesting to see how far the relative position of the two countries in this industry has been affected by an open competition. Add to this that fashion, always capricious and arbitrary, has exhibited of late more than ordinary fickleness in all matters of design, especially in ribbons and trimming. Making every allowance for the difficulty of the time and the extraordinary circumstances under which the manufacturers of silk have been labouring, this is certainly a fine standpoint for studying the condition

PROF.
LEONE
LEVI,
LL.D., ON
SILK
MANUFAC-
TURES, &c.

The cocoon
worm and
wild silk.

and prospects of this branch of industry, and the Universal Exhibition affords us abundant materials for such a study.

The first object of interest in connection with silk is the cocoon, of which there are many illustrations. Over and above the cocoons of France, Italy, and other European countries, which are, generally, varieties of the Bombyx mori valuable specimens are exhibited of the Bombyx arrindia, Scynthia, Ailante, and the Saturnia Fairdebü, shown by Cochin China, Senegal, and other French colonies. Several species of silkworms have been acclimatised and rendered useful in Europe. Only a few years ago the Abbé Fantoni, a Piedmontese missionary in the province of Hang-Kung, in China sent some living cocoons—the Attacus Cynthia and Ailanthus—to some of his friends in Turin, which yielded moth and multiplied both in Italy and France. And there are numerous silk-producing worms which have not yet attained any commercial importance, not having been employed in manufacture. Some have doubtless been tried and found wanting ; but means may still be discovered for obtaining from them a better silk ; and it is all important to see whether, by the acclimatisation of new worms, or of other trees than the mulberry, the silk supply may be permanently increased. Of vegetable silk, a specimen is shown by the Cape of Good Hope of a silk-producing bulb, the Amaryllidea. Brunswigia Josephina, which grows wild all over the country, and might be obtained in any quantity. Wild silk is abundant in India and China. Consul Taylor, in his recent report on the trade of Diarbekir and Kurdistan, referred to a specie of wild silk, called guz and jez, which grows extensively in the Bohtan mountains, and about Rawandoz and Zacho, in the Mount Kaimakhih. The insect seems like a caterpillar, and forms the cocoon in a shrub ; yet it does not die there, but escapes and becomes a butterfly. Though in many respects totally different from the silkworm, the silk is much prized by Kurdish women, who make it into a variety of dresses, the material being very strong. We have no specimen of this at the Exhibition ; but such an instance ought to sharpen the eye of our silk manufacturers, and stimulate them to do what the Cotton Supply Association has done in the way of extending the rearing and cultivation of an article so valuable, and at the same time so attainable, within a zone of many degrees of latitude. On occasions like these how valuable it would be to have a section altogether appropriated to new products, the commercial uses of which have not yet been discovered ! The consuls of different countries, scattered as they are in the most distant localities, might furnish valuable contributions, and scientific commissioners might be appointed to examine and report upon them.

Raw silk, including tram, singles, and organzine, is exhibited by France, Algiers, Italy, Austria, Spain, Portugal, Russia, Turkey, India, Victoria, and other countries, though the exhibition is, as a whole, far from complete. It will be observed that the French and Italian samples are in many cases the produce not of French and Italian cocoons, but of eggs obtained from the East and other places where the disease has not penetrated. And it is gratifying to find that Italian silks made of such seed are yearly acquiring greater perfection. The Japanese seed worked in Italy loses in time its sharpness and want of colour, and accquires the natural softness and elasticity proper to Italian silk. There is something inherent to Italy which renders her, notwithstanding every difficulty, the privileged home of the finest description of raw and organzine silk. The spinning of silk is becoming more and more a manufacturing industry, and everywhere large spinning-mills are being erected, worked by steam-power. Some of the best samples in the French department are from Ardèche; in the Italian, from Milan. Austria, too, has a good exhibition. Russia produces a quantity of silk, principally from Caucase; but the cocoon is sent to Moscow and St. Petersburg, where the manufacture is carried on.

Together with raw silk and organzine, the visitor will see a great variety of sewing silk, or soie à coudre, à broder, raw and dyed, écrues et teintes, as well as bourres de soie, spun, raw, and dyed, for sewing. The infinite variety of shades of colour here exhibited is remarkable, and, with the extensive use of chignons for ladies' head-dress, it will be seen how art is made to supply the deficiencies of nature, and how difficult it will become for keen observers to detect the true from the artificial, in this as in other portions of personal ornaments.

It is not, however, the cocoon, the raw, or sewing silk that forms the attraction in this class. The great wonder is the silk manufacture itself, which is more than ever distinguished for lovely hues and beauty of design. If, on the one hand, the new colours obtained from aniline and other chemical products have supplied a greater variety of tints than could be obtained from vegetable sources, it is quite evident that the genius of the artist is more than ever visible and eminently happy. In such an article as silk, and indeed, in most descriptions of textile materials, a good and

PROF.
LEONE
LEVI,
LL.D., ON
SILK
MANUFAC-
TURES, &c.
———
well-executed design is a primary condition to success. The first element to strike the eye, it is certain to enrich every material; and, when texture and design enter into competition, with the great majority the latter is sure to obtain a decisive victory. Art-designing is itself an important industry in Paris; and to her artists the manufacturers resort in order to produce constant novelties in their tissues, shawls, ribbons, brocades, and embroidery.

Superiority
of French
designers.
But what is it that renders French designers so fertile in imagination and so striking in conception? What is it that enables them to invent designs which either guide public taste or promptly follow that taste and ennoble it with their touch? There is much, doubtless, in a national character full of versatility and quick in perception, in a climate and temperature favourable to the growth of flowers possessing high brilliancy of colour and great perfection of form; but there is more in an artistic education carefully tended and cultivated, not only by the actual teaching of art and design, but by what is still more fitted to awaken the mind to the true and the beautiful, the constant association with the highest models of art in public galleries and churches, in gardens and boulevards. Means of spreading artistic instruction are now provided in the principal States of Europe. In France, schools of design are established in the great centres of manufacture. There science and art are deemed not the luxuries, but the necessities of manufacturing industry. Lyons is rich in her schools, national and martinière (from the name of its founder); and from Paris emanate the highest inspirations of taste, elegance, and invention. The Rhenish Provinces of Prussia abound with art-schools; so do Belgium, Wurtemberg, Switzerland, &c. Every nation is putting forth her maximum energy, with a view to the embellishment and refinement of manufacturing industry and the elevation of public taste. And Britain should not remain behind in a matter so essential.

Illustrations
of remark-
able speci-
mens in
French silk
goods.
The most striking specimens of silk manufacture at the Exhibition are certainly to be found in Lyons and St. Etienne, Let the visitor scan carefully the collective exhibition of the Association des Tisseurs de Lyons (251). Let him observe the splendid tapestry or damask silk exhibited by Messrs. Pillet-Meauzé et Fils (102), and that of Messrs. Methevon and Bouvard (148), equally sumptuous. And what shall we say of the taffeta brocaded silk with lace patterns relieved by wreaths of flowers, or of that other taffeta silk with velvet representing birds, flowers, and feathers, which seem as if you could pick them up? The illustrations of

woven silk will perhaps give some idea of the degree of excellence now attained in this manufacture. The first of these, exhibited by Messrs. Poncet, Papillon, and Girodon (164), is

PROF.
LEONE
LEVI,
LL.D., ON
SILK
MANUFAC-
TURES, &C.

Fig. 1.—PORTION OF A SILK DRESS BY PONCET, PAPILLON, AND GIRODON.

a broché silk robe, the pattern at the bottom representing drooping flowers. The centre large flower forms a new feature in silk weaving. It is raised so as to represent velvet,

PROF.
LEONE
LEVI,
LL.D., ON
SILK
MANUFAC-
TURES, &c.

by a new process, the "velvet" being raised after the silk is woven. The second, exhibited by Messrs. Schulz and Beraud (207), is a robe of taffeta-coloured silk, the pattern

Fig. 2.—TRIMMING OF OSTRICH FEATHERS, BY SCHULZ AND BERAUD.

woven on black velvet. The engraving represents the front half of the dress, the pattern on a smaller scale running round the bottom of the dress. The third is woven in the loom to imitate hand embroidery, representing natural flowers on a satin ground, to be used for chair seats, pillows, or screens. In brocade silks with gold and silver the visitor

PROF.
LEONE
LEVI,
LL.D., ON
SILK
MANUFAC-
TURES, &c.

Fig. 3.—CUSHION AND CHAIR COVER (BY LAMY AND CO., OF LYONS).

will meet with some magnificent descriptions at M. Sagnier-Teulon, of Nismes (81). Beautiful is the satin with feather ornaments exhibited by Messrs. Hielard, and Co.; and so are the gauze tissues with and velvet flowers by Messrs. Josseraud, Févrot, and Co. (121). In moire antique there is something beautiful especially in fancy water patterns. All around the Lyons department the visitor will meet with specimens remarkable for chasteness of design, excellence of material, and elegance of ornamentation. These *tours de force* are doubtless isolated instances of perfection, reached probably at a cost far too high for general application to ordinary articles of trade, yet they serve the important purpose of indicating what may yet be achieved, as well as of facilitating the way to general improvement. And they do find a market especially in France, England, and the United States. Many, in fact, of the most expensive and superb robes made at Lyons, and those, the engravings of which we have given, are exclusively manufactured for an English house, Messrs. Grant and Gask. At the St. Etienne

PROF.
LEONE
LEVI,
LL.D., ON
SILK
MANUFAC-
TURES, &c.

French
ribbons and
velvet.

department, the brocade ribbons of M. Larcher-Faure (129), the velvet ribbons of Messrs. Barallon and Brossard (106), and the ribbons made for fans of Messrs. Dessales and Co. (117), well merit a visit. In silk velvet, both Lyons and St. Étienne have fair samples. The more, indeed, we examine and study the French exhibition of the silk manufacturers, the more we are convinced that, however unfavourable the circumstances may have been as regards the raw material, the French manufacturers have not abated one iota in their efforts for improvement.

Swiss
ribbons and
plain silks.

Switzerland has a good exhibition of exceedingly light and low-class silks. They are plain in taste, but very useful, and sure to find an extensive market. Zurich, the great centre of the tissues, and Bâle, the chief seat of the ribbons, have both acquired much reputation in foreign markets, and at this Exhibition they fully maintain their position of pre-eminence. The most remarkable feature in Swiss silks is the extreme beauty of colour, the lightest and most delicate tints altogether unaffected by the touch of the hand or

Italy.

by atmospheric impurities. Italy, too, exhibits a good deal. She has her old Genoa velvets, of world-wide renown, and she has silk brocade and tapestry of much merit. But the Italian manufacturers, not courageous enough to meet boldly the competition with France, lose golden opportunities for reacquiring the position which they once held. Surely, of all lands Italy should be second to none in purity of

Austria.

design and liveliness of colour. Austria produces tapestry

Spain.

silks of great beauty. Spain has some fine specimens from Valencia and Barcelona. Tunis exhibits good tissues of silk and silver. India has some rich samples of silk tissues,

Russia.

and silk with gold and silver. Russia shows some excellent silks from Moscow; and a good deal is exhibited by Prussia and the Zollverein, especially in silk velvets and ribbons.

Meagre
exhibition
British silk
manu-
facture.

As for Britain, her exhibition is very meagre; she evidently excels in her moire antiques, Irish poplins, and black crape, and she has excellent plain and glacé silks; but she exhibits no specimens where beauty of design is observable, though there are some honourable exceptions. What, for instance, could be more elegant than the *Tissue*

Tissue de
Vere.

de Verre for silk curtains, couches, and chair coverings exhibited by Messrs. Grant and Gask, of Oxford Street? Of all the uses hitherto made of glass, this seems certainly the most wonderful. Who would conceive that that brittle material could become sufficiently flexible as to be woven like a textile fabric? There is something very beautiful in the amalgamation of this lustrous material with the finest silk; and I do not wonder that it has been largely used for the ornamentation of palaces and public buildings. As a whole the British silk manufacture is certainly not so conspicuous at this as at the former Exhibitions, and it is a singular fact that, whilst in 1862 Britain, almost alone, showed great improvement in design, colour, and texture, in 1867 she exhibits no mark of progress. The result of the competition was seen at the distribution of prizes. Five French silk manufacturers were honoured with the Legion of Honour. The town of Lyons carried off the grand prize; and of 12 gold medals four were gained by France, awarded to the Chambers of Commerce of Lyons, St. Etienne, Paris, and Ardèche. Switzerland got two for Zurich and Bâle; Italy one, Great Britain one, the Chamber of Commerce of Vienna one, and Turkey, Prussia, and Russia one each. Of 144 silver medals, 105 were given to France, 13 to Britain, and 10 to Italy. Of 135 bronze medals, 17 went to France, 17 to Italy, 14 to Austria, and 10 to Britain; and of 156 honourable mentions, 57 were awarded to France, 50 to Italy, 9 to Austria, 8 to Britain; and the remainder to other countries. The number of honours granted to any country must, of course, be calculated in proportion to the number of exhibitors; still, it is evident that the position of the United Kingdon is not what we could wish, especially in relation to France, which has taken the lion's share of all medals and honours. How shall we, then, account for this when we look back to the high position Britain had acquired at the Exhibition of 1862? Whence this sudden stoppage? Is it the effect of the high price of the raw material? If so, why has it not operated in like manner in France? Is it the consequence of unequal competition? But why should Britain be behind her competitors? Let us, first of all, clear up the real facts of the case.

Within the last 25 years there has been a great oscillation in the imports of raw silks. In 1840 the imports amounted to 3,759,000 lbs.; from that time they increased enormously, till, in 1860, they reached 9,200,000 lbs. But afterwards there was a considerable decrease, and in 1867 they were not more than 5,800,000 lbs. The greatest fluctuation has taken place in the imports from China, the quantity having first risen from 5,000 bales to 67,000 bales, and afterwards fallen to 26,000 bales. From India the importation has been stationary; and so from Persia. Of Brutian silks the imports have dwindled to nothing, and from Italy they have been reduced to very little.

PROF. LEONE LEVI, LL.D., ON SILK MANUFAC- TURES, &c.

Prizes and medals.

Causes of British inferiority.

Fluctuation in the imports of the raw material.

PROF.
LEONE
LEVI,
LL.D., ON
SILK
MANUFAC-
TURES, &c.

Increased
exports of
raw silk
from
Britain.

Effect of
free trade
on the silk
manu-
facture.

Arrest of
progress
effected by
disease in
the silk
worm.

Nor is this all. In consequence of the disease in the silkworm, France, Italy, and Germany have become great competitors in the British markets for China and India silks; and now, when we deduct the exports, the quantity remaining for home consumption is actually less than it was 25 years ago. In 1840, of 3,800,000 lbs. of silk imported, 3,600,000 lbs., or 94 per cent. of the whole, were left for home consumption. In 1860, of 9,200,000 lbs. imported, upwards of 6,000,000 lbs., or 65 per cent. of the whole, were left for home consumption; and in 1867, out of 5,800,000 lbs. imported, 3,900,000 lbs., or 67 per cent. of the whole, were used at home. Under such circumstances the prices of raw silk have risen considerably. According to Messrs. Durant's circular China silk, which on January 1, 1855, was worth 17s. and 18s. 6d., rose in 1867 to 32s. 6d. and 34s.; Bengal common rose from 7s. 6d. and 12s. to 15s. and 18s. 6d.; Persia, from 9s. 6d. and 11s. 6d. to 15s. and 22s. 6d.; Italian raw, from 19s. and 21s. to 38s. and 40s.; and thrown, from 23s. and 26s. to 42s. and 45s. per lb. And in an industry where the raw material enters so largely in the total value, a rise of 80 or 100 per cent. upon such material left but little surplus either for labour or capital. This is an element which renders the silk manufacture always less profitable than the cotton or woollen, where the raw material is of little value or is indigenous to this country; and we need not wonder if, under such circumstances, these obtain decided preference for the investment of capital.

Following the unsatisfactory condition of the raw material, the exports of British silk have suffered greatly. In 1846, when Sir Robert Peel reduced the duty on silk manufactures from 30 per cent., as it was left by Mr. Huskisson, to 15 per cent., the value of exports amounted to no more than 608,000l. From that time it increased regularly, till in 1856, the value amounted to 1,758,000l. Soon after, the disease in the silkworm appeared, prices rose, and the cheaper descriptions of silk became dearer in proportion than similar articles in wool or other materials. Then, too, in 1860 America, our chief market, became the prey of a fearful civil war, and the exports fell in 1861 to 1,395,000l., and from that time they further fell to 1,028,000l. in 1867. Even the six months ending July 1867 showed a considerable diminution as compared with the similar period in 1866. To a certain extent the check to the prosperity of the manufacture has been as much felt in Lyons as in Spitalfields and Manchester; but whilst England did not get the better of it, France did. Of ribbons, for instance, in 1851 the export from

France amounted to 1,200,000*l.*; in 1855 they rose to 4,700,000*l.*; and in 1861 fell to 1,800,000*l.*, but they have since recovered to 3,500,000*l.* in 1866.

The silk trade in France, as a whole, exhibits a very different progress from that of England as regards the exports of silk manufacture. When the two are placed side by side the comparison is very striking:

——	Exports from England.	Increase per cent.	Exports from France.	Increase per cent.
1851	£1,130,000	—	£7,350,000	—
1855	1,082,000	4	9,650,000	31
1861	1,395,000	28	11,560,000	20
1866	1,318,000	Decreased 5	1,850,000	63

The difference between France and England from 1851 to 1855, and from 1861 to 1866 is very notable.

What, however, alarms the British manufacturer is the fact that, whilst the exports of British manufacture decreased, the imports of French and other foreign manufactures have greatly increased. In 1855 the real value of foreign silk manufacture imported was only 1,800,000*l.* In 1860 it was 2,800,000*l.*; and in 1867, 8,000,000*l.* There is nothing surprising in the fact of such increase, the diminution or abolition of import duty being always followed by a larger trade, by which the community at large is benefited. Only in this case the natural result was still more sudden, from the fact that just when we opened our ports, the American markets being closed, a large portion of French and German silk, which would otherwise have been sent thither, found its way to this country. From these accumulated evils, the manufacturer in this country has been placed under no ordinary straits and difficulty; and there is no doubt that thereby the ability of England to compete with France in certain descriptions of silk manufacture has been greatly put to the test.

The French, Swiss, and Germans have the advantage of a brighter atmosphere, and France, especially, besides producing her own material to a large extent, stands out pre-eminently as the leader of fashion; still, in the processes of manufacture, and in the cost of the raw material, the different countries are pretty much on a par. The wages of labour in this manufacture are very low, both in this and in other countries; and, if they are a little higher in England than elsewhere, that is probably more than made up by her superior power of productiveness. It is not, indeed, by starving the labourer, or by employing cheap and inferior

PROF.
LEONE
LEVI,
LL.D., ON
SILK
MANUFAC-
TURES, &c.

labour, that the British manufacturer will ever be able to meet the competition. On the contrary, the most prominent want in an industry so light and delicate is a higher class of labourers, more educated, more refined in taste, and even more expert in material and texture. As to protective duties of any kind, the idea is quite exploded that any fictitious protection against the competition of foreign manufacture can do much towards propping up native industry. The prosperous maintenance of a manufacture in any country mainly depends on the natural facilities and advantages which the nation may possess for it, and on the energy, aptitude, and skill displayed by the manufacturers themselves. Sound principles of commercial policy dictate that if the foreign manufacturer can produce for us any article better and cheaper than we can produce ourselves, we should let them do it, it being vain and preposterous to think that we should shut the foreigners out to foster artificially any branch of British manufacture. The British silk manufacturer must, like the cotton and woollen manufacturer, learn to be independent of legislative support. He must endeavour to improve his own production by attending better than he has hitherto done to the conditioning of the silk, to the perfect adaptation of the silk he uses to the material he wants to produce, to the proper manipulation of colours, to the novelty of design, and, above all, to the finish of the article. Let it be remembered that the inferiority of British silks is not confined to those tissues where design is the primary element, but that even in the black corded silk, the French are superior. It is very true that the French have to a large extent succeeded, by imparting to their plain silk an artificial weight, which gives to it an appearance and a value beyond its real worth; but that is not all. In truth a higher standard has been attained by France in every description of silks, and the British manufacturer must strain every nerve to place himself in a better position than he seems to be at present, if he will not be ousted altogether in the keen but wholesome competition which has now been irrevocably established.

Great use of shawls.

The shawl seems to be the most useful and most universal of all articles of dress. On the head as a turban, and over the head as a hood, twisted round the neck, folded round the shoulder, or wrapped round the waist as a girdle, at times forming the entire dress, and at other times being but an adjunct of luxury, falling in graceful folds on the person: in every way it is suitable and becoming. In size, too, how different. The shawl used for the turban is of extreme length, often as much as sixty yards. The scarf is of endless variety of length and breadth ; the ordinary plaid from the size of a long shawl to that of a common handkerchief. And in material we have it in wool of every degree of fineness, in cotton and silk, in mixed materials with gold and silver, and in lace of the finest texture.

First in quality and design is certainly the Cashmere shawl, for which the visitor will visit the Indian department. Let him observe the fineness of the material used for the purpose. It is the soft downy substance found next the skin and below the thick hair of the Thibet goat. Then the design, which is ordinarily the pine, with ornaments of great variety ; then the beautiful combination of colours; and, finally, the finish of the article so perfect as a whole. There are shawls exhibited by India of great value, such as the square Cashmere shawl with violet centre, exhibited by Dewansing, and the Dopatta shawl, from Delhi. These far surpass any other for rarity and absolute worth. So jealous is the Maharajah of Cashmere to maintain the reputation of such shawls, that he has recently taken steps against any deterioration in the quality of those manufactured in his dominions.

After India, the visitor had better go at once to examine the shawls exhibited in the French department, just opposite the silk, where, with much that is inferior, he will find many shawls of unsurpassing beauty. France is doing her utmost to imitate the Indian shawl in material, colour, and ornamentation. The specimen given in the Illustration of a shawl manufactured by Lecoq Gruyer, of Paris, is, indeed, a wonderful copy of an Indian shawl, not easily distinguished from the best cashmere. The richest descriptions are made in Paris, the middling in Lyons, and the inferior at Nismes. The shawls exhibited by Messrs. Lacassagne, Deschamps, and Salaville, and especially the one in the centre of the group, are exceedingly fine. A rich velvet shawl, embroidered by hand, with chenille fringe, well merits a visit, and so do the shawls embroidered by machinery. France has a large trade in shawls. The value of exports of shawls from France which, in 1851, was 640,000*l.*, has since increased to about 1,000,000*l.* Austria, too, has some splendid shawls, exhibited by Messrs. Halawatsch and Isbary, of Vienna (14). The Austrian manufacturer gives a precision to his design worthy of imitation. Prussia exhibits great variety of tartan and plaid shawls, but of inferior descriptions.

As for England, the Paisley shawl of superior wool and excellent design, and the silk shawls now produced in Norwich by Messrs. Clabburn and Sons, figure most favour-

PROF.
LEONE
LEVI,
LL.D., ON
SILK
MANUFAC-
TURES, &c.

ably ; whilst the plaid and tartan shawls exhibited by Messrs. Kerr, Scott, and Co., Messrs. Hitchcock and Williams (2), and Messrs. Romanes and Patterson, are unrivalled for brilliancy of colour and variety of clans. In the cases of

Fig. 4.—FRENCH CASHMERE, A PERFECT IMITATION OF INDIAN CASHMERE.

Messrs. Hitchcock and Williams 70 or 80 different patterns are shown, representing the plaids worn by the ancient Scottish clans, together with some fancy plaids, such as the Victoria, Eugénie, and Napoléon. Two gold medals only were awarded for shawls: one of these was given to Dewansing and one to the Chamber of Commerce of Paris. Of 15 silver medals, 11 went to France, three to Britain (of which two to India and one to England), and one to Austria ; of 25 bronze medals, 12 to France, five to Prussia, and three to Britain ; and of 26 honourable mentions, six were given to France and five to Britain.

Prizes and
medals.

Upon the lace shawl, and on lace and net generally, I shall not enter, a lighter and more accomplished hand having undertaken the difficult and delicate task of appreciating their worth and beauty. This much I will say, that the hand-lace exhibited in the French and Belgian departments is really something very superb. A piece of lace is, perhaps, the most ingenious result of artistic skill that can well be conceived. The more we examine the extreme nicety of the operation, the fineness of the thread so well knit together, the fairy-like web woven for it, and the beautiful figures of the pattern, the greater seems the marvel of the achievement; and well may we be grateful to Nottingham for the prodigious feat of performing so nice a work by mechanical agency.

Of embroidery the Exhibition is full, whether by hand or by machinery, so largely does it enter in articles of dress and household furniture. Apart from white embroidery, which will be dealt with in connection with lace, the most prominent description is the gold and silver embroidery used in ecclesiastical vestments and furniture, in the shape of albs, copes, chasubles, cassocks, surplices, and altar-pieces. In these articles France, Italy, Austria, Spain, Russia, and other countries seem to vie with each other in beauty of design and magnificence of material. But let the visitor not miss the Italian specimens. The raised work there is something very fine, and there is no difficulty in finding them, so prominent are they and so beautiful. The art of embroidery in gold and silver is of old date, but seldom has it been carried to such an extent as at this moment. Britain does not exhibit much in this class of articles; and what she has falls far short of the excellence and vividness which distinguish the foreign manufacture. The visitor should note the gold and silver thread used in Indian manufacture, which is not in the shape of a wire, but simply a narrow band beaten on the common thread. In the Lyons department Messrs. Uze, Fils, and Co. exhibit a sample of gold and silver thread of extraordinary fineness. In this class, too, are included small wares, passementerie, or trimming, which fashion has once more revived to an enormous extent. They comprise fringes, girdles, laces, cords, buttons, loops, braids, &c., used in ladies' dresses, carriage furniture, and ornaments. Look at those cases in the French department, with gold laces and other braids and trimmings, for court or livery costumes! See those beautiful buttons of every variety of material in metal, glass, ivory, silk, wool, and cotton, and in the most fantastic shapes! See those coach laces, so chaste and beautiful! What can be conceived more perfect than those

Marginal notes:
PROF. LEONE LEVI, LL.D., ON SILK MANUFACTURES, &c.

Lace.

Embroidery.

Gold and silver embroidery.

Passementeries, or trimming.

epaulettes and other military costumes ? In curtain hangings, too, there is great variety. Paris is the great centre for passementerie ; by the use of always the best material and the exercise of a boundless imagination in design, the French have secured for themselves a decided supremacy. Since the Exhibition of 1851 the exports of passementerie from France has increased from 267,000*l.* in 1851 to 1,400,000*l.* in 1866. Many other countries have excellent specimens in trimming, more especially Prussia, Russia, Austria, Italy, Greece, Nuremberg, and Wurtemberg ; whilst Switzerland has beautiful straw trimming, and France has imitation straw of great beauty. Of Berlin woolwork Prussia has an excellent exhibition ; so have France and Austria. But how is it that England exhibits almost nothing in this important branch, when the exports of small wares, trimming, and fringes are considerable ? The reason probably is that our manufacturers content themselves in producing cheap goods, and, in most cases, without much originality of design. As might well be imagined, the awards in this class are principally favourable to France and Belgium. Of seventeen gold medals, ten went to France, four to Belgium, and one to Britain (to the town of Nottingham) ; of seventy-seven silver medals, forty-eight went to France, eight to Belgium, and four to Britain ; of one hundred bronze medals, fifty-one to France, eleven to Belgium, and nine to Britain ; and of ninety-two honourable mentions, thirty-two to France, fourteen to Italy, seven to Belgium, and three to Britain ; the remainder to other countries.

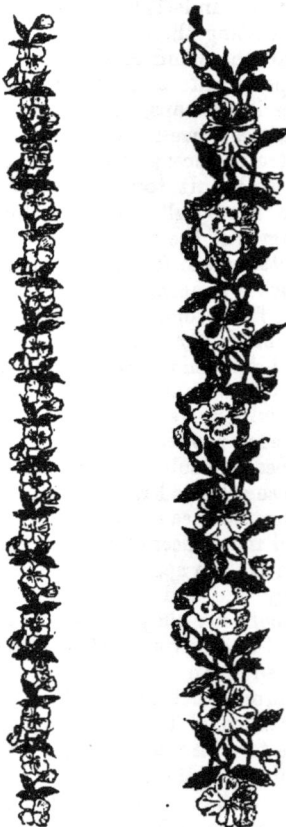

Fig. 5. — HAND EMBROIDERED TRIMMING, BY EMERY, OF LYONS.

Hosiery is largely represented in the French, German, and British departments. France is rich in fancy articles, such as ladies' silk stockings with open lacework and embroidery, mittens, scarfs, and veils. Britain excels in articles really sound and of the finest make; whilst, for bleach and finish, the Nottingham cotton hosiery is unequalled. But some of the largest manufacturers are not represented, and we do not see to the full extent the power of the British hosier to adapt his goods to all the markets of the world. For marvels of cheapness we must visit Saxony; and certainly I was not prepared to find another country producing machine-made articles at lower prices, though inferior in quality, than Britain. Other articles of underclothing—such as shirts and fronts in great variety and beauty, with and without embroidery; stays of the most elegant form; crinolines and jupons—are shown by France in great abundance. Here, too, are fans, some in the finest lace and with exquisite mountings; others adorned with pictorial representations; others of feathers, and others remarkable for cheapness and taste. Umbrellas and parasols are largely exhibited, as well as sticks, whips, and an endless variety of objects adapted for ornaments and for ordinary use. But I cannot attempt to particularise any one of the numerous articles, and the visitor will have no difficulty in selecting the choicest patterns. The prize list gives us some idea of the character of these varied exhibitions. There were six gold medals in this class, of which France took five (two for hosiery, two for buttons, and one for fans); of 82 silver medals, 62 went to France (for her gloves, corsets, buttons, &c.), and only two to Britain; of 129 bronze medals, 78 to France and five to Britain; and of 137 honourable mentions, 48 to France and 28 to Britain, of which, however, the greater part went to India for fans.

As we enter the grand vestibule from the principal entrance the most striking sight on the French side is the exhibition of ladies' dresses by Messrs. Enout and Co. The beauty and excellence of such dresses do not consist so much in the material, though it is always of the finest, as in the make and trimming. The illustration here given is a pattern of embroidered trimming and pansies introduced this season, and made first by command of the Empress Eugenie. It is very splendid, and when applied on taffeta silk in colour, either corresponding to the principal flower, or forming a strong contrast to the trimming, the effect is beautiful. How bizarre, too, are the fancy dresses for balls, close at hand, and how charming are those children's dresses! It is of no use to deny it, the French have a peculiar ability for such things. We may wonder how is it that every nation receives the fashion from France, and why should a dressed doll from the Rue St. Honoré give at once the tone

PROF. LEONE LEVI, LL.D., ON SILK MANUFACTURES, &c.

Ladies' dresses.

Universality of French fashion.

PROF. LEONE LEVI, LL.D., ON SILK MANUFAC- TURES, &c.
to Europe and America? All we can say is that every nation has its own spécialité. England is famous for her minerals and machinery; Spain and Portugal for their wines; Italy for her objects of art; and France for her fashion. Dressmaking in France forms two separate industries. First, are the couturiéres or dressmakers, who work only by measure for private customers, but whose taste and skill are extensively known abroad; second, are the "Maisons de Nouveautés," specially for the sale of ladies' dresses, all prepared, which give forth things very superb and generally cheaper than they can be produced by dressmakers. It is to this class that Messrs. Énout and others in the vestibule belong. The modiste has a distinct profession, and she confines her attention to head-dress in the shape of bonnets and coiffure for balls and soirées. The manner in which the flower, blonde, or lace is to be adjusted is entirely a matter of taste, and the triumph of art consists in the constant renewal of form, constituting in each case a novel and original fashion.

Exports of vêtements from France.
The export of vêtements from France have immensely increased of late. In 1851 their value was about 1,000,000*l.* in 1861 they amounted to 3,400,000*l.* and in 1865 to 5,000,000*l.* But from the United Kingdom also the exports of apparel and slops increased from 1,000,000*l.* in 1851 to 2,000,000*l.* in 1861, and 2,200,000*l.* in 1867. In ready-made clothing the only countries which have some remarkable specimens are France, Belgium, and Austria. Separate articles composing the dress of ladies and gentlemen, a rich collection, is found at the Universal Exhibition.

Hats.
Hats are largely exhibited, with the great desiderata of form and lightness. The specimens at the Exhibition indicate fully the progress which has been made in this manufacture. To say nothing of the common hats covered with silk plush, with the foundation of cork, felt, or cotton, or of hats made of felted wool, I may notice the various descriptions of straw hats shown by the South American States. Malta shows the very cheap straw hat worn by seamen. The Cape of Good Hope has a fibre, the Juncus Serratus, which makes excellent hats, very strong, and im-
Straw hats.
pervious to rain, wind, and sun. Italy has her straw hats and bonnets of exquisite fineness. England too, has an
Caps.
excellent exhibition of chips. Of caps there is great variety. Austria excels in the red cloth cap, with a long tassel. Eastern countries have caps highly ornamented and em-
Bonnets.
broidered with gold and silver; and Britain has the common and extensively-used glengarry. Ladies' bonnets are exhibited in abundance, especially by France, if we can call bonnets the strips of silk ribbon or straw intended to set

off a monstrous chignon. There are at the Exhibition bonnets with ivory and pearls, bonnets composed entirely of feathers, others of glass, others of reeds, bonnets of straw, and bonnets of fancy materials of every description.

Of boots and shoes there is much exhibited; boots made by machinery occupying everywhere a prominent place. Also impermeable boots of indiarubber and other materials. Great novelties are shown in ladies' boots and slippers, both in shape, material, and ornamentation, especially in the French and Belgian departments.

Artificial flowers abound in the Exhibition, and there is something very beautiful among them. The French cases are exquisite. The gold and silver filigree flowers for coiffure, exhibited by Prevost Bernard, of Paris (43) ; the head-dresses of ostrich feather and birds of paradise ; the wild flowers in feathers, by Carchon (65) ; all are very fine. Austria has a beautiful group of flowers ; and so has Turkey and other countries.

In other articles for and of dress there is great abundance. Ostrich feathers of great beauty in length and breadth are exhibited by our colonies, especially the Cape of Good Hope. As for muffs, capes, and furs, it seems that use is now made of the feathers, furs, and downs of beasts and birds of every latitude.

In this important class five gold medals were awarded, four of them went to France for her artificial flowers, preparation of dresses, boots and hats ; and one to Austria for her dresses. Of 76 silver medals, 45 went to France, six to Austria, four to Britain ; of 183 bronze medals, 92 to France, 14 to Austria, and 13 to Britain ; and of 190 honourable mentions, 52 to France, 19 to Belgium, 19 to Italy, and nine to Britain.

But it is time to pass to class 92, comprising specimens of clothing worn by the people of different countries. It is certainly a novel and interesting feature in this exhibition to have all around lifesize figures dressed in the native costumes of almost every country on the face of the earth. I cannot say how far the figures may be taken to represent the ordinary dress of the people ; to what class, high or low, each or any of them may belong ; whether the dress is that of a gala day or of a wedding costume ; but, assuming that, generally, we have before us the customary and popular dress now worn, what a study does such a collection afford ! Setting aside altogether any artistic or ethnologic consideration, the merchant and manufacturer will see in them the most valuable guide for the production of articles of export. It is quite evident that since every country has its own recognisable costume or general style of male and

[Marginal notes:] Prof. Leone Levi, LL.D., on Silk Manufactures, &c. Boots and shoes. Artificial flowers. Feathers. Prizes and medals. Costume of different nations.

PROF.
LEONE
LEVI
LL.D., ON
SILK
MANUFAC-
TURES, &c.
———

female attire, over and above those niceties of colour and texture of dress, which fluctuate according to taste or the whim of fashion, without due attention to these facts we cannot hope for an extensive outlet for our manufactures. It is vain to imagine that old and stationary nations, like India and China, will change their habits and dress to suit the European trader. It is comparatively easy for the French to spread their fashion among European nations in articles of finery; but when England sends articles of ordinary use to nations traditionally opposed to all change, unless she can send them things which they are accustomed to wear, which suit their manner and clime, wear as long and well, and are cheaper than they can manufacture them themselves, they will not buy them of her. Bearing in mind, then, the real mercantile value of such an exhibition, let the visitor see, principally, the materials composing the dresses in such costumes. Where they consist of native cloth, let him carefully examine the texture. Let him distinguish the articles made as piece goods generally from those woven in pieces fitted for use; let him notice the style and make of the dresses, what ornaments are used, how they are worn, and generally the character and type of the design seemingly popular in the different countries.

Morocco.

Suppose we enter from the central garden, by the Rue d'Afrique, into the eastern group of countries, we first alight on Morocco, and there we find a lady with two jackets of orange merino, embroidered with gold and silver, a large broad scarf of silk and cotton of bright colours, a net robe, a coloured silk handkerchief on the head, and velvet shoes richly embroidered with gold. A little further, after passing Tunis, to which I shall refer presently, there is a group, among whom are two Jewesses and a Moresque, the former with robes of beautiful silk velvet, richly trimmed with gold lace, under-vests equally rich in gold embroidery, loose sleeves of silk and gold gauze, silk scarfs on their heads, and a gold and silk scarf wrapped round their waists. The Moresque, with a purple vest and scarlet robe, both richly embroidered with gold, a silk and gold waistband, a scarlet shawl on the head, with a long white-striped scarfs over all.

Tunis.

In Tunis there is a Bedouin Arab, with a brown cloth coat and trousers embroidered with gold, a white bernouse fastened on the head, and a silk shawl as a girdle.

Egypt.

In Egypt we see a Cophte woman, with a mauve silk dress, a black silk mantle, waistband embroidered with gold, a muslin chemise, and head-dress with long veil covering the face, except the eyes. A rich fellah, with a robe of red and yellow silk and cotton lined with calico, a silk shawl round the waist, a fine crimson coat, a white muslin turban, and red shoes. A negress servant, with gold and silk cerise dress trimmed with gold lace, a coarse muslin chemise, and a tulle veil with flower borders for head-dress. And a Barbary Süis, with a white calico dress, a large silk and wool shawl twisted round the waist, a black cloth vest embroidered with gold, and a red cap.

Turkey exhibits a great variety of rich costumes. There is the Albanian, with trowsers of scarlet silk, a full tunic of white cotton, a double jacket of scarlet cloth with hanging sleeves of striped gauze, and a magnificent girdle richly embroidered with gold. There, too, is the Circassian, with a black cloth coat, with gold and silver lace, and a fur cap on the head ; his lady having a purple satin robe with gold and silver lace in front, a crimson velvet jacket with gold, a deep cloth cap, and very singular cuffs in the horseshoe shape.

Turkey.

The costume of China may best be seen from the colony of native Chinese in the park, and it evidently consists, either of a long cloth robe, a black silk jacket, and a small blue cap, or of a dark silk dress and brass buttons, straw-coloured silk trousers lined with blue.

China.

Of Siam there are two illustrations, showing the ordinary dress to be robes of red China crape, calico shirts, and calico scarves round the waist, and huge straw hats in the umbrella shape.

Siam.

India does not exhibit any complete costumes, though she has many illustrations of the different articles which ordinarily enter into the Indian dress. Dr. Forbes Watson, in his able and important work on the textile manufactures and costumes of the people of India, shows, first of all, how general is the use of the turban. Its material is either fine muslin texture, or cotton for the lower classes or silk for the higher. In colour it is red and yellow, green and purple, and occasionally even black ; and is made all of one piece or strip, nine to 12 inches wide and 15 to 25 yards long, with an ornamental border, often with gold thread at the end. The usual male dress a dhotee, is a piece of cloth wrapped round the loins, the end of which, after a couple of turns round the waist, is passed by the Hindoo between the legs and thrust under the folds which cross behind. A longee is also used as a scarf for wearing over the body and shoulders in a variety of ways. It is generally made of plain cotton, with or without coloured borders and ends, or with silk borders ornamented with gold. For female attire, the chief article is the saree, a long scarf which both envelops the body and acts as a covering to the head. As usually worn, one end is passed twice round the waist, the upper border being tied in a strong knot and allowed to fall in graceful folds to the ankle, thus forming a sort of petticoat or skirt ;

India.

PROF.
LEONE
LEVI,
LL.D., ON
SILK
MANUFAC-
TURES, &c.
the other end is passed in front across the left arm and shoulder, one edge being brought over the top of the head. It is then allowed to fall behind and over the shoulder and arm. The Indian costume is very simple ; in most cases it

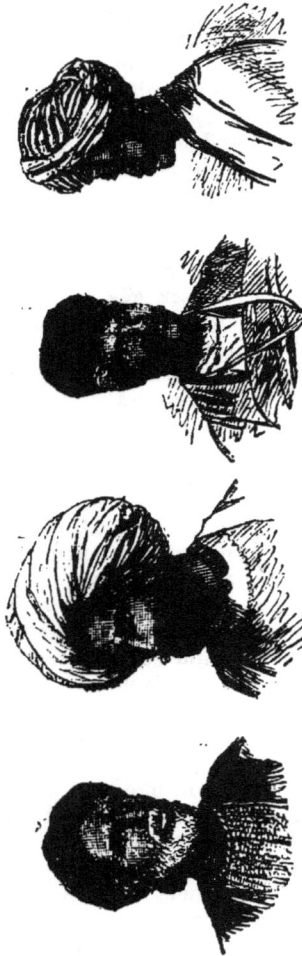

Fig. 5.—MODES OF FOLDING OR MAKING UP TURBANS.

consists of only one article of dress, yet there is great variety in the cloth, and more particularly in the embroidery, which is not easily followed. Illustrations of the turban in different shapes as well as of a longee and a saree, are here appended form Dr. Forbes Watson's work. As an example of imitation of Indian manufacture, the visitor will see in the Dutch East India a cloth called baticks ; a little further he will see in Holland, imitations of such baticks exhibited by M. Tho. Wilson, of Harlem. There is no great difference between

PROF.
LEONE
LEVI,
LL.D. ON
SILK
MANUFAC-
TURES, &c.

Fig. 6.—INDIAN COSTUMES.
" The male figure illustrates the turban-piece and the longee. The female dress shows the long ornamental end of the saree."

them, though the materials used are not quite alike. In the same way M. Sagnier-Teulon, of Nismes in the French department, exhibits a silk tissue with gold, in imitation of Algiers manufacture, the original of which may be seen in the Algiers department. The mode of weaving silk and gold in India and Europe also differs, one using the gold thread by itself, the other using a beaten gold band ; but there are many things which the manufacturer must carefully study ere he can successfully imitate such native productions. The Eastern costume abounds in gold and silver. Gold texture and gold lace from the commonest tinsel to the finest metal, enter very largely into most articles of dress.

Bordering between the East and the West are the Danubian Principalities. There we see the Roumanian mountaineer clothed with leather dress, embroidered with coloured wool ; and the peasant woman with a black woollen skirt, worked with silver, and a jacket of a cotton material called buranqui, sometimes worked with beads.

Greece appears to be in a state of transition from the old national Eastern costume to the ordinary European ; but we still see the full plaited calico tunic, the richly-embroidered vest, and the red cap with gold tassel.

In Switzerland cotton, silk, and lace enter most largely into the usual dress of all the cantons.

A singular collection of costumes of the different departments of France gives an idea that the railway has not yet sufficiently penetrated into the interior of that country, or that the masses of people are proof against the inroad of fashion.

Sweden and Norway exhibit a most picturesque collection of costumes, which a national photographer has beautifully copied. There we see how the coarsest material is rendered useful and becoming by tasteful arrangement and elegant embroidery. To give an instance, there we see a man and woman belonging to the valley of Zatersdalen, in Norway. The man has trousers of fine black cloth, with green stripes, a grey tweed jacket very short in front, with black cloth cuffs and collar. The woman has a dress of cloth, with red and green border and embroidered bodice ; a white cotton jacket, with a broad square collar ; another jacket of thick cloth, with green cuffs, embroidery, and silver lace ; a red cloth waistband, with metal ornaments ; a long scarf of woollen stuff, scarlet and white, and a coloured silk headdress.

Denmark, too, shows some interesting costumes, the clothing being composed of black cloth velveteen or chamois, woollen handkerchiefs, and red damask caps.

Russia, so vast in territory, with so many races and under so many climes, offers illustrations of costumes of a most interesting character. A Tartar of Crimea has black cloth trousers, with surtout fastened tight round the throat, a stuff scarf round the waist, and an upper robe of green velvet with broad gold lace. A lady, his companion, has a robe and jacket of crimson silk with gold lace, a gold girdle with large metal clasps, and an upper robe of green velvet with broad gold lace. The Kalmukian has a finely embroidered woollen cloak, an embroidered skirt and silk gown, a bead collar, and a fur cap. The Cossack has a long coat of red cloth with silver lace, dark cloth trousers, a printed-cotton sash, high fur cap, and a leather girdle. A fisherman of Siberia is dressed from head to foot with clothing made of fish-bladder trimmed with fur ; and other Siberians from the mountains have skin dresses with bead trimming, cap and cape composed of beads and underdress of leather, and coarse linen drawers and shirts. Some of the Russian costumes are shown in the palace ; many more in the park.

Of the American continent, the only illustrations of costumes appear in the South American department belonging to Chili and the Argentine Confederation.

PROF. LEONE LEVI, LL.D., ON SILK MANUFAC- TURES, &c.

Argentine Confederation.

These brief sketches will, perhaps, give a sufficient idea of the great variety of clothing still used by the people of different countries ; and it will be seen that, in the majority of cases, the dresses are not made of superfine British or French cloth, but of native woven goods, often of the coarsest quality, yet strong and durable. In fact, foreign cloth, except calico, is seldom seen among them. How shall we sufficiently account for all this ? Has machinery failed to cheapen the material of dress for the millions of all countries ? Has the ability of England and France, and other great manufacturing countries to make such articles better and cheaper than could be made at home never yet come to the knowledge of the masses of the people ? or have the manufacturers never yet understood properly their proper mission, and consequently failed to adapt their merchandise to the real wants of nations ? Probably all these causes have concurrently operated to hinder the extensive use of machine-made manufactures. As to cheapness, we must remember that the agricultural population has, in every country, always abundance of time and sufficient ability to make their own cloth for ordinary use ; and that, consequently, foreign goods, however cheap they may appear to us, are always dear to those who, having the material on hand, can work it without calculating the value of labour. Then, foreign goods are not, in fact, nearly so cheap as we imagine to the consumer abroad, when the expenses of transport, profits, and charges are added to the original cost, and when heavy import duties are paid upon them. Moreover, as durability is an important element of cheapness, it is quite clear that in this respect machine-made cannot so

Competition between foreign machine-made and native-made cloth.

PROF.
LEONE
LEVI,
LL.D., ON
SILK
MANUFAC-
TURES, &c.

well compete with home-made goods. In countries where fashion effectively controls the manner of dress, durability is not so material an element ; the great majority caring less for an article which will last long than for one which has a fine appearance. But it is far otherwise where the masses are beyond the influence of, or not disposed to bow to, Fashion's behests of change and nothing but change. Much may be said, too, as to the fact that the millions in the interior of these countries have never yet become acquainted with the marvels of mechanical production. Distance, want of communication, and difference of language, have kept them isolated ; and few are the facilities and means afforded to them to acquire what, in many cases, they might consider a real boon. To the necessity on the part of the manufacturer more carefully to attend to the habits of the nations whose wants he means to supply I have already adverted. It is quite clear that if he intends to replace the home-spun goods among the millions in foreign lands he must make his merchandise cheaper than it can be produced where labour is most abundant—better than it can be made with the greatest waste of material—and in colour and pattern every way adapted to the taste and habits of the people, whatever be its state of civilization and comfort.

Demands for costly articles of manufacture.

Such considerations are, of course, quite apart from what is required to meet the demand for the higher classes, the *bon ton* of society. To know what is wanted for such, let our manufacturers obtain an insight into what is paraded in the saloons of the Tuileries, Ministers of State, and Ambassadors. There they will see exhibited, in profuse and surprising variety, the most extraordinary and luxurious dresses, in the most splendid materials and most elegant style, and charmingly ornamented with lace and flowers. And what is the grand lesson deducible from such a display, but that in articles intended for the wealthy and for special occasions, price is not a material consideration, and that the labour and expense necessary in their production should form no obstacle to their attainment. Let it be the aim of the manufacturer in such cases to arrive at true excellence ; and let him not rest satisfied till he produces an article which, like a picture of Raphael or a statue of Michael Angelo, is unique in itself, both in material and design. It is, indeed, by this constant aspiration towards the highest work of art that we can hope to keep pace with the general progress of manufacturing industry in all countries; whilst it should be the ambition of our manufacturers in all their productions, be it in the richest or lowest material, in the simplest or most luxurious design, to have a scrupulous regard to the requirement of art, and the advance of civilisation, and to keep in mind the need of spreading everywhere what is gentle, tasteful, and ornamental.

Before closing this report, permit me to offer a few general observations—first, as to certain defects in these International Exhibitions; and, secondly, as to what seems necessary to promote still further the success of our manufactures. One prominent want I have experienced in examining the articles exhibited has been the absence of all practical information, and of any individual on the spot ready to give it, the Commissioners themselves being, in many cases, quite unable to give any assistance. Generally, no data is given as to quantities produced, nothing as to prices; and though, in some cases, the producers have sent invoices to the Commissioners, the prices so set down afford no guide as to the market value of the articles, since they are more fanciful than real. The catalogue, too, is very imperfect; and most disappointing it is to the inquirer and student to be able only to give a superficial glance at the objects, and to find them always sheltered by the unwonted restriction, " Ne touchez pas, s'il vous plait."

It is, perhaps, a necessity in the case that the real condition of manufacturing industry in the different countries cannot appear from the few specimens exhibited. But if it be advantageous to impress our manufacturers with the sight of the advance made by other countries, it is still more important to put them in possession of the principal facts relating to the condition of such industry abroad, that they may study them for themselves at home. For this purpose it is all necessary to follow up such an exhibition with a careful and exhaustive survey of the economics of manufacturing industry, the rate of wages, the social and intellectual condition of the labourers, and any other items necessary for studying the relative power of the different commercial nations, to sustain the keen competition now existing between them. Even the exhibition of costumes, which shows the real wants of the people and the mode by which they supply themselves with articles of dress, suggests further and deeper inquiry, which can only be made upon real life in the countries themselves.

In concluding this report I would recommend:

First, that a commission should be issued composed of individuals possessing artistic, ethnological, chemical, and commercial knowledge, to examine and report upon the state of manufacturing industry in different countries in relation to the requirements of the masses of the people. A Committee of the House of Commons would not meet the

Side notes:
PROF. LEONE LEVI, LL.D., ON SILK MANUFACTURES, &c.

Defects of Exhibitions.

Absence of information.

Temporary character and passing impressions.

Need of deeper study on the wants and habits of different people.

PROF.
LEONE
LEVI,
LL.D., ON
SILK
MANUFAC-
TURES, &c.

case, as it would be impossible to obtain the necessary information in this country. And the reports of her Majesty's Secretaries of Embassy and Legation on the manufactures, commerce, &c., of the countries in which they reside, valuable as they are, are not sufficiently complete and technical for the purpose.

Secondly. Let works of the same character as that of Dr. Forbes Watson on the costumes and textile materials of India be produced from time to time for all countries, and communicated to our Chambers of Commerce and manu- facturers, together with collections of samples of textile materials woven and produced in such countries.

Thirdly, having regard to the temporary character of such exhibitions, their advantages can best be extended by enriching our museums, extending our galleries, and ex- hibiting to the masses of the people not only models of art and design, but whatever may interest them regarding the condition of life and intelligence all over the world.

Lastly, as regards artistic instruction, it has been my duty to report that in the classes I have more especially examined Great Britain seems somewhat deficient in inven- tiveness and design. Thirty-one years ago, in the Session of 1836, a Committee of the House of Commons was appointed to inquire into the best means of extending a knowledge of the arts and of the principles of design among the people, especially the manufacturing population of the country ; and it is singular that even then this deficiency was particularly manifested in the very branches I have reported upon. A high authority, Dr. Playfair, has just suggested a careful inquiry into the schools of art and design in other countries, and I can only bear my testimony to the necessity of such an inquiry as an important branch of that which I have suggested into the state of manu- facturing industry. Let us give due heed to this salutary warning, and endeavour to extend with all possible speed science and art among our working population.

Great lessons and untold benefits are derived from under- takings of so vast a character as these international exhi- bitions, and not the least of them are the various suggestions to which they give rise, and the impetus they give to the permanent progress of industrial art in all countries.

REPÓRT on LACE, NET, EMBROIDERY, and SMALLWARE MANUFACTURES.—(Class 33.)—By MRS. BURY PALLISER.

1. LACE.

THE excellence of lace making can only be appreciated by those who are acquainted with the difficulties of its manufacture. The laces of Alençon and Brussels are of so complicated a nature that each process is assigned to a different lacemaker, who works only at her special department. Formerly a piece of Alençon lace would pass through eighteen hands before completion ; the number is now somewhat diminished.

The black shawls and flounces of Bayeux are all made in small lengths, and the task of uniting these segments by an invisible seam is one requiring great skill and precision.

Again, Valenciennes lace is of most elaborate workmanship, the pattern and ground are made together with the same thread on the same pillow. One exhibited with the lace in progress has no less than 1,200 bobbins.

The great improvement to be observed in the manufacture of lace is the introduction of shaded tints in the flowers and patterns, giving them the relief of a picture. This effect is produced by varying the application of the two stitches used in making the flowers, the "toilé" which forms the close tissue, and the "grillé" employed in the more open part of the pattern. The system is succesfully applied to the laces of France and Belgium, but it is in France that it has been adopted with the greatest success.

The exhibition of French lace is of the highest order, and its most celebrated fabrics are worthily represented. Alençon point maintains its historic reputation ; the black pillow-lace of Bayeux is unrivalled in elegance and beauty.

The manufacture of black lace, which extends through the department of Calvados, and is carried to the greatest perfection at Bayeux, has now entirely superseded the extinct fabric of Chantilly. The manner of making both laces is the same, and the so-called Chantilly is the production of Bayeux. It is now the most important of the lace manufactures of France, and is unequalled in beauty of design and excellence of workmanship. (*See* Figs. 1 and 2, p. 123.)

MRS. BURY
PALLISER
ON LACE,
NET, &c.

MM. Lefe-
bure's
Alençon
point.

Messrs. Lefébure (57) exhibit a splendid collection of the varied products of their fabric at Bayeux. Among those most deserving of attention is a dress of Alençon point, consisting of two flounces, Fig. 2, and trimmings. The festooned border which surrounds the groups of flowers and foliage is shaded so as to give the effect of being fluted. The design is of great beauty, and nothing can surpass the regularity of the ground or the variety of the open stitches. The price of this dress is 85,000f. (3,400*l*.), and it took forty women seven years to complete. Departing from the old custom of giving to each lacemaker a special branch of the work, the Alençon point of Messrs. Lefébure's manufacture is begun and finished by the same workwoman. The "Pointe," or half shawl, of Messrs. Lefébure is the most effective specimen of black lace in the Exhibition. The pattern, designed by Mr. Alcide Roussel, the special artist of the house, consists entirely of roses. A border of roses surrounds the shawl; and a large bouquet, most elegantly grouped, forms the centre, all exquisitely shaded and standing out in bold relief from the ground, which is perfectly clear, devoid of those small stars, spots, and other accessories called "ornaments" usually placed to conceal the seams that unite the segments of lace, but which destroy the general effect. The price of the shawl is 10,000f. (400*l*.)

There is great beauty in the design and excellence in the workmanship of a bridal veil or "rotonde" of mixed fabric. The ground is needle-point; the flowers application, made at Ghent; a scroll border, in the style of Venice point, surrounds the veil, and ornaments of Alençon point are introduced.

Messrs. Lefébure also exhibit the lace of Malines or Mechlin; and they have been most successful in reproducing the ancient "Rose," or Venice point in high relief. The raised flowers are executed with great beauty, and are surrounded by a pearl, or "picot," of geometrical regularity. The discovery of the way in which this richest and most complicated of points was made has been the work of great patience and intelligence. The reproduction is styled "Point Colbert," in honour of the Minister to whom France owes the foundation of her lace industry. (Fig. 3.)

Point Col-
bert.

Of the black laces of Bayeux (3) there are many excellent specimens. They form the principal feature in the French exhibition. Among them may be mentioned—

MM. Verdé
Delisle.

Messrs. Verdé-Delisle (Compagnie des Indes) (4) have a flounce of ferns, iris, and various flowers, beautifully shaded and on the finest ground; and a dress of similar pattern, of great elegance, but less fine in quality.

They also exhibit a parasol, with ground of extraordinary
fineness; and their black lace "Pointe" may be placed by
that of Messrs. Lefébure: the shading of the flowers is perfect, the grouping admirably light and well composed. In
beauty and correctness of design these two houses far outstrip all others. Each has its own artists; the pattern,
when made, is the subject of consultation and criticism, in
which the heads of the firm, draughtsmen, and workers,
all take their part. It is often the result of years of study;
hence the perfection to which they have arrived. These
patterns have also the advantage of being the special property of the house, and are therefore not reproduced in
ordinary or machine-made lace, as we observe to be the case
where one artist works for the many.

Messrs. Verdé-Delisle also exhibit a magnificent flounce
of Alençon point—the pattern, style Louis XV., bouquets of
flowers in medallions. Their dress of Brussels mixed points
(points mélangés) is very elegant and effective, and of exceedingly low price (150*l*.) In the ecclesiastical court, in
the garden, they have also some good specimens of Cluny
guipure, a chasuble, with the lamb and other attributes in
raised work; and some altar-cloths executed in the same
style.

A Bayeux flounce, rose-patterned of M. Pagny (7), may
be classed among the finest specimens of black lace; and
Bonnet (6) has a fire-screen (écran) style Louis XV., and
some fans of graceful design.

A black lace shawl of M. Lecornu, of Caen (11), is fine
and well executed, but too complicated in pattern for artistic
beauty.

Messrs. Aubry (8) exhibit a black lace flounce, a specimen of the extreme fineness that the ground may be made
to attain. It is technically called "réseau quarante;"
that is, it contains forty stitches to three quarters of an
inch (two centimetres) square. Their black parasol is also
of remarkable workmanship, the flowers being shaded by
the dexterous introduction of a coarser thread upon the
pillow, so as to resemble embroidery. It was made at
Viarme, near Chantilly.

Messrs. Aubry have likewise a magnificent tunic or dress
of white lace, the joint production of Brussels and Mirecourt (Vosges); needle-made ground, with raised ornaments
and flowers superposed. Their coverlet of Cluny lace, with
raised flowers, is also of great merit.

Le Puy, Crâponne (Haute Loire), and the other fabrics of
Auvergne, exhibit no novelty in their manufacture. Black
silk guipure shawls, "dentelles de laine," poil-de-chèvre,

H 2

Mrs. Bury
Palliser
on Lace,
Net, &c.

laces printed in colours, or embroidered with pearls, little varying from previous exhibitions. The success of the Cluny lace (first copied by a manufacturer of Le Puy from old laces in the Musée de Cluny, whence it derives its name) was an injury to the lacemakers of Auvergne and Lorraine, as it led them to forsake their old industries for an article of ephemeral demand. The fashion for Cluny lace has passed away, a circumstance not to be regretted, as the stiff patterns and heavy fabrics of the sixteenth century are but poor substitutes for the graceful and delicate productions of more modern times.

The handkerchiefs, with borders of Venice point and " filet," made in the convent of Notre Dame du Puy (64), are worthy of notice as being most elaborate reproductions of the old fabrics. Gandillot's (58) "guipures d'art " are admirable, as are also those of Violard (60); and the filet of Mdme. Pessière, in class 91, is worked with much accuracy and in great variety. Warée (34), Mirecourt, has pillow-made guipures for coverlets and objects of toilet of excellent workmanship.

In a collection so varied and so splendid it is impossible to designate all.

Pre-ominent
skilfulness
and good
taste of
French pro-
duction.

The exhibition of French lace is only rivalled, but not surpassed by Belgium. This superiority is to be ascribed not only to the skilfulness of the lace workers and the finish and perfection of their work, but most of all to the perfect taste which characterises the productions of France, and is one of the great sources of her industrial richness.

Exhibitors
of Belgium.

Belgium has a magnificent display of its varied manufactures—Brussels, Valenciennes, and Grammont, to which must still be added Mechlin, the prettiest and lightest of its fabrics ; but the fashion for it has died away, and there is little made at the present time. The lace is all laid out upon a lilac ground—a colour peculiarly adapted to set off the dazzling whiteness of Brussels lace.

Brussels
point.

The different kinds of Brussels lace, "point à l'aiguille," and " plat," the production of the pillow, are worked with that unrivalled delicacy and precision which have given to Brussels its world-wide celebrity.

Among the most remarkable specimens exhibited may be noticed a half-shawl of Normand and Chandon (70) in point à l'aiguille, with convolvulus pattern of great beauty ; and another of Verdé-Delisle (79), with guelder roses, ferns, &c., and flounces to match.

In Brussels lace the plat, or pillow-made flowers, are " applied," or sewn upon a ground of Brussels net. Of this kind, called " application " (70), Normand and Chandon (house, Frainais and Gramagnac, of Paris) have a superb bridal-veil; Verdé-Delisle a half-shawl, with bunches of lilac—nature itself; and Hoorickx (55) another, that has not been whitened, of fine workmanship.

The special excellence of this last-mentioned house is "point gaze," of which a dress is an elaborate specimen; the point gaze is worked with great evenness and clearness, and the open stitches with great elegance, but, as a whole the effect is monotonous and the flowers crowded—a common fault in the Brussels patterns. The price of this dress is 50,000f. (2,000*l.*) Two fans (point à l'aiguille) are of most graceful design, and a lappet, with raised flowers, is deserving of notice.

Van der Smissen (74) exhibits application and point, made at Alost, of great freshness and whiteness.

Van Loco (76) has a collection of Mechlin lace from Turnhout (province of Antwerp), one of the few places where this fine effective lace is still fabricated. Mechlin.

The manufacture of Valenciennes lace, after dying out in its native city, was transferred to Belgium, where, from its commercial importance, it forms the principal branch of the lace industry of this country. It is fabricated throughout East and West Flanders. That made at Ypres (West Flanders) is of the finest quality, and most elaborate in its workmanship. It is remarkable for its clear square ground and its improved patterns. In case 52 is a magnificient display, the collective exhibition of all the manufacturers of Ypres, among whom M. Duhayon Brunfaut, who first introduced improvements in the ground and patterns, holds a high rank. Courtrai (West Flanders) has made great advances towards rivalling Ypres, as the laces (69, 73, and 75) will show, and has produced the first half-shawl ever made of Valenciennes lace, exhibited by Verdé-Delisle (79). Valenciennes, principal lace industry of Belgium.

The black lace of Grammont (East Flanders) shows great improvement—the ground firmer, the patterns executed with greater precision, the silk of the best quality. The productions of Mdme. Everaert (5), after French designs, are of good pattern and fine quality. There is a large display of shawls, the collective exhibition of the manufacturers of Grammont (6 to 51), among which it is difficult to select. Those of Van Caneghem (42), Deschauwer (19), and Van Belleghem (39), may be distinguished; but the fault of the Grammont fabric is its heaviness of pattern, which will prevent it, except in cheapness, from competing with the more elegant productions of Calvados. Black lace of Grammont.

Another defect in the Grammont lace is in the workmanship of the leaves. The fibres, instead of being rendered (as in the Bayeux lace) by a silk with a kind of open "grillage," worked on each side to give it relief, is expressed by a simple silk thread, which gives a naked, unfinished appearance to the large leaves of which the Grammont patterns usually consist.

After the productions of France and Belgium, there is little to admire in the lace exhibition of other countries.

Prussia and the states of Germany exhibit no lace, with the exception of some needle-point flounces from Berlin (12), and the coarse pillow-edgings of Nurtingen, in Wirtemberg (Robeck, 5), where the lace industry has greatly extended this last 15 years. Austria has a "Point Imperiale," and some coarse laces of the Bohemian peasantry.

In Spain the lace of Barcelona hardly sustains its old reputation, and the patterns are losing much of their national character.

Sweden has the " torchon " lace of the Dalecarlian peasants ; Russia that of Helsingfors, in Finland.

In Italy is a large exhibition of the black and white pillow-laces of Genoa, poor imitations of Chantilly and other French fabrics, and from Rome is a magnificent example of old Venetian point, of finished workmanship which belongs rather to the Retrospective Collection.

Turkey exhibits specimens of a white silk crochet lace, made at Smyrna and in the island of Rhodes. This work, called "oyah," is also executed in colours, forming flowers and figures standing out in high relief from the ground.

Malta has her black and white guipures, of the old stereo-typed patterns.

In England the Devonshire lace is irreproachable in execution, as will be seen in the elaborate half-shawl of Mrs. Treadwin of Exeter (32), and in various specimens of

Honiton lace exhibited by Mr. Biddle (5), by Miss Radford (29), of Sidmouth. and others. Mrs. Treadwin has been very successful in her imitation of the vandyked collar-lace of the time of Louis XIII.; and Miss Jones (19) has sent a needle-made flounce of most creditable workmanship. Bedford now employs her pillows in making Cluny flounces. Ireland varies little from her usual productions. One of the best specimens of Irish guipure is exhibited in the French Court, a coverlet of beautiful workmanship. It is in the case No. 34, belonging to Warée, of Mirecourt, who has also a lace fabric in Ireland. While we assign to our lacemakers every merit for the beauty and precision of their work, we lament to find so little improvement in their patterns—universally heavy and crowded ; and when we see (18) ostriches and giraffes introduced upon lappets, and lions and eagles upon cuffs and collars, we can say little for the amelioration yet effected by the establishment of schools of design.

In Auvergne a lace museum, "Musée de Dentelle," has been established at Le Puy, containing specimens of the lace of all countries and of all ages. Surely a similar institution might be founded with good effect at Exeter or some other centre of our lace manufactures. There is no teaching like the teaching by example ; and an acquaintance with the elegant productions of other countries would best lead our lace makers to see the deficiencies in our own.

The Republics of Central and South America show indications of lacemaking. In the costume of the Guachos, exhibited by the Argentine Confederation, the linen trowsers are ornamented with a broad border of "filet" or drawn-work. Uruguay has a scarf of the same workmanship. Chili sends a collection of the coarse lace of the old lozenge pattern made by the peasant women of Santiago, and men also appear to work at lacemaking in that province. Venezuela exhibits the finest specimens of this drawn-work lace in some infant's caps and borders of pocket-handkerchiefs, works of great patience and ingenuity, but which come more under the class of embroidery. The finest specimens are from Caraccas. The lace-bordered handkerchiefs of Brazil are of similar workmanship.

2.—Net and Machine Lace.

Nottingham and Saint Pierre-lez-Calais are the principal seats of the bobbin net and machine made lace manufactures. Since the application of the Jacquard cards to the making of lace both fabrics have produced imitations of very great beauty, and at a very low price.

The Calais manufacturers exhibit imitations of every kind of lace, cotton, silk, and mohair ; Valenciennes, Cluny, coloured laces, blondes white and black, silver and gold. Their Valenciennes is excellent ; but the most marked progress is in the perfect imitations of white silk blondes, nearly approaching in whiteness and brilliancy the famed productions of Caen, which, by their cheapness they are fast expelling from competition. Lefort (26), Bacquet (56), and Le Comte (28) have magnificent white and silver blondes and Brunot (40) a dress of white blonde made in a single piece.

MRS. BURY
PALLISER
ON LACE,
NET, &c.
—
Lama and
yak shawls. The finest lama and yak shawls are manufactured at Amiens, the mohair being imported from Bradford, in Yorkshire. The specimens of yak exhibited by Mr. Dognin (3) are remarkably fine in quality, and of good design, and mark a wonderful progress in this class of production. He terms the fabric " Dentelle des Indes." Lyons is the centre of the manufacture of plain and embroidered silk tulles and shawls. These products are exhibited with the silk tissues of that city (class 31.) Among these the collection of Mr. Baboin (31,240) is the most remarkable. The "tulle diamant" of Messrs. Agnellet, of Paris, is a sparkling and elegant material for dresses and bonnets.

Brussels net
now replaces
the pillow
ground. The tulle industry of Belgium consists in its Brussels net, now brought to the greatest perfection. Formerly the Brussels flowers were applied upon a pillow ground made of thread which has cost as high as 400*l*. the lb., and producing the finest and lightest tissue that can be imagined. The invention of Brussels net has superseded the use of this expensive ground, which few workers now know how to make, and has thereby materially decreased the price of Brussels lace. In No. 80, the widow of Mr. Washer, its original inventor, exhibits the Brussels net in its different stages of manufacture. The English cotton of which it is made (670) cost 44*l*. per lb.

The manufacturers of Nottingham exhibit little novelty. The black lace shawls and flounces rival those of Lyons; and the Valenciennes edgings and insertions of Packer and Manton (24) and of Jacoby (16) are equal to the productions of Calais.

3.—EMBROIDERY.

Embroidery. Of works in embroidery we have the specimens of every nation, from the gorgeous productions in gold and silver of the East to the humble moose-hair and porcupine-quill decoration of the Canadian Indian.

Embroidery may be ranged under two classes—white embroidery applied to dress and objects of furniture ; and coloured embroidery, comprising works in silk, worsted, gold, and silver, for dress, furniture, and church vestments.

WHITE EMBROIDERY.

White.
Principal
places of
manufac-
ture. White embroidery is executed by hand and by machinery, with the needle and the crochet-hook, on the fingers and on the tambour frame, which last was originally brought from China.

It is carried to the greatest perfection in France, Switzerland, Saxony, Scotland, and Ireland.

MRS. BURY
PALLISER
ON LACE,
NET, &c.
———
Embroidery
of Lorraine.

In France, the finest embroidery in satin-stitch (plumetis) is produced in the ancient province of Lorraine, at Nancy (Meurthe), and at Mirecourt, in the department of the Vosges. Tarare (Rhône) is celebrated for tambour or crochet work, principally employed for curtains. The specimens of the delicate and elaborate embroidery of Nancy and Mirecourt are exquisite. Among the most remarkable is a morning dress (peignoir) of Lachez-Bleuze (135), Nancy, with rich embroidery of ferns, convolvulus, and wheat-ears.

The shirt-fronts and pocket handkerchiefs of Husson (137), of Féron (92), and Chapron (136), are most perfect in workmanship, and nothing can exceed the beauty of the "point d'armes" and other stitches in the cushion-cover of Lallemant (139), embroidered for H.M. the Queen of the Belgians, and a "guèridon" or stool cover worked by Horrer (138), of Nancy.

Driout and Moret (134), exhibit, from Mirecourt, a fire-screen, "écran." The subject, a group of goats, is a perfect example of the effect of light and shade, given by varying the stitches and superposing them several times over each other. The lights are expressed by satin-stitch, another kind of stitch produces the middle tints, and a third the shadows. There are pocket-handkerchiefs embroidered after the same manner, but the beautiful shading disappears on being washed. Driout and Moret have fabrics in the departments of the Vosges, Meurthe, and Moselle. That at Manoncourt (Meurthe) is for machine-made embroidery.

Juglar (89) has insertion and strips of embroidery upon cambric muslin, resembling the Scotch embroidery— "broderie Anglaise," as it is called by the French. The designs are excellent and the work good.

The best machine-made embroidery is that of Gilbert (129).

Embroidery, as applied to furniture, has made great progress since the last exhibition. In the salle No. 10, class 27, is the collective exhibition of the town of Tarare, the rival of St. Gall and Glasgow for plain muslin, and without a competitor for its tarlatane and its embroidered curtains. In that kind of curtain, placed straight over the window, called by the French "stores," the pattern is displayed to the greatest advantage. Those exhibited are remarkable for their rich, light, and elegant embroidery, and beautiful design. Some are real pictures. Ruffier-Leutner (184), one of the most celebrated houses for this fabric, exhibit a good example of the application of art to industry in a curtain, (Fig. 4.) styled the "Fête des Fleurs," a beautiful composition, of excellent execution, and not of that extravagant cost as to make it unremunerative in a commercial point of view ; the great object is to produce works of good taste at a moderate price. Another of the curtains has the arms of the city of Paris ; and a third, style Louis XVI., with Diana and the emblems of the chase, is equal in richness of design to the Fête des Fleurs.

The curtains of Meunier (185) are also of most artistic design and careful execution. Two, style Louis XV., with pastoral subjects are deserving of special notice.

Among many others are also to be admired those of Brun (186), David (206), Victor Dubois (187), Deschamps (189), Lepelletier (210), and one in colours, by Larivière (212).

Switzerland, the great competitor of France in white embroidery, has a most splendid collection.

This industry was introduced into the canton of Appenzell, in the last century, by a lady who had learned the art in the Levant. St. Gall is the commercial centre of the manufacture. The Swiss work is of the first rank and of a low price.

The pocket-handkerchiefs and shirt-fronts of Staeheli-Wild (21), St. Gall ; the embroidery on jaconet, the petticoats especially, of Baenziger (Appenzell) ; and the insertions and bands executed by machinery of the last named, and of Rittmeyer (18), and Sennhauser (20), both of St. Gall, are worked with the greatest clearness and precision.

But the crochet curtains embroidered upon net form the most important branch of Swiss embroidery.

The "monumental bed" of Schlaepfer-Schlatter (19), St. Gall, is most effective. Altheer (2) Appenzell has a curtain of good design; another representing the Chateau of Arensburg. Alder and Meyer (1) have a flower vase, with arabesque medallion ; that of Ranch and Schæffer (17) is powdered with flowers—all of excellent workmanship, but wanting in the purity and lightness of design of their French rivals.

With Saxony may be associated Wirtemberg ; their productions are similar, and both are known in commerce under the common name of "Saxon embroidery." It was in Saxony the fabrication of white embroidery began, about a century ago, whence it extended to France, Switzerland, and Scotland. The work is confined to the mountainous regions of the Erzegebirge and Voïgtland, and is now in full activity, the girls being taught embroidery in schools under Government inspection.

Plauen, Eibenstock, and Annaberg are the great centres

of fabrication in Saxony; Ravensberg, in the kingdom of Wirtemberg.

Schnorr and Steinhausen (22, Room 27, Prussia) exhibit from Plauen a wonderful specimen of embroidery—an infant's robe in the finest satin-stitch, the pattern (bunches of roses with leaves in full relief) attached to the muslin ground only by the stalks. Bab (1) has handkerchiefs embroidered with raised flowers, and those of Mammen (23), with the infants' robes of Böhler (20) and the machine-embroidered petticoats of Jahn (21), all display the high excellence of the industry in Saxony.

Frünkorn (2), Wirtemberg show the produce of their manufacture near Ravensburg—curtains embroidered by machinery, at very low prices.

The white embroidery exhibited by other countries is scanty. Spain does not send the beautiful cambric of pine-apple thread from Manilla, embroidered with a perfection equalling any European manufacture.

Sweden has some well embroidered handkerchiefs from Lund, and Italy various others of good workmanship but nothing approaching in excellence to the produce of France and Switzerland.

Most to be remarked in Italy are the "macramé," or towels, made at the Albergo dei Poveri, at Genoa, with long fringes plaited in geometric patterns of great ingenuity.

There is no Scotch or Irish embroidery exhibited; but some embroidery upon cambric muslin is sent from Bengal, worked, like the Scotch, with great regularity.

It is difficult to decide whether to class as lace or embroidery the elaborate workmanship exhibited by Persia in the veils worn by the women when they go out of the house. The veils, which are of cotton, have an aperture for the eyes, about 4 in. long by 1 in. wide, of the finest lace on drawn work, imitating the open-work stitches of Brussels or Alençon lace.

In white embroidery, France holds the first place. Switzerland can rival her in the quality of the work; and both that country and Saxony surpass her in cheapness; but neither can equal her in elegance of design or excel her in the perfection of workmanship.

COLOURED EMBROIDERY.

From the East we derive the most elaborate specimens of coloured embroidery, as applied to dress and furniture. The rich works in silver and gold of Europe are more specially dedicated to ecclesiastical ornament, and court or military costume. Turkey, Egypt, and Morocco, ancient seats of Eastern luxury, cover with embroidery every article of domestic use.

Of these Turkey sends a gorgeous collection—slippers, purses, tobacco-pouches, caps, handles for hookahs, housings for horses, all in the richest embroidery of silk, gold and silver upon velvet and other tissues. Some covers for coffee tables and portières for doors are embroidered upon cloth. The Albanian costumes are one mass of gold.

A violet velvet carpet for prayers and one of lilac velvet with gold scroll and silver border are among the choice specimens exhibited by the Viceroy of Egypt, together with a cloth covered with large characters in gold and silver and housings superbly embroidered.

In Morocco is a variety of stools or cushions, and a large piece of red and black cloth, all embroidered with gold.

China and India are no less skilful in embroidery, but vary little from their primitive type. The Chinese, patient and laborious, execute, with twisted or floss silk, embroideries of the greatest accuracy. The Imperial dragon, embroidered in gold on crimson satin, and flowers and birds executed on white or coloured silk or satin, have, from the extreme care and cleanliness given to the work, a freshness and beauty unsurpassed.

The Indians embroider with great lightness and regularity. In the collection from Bengal are the delicate silk-embroidered net shawls of Delhi, muslins embroidered with beetles' wings, bags (joolee) of gold from Agra, the shubgara or coloured silk gauze shirts embroidered with gold from Central India, shawls embroidered with gold from Bombay, fans, saddle-cloths, &c.

Russia produces some fine specimens from Tiflis, a sofa-cover, pillows, and bolsters (9), embroidered in gold, and coloured silks upon crimson velvet, designed in good taste, and executed with that skilfulness of work for which the Georgian women are celebrated.

Roumania exhibits, from Bucharest, the leathern cloaks and vests of the national costume, gaily decorated with coloured worsted embroidery.

Canada sends tobacco-pouches, slippers, boxes, and various articles embroidered with moose-hair and the quills of the porcupine.

The military and church embroidery of France is mostly executed at Lyons and Paris, and is the first of its class.

The vestments of Barban (110), Lyons, are of great magnificence; a chape of silver tissue embroidered with gold, and a chasuble of gold tissue, with figures in high relief, enriched with jewels, are among the finest specimens in the Exhibition.

Biais (65), Paris, exhibits a chasuble of cloth of gold, embroidered in gold, with vine leaves and wheat, and several others equally elaborate in the styles of different epochs.

Henry (31, 151), of Lyons, has church embroidery of the finest workmanship.

Melotte (60), of Brussels, gives but one specimen of his art—a velvet banner embroidered with gold.

Milan, so celebrated in the Middle Ages for the richness and perfection of her works in embroidery, exhibits (48), some fine church ornaments by Eugène and Giuseppi Martini ·—a chasuble of white satin embroidered with silk, the pelican in relief in gold, and many others.

The ecclesiastical embroidery of Roumania is very rich. A large entombment, worked in gold, with the lengthened figures of the Byzantine school, bears great resemblance in character and style of workmanship to a similar subject (5) exhibited in the Russian Court. Brazil sends a well-executed church banner, the work of the inmates of the Foundling Hospital at Pernambuco.

Various are the smaller objects of embroidery, difficult to class.

In France, Mdme. Lefay (127) exhibits a tulle train embroidered with vine-leaves and grapes of gold, and another in green and gold, perfect in execution, but faulty in pattern. A tarlatane ball-dress embroidered with poppies, from Tarare, is well executed. Asselineau (101), two bands of coloured silk flowers upon white ground. Poiret (99), butterflies and flowers embroidered in coloured silks and wools upon a buff canvas he calls "Natte de Panama." Heilbronner (100) has works on canvas of great beauty. Henry (142) upon cloth styled "broderie Turc," and various excellent "ladies' works" and "filet." Richter (20), in Austria, has the best variety of ladies' works in the Exhibition—a cushion of black velvet with twist of gold and silk flowers, a chair, and numerous others.

Zelgar (20) exhibits a needlework picture of the Emperor on horseback, Italy, a portrait of Victor Emmanuel, historic paintings, pictures to imitate engravings, &c.—all works of meritorious patience, but of little interest or utility.

4.—SMALLWARE MANUFACTURES.

Called by the French passementerie, comprising every kind of trimming for dress, furniture, and liveries, carriage lace,

gimp, buttons, cords, &c. This industry is in great prosperity, and employs a large number of women and children.
It is made by hand and by machinery. France is the
principal centre of its manufacture and the only country
which sends a large collection to the Exhibition.

The carriage and livery lace of Cagnet (123) are the best
of their class. The epaulettes and gold-lace embroidery for
military uniforms of Truchy and Vaugeois (68) are first of
their class; and the tissues in gold and silver, for furniture,
of Louvet (71), Passementier to the Crown, make a brilliant
show of well-arranged colours. Alamaguy's passementerie
is of remarkable beauty (81); that of Weber (69), is to be
remarked, with the subject in passementerie of Adam (70),
the buttons of Najean (76), and those of Pariot Laurent (79),
with many others. Mottet (75) has some effective trimmings with glass beads.

In Prussia is some well-shaded carriage lace by Scharf
(5); and the passementerie exhibited by Drachster (5), in
Austria, is good.

The military gold lace of Bavaria, and that of England
Davies (8), are of excellent workmanship.

Fig. 1.—SILK LACE OF SPAIN.

Fig. 2.—POINT COUTURE, A REPRODUCTION OF VENICE POINT LACE.

Fig. 4.—EMBROIDERED CURTAIN OF TARARE.

Fig. 3.—AURBLAN POINT FLOUNCE.

REPORT on TOYS.—(Class 39.)—By
G. C. T. BARTLEY, Esq.

THE collection of toys in the Paris Exhibition is not a fair representation of the state of this trade at the present day; there is almost a total absence of ordinary and practical playthings. Great attention has been paid to dolls and mechanical toys, more particularly in the French Court. The German States do not send so good a sample of their great trade in these juvenile articles as might have been expected. Altogether, it is to be regretted that the subject of toys has not received the attention which it deserves. *How represented.*

The following countries exhibit. The figures in the first column indicate the number of exhibitors of toys; those in the second the number of exhibitors of games; and those in the third the number of exhibitors of articles grouped with this class, which cannot be considered either toys or games :— *Number of exhibitors from each country.*

France	23	—	—
Holland	—	—	1
Prussia	7	—	—
Baden	—	—	1
Wirtemberg	3	—	—
Bavaria	8	—	—
Austria	2	—	—
Switzerland	3	—	—
Spain	—	1	—
Denmark	—	1	—
Russia	2	—	—
Turkey	—	—	2
Egypt	1	—	—
Tunis	—	—	1
Morocco	1	—	—
Japan	1	—	—
United States	—	1	—
Great Britain	1	5	—
English Colonies	—	1	1
Total	52	9	6

In the following pages a brief outline is given of the merits of the exhibits of the various countries.

FRANCE.

France has the largest number of exhibitors, and all, with one or two exceptions, reside in Paris. The most important French toy is undoubtedly the doll, and hence the visitor is not surprised to find that it is the chief article *French dolls.*

in the cases round the attractive, though crowded and confined, French Toy Court. The manufacture of these puppets is carried on in Paris to a greater extent than in any other city in the world; and as regards magnificence of attire and display of fashion, nothing can approach the French doll. To English feelings such a display is not an advisable way of educating the mind of a child; and, if a doll is to represent a baby, it is absurd for it to be dressed in all the grandeur of a full-grown and fashionable woman. At the same time, it must be borne in mind that the French doll manufacturers have an object in thus dressing their dolls, which is more important than their use as toys. They are sent to India, and all parts of the world, to serve as types and models of the Paris fashions; for on arriving at these places their first use is to be studied by the dressmakers; and, when useless to them in this respect, they descend to the children for toys. These two uses to which French dolls are subjected, though, perhaps, an economical commercial arrangement, are quite opposed to the production of a doll suitable for the hands of a child, and may account for the total unfitness of most of those exhibited in the French portion of the Exhibition to be classed as toys at all.

The manufacture is in itself a very interesting process, though difficult to witness, owing to the various portions being generally carried on in different places. M. Jumeau, at 8, Rue d'Anjou au Marais, is one of the largest makers in Paris. He employs many hands, the greater number being women, who are scattered in all parts of the city. The heads of his dolls are porcelain, and most of the bodies of sheepskin, stuffed with sawdust, except the hands, in which iron fittings are inserted, to enable the fingers to be moved easily. The process of cutting the leather is peculiar, being done by hand, with an iron stamp set in boxwood. The stamps, of course, vary in size, and several of different shapes are required for each doll.

When the leather is cut, the next process is to sew the parts together; this requires a regular apprenticeship, more particularly for the fingers, which need great care; after the various parts are sewn up, the body has to be stuffed and the limbs attached. The doll is then ready to receive its head; the manufacture of this part is totally distinct, and similar to that of ordinary porcelain. Cheap heads and shoulders are all in one piece, and their eyes are simply painted; while the superior description are made separate from the neck and shoulders, to enable the head to move on a sort of joint, and glass eyes are inserted into the sockets left for this purpose. The last thing is the hair, and in this branch we much excel the French. At this manufactory, owing to the heads being of china, the hair has to be put on as a wig, and cannot be inserted so naturally as when the head is of wax. Human hair is rarely, if ever, used in Paris, the general material being mohair for the best and a sort of fur for the cheaper style of doll. The dolls, when completed, have to be dressed, and this process varies with the fashion; it would not do for a French doll to be behindhand in this respect. At M. Jumeau's establishment the same style is not used for more than a month. All the dolls' clothes are made on the premises, where a roomful of young women is continually at work for these small fashionables.

The dolls exhibited by M. Jumeau are not his best specimens, nor can they be looked upon as giving a fair idea of his general style. Some of the smaller ones which are put in the less attractive parts of the stall are good. The three figures at the back of the case are got up in an elaborate and brilliant manner, representing ball costumes; but they are certainly not commendable as toys, or suitable to the taste of English mothers for their children. The small boxes of dolls' clothes, or the dolls' trousseau, are good toys, and from the variety exhibited, and the very large numbers manufactured, it is evident that they are popular.

M. Jumeau has not exhibited any of his mechanical dolls, saying "Mamma" and "Papa," and crying when laid down. These specimens are well worthy of a corner in the Exhibition. He also arranges the works, and dresses a large number of walking dolls, the patent for which is American, and for this reason he does not exhibit them.

Some of the dolls most fit for children are exhibited by MM. Huret and Lonchambon. The young lady in white on the right-hand side of their case is modest looking, and quite a child's doll. The dresses are well made, and there is no air of careless finish to be detected; all have the further advantage of being of gutta-percha, with articulated joints; by this they can be made to sit, stand, and move their arms in many positions. The doll's-house furniture exhibited in this case deserves mention as being among the best in the French Court. It is imitation inlaid wood, and though the finish, on examining the internal work, does not bear comparison with the best exhibited by Mr. Cremer, yet the patterns and style are commendable.

M. Rohmer's dolls, in a case outside the Toy Court, are both well made and have pretty faces; the hair is not good or put in naturally.

The finish of the collection of M. Au Bengali is not so perfect as those just mentioned; even the walls of the doll's-house in which the specimens are placed, though elaborately enriched, are made of wood so slovenly put together as not to be properly planed.

The case exhibited by M. Rémond contains a collection of gorgeously apparelled ladies. A bride is prominent in the midst, with a long train of white silk and orange-blossom; she is surrounded with fashion if not with beauty; some dolls using their eye-glasses, and others coquetting in imagination in a variety of attitudes, all, however, having a style which no one would care to encourage in a child. The novelty in this case is the carte-de-visite photographs of these young ladies. At first sight they might be mistaken for the portraits of ladies moving in the grandest sphere, but on a closer inspection the dresses and features of M. Rémond's group are recognized, and these magnificent persons are but the photographs of a few dolls. The same maker exhibits a well-arranged and nicely made doll's toilet table; the brushes, glasses, pomade-jars, jugs, basins, mirrors, &c., are so compact and tastefully placed as to make it an attractive toy.

In a very conspicuous corner outside the Toy Court M. Simonné has a case, and it is a pity that the space is not better filled. The dolls are stiffly arranged to represent a court ball. Some of the dresses are good, though the style is not at all pleasing. Most of the ladies' heads must have come out of the same mould; and the gentlemen's faces resemble one another in a remarkable manner. This show is grandly attempted, but the result is not happy.

The doll's clothes of Mdlle. Beruse are among the best specimens of neat work and taste in this branch of the Exhibition; the case, in fact, being like a portion of a first-class ladies' outfitting warehouse; the various miniature articles of clothing are nicely arranged, and in every respect the collection is worthy of examination. The few dolls which are placed to show off the clothes are also greatly to be admired.

In mechanical toys the French greatly excel, and without doubt these form the most attractive and popular portion of the toy display. Everybody is at once taken with them, and, although the larger ones are not strictly toys, yet they serve as specimens of the great perfection which has been reached in adapting clockwork machinery to the delicate movements of the body. The large trophy is exhibited by M. Theroude, and some of the examples are remarkably good. A shepherd, near the top, almost life-size, is seated on a rock, and plays the flageolet, moving his fingers to the stops on the instrument, and, though this movement of the fingers has nothing to do with the formation of the varying sounds, all of which come from within the body of the man, yet the action is so natural that probably many persons would be misled. A very similar specimen, of a black man playing the flute, is exhibited below him on the trophy. He stands naturally, even gracefully, and the movements of the head and fingers are remarkably true, considering the number of joints, and consequent angles, through which the clockwork has to act.

The figure which, perhaps, most young people regard with the greatest attention is that of the large black monkey playing on the violin. This is very clever, for it really produces sounds with the bow, although the fingers of the left hand do not form the notes on the strings of the instrument, as some visitors have imagined. Its movements are easy, and at the same time comical; it turns its head, and opens and shuts its lips.

There is a smaller monkey, which sometimes is placed on the trophy. He is dressed in a glittering costume, and represents a dancing-master with his fiddle. His performances are even better than the former, as he leans his head on his instrument in the most absurd manner. He is well worth a visit: as also is the funny, little, smartly-dressed man playing at battledore and shuttlecock, who is a great favourite.

Besides these which are individually noticed, there are numerous small toys on the same principle exhibited by this maker, such as chickens running round and flapping their wings, dolls drumming as they ride along, dolls on horseback; goats, small monkeys, and hares all going through a number of evolutions.

Another exhibitor of good mechanical toys is M. Verdavainne. His two organ men, one small and the other about 3 ft. high, are clever and amusing, as well as many of the small figures which are exhibited in motion on the table placed in the middle of the Toy Court.

Amongst the mechanical toys must be classed those in tin, exhibited by M. Dessein. They are in several ways interesting, and worthy of remark. He manufactures a large number of toy railway engines and carriages, omnibusses, steam-boats, and metal articles used in houses. The prices are almost incredible—a train, without clockwork movement, consisting of locomotive, tender, and one carriage, all in separate portions and made to run quite evenly, is sold wholesale in a neat cardboard box for five sous, or two-

Marginal notes:

MR. BARTLEY ON TOYS.

The playing monkey.

M. Verdavainne's mechanical toys.

M. Dessein's mechanical toys. Remarkable cheapness.

pence halfpenny. The jury when examining these goods, could not believe that the articles were manufactured at the prices stated, owing to the value of the metal employed; but on examination it appears that, by an ingenious application of old biscuit-boxes and sardine-cases for the stronger parts of the toys not requiring painting, a fair profit is obtained even at these prices.

The process of manufacturing.
The manufactory of M. Dessein, at 13, Rue Chapon, is worth a visit for those who are sufficiently interested in seeing the whole process by which these tin toys are made. He employs about 50 workmen and women all the year round, and most of them are engaged at the manufactory. Some stamp out pieces of tin of various shapes by the thousand; others, by an ingenious machine, are enabled to fold these strips of tin into the shapes required at the rate of a thousand an hour; others cast the wheels and mould portions of the toys; the number and variety of these operations are surprising. When all the various portions are made they are transferred to the hands of more skilled workmen, whose business it is to solder the parts together. This is done with equal rapidity. Each workman has a tool consisting of a hollow handle, having a pointed piece of copper attached to one end of it, while to the other end two pipes are attached, one containing air and the other gas. These mix and issue at a jet close to the copper, and when lighted the Bunsen's burner thus formed plays on the copper and keeps it sufficiently hot to melt the solder. The workman, after having put the portions of the toy together and moistened them with a solution of chloride of zinc to make the solder adhere, touches a piece of the latter substance he has before him with the pointed end of the copper, and thus takes up a globule for use, the whole process very much resembling in rapidity and effect the sealing together with wax of two pieces of paper. When the toys have arrived at this stage of completion, the next process is to paint them, and this is done chiefly by women. They are first put into an oven, to make them capable of receiving the paint. The colours come chiefly from Germany, and are ground and mixed on the premises. The painting varies with the nature of the toys, some having several coats, and being finished off finely with a camel's hair brush: but the cheaper class necessarily receive less attention, and have only one coat. When painted they are again baked, and the colours thoroughly hardened. The last process, in most cases, is putting in the mechanical works, and this is done chiefly by M. Dessein himself. It, of course, requires considerable skill. The cheapest train, with locomotive, having clockwork movement, and capable

of running round a table, is (wholesale price) three francs fifty centimes, or under three shillings—this includes locomotive, tender, and two carriages, packed in a cardboard box. MR. BARTLEY ON TOYS.

At M. Dessein's manufactory about 10,000*l.* worth of toys are made annually, entirely of tin; and considerable credit is due to this manufacturer for the ingenious utilization of various sorts of waste material. Many tons of tin are used, the new metal required being imported from England. It may seem incredible, but not less than a quarter of a million of toy trains, or a million of railway carriages, must be made at this one manufactory in the course of a year. A very large portion of them go to England. Amount manufactured.

The mechanical figures with wheelbarrows holding flowers, exhibited by MM. Lamour and Roullet are novel and clever. These consist of a boy with clockwork inside him to enable his feet to move in the natural manner of walking. On being wound up he therefore walks along, pushing his barrow before him. It is a charming little toy, and to be regretted that so high a price has been put upon it. Walking mechanical figures.

The Mechanical Singing Birds.—In this display, all the articles of which are exhibited by M. Bontemps, there is nothing of special novelty, though the tunes sung by the various birds are very natural. One bird in particular, in a brilliant gilt cage, placed about the middle of the case, is an object of great interest; besides going through its warbling notes, it turns from side to side, and at the same time moves its head in a very birdlike manner. The price of these toys, if such they can be called, is of course high, and precludes them from general use. M. Bontemps is the only exhibitor, and it is due to him largely that these singing birds have been brought to their present perfection. The specimens exhibited are numerous, and embrace birds of different plumage and song. Mechanical singing birds, by M. Bontemps.

Conjuring Tricks.—All those exhibited, with trifling exceptions, are by M. A. Voisin, who is a manufacturer of these articles. The tricks which are made in the greatest numbers are of the well-known character—such as the inexhaustible bottle, the egg-cup, the magic tree, &c. The trade and consequent manufacture of these articles—which, though classed with toys, can scarcely be said to come under the heading of either toys or games—appears to vary very much; it rises and falls according to the popularity of a clever wizard, and at the present time is not very flourishing in England. Conjuring tricks by M A. Voisin.

Military Toys.—Those exhibited by M. Andreux are good, and no manufacturer equals him in finish or design— many being, in fact, quite models of guns and artillery. Military toys, by M. Andreux.

Miniature cannons and gun-carriages, swords, military equip-
ments, and drums are the chief articles he makes, though he
also exhibits ships, and tin toys moving by clockwork.   This
manufacturer has several places in Paris, and employs about
40 workmen of different kinds.   The whole of them are
paid by piecework, and the lowest wages are 4s., the highest
10s., a day.   A great peculiarity of these toys is the number
of pieces each contains when complete, considering the low
price at which it is necessary to produce the finished article.
Guns about two feet long, firing caps, well made and
polished, are sold for a little less than 15s. a dozen.   Now,
in the lock alone there are eight distinct pieces of metal, all
of which have to be cast, fitted, polished, and put together
before the lock is made ; this must then be attached to the
stock by several rivets and nails, then arranged to suit the
barrel ; yet the whole, including the material, after passing
through 10 hands, is sold for less than 15d.   The workman
who mounts the locks and barrels must finish at least 150
guns a day in order to gain a livelihood.   The polishing of
the various metal parts is done by steam, and the polishers
(paid by the piece) obtain higher wages than any other workmen in the trade.   The wooden stocks are polished chiefly
by women.   About 70,000 toy guns are manufactured at this
establishment in the course of the year.   The number of
military toys has very much decreased of late years, the
present notion being in favour of giving children toys more
suggestive of the arts of peace.

The wooden gun-carriages made here are beautifully
finished ; all the best, as well as the superior guns firing a
charge, pass through M. Andreux's hands for careful examination, in order to prevent a chance of accident.   There is
considerable fashion even in toys, as was particularly noticeable after the war last summer.   At that time, every one
being interested in the Prussian fire-arm, M. Andreux produced a toy needle-gun ; and so great was his success that
he sold 38,000 of them in three months.   To produce some
portions of the guns, and particularly the last-mentioned
needle-gun, requiring short tubes with indentations of great
exactness, to slide one within each other, very ingenious and
expensive machines are used, which first cut the piece of
iron into the required shape, and then roll it up in a most
astonishing and rapid manner.   The method and machinery
employed in shaping the wooden stocks are, perhaps, the
most curious part of the manufacture.   It is all done by the
circular watch-spring saw.   A tree 20 feet long is first of all
longitudinally cut in half, and the rough shape of the stocks
is drawn on each flat side, as close together as possible.   The

beam is then cut into the lengths indicated, and, with a rapidity that is almost incredible, the workman glides the block so that the saw cuts along the lines drawn on the beam. By this means the rough stocks are shaped out by dozens, one workman being able to produce about 500 a day.

Miscellaneous Toys.—Only a few are exhibited, and the best of these are in the case of Messrs. Duvinage and Harinkonck, otherwise called " La Maison Alphonse Giroux." A Roman car, laden with arms and military implements, drawn by a yoke of oxen, is carefully made, and the oxen are fine creatures. It is a pity that there is no arrangement on their feet to enable them to be drawn along the floor. The woodwork of the car is well carved, as also the Roman soldiers standing by its side. Close to this is an elephant, likewise loaded with Roman soldiers, and really quite a zoological model. The same case contains other animals coated with skin equally good.

The metal toys exhibited by M. Dehors, just outside the court, are very good. Knives, forks, dinner services, and every description of dolls' plate, both in metal and china, are to be seen here. Several of the specimens are in aluminium bronze ; and these, from the beauty and gold-like appearance of the metal, are most attractive. A few of the moulds used in the manufacture of these articles are also exhibited. The little toilet services have great charms for children ; they are so nicely made ; and, though superior to most, are not quite so elaborate as some in the neighbouring cases. At the top of this stall, though so high as to be almost invisible from the reflection of the glass, is a set of remarkably good fur animals. It is a pity that they are so much out of sight.

The miscellaneous toys of M. Simon are certainly superior to his dolls already mentioned. The horses and jockeys are nicely made, also the military toys, including the soldiers' tent. A remarkable canteen is placed here, though its size and general arrangement make it more fit for practical use than for the imaginary requirements of dolls.

The playthings exhibited by M. Schutz are different from all others in the Exhibition. They have some sort of movement, though not a clockwork one. This is managed either by the wheels setting parts in motion or by strings passing through the figures. A cart full of animals at the bottom of this case makes a capital toy. The animals can be taken in and out, and as the cart is pulled along a monkey goes through various comic evolutions. Every variety of figure is to be seen—dancing-men, monkeys, grotesque dolls, &c. ; all are well finished and tastefully dressed. About the best toys here are two peasants made to represent hawkers, carrying large baskets of household wares on their backs. These baskets can be packed and unpacked, and so form an amusing toy.

M. Rémond has a few miscellaneous toys, besides dolls, though these latter, as already stated, form the more important part of his case. A mechanical train is conspicuous, as also some fair carts, horses, and military toys. In the centre of the court is a round table, on which the prolific top exhibited by M. Caumière is continually spun by an attendant. This top is of Japanese origin; and the number and variety of ways in which it may be spun, and the skill required in spinning it, make it quite an attractive plaything, even to grown-up people. Amongst the French miscellaneous toys, though placed in Class 91, owing to their cheapness, must be included the exhibits of the following makers:—M. Feliker, a collection of the cheapest toys, such as rough dolls, rattles, whips, &c.; M. Clavel, a number of wooden toys, such as cannons with large wheels, windmills, trumpets, &c., all quoted by the gross, at wonderfully low prices; M. Thael, animals made in plaster, of very original and grotesque shapes, evidently invented by the maker; M. Bunant, gutta-percha articles, including dolls, balls, rattles, &c.; and, lastly, a number of children's colour-boxes, of all prices and sizes, warranted to contain no poison. Little thumb-palettes, with half a dozen colours and a brush attached, sold for about $1\frac{1}{2}d$., are likely to be popular.

Games.—There are only one or two unimportant French games exhibited among the toys; and these are by M. Giroux, who has an elaborate display, in Class 26, consisting of a small cabinet with about a dozen drawers, all compactly filled with games, chiefly in ivory; the case forms an elegant piece of furniture; and, though there is nothing novel about the games themselves, the skill displayed in arranging so large a number calls for remark.

HOLLAND.

The exhibition of toys from this country is trifling, and consists of eight coloured cardboard figures, made for the Indian Theatre. They are grotesque and comical, having rivet-joints similar to the dancing donkeys so popular a few months back.

PRUSSIA.

The Prussian collection of toys is not so extensive as might have been expected.

Mr. Söhlke, of Berlin, sends an assortment of well-made metal toys, consisting chiefly of dolls' house furniture, such as candlesticks, lamps, chairs, tables, stoves, and English fireplaces, &c. There are also boxes of metal figures, fairly modelled carts and horses, and a few military toys.

The articles sent by Mr. Osius are entirely of fretwork ; some of the little chairs, tables, pianos, and other pieces of dolls'-house furniture are beautifully made and worth noticing.

M. Scheibner's collection of ordinary German toys has no novelty.

On the opposite side of the gallery are Mr. Kirschkamp's dolls ; and although their finish is not equal to that of the French, yet they have a childish style which makes them more fitted for toys than their gaudy neighbours.

The elaborate glass case of figures and animals sent by Mr. W. Simon, although in detail ridiculously out of proportion, deserves to be remarked. The animals in many cases, horses and cows (only up to the waist of the man leading them), are beautifully made, as well as the trees and buildings in the background. The toy, however, is too big and clumsy for use.

In another room will be found a small collection of glass marbles : these are made in enormous numbers and in an infinite variety of design. The process of manufacture consists in rolling a piece—or " cäne," as technically called—of coloured hard glass within a globule of soft transparent glass ; the pattern varies with the colours of the " cänes " and the number of turns, &c., given to it during the process.

WIRTEMBERG.

There can be no question as to the very great superiority of the Biberach tin toys over all others manufactured, except as regards the prices, which are very much higher than those charged by M. Dessein, in Paris.

Rock and Craner's case is full of beautifully-modelled toys in tin, including every description of carriage, cart, cab, omnibus, perambulator, &c. On examining them one is struck with their firmness and solidity, and the evenness with which all the animals and carriages run. The former are now arranged with small wheels in those feet which touch the ground ; this is a great improvement on the clumsy flat board set on wheels on which the horses used to stand. Great attention is paid to the mould in which the animals are made—the exact similarity of the four horses in the drag is to be regretted, but no fault can be found with their shape. English visitors will be struck with the Hansom cab, which is decidedly not a German toy ; but at this and other manufactories in Germany, carriages, carts, &c., are often made

MR. BARTLEY ON TOYS.

from models supplied by the large foreign toy-dealers for their own market.

Tin dolls' house furniture. H. Blumhardt and Co., Stutgard.—The objects exhibited by this company are almost entirely dolls' house fittings. They are good, and have the great advantage of being firm and solid. The dolls' houses themselves are, of course, finished chiefly after the German fashion, and the stoves are rather out of proportion to the rooms; but in this case, as in that of Rock and Craner's, nationalities are studied for the various markets supplied.

Carl Gross, Stutgard.—This maker has a most miscellaneous collection of all sorts of wooden toys—horses, carts, stables, conjuring tricks, tool-boxes, and a few turnery goods. By the side of the bright tin toys these look rather rough; and in fact, there is nothing very remarkable in this overfilled and badly-arranged case.

BAVARIA.

Pewter soldiers. There are eight exhibitors from this country, and a considerable collection of toys of different descriptions. The larger number are the well-known pewter toys shown by M. Hafner and M. Allgeyer. Both these exhibitors have sent a large number of soldiers of all nations. An Englishman will easily recognize the uniform of the Foot Guards by their red coats and bearskins. The variety of uniforms shows that the trade is pretty extensive, and made to suit the nationalities of different markets.

Coronation coach. The most striking object in this class in the Bavarian Court is the coronation coach for the Emperor and Empress, exhibited by Mr. Birkman, of Nuremberg. It is drawn by eight horses, every part made entirely of metal, even to the reins and harness. On the roof are figures of fairies in wax, but badly modelled. The carriage is most elaborate, but is not to be compared to the perfection of those from Biberach exhibited a few yards off. The toys sent by M. Issmeyer are **Magnetic fish, &c.** mostly of tin, such as magnetic boats, fish, swans, &c. Some of these are well made, and as toys, are always popular with children.

The Swiss cottage exhibited by M. Finkh has many points to commend it, though rather large and clumsy. The animals are nicely modelled, and the peasants are in keeping with them.

Nuremberg shops. One of the special manufactures of Nuremberg is that of models of shops; and those sent by M. Hacker convey a tolerable idea of a toy which is always in demand. Grocers' shops are the most popular, from their having a number of drawers which open and shut, and so give plenty of occupation to children. From photographs in this case, it appears that all sorts of shops are made to order. Those exhibited here as specimens are very elaborately got up. The pastry-cook's at the bottom, though one of the most attractive, is not so usable as the others.

The paper toys of Messrs. Hunt and Hoffman, of Nuremberg, should be looked at. They consist of separate pictures of men, animals, carts, trees; each is painted on stiff cardboard, with a block of wood glued to the foot in order to enable it to stand easily. The position of the figures, &c., can be moved as desired to form different views, and to give scope to the imagination and ingenuity of the child.

The horn snakes of M. Wohlgeschaffen are good specimens of these curious toys. They are made with a particular-shaped tool in a lathe with considerable rapidity, and, consequently are inexpensive, although they appear of intricate workmanship.

The games of roulette as exhibited by M. Xavier Wahlge-schaft, of Nuremberg, have not the finish and delicacy which one would expect from that maker.

AUSTRIA.

The case of toys sent to M. Liebscher is one of the most interesting in the Exhibition. His toys are chiefly mechanical, though totally different from those in the French Court; and most have a musical snuff-box concealed in them. One is made to represent Blondin crossing the high rope with a wheelbarrow. A little figure trundles the barrow across the rope while a tune plays. Another toy consists of a group of persons sitting round a piano; one of them beats time, another plays, others listen, and music is heard from the instrument. Ordinary toys are also exhibited, such as horses, carriages, animals, balloons, and dolls' house furniture in wood. Besides these, there is a collection of clockwork pictures. In one a schoolmaster flogs an urchin while a boy draws a donkey on the wall behind the teacher's back; in another three fiddlers play away and nod their heads; and in a third a balloon ascends in the background of an elaborate landscape.

SWITZERLAND.

This country has three exhibitors. M. Rous's collection of dolls in Swiss costume is interesting, and the dresses are nicely made. On close examination, the visitor will find a beautiful model of a gun and gun-carriage, by M. Benoit, placed in the middle of the case.

Hunt and Hoffman's paper toys.

Horn snakes.

Roulette games.

Mechanical and other toys.

Switzerland.

DENMARK.

From Copenhagen there is one exhibitor of an elaborately-carved set of spillekens. These are quite models of almost every sort of implement, such as spades, rakes, hammers, picks, billiard cues, scissors, laders, flags, &c.

RUSSIA.

Russia.

The Russian toys are not numerous; but the india-rubber balls and cords for gymnastic exercises are of good and elastic material and well made. They are exhibited by the Russo-American Company for the manufacture of india-rubber at St. Petersburg.

EGYPT.

Egypt.

The Egyptian toys are rather remarkable, though rude and original. A large collection was sent; but many, being somewhat cumbrous and not deemed worthy of careful packing, were broken on the road, and so are not exhibited. This is to be regretted, for the remnants show that an entire collection from this country would have been interesting. Included in this class are swinging bassinets, cradles, and small go-carts for teaching children to walk. All of them are of a somewhat curious make.

TUNIS.

Tunis.

The only object from this country is a playing die found in the excavation of Carthage, and exhibited by his Excellency Prince Mohamed. It is of stone, rather large, being somewhat more than half an inch cube, and is in a perfect state of preservation; the edges are rounded, but all the sides have the numbers distinctly remaining on them.

MOROCCO.

Morocco.

The trumpets and tops from this country resemble very much those sold at our small shops and fairs; they are painted in brilliant red and green colours alternately in rings. Some are pegtops, having iron pegs, while others are more like teetotums, to be spun with the fingers.

JAPAN.

Japan.

A curious and interesting case is sent by the Japanese Government containing toys of all kinds, rattles, dolls with moveable eyes, others of white earthenware with comic faces, cups and balls, little boxes of kitchen articles, &c. Owing to their being sold, it is impossible to induce the custodian to give any information concerning them.

UNITED STATES OF AMERICA.

This country has but one exhibitor, and he has sent a few geometric puzzles. These are good, and of considerable merit, as they make an immense variety of figures and give scope to the imagination and ingenuity of the child. It is to be regretted that a fair representation of the toy manufacture in America has not been sent to the Exhibition. Many clever playthings are made on the other side of the Atlantic—as, for example, the "walking doll" referred to in connexion with M. Jumeau's exhibits.

ENGLAND.

The only exhibitor of toys in the English space is Mr. Cremer, who displays a fine collection of English manufactured goods in this class; the most striking portion of the stall is the dolls, dolls' houses, and dolls' wardrobes. England excels in the manufacture of the best class of dolls, and more particularly those in wax; they are all children in face and dress, and are superior as toys to the make of any other country. Those exhibited by Mr. Cremer are most pleasing, and the modelling of the faces, hands, and feet, shows that no pains or expense is spared in producing the best moulds. The clothes exhibited are quite perfect, everything being made to be put on and taken off. The sleeping apartment of Mr. and Mrs. Doll is a capital example of an English doll's house of the most luxurious kind, though as a toy it is inferior to the model kitchen below; this has a kitchen-range and sink supplied with water and every requisite utensil, even including a working filter. The doll's wardrobes are to a certain extent a novelty, or, at any rate, the perfection in which they are exhibited in this stall. The rag dolls at a slight distance can hardly be distinguished from wax, so well are their faces coloured. The models of ships and boats are popular English toys, as might be expected in a maritime nation, and some of those exhibited are well worthy of note, more particularly a model of the Henrietta, the yacht which won the ocean race last year.

Games.—The exhibitors of games in the English division are not numerous. Cricket is represented by Messrs. John Lillywhite and E. J. Page, both of whom have sent excellent specimens of the requisites for this game. The racket bats, balls, and shoes of Messrs. Jefferies and Malings are made with great perfection, as also those exhibited by Messrs. Cremer, Page, and Lillywhite. It is remarkable that this game should be represented by more English exhibitors than the national sport of cricket. A pair of porphyry curling stones from Edinburgh will be found among the English games, they are exhibited by the Lord Provost, and are beautiful specimens.

Mr. Cremer's games are numerous, croquet being the most important. His miniature billiard-tables are well finished, and it may be remarked that this game has come into fashion in consequence of a table exhibited by this maker in the Exhibition of 1862.

A new game, styled "A Summer Excursion," though not well arranged, seems to have its merits, it was invented by the Rev. C. Mackenzie, of the Polytechnic.

BRITISH COLONIES.—CANADA.

Colonies.

Mr. Peacock, of Montreal, exhibits a set of cricket stumps, bails, and five bats, which are well and strongly made, though somewhat clumsy. There would appear to be a considerable demand for these things in Canada.

REPORT on APPARATUS and METHODS used in the
INSTRUCTION of CHILDREN.—(Class 89.)—By the
Rev. Canon NORRIS, M.A.

REV. CANON
NORRIS
ON MEANS
FOR IN-
STRUCTING
CHILDREN.

Paris, May 1867.

THE educational department of the Exhibition is divided
into two portions—Class 89 contains all that concerns the instruction of children; Class 90, what concerns that of older
persons. The report which follows relates exclusively to
Class 89.

France, Prussia, Saxony, Sweden, Denmark, Austria,
Spain, and Italy are the nations of the Continent which have
contributed most largely to this portion of the Exhibition.

Taking these nations in the above order, I shall briefly
notice such of their contributions as have seemed to me most
deserving of our attention.

I. FRANCE.

France.

Beyond all doubt the most striking and the most instructive
sample of French primary instruction is to be found in the
large building in the park (near the Grande Porte) dedicated
to the iron-works of Creusot. Here Messrs. Schneider and
Company exhibit a most complete account of their magnificent
schools. The statistics, methods, rules, time-tables, and works
done by the scholars are ranged along the west wall. The
schools are maintained chiefly, but not exclusively, for their
workpeople's children. These pay 7d. per month; strangers,
14d. There are 2,219 boys and 1,846 girls in attendance.
The boys are taught by twelve masters, the chaplain attending to give religious instruction: the girls, by the Sisters of
St. Joseph de Cluny.

Schneider &
Co.'s schools
at Creusot.

Each of the two principal schools numbers about 900, and
is divided into nine classes. The mean age of the highest
class of boys is fourteen; of girls, thirteen; the mean age of
the lowest class of boys, is eight; of girls and infants, four.
The course of instruction is fourfold:—

1. *French,* occupying ten or twelve hours in the week.
Under this head come reading and committing to memory;
and for the older children grammar and composition.

2. *History and Geography,* occupying about three hours
per week of the girls' time, and from eight to four hours of
the boys', the younger boys giving more time to it than
the elder. A course of Bible history is included in this
department.

Rev. Canon
Norris
on Means
for in-
structing
Children.

3. *Science,* occupying five hours of the girls' week, and from six to ten of the boys'; in the girls' school "Science" means arithmetic and bookkeeping; in the boys' school it means arithmetic and geometry throughout, and for the elder boys it includes one hour of natural philosophy and mechanics, one of chemistry, and two of algebra.

4. *Arts,* occupying twelve hours per week in each school. For the girls an hour every day of needlework and another of writing, with two hours of music; for the boys, writing, drawing, and music. On Thursdays and Sundays the children have holidays, with home tasks, which are corrected the next morning.

Good marks are given for conduct and for lessons. These are carefully registered in the teacher's journal, together with his private observations. In August every year the marks of the year are counted up and added to the results of a general examination; the result determines the prizes. To these the boys look forward with much interest; but a far greater incentive to industry and good conduct is the admirable system of *patronage.* To the most deserving boys who leave the school an honourable career is opened in the company's employment as clerks or as engineers, to the next most deserving employment as workmen, while the undeserving have to seek their living elsewhere. This patronage is exercised rigorously according to merit: the poorest boy in the school knows that he may rise to situations of the highest responsibility in the company's service. To this the company ascribe the very remarkable success which has attended the schools. Punishments are seldom needed. Where loss of marks fails to suffice, a letter is written to the parent, and the child's attendance at the school is suspended for a while. In 26 years not more than three cases occurred in which final expulsion was found necessary.

In 1863 a night school for adult workmen was instituted, with an attendance of 100; last year the attendance had risen to 260, and they had asked to have special lessons in machine-drawing. The result of the children's work, drawings, needlework, and copy-books seemed to me admirable.

From the Creusot school I pass into the main building. There, near the Rue des Pays Bas, is to be found the rest of the French educational exhibition. On the wall will be seen

very complete plans of school buildings by M. Uchard, an architect (under No. 8 of the catalogue). The question of

ventilation is yet unsolved in France as in England. Ventilators in the roof are condemned, and ventilating flues running alongside of the smoke-flues preferred. But the success of this system depends on the length of the flue; and here the

French schools, two or three stories in height, have a great advantage over our single-story schools. Where the rooms are one over the other several stoves combine in winter to increase the upcast draught, and the air-flue sucks the vitiated air through the floor-grates very powerfully ; while the warm air chamber of the stove is continually sending a fresh supply into the room. In summer, when the stoves are not lit, valves into the air-flues may be opened in the walls near the ceiling. A specimen of one of these ventilating-stoves may be seen under No. 105. But an open grate (such as those made by Hyde, of Winchester, with hot-air chambers behind them) would fulfil the requirements of this system of ventilation quite as well.

Passing to what concerns instruction, Taupier's method of teaching writing (No. 51) well deserves attention. His copybooks are published by the great school publisher, Hachette (Boulevard St. Germain, 77). As in the best copybooks of all nations, the child traces a few lines over pale letters before he trusts himself to write unaided, pale lines guide the slope of the letters, and their spaces also, throughout the earlier books. The more advanced copybooks embrace invoices, addresses of letters, elements of grammar, &c. *Copybooks.*

In arithmetic, admirable facilities for teaching decimal weights and measures, the relation of the whole to its metric base being made obvious at once to the child's eye, may be seen in M. Demkes' staircase (No. 76), and in M. Carpentier's cabinet (No. 79). This last is most complete, having a pair of scales in which the several equivalents can be made manifest to the child's eye, each being also brought into relation with the base-metre. *Arithmetic.*

In geography, Gervais's atlas of outline maps, to be filled up and coloured by the pupil (No. 22), should be especially noticed. The maps are most beautifully engraved, with the mountains in admirable relief, and cost only a penny a piece. (M. Gervaise, Rue du Rendez-vous, 53, Paris.) *Geography.*

Among the results of scholars' work but little needlework appears.[*] The results of the boys' work are very satisfactory. The portfolio of drawings, especially the machine drawings, from M. Barbier's school in the Rue Neuve-Coquenard, Paris (No. 197), as well as some excellent drawings and maps from the Algerian schools of Oran, well repay attention. But if an Englishman wishes to see the mag- *Needlework* *Drawings.*

---

[*] Last month a law was passed requiring all communes of more than 500 inhabitants to have a separate *girls' school* under a mistress, and all smaller communes to provide a sempstress for their mixed schools.

K

Technical instruction.

nificent effort which France has made in the last three years to connect together the school and the workshop, he should pass on to Class 90, and there examine the results of the "enseignement secondaire spécial," to which the law of June 1, 1865, is giving such a completely efficient organisation. The professional and technical schools take up the children at the point where the primary school leaves them. Here the girls learn bookkeeping,* wood engraving, porcelain painting, millinery; the boys machine drawing, physics, and generally the principles applicable to whatever trade they are about to engage in. It is clear that the necessity of this kind of education for artizans is better appreciated in France than in England. These schools do not, it is true, belong to Class 89; but this higher course of instruction is beginning to react downwards, on the primary schools, requiring of them a more scientific teaching of the A B C of design. Some results of this may be seen from M. Delahaye's primary school in the Boulevard des Batignolles, 24 (No. 201).

Evening schools.

The rapid extension of *evening schools* all over France in the last two years has been most remarkable. In April, 1866, M. Duruy was able to report 22,980 evening schools for men and 1,706 for women, attended by 552,939 men and 42,567 women. These are mainly supported by voluntary effort—three-fifths of the schools being gratuitous. The law of last month offers a premium to any teacher of a day school thus volunteering to open an evening school.

Prussia.

II. Prussia.

Maps, books, &c.

In a white house in the park a room has been furnished by the Prussian Government with all that a school needs. It might, perhaps, have been better done in some respects; but the admirable wall maps of Kiepert, published by Reimer of Berlin, cannot fail to arrest attention. There is an excellent school atlas by Diehl, of Darmstadt, price 1s. 2d.; and another by Haester, still cheaper. The reading-books, carefully prepared in a graduated series by the teachers of the Münsterberg normal school, are marvellously cheap. So also are the very complete sets of arithmetic books by Böhme, used all over Prussia. Böhme also exhibits some curious tin slides, to be used in infant schools instead of the ball frame.

A school at Ahrensberg sends a quantity of needlework, done by the scholars, of the highest excellence, and giving evidence of very sensible teaching—no fancy work, all of the plainest utility.

---

* The bookkeeping of the French tradesmen is almost entirely intrusted to women.

Diagrams for teaching the working of pumps, &c., and of the electric telegraph, may be seen on the walls.

III. SAXONY.

In a little temple in the park is a modest but very excellent exhibition of school books and apparatus sent by Saxony, the cradle of German education; for here in the 16th century were sown the seeds of that system of popular instruction which has since spread over Germany. In the centre is a model of the Gymnastic School of Dresden. On the counters and walls are to be found Lange's excellent altas (Leïpsic), giving a full account, physical and commercial, of Saxony; Delitsch's elementary Atlas of the World, a marvel of cheapness (six maps for 14*d.*); Lüben's Atlas of Botany, which they seem to teach carefully in the Saxon schools; Schnorr's Bible woodcuts; and much else worthy of attention.

IV. SWEDEN.

The Swedish Government has furnished the lower chamber of a most picturesque little wooden house so as to represent one of their small village schools. Since 1842 education has been obligatory in Sweden; the entire absence of dissent makes it possible for the Government to work the schools through the ecclesiastical organization of the country. Each parish is rated according to its requirements, as reported by the clergyman and approved by the inspector. If we may judge by what is here seen, the furniture is of an almost sumptuous kind. Each child has a small desk and seat to himself; the desk holds his books, &c.; the seat has a back. The teacher thus passes freely among all the children. In the larger schools of more thickly-peopled countries this would be of course impossible.

The maps of Scandinavia are perhaps the most striking school maps in the whole Exhibition. They are by Mentzer of Stockholm (No. 11). The stove is of earthenware, as in their houses, warming the air by conduction, not by radiation.

V. DENMARK.

From Denmark I find a very complete collection of scholars' work from the various primary schools of Copenhagen. The boys' drawings and writing books are good, the girls' needlework admirable. In all the schools the English character of writing is taught as well as the German.

An excellent adult night school, supported by voluntary subscriptions, for teaching drawing, also sends good results.

REV. CANON NORRIS ON MEANS FOR INSTRUCTING CHILDREN.

In England a school for teaching drawing would hardly draw forth the charitable contributions of our gentlefolk.

VI. AUSTRIA.

Austria.

The well-stored assortment of school apparatus sent by the Austrian Government is nearly all under glass, and difficult to examine.

Globes, &c.

The best globes of every size and price are from Austria. Steinhauser's maps of physical geography, Frobel's "Kindergarten," Patek's apparatus for teaching arithmetic, from the St. Anna School at Vienna, all deserve notice. I never saw in an English school the Vienna frame for teaching vulgar fractions. It is like a ball-frame, only on the wires, instead of balls, you have divisible reeds. The uppermost is undivided, and represents the integer. From those below, which are divided into fractional parts, and run on the wires, the child sees at once (for example) that three-fourths are equal to six-eighths, greater than two-thirds, less than four fifths, &c.

Drawings.

In large portfolios are to be found specimens of drawings in every stage. Better methods of teaching drawing in connexion with ornamentation can hardly be conceived. In this respect the Austrian exhibition seems to me unrivalled.

Telluriums and planetariums.

I may also mention very cheap telluriums and planetariums, from 30s. to 5l., sold by Felkl, of Prague. By lighting the lamp and turning the handle, the whole theory of day and night, of the seasons, and of eclipses, is shown to the child at once. One of the cheaper sort might well be in every village school. All the Austrian school apparatus seems to be far cheaper than that of France or England.

Spain.

VII. SPAIN.

In the upper room of an elaborately carved and turreted house in the park is to be found the Spanish school exhibition. Without an interpreter it is difficult to understand it.

School-desk.

The eye is at once caught by a school-desk, long enough for five children, supported by five simple cast-iron standards. Instead of a bench, as in England, with all the attendant inconvenience of stepping over, there are five round seats, each seat resting on a continuation of the iron standard, like so many music-stools before a pianoforte. When the class is told to stand, each child stands at once *by the side of* his seat, and can leave or resume his place without difficulty. When used for needleworks, cushions are attached to the desk, to which the girls may pin their work. Under No. 87 will be found a cheap box of geometrical solids of walnut-wood, the best, perhaps, in the Exhibition.

Morenilla's method of teaching reading (No. 73), and Iturzaeta's writing copies (No. 91) appear to be good. Avendaño (No. 88) is their great publisher of school books at Madrid, and Bastinos, of Barcelona (No. 33), is a well-known house for all sorts of school apparatus. There is a society (or junta) of noble ladies at Madrid who maintain a normal school, and have founded numerous elementary schools, also represented, though inadequately, in this exhibition.

REV. CANON NORRIS ON MEANS FOR IN-STRUCTING CHILDREN.

VIII. ITALY.

Italy.

The exhibition from Italy indicates a rapid and satisfactory progress in the last few years. The Minister of Instruction and Worship sends a very complete assortment, including a full account of their recent legislation in favour of education. Paravia, the great publisher at Turin, sends text-books of every sort; those of Lambruschini and of Carbonati are reported to be excellent. Perrin, of Turin (No 13), sends copy-books as good as any in the Exhibition, to be had for half the cost of English copy-books. Luca, of Naples (No. 38), sends very good books on geography. All their older educational societies have been recently consolidated into the Italian Association for the Education of the People, which (under No. 21) exhibits good evidence of progress. The architectural and ornamental drawings from the schools of Naples, Venice, and Padua are most beautiful.

It is to be regretted that some other countries in which education has already made, and is now making, great progress, are so inadequately represented.

BELGIUM sends but little:—The school-books of Braun (No. 2) and of Willequet (No. 16), Joly's Atlas (No. 11), and Callewaert's (No. 3) should be noticed.

Belgium, &c.

HOLLAND and SWITZERLAND, both nations honourably distinguished for what they have accomplished in the cause of popular education, send nothing.

Canada.

CANADA sends excellent school-books (note especially the commercial copy-books) from the upper province and school apparatus from the lower. There is also an interesting model of the village of St. Anne, showing the great agricultural school and its system of husbandry. The model was made by the teachers of the institution.

St. Anne.

UNITED STATES OF AMERICA.—Nothing belonging to this class had arrived at the date of this report (May 14).

Such are my principal gleanings from my month's study of this portion of the Exhibition. But, in conclusion, I must record my strong impression that any educational exhibition

Conclusion.

REV. CANON
NORRIS
ON MEANS
FOR IN-
STRUCTING
CHILDREN.

of this kind must be, from the nature of the case, unsatisfactory; as a test of comparative progress it is clearly untrustworthy. Nations whose administration is highly centralised are sure to appear to advantage as compared with those which trust chiefly to voluntary effort; and of the work done it is the *material, i.e.,* the least important, results only that can be properly represented. How, for instance, can a teacher's success as a disciplinarian be made to appear in such an exhibition? Even of the mechanical appliances a trustworthy judgment can hardly be formed unless one has a practical teacher by one's side to answer the question, "How do they work?" And of the real tools of a teacher, his school-books, it is of course impossible to make any profitable examination while standing before a glass case. Still Class 89 contains abundantly enough to interest an English schoolmaster, and the above report may perhaps help to direct him to what will best repay his attention.

REPORT on APPARATUS and METHODS used in the INSTRUCTION of the BLIND.—(Class 89.)—By EDMUND C. JOHNSON, Esq.

CLASS 89 contains many interesting appliances and methods for the instruction of the blind, exhibited by the undermentioned countries :—France, Austria, Italy, Prussia, Holland, Belgium, Denmark, Würtemberg, Spain, Sweden, Italy, America, and England.

It is proposed in this report to give a short summary of the principal objects of interest in each country, under the following heads :—I. Books or treatises on the education of the blind. II. Apparatus used in the instruction of the blind. III. Results of manual labour in the workshops and schools.

Austria and France occupy the first positions in this section of education.

AUSTRIA.

Das K. K. Blinden-Erziehung's Institut, in Vienna, is a school established by the State, having a central government and schools in union throughout many parts of the empire. It contains about 200 pupils, under the direction of M. Pablasek, a very learned and philanthropic professor. The male and female pupils are lodged, fed, clothed, and instructed in reading, writing, arithmetic, geography, music, basket-making, matmaking, turning, ropemaking, blind-making, and needlework. The musical instruction includes vocal and instrumental music and composition. An asylum and workshops for the employment of the pupils of this school above age have also been established at Vienna, and found to be of the greatest utility. Mr. Mathias Sohlentung tells us in his report :—" At present there are 75 workers " —43 males and 32 females. The most productive of the " trades are basket-making, bookbinding, and knitting. The " expense of keep per head is about 21*l.* The profits of the " musicians," says the report, " who play in cafés and " restaurants, are very considerable. They induce many of " our best pupils to leave as soon as they become useful to " the charity."

Austria State School

There are two itinerant groups of blind harmonists in Vienna who subsist in this manner ; one a mixed band of instrumentalists and the other a society of harpists, who have

Itinerant blind musicians.

been instructed by Mr. Zakreiss, the professor of that instrument at the Royal Institution for the Blind.

Attention to intellectual education, rather than to gain a good livelihood by manual tradal employment, has hitherto been the principle of action in the treatment of the blind at Vienna. It is, however, a subject of congratulation that the Germans are gradually working round to the English and American systems of teaching the blind useful manual labour, with moderate primary intellectual instruction. Dépôts for the sale of work are opened in Vienna, in connection with the Home; and also an Infant School.

I. Three treatises are exhibited:

a. "The Blind from the Cradle to the Grave," by M Pablasek, Director des genannten Institutes, Wien, 1867. A work of considerable merit, including the latest results of his own experience, with full directions as to the primary and secondary education of the blind.

b. "Reports of the Blind Institution of Vienna."

c. "Sketch of the Life of J. W. Klein" (late director of the Imperial School for the Blind): an interesting memoir of one of the great German philanthropists, the originator of blind schools in Germany—he and Valentine Haüy, of France, being the pioneers in this branch of primary instruction.

II. Apparatus for instruction:

a. Zum Lesen mit lateinischen Alphabet, von M. Pablasek. A frame and letters for teaching the alphabet.

This is a very useful little box, about one foot in length, and a foot in width; the lower part being divided into small partitions, like a compositor's desk, each containing a letter stamped in relief. The metal of which the letter is composed is light and firm, half an inch in length and two-thirds in breadth. The characters employed are the common Roman type (lower-case letter), together with numerals and stops. The inferior edge of each letter-plate is stamped with a small dot, which indicates the position in which it is to be held, the dot downwards. The upper compartment of the box is furnished with a series of slides, into which letters can be inserted when words are spelt; and a small slip of wood, with two screws, holds the letters together when the page is completed. A blind child, by this simple apparatus, can be taught the exact form of each letter, *in relief;* can practise the combination of letters in the formation of words, and exert any amount of pressure with the finger upon the type, without destroying or detracting from its sharpness.

The frame forms a sliding drawer or cover to the box, and can be obtained at the Imperial Blind Institution, at Vienna, price 1*l.* 18*s.*

b. Stacheltypen von J. W. Klein, a machine for embossing, with type made of pins' points. This is the apparatus used in the blind schools of England and other countries, where the ordinary Roman letter is employed. It consists of a box of type, with metal lines, between which the type can be worked. The letters are too fine, as to points, for the use of ordinary blind children, and the machine is too costly (12*s.* 6*d.*) to be used with advantage by the poor.[*]

MR. E. C. JOHNSON ON MEANS FOR INSTRUCTION OF THE BLIND.
—
Embossing machines.

c. Braille Punktypen von M. Pablasek, a small embossing press on Braille's system. This is a compact little box, containing the necessary type for a correspondence between blind persons. Its portability is a great recommendation, as it contains a reserve of type (made in France), an embossing desk which folds into a small compass, and a " guidemain " to receive the type. It is highly to be recommended as a portable desk : and other type than that of M. Braille can be substituted when required. Price 1*l.* 8*s.*, complete.

d. Zur Markirung der Spielkarten fur Blinde von J. W. Klein (for marking playing cards) is a little instrument of but small value in an educational point of view.

III. The results of the manual labour of the pupils are not very remarkable. The basket-making department exhibits four different specimens of round, flat, and split skeinwork. The price is too high to command a market, whilst the colours introduced are by the hand of the masters. The window-blinds, manufactured with small spills of wood joined together by string, are novel features in this Exhibition. They are cheap and well made, and merit especial notice. It is in its turnery that the Imperial School at Vienna excels. The specimens consist of boxes, egg cups, needle-cases, and various objects turned by the blind, which for beauty and cheapness cannot be surpassed.

Result of manual labour.

Switzerland, France, Austria, and Prussia are the chief countries in which turnery is made an occupation for the blind.

Various specimens of female work may also be noticed, such as knitting, netting, shoe and slipper making ; though inferior to the productions of other countries.

There are three private schools in the empire of Austria, which exhibit in class 89—viz., 1, Linz ; 2, Pesth ; 3, Brünn (Moravia).

Private schools.

1. The school of Linz is an institution supported by private subscription, with a small rate in aid from the Government.

---

[*] N.B.—The ordinary writing-desk of England, as in operation at the School for the Indigent Blind, Southwark, is more perfect in its construction, and is less costly.

MR. E. C.
JOHNSON
ON MEANS
FOR
INSTRUC-
TION OF THE
BLIND.
Books in raised letters are exhibited, in the ordinary lower-case type, well embossed, and moderately cheap. Portions of the Bible form the only literature in use at this school.

The industrial products are few; straw mats, cane-work, string, knitting, and sewing are the only specimens exhibited.

2. The school of Pesth is the single establishment in Hungary for the instruction of the blind; and, like that at Vienna, is under the direction of the Government. A few embossed books, in the Roman character (Magyar reprints from similar works in German), and some well-made string and stockings, indicate considerable progress in primary instruction amongst the Hungarian blind.

3. The school of Brünn (Moravia) is, perhaps, the most remarkable of the private blind schools of Austria. It is supported by voluntary subscription, receives a small subsidy from the municipality of Brünn, and is especially devoted to " instruction in manual labour;" it resembles an institution for promoting the general welfare of the blind founded in London by the well-known Miss Gilbert.

Shoe-
making.
The specimens of shoemaking are wonderful—indeed so startling, that if they be really the work of the blind, they are deserving of especial notice. Hemming, marking, sewing, and plain needlework are brought to the highest point of perfection in this establishment.

FRANCE.

France.
History of
the Institu-
tion Impé-
riale des
Aveugles
de Paris.

Valentine
Haüy.
L'Institution Impériale des Jeunes Aveugles de Paris.— As long ago as 1784 ten or twelve poor blind musicians were executing a discordant symphony in one of the streets of Paris. Crowds of people were attracted by this novel exhibition, but more particularly a simple passer-by of the name of Valentine Haüy. The philanthropic mind of this great man at once conceived the design of regularly educating the blind. About the same time a young German lady, Mdlle. Paradis, who had been blind from the age of two years, arrived in Paris, accompanied by a blind instructor, of the name of Vesinburg. Haüy fortunately made the acquaintance of Mdlle. Paradis, whom he found both intelligent and useful in drawing up " Un Plan " Général d'Institution pour les Enfants Aveugles." Chance also threw in his way a young man named François Le Seur, who, blind from his birth, had up to the age of sixteen subsisted by begging at a church door. At the period when Haüy found Le Seur, the latter had begun a course of self-education—half his day being devoted to intellectual exer-

cises, and the other half to begging in the streets. Valentine
Haüy, struck with these two remarkable instances of energy,
drew up a memoir, which was read before the Société
Philanthropique, of which Lenoir, the celebrated lieutenant
of police, was president. The society at once sought out
twelve blind children, and placed them under the care of
Haüy. A little house was taken in the Rue Coquillière,
and the Academy of Sciences was called upon to determine
on the best mode of instruction; whilst Valentine Haüy
invented characters in relief, taught the blind to read, and
set to work to print books in raised letters for their instruction in music and geography. The report of the Academy
does not make any mention of *manual labour*, though it is
believed that the blind children, even at this early period,
made tape and small baskets.

Mr. E. C.
JOHNSON
ON MEANS
FOR
INSTRUC-
TION OF THE
BLIND.

In a short time the Royal Academy of Music gave a
concert at the Palace of the Tuileries in behalf of the institution; and in December 1786 the blind children were
admitted to the Palace of Versailles, and " displayed their
" proficiency " before the King and Queen, " who lodged
" and entertained them in the château for more than eight
" days." Immediately after this Haüy published an essay,
" Sur l'Education des Aveugles," a book which was printed
partly *in relief* by his pupils. In 1787 his school numbered
thirty pupils, some of whom paid a small monthly subscription, the rest being totally indigent. Various manual works,
such as knitting, netting, string and rope making, were
taught with various success; the instruction in music taking
the first rank, under the constant care of the celebrated
composer, Gossec. In 1787 the musicians of the school of
Haüy took part in a grand religious service at the Church
of St. Eustache, many of the pupils making their first
communion, and chanting a mass which had been written for
them by Gossec. In 1788 the pupils of Haüy augmented
to the number of fifty; and on the Feast of St. Valentine a
temporary chapel was erected in the establishment, where a
full choral service was performed by the pupils, in which
the blessing of the Almighty was invoked, and their voices
raised in prayer, " Pour le vrai bonheur de l'institution, et
" pour son père adoptif." Amongst the pupils was young
Gailliod, who had been admitted into the school at the age
of nine years. His great aptitude for music soon enabled
him to become an expert organist as well as a skilful player
on the violin. In 1789 Haüy determined to admit *seeing
children* to some of the advantages of the institution; and,
on small payments, upwards of a hundred were (strangely

Mr. E. C.
Johnson
on Means
for
Instruc-
tion of the
Blind.

enough) instructed in music and in the primary branches of education *by the blind*. These classes only lasted until 1791. All was going well with this blind school until the Revolution, which threatened to overthrow all the charitable institutions of France. " The blind, imitating their seeing " confrères, cried aloud for liberty and independence ;" and a little emeute took place in the establishment, which, after some difficulty, was suppressed by Haüy. But a greater danger menaced it. The Philanthropic Society became daily weakened by the dispersion of its members, and it ceased to contribute funds for the support of the blind school. These were hard times for Haüy, who, failing in his applications for relief from wealthy demagogues, turned with a heavy heart to the Government. Assistance was for a long time refused. At length, " by a decree dated July 1791, the National Assembly assigned the house and funds of the Convent of the Celestines to the wants and necessities of the deaf and dumb and the born blind. Thirty blind and thirty deaf and dumb children were boarded and lodged in the institution. This singular arrangement of mixing the two classes of unfortunates introduced a novel and undesirable feature in the institution ; and no less than nineteen masters and mistresses were appointed to supervise thirty blind children. The establishment was next transferred to the religious house of St. Catharine, in the Rue de Lombard, where it fell into the greatest confusion ; and it was not until 1795 that the National Convention once more gave an impetus to the undertaking. The school changed its name to that of " Aveugles Travailleurs," every pupil being instructed in a trade, and, after a residence of five years, leaving the establishment with a gift of 300 f. The poor blind gained but little by this apparent liberality, as their portions were paid in worthless assignats.

When the first years of the Directory gave hopes of returning order and confidence in France, the blind school participated in the temporary amelioration of affairs. The Hospital of the Quinze-Vingts and the Aveugles Travailleurs were united, and in 1801 the trade workers were transferred to the former institution. Haüy, thoroughly disgusted, resigned his place, and the affairs of the blind fell from bad to worse. The manufacture of cloth, which for a long time had been declining, was discontinued in 1803, and but two hours a day were devoted to instruction, of a very imperfect character. In 1805 the Government once more turned an anxious eye upon the institution, reviewed the work that Haüy had so

Dr. Guillie. well begun, and in 1814 appointed Dr. Guillie head of the establishment. By his able advocacy the institution was separated from the Quinze-Vingts, and M. Dufau was nominated as second instructor. To the great talent of M. Dufau, who was called to fulfil these important duties at the early age of twenty, the institution is indebted for its present prosperity; and it is not too much to affirm that to his fostering care, his large and comprehensive intellect, his deep research, both in the moral and intellectual capacities of the blind, that such good results have been achieved. In 1816 the institution was transferred to the ancient College of Les Bons Enfants, in the Rue St. Victoire; and in 1817 Guillie placed the school in certain train for success. Thus in 1819 and 1820, many books were embossed in the asylum: among others an English Grammar, two volumes of English extracts, a Latin grammar, an Italian grammar, two volumes of extracts from Italian authors, a Greek grammar in two volumes, a volume of extracts from Greek authors, a Spanish grammar, two volumes of geography, and many books on religious subjects. In 1820 the embossing-press of the school produced other works, including the Catechism, choice extracts from Latin authors, and two volumes of Horace and Virgil. It is somewhat remarkable, however, that the press of the institution did not produce any treatise on arithmetic or history; and that pupils only learned music and composition by methods used at the Conservatoire. The orchestra, even at this time, was worthy of public attention. The manual employments, both of the male and female pupils, included the manufacture of purses, knitting, slippers and shoes, in " peluches de laine," brooms and whips. The boys worked at the loom stuffed chairs, turned; and manufactured straw mats. Dr. Guillie was very anxious to establish an asylum in the country, where the pupils who left the institution could work in little gardens, follow a particular trade, and become members of a self-supporting community; but this excellent plan was never carried out. Dr. Guillie retired in 1821, and was succeeded by Dr. Pignier, who received the title of Director. M. Dufau, however still remained in the establishment as professor, and continued to give his lectures in grammar, rhetoric, and philosophy. The little orchestra received fresh encouragement from Habeneck, Da Costa, Dauprat, and Guillou, who gave their gratuitous services as professors, and in 1832 a blind pupil became organist at one of the principal churches. The years 1825 to 1829 were of great importance to the institution, in consequence of the introduction of a new system of writing and printing—the system of embossed points.

MR. E. C. JOHNSON ON MEANS FOR INSTRUCTION OF THE BLIND.

M. Dufau.

Pointwriting and printing.

M. Charles Barbier was the first person who entertained the idea that the blind might be taught to write, and yet read their own composition " sans connaître la figure des lettres, " l'usage de la plume ou du crayon, les règles de l'orthographe, " ni les difficultés de l'épellation."

The Abbé Carton, in his admirable work on " Les Etab- " lissements pour les Aveugles en Angleterre," gives the following tabulated plan of Barbier's system :—

1st line	a	i	o	u	é	è						
2nd ditto	an	in	on	un	ea	ou						
3rd ditto	be	de	gue	se	ve	ze						
4th ditto	pe	te	que	che	fe	se						
5th ditto	le	me	ne	re	gn	1 mo						
6th ditto	ci	cin	ien	ste	+	ment						

" Il ne fallait pour tout instrument qu'une règle rayée dans son milieu, de six lignes parallèles et creusées dans le bois sur laquelle on posait le papier qu'on retenait par une espèce d'agrafe, ou sur laquelle on mettait une réglette platte en cuivre percé de carrés."

This novel method was further developed by a young man of the name of Louis Braille, who after much labour and thought perfected a system of point-writing, which has since been widely adopted in France, Switzerland, and Spain, and is daily making immense strides in the schools of other countries.

ÉCRITURE À L'USAGE DES AVEUGLES, PROCÉDÉ DE MONS. L. BRAILLE,
PROFESSEUR À L'INSTITUTE DES JEUNES AVEUGLES, À PARIS.

A	B	C	D	E	F	G	H	I	J
1	2	3	4	5	6	7	8	9	0

K	L	M	N	O	P	Q	R	S	T

U	V	X	Y	Z	ç	6	à	è	ù
					oin				ien

an	in	ðn	ûn	èu	ou	oi	ch	gn	u
à	ê	î	ô	û	ë	ï	ü	œ	w

,	ì	ð	œ		signe
	ian	ion	ien		des nombres.

e	è	:	.	?	!	( )	«	*	»

1	2	3	4	5	6	7	8	9	0

MR. E. C.
JOHNSON
ON MEANS
FOR
INSTRUC-
TION OF THE
BLIND.

Claude
Montal.

Pianoforte
tuning.

M. Dufau lost none of his energy and perseverance as years rolled on; for we find that in 1830 he took by the hand Claude Montal, a pupil of the school, and advanced him to the position he now occupies. Montal obtained permission to be instructed in the tuning of pianofortes, and ended by becoming a renowned maker of that instrument. His example led M. Dufau to train others in the same branch of trade. At the present time many blind pianoforte-tuners have created for themselves a lucrative " métier " in Paris and other parts of France.

In 1839 a new site was appropriated by the Government for the purposes of the charity, and the first stone of the present school was laid with much éclat. The whole establishment was reorganised, and M. Dufau, after twenty-five years of professorship, was raised to the position of director; M. J. Guadet, the present active chef de l'enseignement being created " instituteur," and the old mistress of the house replaced by the intelligent Mdlle. Cailhe. In 1843 professors and pupils took possession of their new abode, and the Institution " des Jeunes Aveugles " attained its present position. Full of years and of honour, the veteran director, M. Dufau, retired into private life at the beginning of the year 1855, and he has since enjoyed the affection and respect of all who know him. He still lives at Versailles, takes a deep interest in the welfare of the blind, and assisted the Commissioners of the London Exhibition in 1861, and the Paris Exhibition in 1867.

Object of
the Paris
Blind
School.

Studies.

The chief object of this excellent charity, the only one in France subsidised by the Government, is to rear blind children of both sexes—to give them an education according to their several capacities—and to instruct them in a trade or liberal profession. It may fairly be considered as the parent blind school of France, as all the other institutions of the country adopt it as a model, and are regulated by its rules and practices. The studies are divided into three divisions :—I. Intellectual. II. Musical. III. Industrial.

Primary
instruction.

I. THE INTELLECTUAL INSTRUCTION IS OF TWO KINDS —primary and secondary.

The primary consists of reading, grammar, arithmetic, sacred history, natural history, and the elements of geography. The secondary includes the higher portions of grammar, composition, arithmetic, geometry, and the rudiments of physics. Every class is under the direction of a seeing professor; whilst those of the children who show peculiar talent are taken to lectures at the college of France or the Sorbonne. A good classical library has been formed in the institution (embossed in relief by the blind pupils), which is often increased by the addition of the newest literary and standard works.

II. MUSICAL INSTRUCTION is the great feature of the establishment. Ten blind professors are permanently retained in the school, who give their entire time and attention to the pupils, and form the nucleus of the orchestra. Instruction is given both on the pianoforte and organ; and many of the advanced pupils gain lucrative appointments as organists at the different churches in Paris and the provinces. Vocalisation and the theory of musical composition are also taught to the elder pupils with considerable success. *The occupation of pianoforte-tuner* arises out of this section, and has been attended with such favourable results in France, that it would be well for other countries to recognise this branch of lucrative employment for the blind.

Claude Montal, the son of a saddler, was the first blind man in France who turned his attention to this subject. He was born at La Palisse, on June 28, 1800, and became totally blind at the age of five years. Soon after he showed remarkable precocity by tracing letters with a pin upon paper, and in this way teaching himself to write. His love of music was very great, and he soon manufactured a violin on which he played several little airs. Added to this, he learned the flageolet and other instruments, and obtained a fair idea of arithmetic and mathematics. He was admitted into the Paris blind school in 1816, where he made great progress, both in music and in manual labour. Here he became acquainted with Turcas, who helped him in his studies. One day Turcas and Montal, finding the pianoforte of the institution somewhat out of tune, attempted to arrange it; and, though successful, got into disgrace with the director for what was called their meddling propensities. Turcas, nothing daunted, purchased an old instrument, upon which he and Montal practised the art of tuning. The organ of the chapel was next experimented upon, and the director intrusted its reparation to Montal. The two blind men not only executed this work, but adapted a new set of pedals to the old instrument. Montal from that moment determined to create an independent position for himself. He left the institution, took regular lessons in tuning, and subsisted by giving instructions in grammar and arithmetic, the violin and pianoforte, at the low rate of from eight to ten sous a lesson. He was fortunate enough to make the acquaintance of M. Laurent, one of the professors of the Conservatoire, who recommended him, as " le meilleur accordeur de Paris," to

Marginal notes:
MR. E. C. JOHNSON FOR INSTRUCTION OF THE BLIND.

Musical instruction.

Pianoforte tuning.

Claude Montal.

MR. E. C.
JOHNSON
ON MEANS
FOR
INSTRUC-
TION OF THE
BLIND.
Zimmerman and Adam. These eminent composers procured him plenty of work. In 1842 Montal gave some public lectures on the art of tuning, and published his little book entitled " Abrégé de l'Art d'Accorder soi-même son Piano." This had a great success in the artistic world, and subsequently led Montal to commence the manufacture of pianofortes, in which he succeeded beyond his most sanguine expectations. From small beginnings he ultimately became one of the great piano-forte makers of France, and was even appointed fabricant to the Emperor and Empress.

Method of
teaching
pianoforte
tuning.
" It requires three years," says M. Guadet, " to train a blind man to become a good tuner." In the first year a correct notion of the exterior form of the square, the upright, the oblong, and the grand pianoforte is acquired, every part of which he is made to touch and examine. The instrument is then taken to pieces, and its mechanism thoroughly explained, the name of all its parts committed to memory, and their readjustment in the formation of a perfect instrument. After this preliminary work (more necessary for the blind than the seeing) the professor points out the position and order of the pegs in different pianofortes, and the mode in which the strings are applied. At this point the special instruction in tuning begins. The sound which the ear most easily appreciates is that of unison. A note is produced by the tension of one string ; a second string, and then a third, is extended, until perfect unison is arrived at. In this way the tones of thirds and fifths are produced, until the ear of the blind man can thoroughly appreciate concord and discord. " The object of this work is to make the hand dexterously " subordinate to the ear." Thus the pupils learn to make octaves, fifths, and thirds. " In that which concerns the " division of the strings into the required number of octaves, " the professor explains how the intervals are adjusted, as " on this depends the entire equality of tone throughout " the perfect instrument." It requires immense application and patience on the part of the pupil to acquire this precision. The division once made, the pupil fills in the strings, octave by octave, regulating by the octave above and below the harmony of the whole. It is obvious that some knowledge of music must be superadded to this mechanical employment.

" In the second year the pupil is allowed to tune the pianofortes of the establishment, under the guidance of a professor. The institution possesses twenty-one pianofortes on the boys' side and eleven on the girls'—thirty-two in all. An hour and a half each day is devoted to tuning, which accustoms the learners not only to tune well and quickly, but to keep the instruments in perfect condition."

During the third year the pupils are sent to the workshops of large manufacturers—have the advantage of examining every kind of pianoforte--get accustomed to exercise their trade in fresh localities, and gain that confidence which they so much require when going about alone to tune instruments in private houses. " They also live amongst the seeing and " learn to compete with them in their work." There are many reasons why blind men should be good pianoforte tuners. They have more delicate ears than the seeing, and are for the most part musicians ; whilst the generality of seeing tuners in France are simple mechanics. In the Paris blind school they receive a theoretical instruction in music at the same time that they are executing their manual calling of tuners.

" En définitive," says M. Guadet, " toutes les fois qu'un art ou un métier sont tels que la cécité n'y est pas un obstacle, que l'aveugle peut les exercer à avantage égal avec les voyants, qu'ils sont de nature à faire disparaître la différence qui existe entre eux, cet art, ce métier, sont favorables à l'aveugle, il faut se hâter de les lui donner. Or, en fait d'accord des pianos, l'aveugle n'a aucune infériorité, il a cer- tains avantages, au contraire, l'expérience le montre chaque jour, il faut donc faire des accordeurs; il n'y a pas à craindre que le travail manque aux accordeurs, il faut donc en faire autant que les circonstances le permettront."

THE ORCHESTRA OF THE PARIS BLIND SCHOOL demands our special notice. The professors of the institution form the nucleus. " The one who is at the same time chief of " the orchestra is also professor of the first violin ; another " of the second violin ; a third and fourth, the violoncello " and bass ; a fifth, the contrabasso ; a sixth, the first " clarinet ; a seventh, the first flute ; and the eighth, the " trombone." All these professors aid in the instruction and performance of the band, which is not considered complete without them. The band consists usually of three first violins, three second violins, two alto violins, four basses, two contrabassi, two flutes, two clarinets, two hautboys, one bassoon, three horns, one trombone, one ophicleide, timbrels, large drums, triangle : thirty performers in all. The num- ber, however, is frequently augmented to thirty-six per- formers, many new pupils having lately been admitted as members of the band.

The mode in which they execute a piece of music, overture or solo with orchestral accompaniments, is the following :—

SUITE DU PROCÉDÉ L. BRAILLE MUSIQUE.

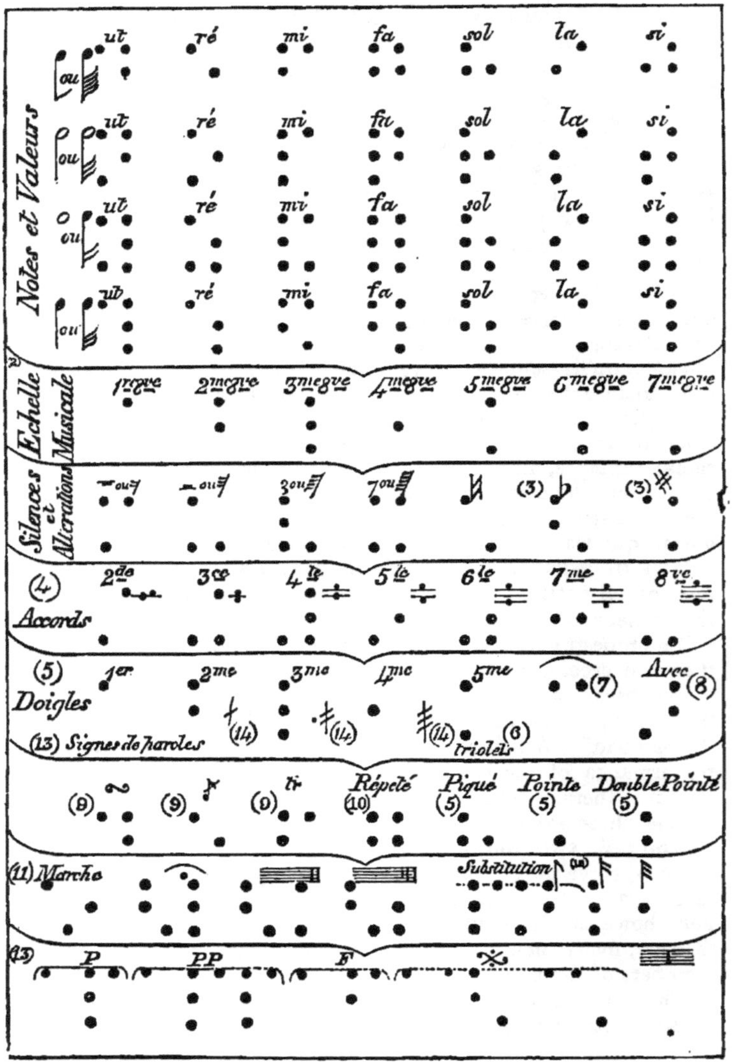

Their chief writes the notes of the *morceau* to be performed in Braille's system of pointed notation; reads with his finger from the raised music the first bar of the score of the first and second violins, which is taken up by the blind pupil, who produces the bar upon his instrument. Thus the master is enabled to judge whether it has been properly understood. He does the same with the second violin, the altos, and the bass, and for the other instruments. The bar or movement is then played in concert, and the proper time and measure determined upon. The next bar is studied in the same manner, and so on throughout the piece.

At the next rehearsal he continues his instruction, and then puts together the various morceaux that have been learned during the two sittings, superintending the practice and rehearsal of the entire orchestra until it is able, by memory, to perform the " motive " with precision.

" It is with difficulty that seeing players can be brought to understand how the executants remember their different parts, know when to stop, and where again to resume their accompaniment — how each instrument and each part are completely under control, and how they succeed in proper time and proper measure. All is done with a precision and an enthusiasm seldom witnessed in an orchestra of seeing performers, spite of the bâton of its leader or the well-written score of each instrumentalist. It is precisely because the blind need not this assistance, and require neither bâton nor music to read from, that they play with precision and correctness and reproduce their several parts with feeling and spirit."

The difference between blind and seeing musicians is now pretty well understood. The blind are obliged to learn by heart all the music they attempt to play, whilst the seeing often execute at sight. The first, though they may play little, are conversant with every portion of their study and well grounded in its theory; whilst the second read rapidly and execute fluently, but may understand or retain little of what they so hastily acquire.

III. THE INDUSTRIAL WORK OF THE PUPILS is best explained by reference to the objects exhibited at the Exhibition in class 89. They consist of baskets, various specimens of turnery, string-making, chair and cane work, knitting, netting, and the usual trades and employments of the blind. These specimens are very well and neatly executed, though the work of the blind girls takes the lead in excellence and finish. Many objects of turnery are worthy of notice, particularly a pair of candlesticks, a pair of cups (St. Lucie), a pair of ebony candlesticks (Louis XVI.), a pair of antique

Mr. E. C. JOHNSON ON MEANS FOR INSTRUCTION OF THE BLIND.

Difference between blind and seeing musicians.

Industrial work of the school.

Mr. E. C.
JOHNSON
ON MEANS
FOR
INSTRUC-
TION OF THE
BLIND.

ebony cups, and several wooden cigar cases. The work of the girls includes every variety of tricot, crotchet, and needlework, all excellent of their kind ; whilst chessboards, embossed playing cards, and tablets for marking cards complete the catalogue.

One peculiar feature of this exhibition is its historical nature. M. Guadet, the Chef d'Enseignement, has collected together a most interesting museum of all the appliances and apparatus used in the instruction of the blind since the middle of the last century, arranged in the following order :—

Writing machines.—Haüy's handguide, 1784; Heilman (a blind man) handguide, 1788; Gatteaux, engraved plate for teaching formation of letters, 1794; De Pongus, handguide ; Becke (blind man), handguide, 1852 ; Fournier (blind man), handguide ; Challons, process of writing in relief; Guerault (blind), plan for directing the fingers; Duvigneau (blind) handguide ; Bruno, handguide, 1854 ; Dufau, regulating slate; Gall, Edinburgh typhlographe ? Hurtlendy (blind), typhlographe ; Bird (blind), typhlographe; Masse (blind), typhlographic slate; Balleu (blind), key typograph; Hughes, typograph; Levitte, typograph of Hughes adapted to the use of the French language; Schiott, typograph ; Braille, reglette for writing in the ordinary characters; Foucault (blind), instrument for writing in relief in the ordinary characters; Foucault (blind) perfected instrument ; Barbier, tabular system of writing, 1821, and other instruments; Braille (blind), three machines for printing in relief, pointed system; Fournier (blind), an instrument for writing on Braille's system ; Laas d'Agneu, arithmetical calculating instrument on a modified system of Braille, calculating boards.

Geographie.—Weissembourg, aveugle, carte géographique, 1810 ; Guillié, cartes géographique, 1819; Dufau, carte géographique, 1824 ; Laas d'Agneu, carte géographique, 1835, cartes géographique gravées, 1847 ; Levitte, cartes géographique, obtenues sur planches autographique, 1866 ; Levitte, quatre planches d'images en relief pour servir à l'étude de l'histoire naturelle ; David, un cerf et un éléphant plastiques, spécimens d'une collection des principaux types d'animaux réduits au dixième pour servir à l'étude de l'histoire naturelle, 1863 ; Pignier, figures géométriques, 1833 ; Levitte, planches autographiques pour l'impression des figures géométriques, 1867 ; Types de Haüy, Essai sur l'éducation des aveugles 1786 (relief noircé); catechisme de Paris (types abréviateurs); Guillié, notice historique sur l'instruction des jeunes aveugles, 1819 ; élémens de lecture, 1820 ; fantaisie pour la clarinette (specimen de notation musicale par lettres) 1831 ; Société Biblique, histoire ancienne, 1841 ; Philadelphie, solfège de Gauthier, 1841 ; Dufau, arithmétique de Dufau ; Barbier, specimen d'impression, 1827 ; Braille procédé pour écrire au moyen de points les paroles, la musique et le plain chant, 1829 ; Le même, deuxième édition corrigée, 1837 ; histoire naturelle ; methode de piano par Kalkbrenner ; group photographique de l'orchestre et du chœur de l'institution.

Travaux des Elèves. — Atelier de Filets : Epervier goujonnier de vingt mètres ; tambour à mailles carrées ; verreux ; bourriche.

Atelier d'empaillage et de camage des chaise.—Un Siège en paille ; un Siège en canne.

Atelier des Tourneurs.—Paire de flambeaux néo-grec (bois de rose). Paire de coupes (Sainte Lucie). Paire de flambeaux Louis XVI. (ébène). Paire de coupes antiques en ébéne, sur piedestaux en bois de rose. Deux porte cigarres fantaisie (ébéne). Ouvrages des filles : tricots divers, filets divers, crochet.

Guadet, L'Institut des Aveugles de Paris, son histoire et des procédés d'enseignement. L'Instituteur des Aveugles (8 vols).

Jeu de dames, jeu d'échec, jeu de cartes, tablette à marquer les cartes—à l'usage des aveugles.

Number of pupils at present in the school, 202—135 males, 67 females.

The points worthy of especial notice in connection with the Paris Blind School are three in number :—

1. Adoption of the system of Braille, both in printed books and as an ordinary mode of writing and embossing.

2. The musical instruction and the instrumental band.

3. The encouragement given to blind pianoforte-tuners and their advancement in the world.

The jury have awarded a gold medal to the Institution des Jeunes Aveugles ; silver medals to Mr. Guadet, Mdlle. Cailhe, and Mr. Siou, a blind pianoforte-tuner ; and a bronze medal to Mr. Levitte for his typograph of Hughes, adapted to the French language.

M. Colart Venoit has separately exhibited his machine (88) for enabling the blind to write music, Mr. Duvignau (89) his " guide main," Mr. Renaux (90) his " guide main " et " porte " plume encrier," and Mr. Sinet his " regulateur des mouvements des doigts."

The Blind School of Mulhouse has also sent specimens of its work to the Exhibition, a portion of which is shown in the Mulhouse cottage in the park, and the rest in the case

Mr. E. C.
JOHNSON
ON MEANS
FOR
INSTRUC-
TION OF THE
BLIND.

of the Paris blind school (87). The cane, straw, and mat work is worthy of attention, as well as the well-embossed books in Braille's system.

PRUSSIA.

Although the educational departments of North Germany are well represented in the Paris Exhibition, it is a matter of regret that the great blind institutions of that country have failed to exhibit any appliances for the education of their inmates. In the Prussian schoolhouse, which forms so interesting an object in the park, Mr. Hebold, of the blind school at Barley, exhibits a useful little machine by which the blind can write. It consists of a small desk in wood, a perforated line, which receives a pointed style. The mode of writing is best explained by a glance at the accompanying diagram (*see opposite*).

The great difficulty in this method of writing is to teach the blind the necessary form of the letters. The specimens of embossed books, published in Berlin, in the ordinary Roman capital letter, are well and clearly printed. They consist of primary elementary works, and are well adapted for schools. Their moderate size and price are also great recommendations.

WÜRTEMBERG.

One of the most interesting groups displayed under class 6, in the kingdom of Würtemberg, is the collection of embossed books by La Société Biblique de Stuttgardt. It consists of sixty-three volumes of the Bible embossed for the use of the blind, printed in Roman capital type, bound and numbered, price 130f. This collection was commenced in 1840 by the publication of the Gospel of St. Luke, and continued until the New Testament was complete, in 15 volumes, in the year 1859. In the spring of 1863 all the sacred book was embossed, and published in sufficient numbers to satisfy the demands of all the German blind schools.

The embossing was carried on at Stuttgardt until 1856, since which period M. Alphonse Kochlein, himself a blind man, has continued it at the school of Illzach, in Alsatia. Five thousand copies have already been printed—one thousand distributed in Würtemberg, and four thousand throughout the rest of Germany, particularly in Prussia, Saxony, Hanover, Bavaria, Switzerland, Alsatia; a complete copy being also sent to China. The society has sold most of its works at two-thirds of their cost, while the poor and deserving have received copies gratuitously. " The ordinary type in which " these bibles have been printed," says the official report, " is of great advantage to the blind, as they are thus taught

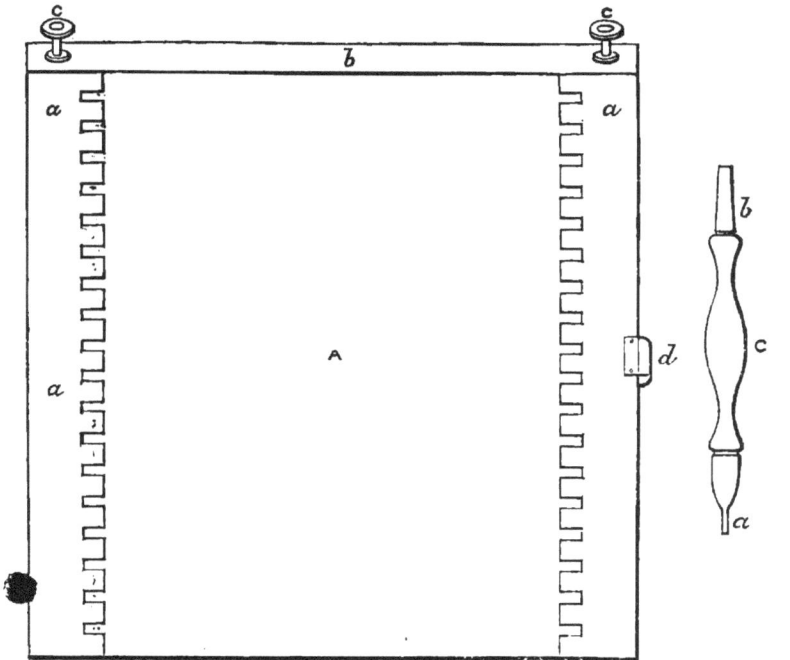

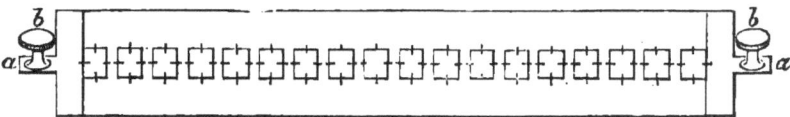

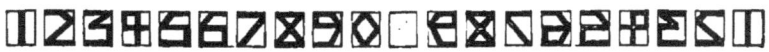

" in the same way as a seeing child. It has a great advan-
" tage over the system of Moon, a species of stenographic
" writing, like that of Braille, as instructors are not obliged
" to learn arbitrary characters." This library for the blind
received honourable mention at the last Exhibition at
Munich.

BELGIUM.

The Royal Institution for the Deaf, and Dumb, and Blind,
at Liège, is the only Belgian blind school represented at the
International Exhibition. Pupils are admitted between the
age of eight and 15, and day scholars are allowed to profit
by the advantages of the institution. A payment of 375f.
is required on admission for the poor, and 450f. for those
in a better condition of life. The education for the blind
consists of religious instruction, reading, writing, grammar,
arithmetic, geography, and music, &c. ; whilst that of the
deaf and dumb includes " la langue mimique " articulation-
drawing, modelling, and sculpture ; each scholar being
apprenticed to a trade. A night school for old pupils is likewise held within the building. In 1865 the establishment
contained 31 dumb boys and 16 girls, five blind boys and
four blind girls.

Dumb.—Twelve tailors, eight shoemakers, seven turners,
four printers, 16 workwomen.

Blind.—Three upholsterers, four straw-plaiters (boys),
four straw-plaiters (girls).

The straw-plaiting of the blind deserves some notice,
especially the well-made hats and caps, mats, and small
baskets. The tailoring of the dumb pupils is not, however,
to be compared to results shown in other foreign schools.

The exhibition is below par, when compared with that of
other countries, and lacks that care and completeness so
remarkable in the schools of France and Austria.

HOLLAND.

The Rotterdam Institution for the Blind is the only Dutch
school represented at the Paris Exhibition.

The display is so carelessly arranged, and so few details,
as to its organisation and object, are furnished to the jury,
that it becomes a matter of impossibility to decide as to its
actual condition and progress. A few embossed books, in
Moon's artificial characters, printed for the Dutch in
England by Mr. Moon, of Brighton, form the only appliances exhibited for instruction.

The industrial results include poor specimens of mats in
cocoa-fibre and rope, some fanciful flower-stands in round
canework ; baskets indifferently finished, coarse beadwork,
strung together by the female pupils ; large over-shoes made

of list, and a few brushes. The deaf and dumb have also contributed some very elementary specimens of drawing and modelling. It is evident that, throughout Holland, industrial occupation for the blind takes the lead in all their schools and asylums. The jury, therefore, awarded an honorary mention to the institution at Rotterdam, which has only been established since 1858, not so much for its exposed results as for its good intentions.

Mr. E. C.
Johnson
on Means
for
Instruc-
tion of the
Blind.

DENMARK.

The Institution for the Blind at Copenhagen is ill represented at the Paris Exhibition of 1867. This is a matter of some regret, as the institution has done, and still continues to do, much substantial good amongst the poor blind of Denmark. It is patronised by the Royal family and the State, and counts amongst its well-wishers and supporters Mr. Schott, Mr. Guldberg, Dr. Melchior, and Mr. Moldenhawer.

The institution was established in 1857, by a vote of the Folkething, under the direction of a council of five persons —three appointed by the State and two by the Philanthropic Society. It receives and educates 60 poor blind children between the ages of 10 and 12 years. A payment of nearly 40*l.* a year entitles the richer class to a share in the advantages of the charity. The blind school was opened on Nov. 6, 1858, and has made fair progress though the objects displayed are few, and for the most part unimportant, considering the position of the institution. They consist of specimens of embossed books, well executed in pointed lower-case Roman type, and cheap in price ; the specimen most worthy of notice being a new volume, " Study for the Violin by Spohr," printed at the school by blind embossers.

The following works have also been embossed in the Braille system :—For pianoforte : Sonatas of Kulhàn, Clementi ; fantaisies of Mozart, Haydn, Beethoven. Exercises of Czerny. Studies by Lomoine (work 97).

For violin : exercises of Rode and Kaiser.

There is, likewise, a sister institution in Denmark for " blind workers," which has received a considerable impetus since the opening of the blind school. Established by a charitable society called the " The Chain," in 1811, it has since held bazaars and opened shops for the sale of work executed by the blind. In connection with this charity a preparatory infant school for the blind has been founded, which promises to be a great success.

The specimens of geometrical and general diagrams embossed on paper by the male pupils are clear and well defined, and must be useful aids in the higher classes.

The writing-frame of Mr. C. E. Guldberg, for correspondence in the ordinary lower-case character by means of a pencil (the blind to correspond with the seeing), is the only apparatus exhibited. It is thus described by the inventor :—" A hand-" guide for writing with a pencil in the ordinary caligraphy " of the seeing." The writing, when reversed, is slightly in relief, but can only be useful in communicating with the seeing. The frame is composed of a little desk, with a slide, which moves from right to left, and *vice versâ*, between two parallel bars of wood. The moveable portion contains an angular and oval aperture, in which letters are formed with the point of the pencil. In this respect it resembles the instruments of Mr. Gall, of Scotland, and Mr. Hebold, of Prussia, and, in common with them, consists of " a hole " which changes in form by means of four slides in which " letters are formed." (*See opposite.*) It is very cheap (4s. 6d.), can easily be put into the pocket, and is useful for an expert blind man who has lost his sight late in life.

The opinion expressed of this machine by M. Guadet, Chef d'Instruction dans l'Ecole des Jeunes Aveugles à Paris, deserves to be mentioned :—" La machine de M. C. E. Guld-" berg procédé du typhlographe dont elle est une regularisa-" tion ingénieuse, mais aussi, il faut bien le dire, une " complication pousée à un assez haut degré."

There is no opportunity of judging as to the proficiency of the pupils of this school in manual occupations, though it is stated that basket-making and other trades are making progress.

ITALY.

Only two Italian blind schools are represented at the Paris Exhibition, those of Milan and Sienna.

MILAN. This school, under the direction of Signor Barozzi, is supported entirely by private charity. It is a fine building, situate in one of the best parts of the town, and contains 100 scholars, varying from the age of 10 to 45. It com-

bines a school for primary instruction, and a normal training school for masters, with pupil-teachers. A high degree of proficiency is attained, both in intellectual progress and manual labour, whilst the musical education has reached a

perfection almost equal to that of Paris. Its orchestra, conducted by a blind leader, numbers upwards of 40 executants, and is the great attraction of the establishment. The male pupils are mostly engaged in learning music and French, as manual instruction is made a secondary consideration. They

are, however, taught cordwork, the manufacture of nets, chainwork, brushes, baskets, embossed printing, and the

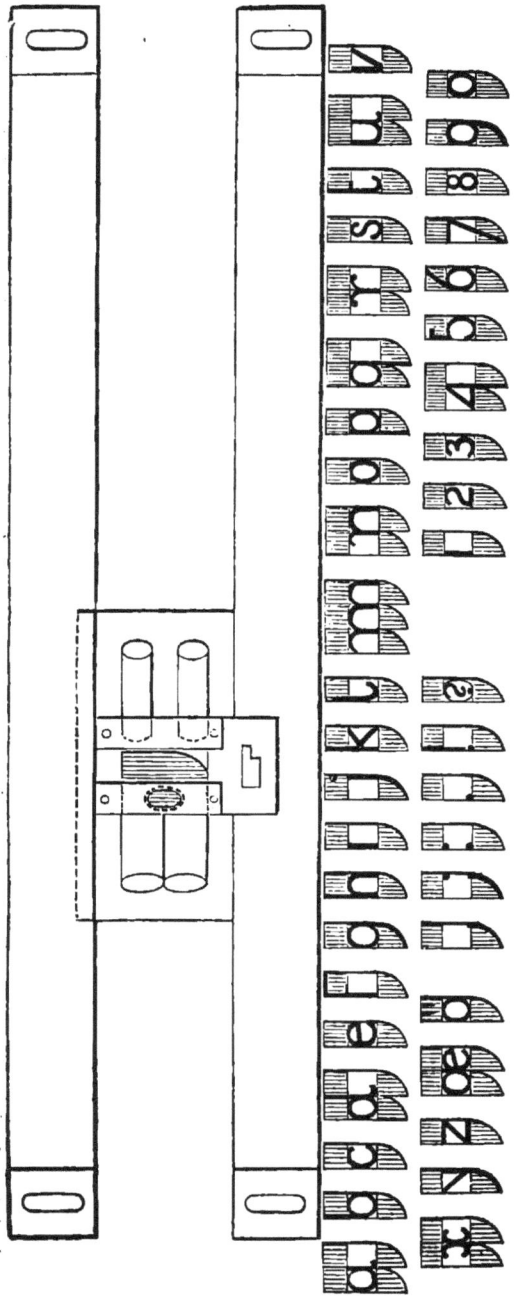

ABCDEFGHIJKLMNOPQRSTUUIJYZ
ÆØ

WRITING FRAME AND LETTERS.—MR. C. E. GULDBERG, OF COPENHAGEN.

Mr. E. C.
Johnson
on Means
for
Instruc-
tion of the
Blind.
weaving of elastic bandages. The females are employed in similar occupations, but more particularly in the manufacture of worsted carpets. A singular class is held by Signor Barozzi, in which he teaches the form and value of the different coinages of all countries. A well-chosen collection of embossed books, in the lower-case type, is exhibited, including a grammar, theory of reading, national stories, French grammar, selections from Italian authors, arithmetic, geography, principles of music, essay on writing.

Vensali
Cesari's
embossing
and writing
frame.
A collection of reports, contributed by Signor Michael Barozzi, contains ample accounts of the condition and management of the school. The embossing and writing frame invented by Vensali Cesari also finds a place here. It consists of a desk-frame fitted with a sliding bar, to which is attached a small moveable plate, with slides, somewhat resembling the machine of Mr. Guldberg, described in "Denmark." It is, however, of so complicated a nature that it can be but of little use except in the hands of an expert.

The specimens of basket-work, string, chair cane-bottoming, and slippers, merit especial attention, as they prove that industrial work is making considerable progress in Italy. The
Industrial
work.
most remarkable object, and one that has attracted the especial attention of the jury, is a handsome carpet, made in coloured worsted by a blind pupil of the establishment. It
Carpet.
is unlike those manufactured in England by the blind, being, in fact, a specimen of what is called "berlin-wool work," executed with a needle in stiches, on a moderately fine canvas. There are ten different colours blended into a beautiful design, worked from an embossed pattern on paper. The arrangement of the pattern is by numbers and points embossed on paper—the numbers standing for the colours, and points for the stitches.

The jury awarded the eighth silver medal to this school, which has only been established since 1840, and a bronze medal to the pupil who executed the carpet above referred to.

Sienna
Blind
School.
SIENNA.—The blind school at Sienna is entirely in the hands of a friar named Padre Pendola, and Signor Luigi Tofani. These two men have devoted their time and attention to the cause of the blind and deaf and dumb, and from their own private means, together with occasional help from the Government, have succeeded in carrying on their charitable work. At the present time sixty blind pupils are fed, lodged, clothed, and instructed in this school. The exhibition of results is not favourable when contrasted with the great school of Milan, yet it is worthy of notice as being the creation of these two gentlemen. Deaf and dumb children are

also lodged, clothed, and instructed in the same establishment; some of whose works have attracted attention, particularly the wood-carving, framework, and engraving, for which bronze medals have been awarded.

SWEDEN.

In the picturesque house allotted to the products of Sweden and Norway, in the park of the Exhibition, some very remarkable manufactures of the blind, and various educational instruments, are exhibited; amongst which, list-shoe work, string, knitting, and baskets may be mentioned, though for the most part clumsily but strongly made. Several embossed books are also exhibited in large lower-case and awkward-looking Roman type, each letter printed at great intervals, and occupying much space. The embossing, however, is sharp and well raised, and easily felt. There are also rough writing and calculating boards, in which arbitrary characters somewhat resembling the following are employed:— *Remarkable manufactures.* *Writing and calculating boards.*

$$\times \;\; \boxed{} \;\; \boxed{}\boxed{}$$

From the want of a proper attendant to explain the working of these frames, it was difficult to test their utility. One in particular consisted of a number of longitudinal and circular holes, ranged alternately, with type of corresponding dimensions, which, when fitted, denoted sentences, arithmetical sums, or algebraic figures. The board presents somewhat the following appearance,

$$\| \circ \| \circ \| \circ \| \circ \| \circ \| \circ \|$$

$$\| \circ \| \circ \| \circ \| \circ \| \circ \| \circ \|$$

and is not unlike the ordinary calculating-board used in the Alston Asylum at Glasgow. The maps and other writing-frames are of the pattern used in France, and therefore present no originality of design. The jury awarded a medal to this section, and was informed that a small blind school existed in Stockholm with a large parent institution in Christiana, under the direction of Messrs. Roggew and Angell.

SPAIN.

Two schools are represented from this country—viz., those of Madrid and Barcelona.

THE BLIND SCHOOL AT MADRID contains an equal number of blind and deaf and dumb pupils, under the superintendence *Madrid Blind School,* of M. Ballesteros, who, after much personal labour and indefatigable zeal, has obtained considerable success. The description of this charitable work is graphic and touching, and merits the reward it has attained.

He tells us that, " in 1834, he was touched by the wretched " condition of many poor blind beggars who infested the " streets of Madrid, and who shocked the ears of the passers- " by with their insulting language and disgusting bearing." Having had considerable experience in the education and treatment of the deaf and dumb, he determined to try his hand at the blind; and, in co-operation with the Société Economique de Madrid, partially educated some eight or ten blind children, at his own expense, in reading, writing, arithmetic, geometry, and geography. The Queen of Spain then gave her patronage to his school, and in 1836, 26,000 livres was voted for its maintenance. It appears that since that period suitable premises have been obtained in Madrid, and that all modern appliances have been introduced with complete success. Amongst the apparatus exposed in the

Exhibition are various writing and embossing frames used throughout France and England ; but, as they are not of Spanish invention, it will be unnecessary to describe them in detail. They indicate, however, a strong desire on the part of the Spanish Government to employ all available aid from other countries for the use of their own people. The ordinary Roman letter, and M. Braille's system of writing and printing, find equal favour in Spain. Several books on the former system are exhibited, well and cleverly embossed by the pupils of the school, particularly a " System of Musical Instruction for General Use." The books in Roman capital and lower-case character include some well-selected editions of standard authors in music, geography, and religion. The manufactures of the pupils are confined to the making of slippers, a few poor specimens of turnery, together with cord and string work. Music appears to form a considerable feature in the establishment, though it has not attained to so high a position as at the Barcelona school.

Some of the works supplied by the deaf and dumb inmates of the same establishment are worthy of notice; to which, and the products of the blind, the jury awarded honourable mention.

THE BLIND SCHOOL OF BARCELONA.—It would be difficult for a stranger to judge of the working of this school by a casual inspection of the very poor specimens of manual work exhibited at the Exhibition. There are many embossing frames of French and English design, some good books, printed in raised lower-case type, arithmetic boards, specimens of embossed correspondence, and musical composition. A violin, manufactured by one of the blind pupils, is by far the most curious of "les travaux d'élèves;" whilst the worsted and string work is insignificant when compared with those exhibited by the blind of other countries.

The author feels that he cannot do better than quote from one of his own works[*] the personal impressions which he received whilst visiting this school a few years ago in company with his blind friend, the late Viscount Cranborne, whose untimely death was a sad loss to the indigent blind of England.

At that period the school of Barcelona had made great progress in the musical instruction of the blind, and had produced some remarkable musicians. It may be said to have given the impulse to the London School for the Indigent Blind in the formation of their orchestra of blind musicians, which has since been so peculiar and interesting a feature in that establishment.

"During the summer of 1854 I visited the blind school of Barcelona, the most complete of its kind throughout Spain, and was much pleased and astonished at the progress made in the education of the blind, The school is situated in the Platza Santa Anna, in an old convent, which has been allotted by the Government to the uses of the Corporation of Barcelona, who have established there a very large school, divided into several sections, for the general instruction of the children of young and of more advanced ages, and likewise for those afflicted with partial or total blindness. Unlike charitable schools in other countries, it is devoted exclusively to mental and musical instruction, neither food nor clothing being found; whilst the attendance, not being compulsory, is somewhat irregular, the number of pupils depending greatly on caprice, the state of the weather, or extraneous circumstances. The hours of attendance are nominally from nine to twelve and from three to six, with several intermissions on fête days and holidays, which, being of frequent occurrence in so Catholic a country as Spain, makes it difficult for visitors to find both masters and pupils at work.

" The establishment will accommodate a large number of scholars, though there are but about sixty or eighty blind pupils, who attend irregularly. Forty-five to fifty males and twelve to fourteen females is the ordinary number that can be got together, except on particular occasions. The

MR. E. C. JOHNSON ON MEANS FOR INSTRUCTION OF THE BLIND.

Report of visit in 1854.

---

[*] "An Inquiry into the Musical Instruction of the Blind in France, Spain, and America," by E. C. Johnson, Esq.

3.

Mr. E. C.
Johnson
on Means
for
Instruc-
tion of the
Blind.

locale is very Spanish, being fragrant with the fumes of garlic, and very al fresco as regards furniture and school accommodation. On the boys' side there are several small cells, once the sleeping-chambers of bygone friars, but now devoted to the practising on one or other of the many musical instruments on which the pupils are taught. There are three larger rooms for the masters, who give separate instruction to their various classes in music—that being the chief feature in the education—a greater portion of time being devoted to its acquirement than to anything else. Indeed, as far as the males are concerned, there is little else in which they are proficient. The head master or director of the school spoke French, and therefore was enabled to carry on a conversation with me. I attended his class of instruction in the morning and was astonished at the proficiency of his pupils. He began to teach a portion of a mass by Palestrina, and had, ere I left, almost succeeded in perfecting them in the task. This little troop consisted of two violins, a cornet, clarinet, French horn, and two flutes. The music was called out by the professor : those who understood notes or written music being told the notes they were to produce, others only taking up the air by ear. Little is done to teach the full theory of music, though in a few instances it has been done ; and it is now in contemplation to effect so desirable an end more generally. The acute ear of the Spaniard and his innate love of music seem here doubly developed, and to become a source of unceasing amusement. There is a degree of cheerfulness and vivacity about the Spanish blind which surprised me ; they seem less helpless than their northern brothers in affliction, whilst their gaiety of manner is no doubt dependent on the vivacity of the national character. Their deportment is very Spanish, and they possess a self-confidence and a nobleness of bearing seldom found among the inmates of similar schools in other parts of Europe. They appear to belong chiefly to the lower orders, though some are well dressed and clean, while others forcibly reminded me of the acute, handsome, and sunburnt subjects immortalised by the brush of Murillo. The two under masters also gave instruction in music, and in the other branches of education ; whilst a very intelligent priest attended to the moral and religious training of the little community.

" The music is not only read to the younger pupils, but intoned by the masters, whilst many of the learners write down on paper, by means of the frame and style of M. Braille (the French dotted system), the notes they have to commit to memory. Great care is taken that part music shall form

the chief subject of instruction, as the directors wisely foresee that if the blind are taught to play out of class, they will
only, in after life, become itinerant street-players, and crowd
the town as beggars. Many pupils write fluently on the
Braille system, though there seems a great objection to its
free adoption, arising from its arbitrary character; and they
only wait the arrival of machines from England to commence
work with our ordinary writing-frame. No trade or other
manual employment is taught amongst the males; and,
indeed, it is feared that they would be little inclined to avail
themselves of such instruction if offered to them. It is,
however, in contemplation to establish a more permanent
school, after our English models, when it is expected that
the Government and municipality will not only help it with
funds, but will cause the pupils to be instructed in industrial
work. At present the Spanish Government only affords the
building, the town furnishing the necessary means of carrying on the schools.

"The most intelligent male pupil was one Casa Pugiberti,
twenty-one years of age, and blind from birth. He had
been three years under instruction—wrote well both prose
and music—played on two instruments—was well informed
—and of rather a better rank of life than his fellows. He
appeared much delighted at the visit of an Englishman, and
was very grateful for the interest taken in his doings.

"The female portion of the school was on a much smaller
scale than the male. The instruction was conducted by a
mistress, whose sole duties consisted in teaching her pupils
knitting, making beadwork, sewing, and netting. A peculiar
manufacture of gimp was carried on by one pupil which, I
think, might be introduced into our English schools with
advantage. It seemed to be very easily and quickly performed, and to be a pleasant work. One old woman was
very dexterous with her fingers, and threaded her needle
with her tongue, as other blind persons frequently do. The
priest above-mentioned instructed the females in what seemed
to be a mere repetition of prayers and hymns, and the topo-
graphy of the town. But he had made some excellent raised
maps in wood and cardboard, and has thus taught his pupils
to find their way amongst the intricate and narrow streets
of Barcelona. There seemed to be an indisposition to introduce embossed books; though, after a long conversation
with this priest, which was interpreted by a gentleman, a
member of the municipality of Barcelona, he appeared to
concur in my views of a literature for the blind, and begged
me to send him some type from England, that he might
print books on religious subjects in the Roman capital letter.
This has since been carried out.

Mr. E. C.
Johnson
on Means
for
Instruc-
tion of the
Blind.
 " The great evil of the whole institution is the admission of cases not totally blind. The same objection holds good here as in England ; as the seeing lead the blind into mischief, and rather trust to what little sight is yet left to them, than to proper oral and manual instruction. Some of the cases possessed a considerable amount of sight, whilst others were completely blind; the blind, as usual, being the more patient and persevering, and becoming the chief proficients in their art.

" The band consisted of twenty-three blind musicians— viz., ten violins, two contrabassi, two clarinets, two horns, two cornets, two flutes, one trumpet, one fife, and one drum. The selection of music consisted of lively airs and operatic morceaux, which were performed with great regularity and precision. The performance of a boy of ten years of age on the flute and the fife was very surprising and perfect of its kind ; whilst the violins and cornets were handled in a manner that did the players great credit. The band was conducted by the chief professor, who beat time on a piece of board, occasionally walking amongst his blind pupils, and giving oral instruction as he passed. I received the very greatest attention and civility from the Court of Directors, all members of the municipality of Barcelona, none of whom had ever seen a blind school out of their own country, and who were therefore anxious to have the opinion of any one at all connected with a foreign school."

AMERICA.

America.
Dr. Howe's
literature
for the
blind.
Dr. Howe, of Boston, has contributed specimens of his literature for the blind, printed in what is called American character, viz.—small lower-case type. His books are so clearly and beautifully printed, and the texts so well chosen, that it would be difficult to speak in too high terms of his collection. The number of volumes, and the full description of Dr. Howe's labours, were so fully recorded in the report of the juries of our first Exhibition, that it will be unnecessary to recapitulate them here. The jury of 1867 have, however, marked their sense of Dr. Howe's valuable labours in the cause of the blind by according to him, as director of the Boston school, a silver medal.

ENGLAND.

England,
almost un-
represented.
England, which is so rich in institutions for the blind, is almost unrepresented at the Exhibition. This is attributable to a want of harmony and concert amongst the various schools and societies in England ; to the dread of intrusting their interests to other hands than their own ; and to the

opposition which is so strong an element amongst the lovers of particular systems for teaching the blind to read. Neither the noble School for the Indigent Blind at Southwark, with its 200 pupils, its grand tradal resources, and its wonderful educational appliances, nor Miss Gilbert's society, with its host of blind workers, have thought proper even to apply for space in the Exhibition building; while the St. John's-wood and Bristol blind schools are nowhere to be found in class 89. This omission has placed the English blind in a very unfavourable position on the Continent.

Two exhibitors have however feebly proclaimed the nakedness of the land. They occupy Nos. 4 and 8 in the catalogue and have been passed over by the jury as unworthy of special praise.

No. 4. James Gray.—A map in relief for the blind, consisting of an ordinary printed wall-map, with the divisions of the countries, counties, rivers, &c. marked with different sized string, gummed on the paper. As the work of a blind man, it is curious and interesting.

It has been remarked that Tangible Geography seems to have made but very little progress of late years. Although a blind man may gain a tolerably correct idea of space, form, and even colour, few attain a marked proficiency in it. The resources, position, and size of countries can be mentally appreciated; but the reduction of large tracts of country to the small scale of a map baffles the blind man more than any other study. The question arises whether he can at all realise by touch, or take in mentally, what the seeing conceive when looking on a flat painted surface. Amongst the English blind this is far from the fact; they learn the names of cities, districts, mountains, and rivers, but fail to carry in their mind's eye the whole scheme of a diagrammatised country. In the writer's experience, founded on the observation of the habits of a very large blind school, instruction in mental geography is far more useful than even the simplest of raised maps.

No. 8. Milford's apparatus includes a "New and Easy Method of Reading for the Blind," in Roman characters, on a vertical system; and a "Hand-Guide for Writing."

" In this system," says the author, " the reading is down-
" wards, the letters being arranged like figures, one under
" the other; the words being separated, as usual, by spaces.
" If the word does not finish at the bottom of the column it
" will continue on to the next. The blind reader, when he
" gets to the bottom of a column, will run his finger up the
" channel made by the rows of letters, which will guide him

MR. E. C. JOHNSON ON MEANS FOR INSTRUCTION OF THE BLIND.

James Gray's map.

Tangible geography.

Mr. Milford's vertical system of reading.

" without difficulty to the next. Feeling the letters from " the top, they are more easily recognised from the side."

Mr. Milford tells us that the vertical system is proposed because it possesses mechanical aids in a greater degree than any other known plan.

" 1st. The letters, on this system, are always at equal distances from one another; also, the spaces between the words are alike.

" 2nd. Each page will contain the same number of columns throughout the book. These will be found great helps to the reader.

" 3rd. According to the present system of reading in horizontal lines, the motion of the hand to and from the body is fatiguing; upon the vertical or downward plan, it would be much reduced and more natural, therefore less fatiguing, the arm having little or no motion from the body.

" 4th. The sensitiveness of the feeling is impeded by the side motion, the edge (or less sensitive part) of the finger coming first in contact with the letters. In the vertical plan the forefinger would be employed alone; and this finger, I think, will be allowed by all to be the most sensitive. At the same time the top of the finger would come directly over the whole letter, which would therefore be the more easily recognised, no other letter touching it on either side.

" 5th. In the horizontal system, when Roman characters are used, the letters are approached sideways—the most difficult for recognition. In the vertical plan the letters are approached from the top—the most easy of recognition. This I consider a great advantage over the side motion in many of the letters—such as B, D, E, F, I, K, L, M, N, H, R, U. These, when approached sideways, would at first appear like i's to the touch, on account of their straight sides. As an instance of a small letter, take *m*; the first line to a blind man (reading horizontally) might appear to be *r*; he then moves on to the second, which will make it appear an *n*; and it is not till he feels the third arm or stroke that he knows it to be an *m*; whereas with the downward motion the bows would have been felt at one and the same time. The same may be said of most other letters.

" Some people will say this is all quickly done; but no matter how quickly, still it has to be done, and a blind person reading will only pass one bow at a time, and his mind must add together the several sensations before he can ascertain the letter. But in approaching from the top the letters are more easily recognised and more quickly felt by the most sensitive part of the fore finger."

" Any other type may be printed on this system with advantage and any abbreviations may be introduced."

MR. E. C.
JOHNSON
ON MEANS
FOR
INSTRUC-
TION OF THE
BLIND.

SPECIMEN OF PRINTING.

T	H	V	
H	E	I	T
E		N	H
	G	G	E
E	R		
L	E	W	C
E	A	O	R
P	T	N	E
H	E	D	A
A	S	E	T
N	T	R	I
T			O
	L	I	N
T	I	N	

Mr. Milford deserves considerable credit for his philanthropic views, particularly as he is a champion for the use of the ordinary type of the seeing. His books are well and clearly printed, and the type used is of the same form as first introduced by the Rev. W. Taylor of Worcester, in printing some of his early books for the blind at the press of Messrs. Taylor, Queen-street, Lincoln's-inn-fields.

Mr. Milford is not so happy in his writing machine for the blind. It is too large and expensive to be of practical utility in ordinary blind schools. His telegraphs for the deaf and dumb are, on the other hand, very useful little instruments, and both portable and moderate in price.

REPORT on LIBRARIES and APPARATUS used in the IN-
STRUCTION of ADULTS.—(Class 90.)—By the Rev. M.
MITCHELL, M.A., and one of Her Majesty's Inspectors
of Schools.

IN reporting on the special objects exhibited in Class 90
of the Paris Exposition considerable difficulties are experienced, as in reality the principal subjects of the class are
not such as come under class exhibits. Libraries and
material for the instruction of adults, whether in the family,
the workshop, or societies, differ in no respect from the
libraries of ordinary life, or the materials of ordinary school
teaching. Every adult who is ignorant must be taught as an
ignorant child is taught, and with the same material and by
the same processes. Every educated adult of the working
classes will make use of the same books as other educated
people, either for the pursuit of such special branch of knowledge as he may require, for general education or for pleasure.
There is, therefore, no special peculiarity for working class
education. This report, then, will be confined mostly to
relations on the progress of education amongst the working
class; the statistics of the several counties that have exhibited, as far as I have been able to secure them; reports on
the societies for mutual education of each State, the progress
that has been made, the establishments formed, and in some
cases of artistic production, the results obtained. I shall
show what other nations are actually doing, by what means
they propose success, what are the actual results, why some
people succeed in a certain progress, why others are kept
back, either retrograding, or not making those advancements
which the age and general spirit of the time require.

It is especially important that England should address
itself to this knowledge, as an opinion prevails that the last
ten years have not developed so much artistic and mechanical
power in our manufactures as has been the case amongst
other nations. A very deep feeling pervades the minds of
many of the jurors of classes that the education given in
other countries, specially adapted to manufacturing life, is
very much more extensive and very much more real and
suitable than is to be obtained amongst ourselves, and that it
would be well for us to examine what is the best in other
countries, that we may adopt their excellencies and remedy
our own defects.

REV. M.
MITCHELL
ON
LIBRARIES,
&c.

The true
education of
England.

In such examinations jealousy on either side should be carefully avoided; and if we, comparing ourselves only with ourselves, are not always wise, yet we should remember that a depreciation of English art and education from mere inspection of the Paris Exposition may lead to very unjust conclusions. The intelligence of a country is not altogether best displayed in exhibitions. Certain excellent qualities, no doubt, are developed; certain arts and manufactures; certain qualifications and teachings; but the spirit and power of a nation, the development of its mental activity, its force and strength, are best shown in the energy of its people, ramifying into all parts of the globe; in its extensive and numerous factories, in its exports and imports, in the admiration of other States for its institutions, in its power of self-government and control, by the conduct of the people when in masses, and by the numerous daily and weekly journals supplied to an ever-increasingly intellectual population such as no other State can show. These real results of education are worth a thousandfold more than all the copy-books or artistic drawings in the world. These evidence a people by no means uninstructed in the higher and more elevated moral and civil duties of citizenship; and that country cannot be said to be indifferently taught whose people, for the most part, have inwardly grafted within them the idea that respect for law and self-control in the subject are of more consequence to a State than power in the prince or ruler.

Still, there is much yet to be done before we ought to rest contented. A work has been commenced, progress has been made, the nobler branches of education as a rule, have been acquired—the higher parts of the law. Why should the mint and cummin be neglected? And if our trade suffers from the want of art-education, as is generally thought by those that ought to think; *i.e.*, people who really understand the matter—it will be surely wise not to blind ourselves to the fact, but to take all possible means to remove the stigma.

The president of the Institute of Civil Engineers at the dinner of that society last May, stated:—" I am reluctantly " compelled to admit that in machinery a more rapid ad- " vance towards excellence and a greater number of new and " successful combinations have been made by foreigners " during the last ten years than by the people of this " country." And the special correspondent of the *Times* (May 13) reports that " at the French Exhibition the French, " the Austrians, and the Belgians have not only come up to " us, but have beaten us in ironwork. In textile fabrics a

" similar inglorious tale has to be told. In our woollens we
" show scarcely any advance, and in our silk manufacture we
" have decidedly retrograded."

Viewed in the light of exhibiting the vast reading powers
of the nation, we may point to that large collection of daily
and weekly journals, a single number of each of which
occupies so conspicuous a place in the English department.
It tells a great tale, the number of thousands of every sort of
paper, with political and scientific, and, in fact, all knowledge
thus scattered broadcast through the length and breadth of
the land ; and it affords no small proof of the actual morality
of the nation that, of all this vast number of journals, the
very smallest minimum alone is found that infringes the rules
of morality or inculcates doctrines subversive of Government
or good order.

Among these journals, perhaps the one of most educational
value is the *Illustrated London News.* The advantage of
aiding the description through the picture is so great that
one might conceive that, by aid of this journal, anyone of
ordinary sense, however secluded, but able to read, might
perfect his knowledge himself, and in the course of years
have picked up more acquaintance with every subject of
information than in the last century even the literary classes
could obtain. It is gratifying to state that this periodical is
extensively circulated amongst their schools by the clergy
of all denominations.

This report on Class 90 is necessarily very imperfect ; circumstances rendered it impossible to complete it satisfactorily.
There were great difficulties, in many cases, in discovering
the exhibits and in finding the proper persons to display and
explain their merits; and thus many valuable objects have
been, perhaps, unfortunately omitted. Our report relates,
also, to little except the expositions of the chief European
countries. The Asiatic and African contributions are not
numerous, nor those of America ; while the languages of
Turkey and Greece preclude the ordinary visitor from
deriving any other pleasure than that of curiosity to see the
productions of each country. I shall take the exhibition in
its order of place in the building, beginning with France and
ending with Great Britain.

It will be found that considerable similarity of motive
actuates all the authorities and all branches of society among
continental nations. They all use one word, " progress;"
they all endeavour to extend education amongst the people,
to all its members, and to improve that education in all its
forms and subjects ; they are not content with the minimum,
they demand and enforce the maximum ; they suffer no

class jealousies to interfere; they believe in education, and they confirm their belief by the testimony of its good results —of the moral as well as intellectual advancement of their several peoples.

FRANCE.

The French Education Department of the Exposition counts 500 exposants; it 1862 it counted 180; and on this occasion twice as many sought admission in vain. This branch of the Exhibition establishes two grand facts:—1. Great progress in the last five years; and, 2. Much greater to be expected from present institutions for the future.

While the buildings and materials of instruction have increased and improved, the instruction itself has not remained stationary. Its subjects have been enlarged by making instruction compulsory in several branches to this date only recommended, and by the better methods of teaching now introduced. Instruction is given in agriculture, and horticulture, and gymnastics; but more particularly has it advanced in respect to adult education, only lately offered to those who either by their own or parents' fault or exigencies have grown up in ignorance; and in its higher branches also to those desirous further to improve their minds. The recent introduction of living languages, of commercial geography, of laws relative to workmen, and of industrial economy, will give an immense impetus to education all through the country.

In respect to art schools, the workmen comprehend no less than the masters that the destiny of one part, at least, of their occupation depends upon the superiority of their taste, and it is the strength of this shared opinion of workman and employer that has compelled the foundation of technical schools to supply the inefficiency of apprenticeship.

The object of this technical teaching is to prepare for a certain profession or trade, &c. It is, in fact, an apprenticeship. Education, however, is little without books; hence the foundation of libraries. There are 8,000 in France, lending 500,000 volumes a year, attached to communal schools. These are supported by the State, and aided by the exertions of individual societies.

Many publishers have commenced issuing very cheap, excellent libraries adapted to this use. They include most of the classical works of their own language, together with many translations from Greek, German, Roman, and English authors.

A very important step is in progress in France, through the influence and position of M. Duruy, the Minister of

Public Instruction, to whom France already owes so much.
He found that the French language was unknown in many
districts of France, whose inhabitants speak only a patois,
entirely their own. He now requires that French shall be
taught in all the schools. Again, he has considered that
France is bordered by several nations, and he is taking steps
to have the teaching of the neighbouring language in each
communal school. Thus the east and north learn German :
the south, Italian and Arabic ; the west, Spanish ; and the
north-west and seacoasts, English. It is a great satisfaction
that France possesses so enlightened a Minister, and to know
that he will not be thwarted by the feeling either of the
ruler or the people in developing his noble plans ; for France
has begun to believe in free trade, and to act on that belief.
Free trade is commercial rivalry and contest, and the crown
of victory will be gained by that people whose industrials are
the most intelligent and laborious.

Very ample reports of the state of education in France,
in four volumes of most complete and well-arranged statistics,
leave nothing to desire in respect to information upon its
condition. Elegantly-bound copies of these and former publications of the Minister of Public Instruction will be found
in the educational French department. They contain accurate
accounts of each of the sixteen academies, extended over the
whole of the country ; maps also of educational progress,
similar to one originally produced for our own country by the
late Mr. Fletcher, Her Majesty's inspector of British schools,
which once attracted so much attention.

It appears that in the 37,510 communes of France there
are 694 which possess no school ; but considerable progress
is being made to fill up this gap, as in the last two years
schools have been built in 162 communes. Altogether in the
same period there have been erected in France 1,202 schools,
and 135,014 pupils have been added to her scholars.

After inquiries, it has been ascertained that of the 4,000,000
children, between 7 and 13 years of age, rather less than
700,000 do not attend primary schools ; in 1865 it was
found that 440,000 received no instruction at all, so that
250,000, in round numbers, have received instruction either
at home or in establishments of secondary instruction, or
from illness, &c., were incapacitated, or, perhaps, were only
just seven, or had left school before 13 years of age.

In 1865 the half of the children attended the whole year
at the schools.

On Dec. 15, 1866, there were 28,546 evening classes. In
the last year 600,000 adult scholars attended these classes,

of whom more than half either acquired entirely or completed the elementary education given in the primary schools. To establish the necessity for adult schools the Minister, M. Duruy, obtained statistics which proved that the mean for all France of those who did not sign their names at marriage was for men 25·88 per cent. ; for women, 41·02— the general mean being 33·45 per cent., or as nearly as possible one-third of the population. But in certain departments the number amounts to 51, 61, 67 per cent. men, and 75 to 80 per cent. women in that deplorable state. The Minister winds up an admirable resumé by detailing improvements in course of being effected, which will enable every subject of the empire to attain education, at least as far as primary instruction is concerned—that power so equally indispensable for all moral excellence as for all professional progress.

Duties of the State.
On the Administration, he adds, devolves the care of multiplying normal schools, of ameliorating instruction, of perfecting the methods, of rendering the teaching more practical, producing better results, increasingly adapted to the wants of the rural populations, and more especially to elevate the schools for girls from the inferior position they at present hold ; for these young girls will be one day mothers, and it is upon the knees of the mother that the child receives its first best lessons. The report is divided into two parts, 1, public ; 2, free education.

Part 1. State education.
Part 1. Public or State Education. — The number of schools in the communes in 1865 was 38,629 :—

Held by laymen	- 19,044	} Boys.
By congregationists	- 1,907	
By laymen	- 14,469	
By lay-females	- 1,647	} Mixed.
By female congregationists	- 1,099	

—	Schools.	Boys.		Girls.		Total.
		Paying.	Gratuitous.	Paying.	Gratuitous.	
Ecoles Laiques	35,560	1,176,491	512,778	236,902	76,869	2,003,049
Ecoles Congregationists }	3,069	113,634	208,570	18,509	7,901	420,614
Total -	38,629	1,290,125	793,348	255,411	84,770	2,423,654

The number of teachers equals the number of schools.

The number of girls' schools is 14,721; Laiques, 6,399; Congregationists, 8,322.

	Number of Children.		Total.
	Paying.	Gratuitous.	
Laiques - - - -	222,923	114,381	337,304
Congregationists - -	342,723	373,861	716,584
Total - - -	565,646	488,242	1,053,888

The congregationist schools are those conducted by religious bodies; and these tables show that two-thirds of the girls are included in these schools, while only one-tenth of the boys attend them.

The number of infant schools is 2,484; 567 under laymen, 1,917 by religieuses :—

	Boys.		Girls.		Total.
	Paying.	Gratuitous.	Paying.	Gratuitous.	
Laiques - -	8,014	30,151	8,394	24,288	70,847
Congregationists -	27,532	106,940	30,617	108,452	273,541
Total - -	35,546	137,091	39,011	132,740	344,388

The total expense of primary instruction amounts to 70,405,125f. 25c. The 25c., about 2½d., is amusing after 70,000,000f. Towards this expense the payment of scholars has been ;—

		Francs.
Boys, or mixed	- -	- 14,351,287·43
Girls	- - -	- 4,913,225·15
Infants	- - -	- 351,666·16
Adults	- - -	- 348,883·98
Total -	-	- 19,965,062·72

i.e., in round numbers, about 800,000*l.* out of the 2,800,000*l.* of the whole.

For ordinary expenses—

	Francs.
The communes have furnished	- 15,943,534·32
The departments - - -	- 4,503,575·06
The State - - -	- 4,108,881·06

And for extraordinary expenses—

The communes - - -	9,800,034·23
The departments - - -	1,036,714·69
The State - - - -	2,066,364·99

The remainder is provided by legacies, donations, &c.

Part 2.
Private
education.

Part 2. Free schools, or not connected with the State, there were in the year 1865—Boys, 2,979; mixed, 541 : Total, 3,510. Of these 2,864 are conducted by laymen, 646 by congregationists. They are attended by :—

	Boys.		Girls.		Total.
	Paying.	Gratuitous.	Paying.	Gratuitous.	
Laiques - -	123,271	10,101	3,096	803	137,271
Congregationists -	34,757	55,190	728	1,298	91,973
Total - -	158,028	65,291	3,824	2,101	229,244

Girls schools :—

	No.	Paying.	Gratuitous.	Total.
Laiques - - - -	6,983	266,881	19,028	285,909
Congregationists - -	5,856	287,037	156,738	443,775
Total - - -	12,839	553,918	175,766	729,684

Infant schools :—

	No.	Boys.		Girls.		Total.
		Paying.	Gratuitous.	Paying.	Gratuitous.	
Laiques - -	396	7,885	2,233	7,403	1,940	19,461
Congregationists	692	10,026	15,474	11,341	18,078	54,919
Total -		17,911	17,707	18,744	20,018	74,380

Of 4,436,470 children who have attended school, 2,826,952 have paid, and 1,609,518 been received freely or gratuitous. In 1865, 657,401 children left school, of these—

Did not know how to read and write -	91,170
Could read and write only - -	170,838
In addition, knew arithmetic - -	286,202
Had general instruction - -	109,191
Total - - -	657,401

Of these, the two first classes, making a total of 218,602 or 34 per cent., *i.e.*, one-third of the whole, receive so little instruction that in a few years they will have forgotten all they ever learnt.

To diminish this ignorance adult schools are now much encouraged, and have made extraordinary progress. In 1863-4 there were 5,623 schools ; on January 1, 1867, they amounted to 28,546, *i.e.*, an increase of four-fifths.

The most enlightened populations of France are those bordering the Rhine ; the least instructed those of Brittany, the centre, the Landes, and Corsica.*

The reports upon these adult schools have been lately thus summed up by M. Duruy, Minister of Public Instruction, at the distribution of prizes awarded by the Polytechnic Institution. It appears that 40,000 teachers have opened 32,383 evening schools, at which 830,000 adults attended. More than a third of that number were absolutely illiterate, or very nearly so ; 23,000 only left the schools in nearly the same state of ignorance as when they entered ; but all the others— that is, more than 800,000—acquired the elements of knowledge. Nearly 13,000 teachers gave their gratuitous services ; 9,000 spent out of their own pockets a sum of 235,000f. to promote the undertaking ; 10,000 municipal councils granted funds during the present year ; and the total amount obtained, exclusive of the State subsidy, was 1,860,287f. Having stated the methods of examination, he observed, writing, orthography, and arithmetic are in progress, and so are morals ; for these young men, for the greater part, consented to stand the test of examination only from a grateful feeling towards their teachers. M. Duruy further observed that, owing to various causes, but especially to popular instruction, the moral habits of the population have greatly improved. (*Times*, Friday, May 24, 1867.)

After thus reviewing the whole state of education in France, let us now proceed to describe some individual establishments.

A sort of branch of the Ecole des Arts et Métiers, the Ecole Centrale d'Architecture, 59, Rue d'Enfer-Ancien, Hôtel de Chanlues, founded and opened in 1865, is one of

Marginal notes: REV. M. MITCHELL ON LIBRARIES &C. — Summary. — Reports on individual establishments. Ecole Centrale d'Architecture.

---

* I cannot sufficiently express my obligations to M. Charles Robert for his general politeness in every matter relative to the subjects visited by the jury, and am further much indebted to him for furnishing the four large volumes from which the above statistics have been culled. M. Robert is the secretary of the department, which must owe much to his intelligence, activity, and zeal. He was also the president of the jury of Class 90, and occupies a very high position in his country, being Conseiller d'Etat and member of several orders.

the most interesting establishments of Paris formed in the last 10 years. It is under the patronage and assisted by the influence of the very highest authorities. It is an especial object of attention to M. Duruy, the very able and enlightened Minister of Public Instruction; and M. Charles Robert, the secretary of that department, well known for various works on education and of very advanced views, has constantly attended the meetings of the schools, representing at once the Minister and his own opinions. It is sufficient to manifest the esteem in which the idea and method of carrying out the institution is held to state that M. Dupont de l'Eure is the president, and made most valuable addresses at the commencement of each session—valuable in every point of view, applying not merely to art as practised in France, but to general art all over the world.

It is only necessary to name MM. Lecoq de Boisbaudran and Pierre Chabat, and MM. Viollet le Duc and Bellange, as their colleagues to prove the great importance attached in Paris to this establishment.

M. Emile Trelat is the director, assisted by a staff of more than 30 eminent professors.

The nature of the course of instruction will be best understood by naming the chief subjects to which professors are appointed. They relate to—1, the stability of constructions; 2, stereotomie; 3, chemistry; 4, general physical science; 5, geology; 6, natural history; 7, hygiène; 8, history.

The whole establishment may also be considered as a branch of the Conservatoire des Arts et Métiers—a specialty for architecture. The pupils are admitted after examination to prove they are already grounded sufficiently in the subjects, and have aptitude for the studies of the institution. The course lasts three years, and the time of instruction is nine months in each year. The pupils live at home, and the hours of work last from half-past ten to half-past four each day, with an interval of an hour for lunch.

The establishment includes several workshops conducted by able instructors. Thus the teaching from the professor's chair directs and advances the labours of the pupil in the workshop, and the labours of the workshop enable the pupil to comprehend the lectures of the professor.

It is not possible to enter into all the details of the establishment. It is sufficient to state that, the course of instruction having been successfully followed for three years, the student, after a very strict examination, receives a diploma, which may be called a degree in architecture, and will, no doubt, obtain its place among the highest ranks of scientific honours.

But the architect, like the poet, *nascitur non fit;* and if it happens that few of the students become rivals of Bramante, Michael Angelo, or the cathedral architects of the mediæval period, still will these studies and this institution show no unsuccessful result if they only form a higher class of builders, and minds better able to comprehend and improve upon the ordinary plans and workings of the common-place and domestic constructions of the day. Every trade and profession has an artistic side or point of view. As in every trade there are artists so among those devoted more especially to art, many, alas! will be found whose will and hope have not been seconded by their power. The " Anch' Io son "* of Correggio, how many a delusive dream has it produced, from which the awaking is poverty, misery, and the regret of ambition thwarted, and a life misspent and a failure! Beautifully does M. Dupont de l'Eure express his view of the artistic life and feeling. Let me quote his words (November 1865) delivered at the opening of the institution :—

" An architect, gentlemen, is an artist. An artist—noble expression! by most how little understood! Still, it is as requisite to affix a signification to the word, and a condition to the man, amongst those who exercise and develop their ideas, as it is to acknowledge the position and duty of the man of science or of one engaged in industrial labours. I must endeavour to develop it.

" I have before me, in my mind's eye, one who has culled the facts of history—the past and the present; who has gained large knowledge of the experiences of the human race; who, by heaven-born gift and own personal effort, has arranged in order these facts and this experience, who classifies them on a system, and deduces therefrom their laws of action; that man is a philosopher—a savant.

" Another passes before me, who, with science for his weapon and experience as his guide, conquers, by methods known to himself alone, the facility of fabricating, bringing into general use, and cheapening any number of similar products; he is a producer—a workman—an *industriel.*

" All the world understands these two; but as regards the artist it is a different affair. He who conceives or adopts a thought, and expresses it beneath a form essentially and especially his peculiar ; who calls, as it were, spirits from the vasty deep of his own unfathomable being (and they do come at his command), he is the artist, the lone man wandering ever amongst the lovely, to others undiscovered yet beautiful

---

* " Anch' Io son pittore," as he regarded at Bologna the " St. Cecilia " of Raphael.

prairies of his own creation, sustained by his own genius and living for his own work. And what *that* work?—A creation responding to his own ideal—that something to him and to his sympathisers—*the* thing of beauty and *the* joy for ever. Every idea laid hold of by the artist should develop itself so as to reach the senses of others ; that is the chief end of art. To express and bring out ideas ; to render them lucid, comprehensible, penetrative, attractive, and with power to seize hold of and retain the affection ; such is the rôle, the profession, the work, the life of the artist.

" To follow the highest artistic profession is not in every one's power ; yet each one may become for a time an artist, and for a particular purpose, object, and pursuit, according to his abilities. Lavoisier, Arago, Humboldt become artists when they clothe scientific discoveries in forms of language sensible, as it were, to the touch, comprehensible and attractive to the multitude—weaving, as by sorcery, the spell of words around the intellect and conjuring up to the imagination mazes of delight.

" The journalist, the advocate, the orator become artists whenever they excite to action and to life a multitude roused by eloquence to urge them on and on by cheers of approbation or hound them down with groans of dissent. For that speaker is an artist, whether Michael or Lucifer, who excites emotions, either false or true. But woe and misery to the false one !

" Again, the potter modelling a vase after his own idea, adding each secondary beauty in such a manner as to enhance the value and effect of the whole, having expended time, and thought, and knowledge on the production ; who puts before the world the rare specimen of his craft by which the senses and the eyes are entranced, and which, not satisfied with mere sight, our very hands tremble with anxiety to embrace, fearful least we should not grasp the whole idea ; he, too, is an artist.

" In like manner with the furniture-maker, carriage-builder, saddler, armourer, glassmaker, and all other trades. Whenever the producer exhibits any object that is not the mere product of a mechanical process, a something which bears the stamp of an individual mind and which acts on the feelings of the beholder by the medium of the senses, that is an art-treasure, and the maker an artist.

" And so, gentlemen in every occupation an artist may discover a field for his labours. He belongs not to any confined range. 'The world, the world is his.' Some professions and occupations seem especially the artist's home ; yet even in these the professors too frequently are not artists; while, on the other hand, the true artist may often be successfully sought in occupations remote from the ordinary notion of artistic life. I have thus endeavoured to define the nature of a man who executes a good work, and name him 'artist.' I use the word not in its professional sense, I apply it to the individual—to the man who creates a beauty in the shoe as to him who holds the pencil, the palette, or the chisel. 'He is an artist.' What means the phrase? It means that such a man does not necessarily follow the rules and common-places of his order; that when he undertakes a work he does not say, 'How does my 'compère make this?' but, 'How ought this to be made 'that it may be duly and rightly fashioned?'

"The world is continually peopled, for him, with virgin ideas; he is constrained to grasp their newness. Does he construct a house or build a coat, he consults how he may be able to cause either to accord with the peculiarities of the habitant or wearer; he does not utilise over and over again a certain form which conventional custom has already sanctioned; he seeks freshness and novelty. Whatever his work, be it small or large, he desires to fashion it as an express article, as a thing with an individuality. Such is the true criterion of the artist. Cursed is he if he be led astray from his true instincts. Ah! wretched man! if, contrary to his nature, he be drawn by circumstances of his position or compelled by destiny to enter upon the busy, bounded field of regulated industry. Powerful benefactress as she is, what can she do for him in the uninterrupted pathway of ever reproducing similarity? No production passes from his hands unless peculiarly appropriate to its distinct individual employment; not allowed to act thus, he nevertheless yields not; he takes a middle course, he becomes a semi-art producer. His models increase in number, and their reproduction costs increased expenditure. More business-like rivals contend with him in similar but inferior goods; these sell for less than would remunerate the actual but misplaced labour of our artist, and he dies a ruined and a soured man.

"Let us not, then, attempt in the same individual to fuse art with industry. Leave the artist what he is, but seek to utilise him. Let us preserve the artist; let us reward and bless him; let us elevate his thoughts and views; let us open to him the most extended horizons, that he may have power to expand to his soul's desire, for his work is, and will ever remain, the most engaging of those legitimate attachments that thought and labour procure to man."

After this he procceds:—"The true excellence of the
"artist is not to be acquired by learning; technical instruc-
"tion can be taught, the poetic ideal—not. But we can
"instruct a man in the fixed methods of art-production;
"that particular process by whose virtue the artist will be
"enabled to utilise the personal gift which God, the all
"Divine, has given him, by which he sees all things in such
"light, and receives such impressions as are his, his only,
"and therefore which he alone invents and produces to the
"world. If a man be not nature's artist, no teaching can
"make him one. The jewel must be there before it can be
"polished; and the use of art teaching is to place a man
"in such favourable conditions as to enable him to develop
"all his faculties. The poet must know to read and write
"and the rules of grammar; so the architect must be able
"to draw, that he may be taught by successive stages to
"mount to the higher currents of artistic thought, where the
"views of the art enlarge at the same time as the spirit of the
"man expands and the ability of expression is acquired."

To those who have criticised the idea of forming this
establishment, he replies:—"On every occasion of new ideas
"arising, on the one side clear-sighted, on the other narrow-
"minded, people express opinions. 'You go too far,' say
"some. 'You are not sufficiently advanced,' say others.
"May we not content ourselves, therefore, in believing
"that we are in the right path? If teaching be requisite,
"it cannot be too high or too complete. Each scholar will
"take what he can turn to his own advantage. The strong
"will become stronger, the weaker at least receive in part
"the benefits offered to all." To the other party he adds:
—"Instruction is a stimulant to the aptitudes of the true
"artist, not a repression. How great the error, how grave
"the fault, to believe that inspiration resides beneath the
"calm of ignorance, beneath that dangerous quietude in
"which reverie usurps the place of thought, since to replace
"thought by reverie is to confound poison with nourish-
"ment!" The conclusion of this most valuable address
advises the students, "in no position is work more necessary
"than the artist's; in none is it so difficult. All is lost
"unless safety comes through belief in work. At the first
"entrance on art all is agreeable, but if the student does
"not bring a permanent habit of labour all goodness rapidly
"becomes degraded. If a man hold not firmly to exertion
"he remains for ever an infant—a uselessness for ever."

Another adjunct to the Ecole des Beaux Arts et Métiers
is L'Ecole Municipale de Dessin et de Sculpture à Paris;

director, M. Levasseur, Rue Volta, 37. It furnishes in the labours of its pupils exhibited abundant evidence of the value of the institution. The methods of teaching are excellent, and the results correspond. It has been established many years, and each year been attended with increased success. The drawing and casts in plaster and models in clay executed by the students are exceedingly satisfactory and real. Careful teaching and careful study are manifested. The schools are held on two evenings in the week. The direction of visitors to the Exhibition should be particularly addressed to the species of triumphal arch leading from the Rue de Flandres to the French Education Court—a work of considerable artistic merit in itself, and rendered more so by the plaster casts and statues which adorn and add to its effect. All these are the work of the students of this school of art, and very worthy of much attention.

The work is not merely well done in this establishment, but very rapidly. A man cannot be said to have acquired his proper knowledge unless he has it, as it were, at his fingers' ends ready to apply it at the moment required, and equal to any emergence he is called upon to supply. This is especially the case in Paris, where decorative art is so much needed, and so rapidly, for the various fêtes so frequent and so magnificent in their decorations and display.

The theatre too and the churches require, and provide support for, many artists thoroughly acquainted with decorative and scenic art; while every article of furniture, hangings, glass, jewellery, china, &c. demands for its production an amount of artistic skill and facility of execution from numerous hands not to be equalled in any other city in the world.

The rapidity of execution, as well as the completeness of the result, was tested at an entertainment given by M. Le Ministre de l'Instruction at his palais to the jurors of the Exhibition. Several of the students were invited to show their ability in clay modelling in one of the rooms prepared for the purpose, and in the course of a very short time—from one to two hours—had modelled in clay very excellent and very artistic productions from memory and from copy. In this short time frieze-cornices, and even busts, were executed by young men of 20 that would have been deemed artistic in England, but which here seem only the natural accomplishment required for the development of certain trades. Our own school of design at Kensington is following a similar course, and with an enormous success; but France, the nation, has been artistic for 300 years. Our own art-life in this sense, as a nation, was not born 30 years ago. To produce real art-study amongst the masses these must have been accustomed to live amongst art-works, as part of their daily existence. Art-works will be required in England whenever such advance has been made; and art-producers, similar to these students of the Ecole Municipale de Paris, be able to cultivate with success and profit the excellences which science and skill alone evolve, and which only high payment can remunerate and foster.

The French nation are so convinced of the value of art, both morally and commercially, that in most of their large towns schools have been formed and buildings erected and supported at great expense both of individuals, the municipality, and the State. Several of these schools exhibit productions that may rival those of the great establishments of Paris, in which city there are many others of nearly equal importance to this of M. Levasseur. These schools are not conducted by mere drawing-masters, but are under the superintendence of elegant and accomplished artists.

Thus, M. Schrieber, of St. Quintin; M. Le Coq de Boisbaudran, Paris R. Ecole de Médicine; M. Lequien, Rue des Petits Hôtels, 19, Paris; M. Deuilly, of Metz: M. Gallard, Toulouse, &c. show very excellent designs.

Nor are females excluded from the cultivation of art, as is proved by the results from the establishments of Mdlle. de Morandan, sister to Mdlle. Rosa Bonheur, Rue Dupuytren, Paris; Mdlle. Levasseur, Paris; Mdlle. Jacquemart, Ecole de Gravure pour les Jeunes Filles à Mulhouse, and others.

The establishments at Turgot and Ivry seem to combine the commercial and artistic schools in one system of instruction, and very successfully. They are under the able direction of M. Pompée, and the works of the pupils have been deemed worthy of the highest mention by the jury of the class.

I must not omit to point out the very excellent drawings exhibited by the Ecole des Frères Chrétiens, 27, Rue Oudinot, explained as was the manner of teaching by their very able, intelligent, and evidently most amiable and excellent instructor. I refer to them with regret to think how few schools of the working class in this country could produce such results, or show such careful teaching. I know, too, that the schools are so well taught in other respects that few can produce more lively and intelligent pupils in every branch of ordinary education.

The Ecole Centrale Lyonnaise seems to have originated as another offshoot, or in consequence of the success of the

Centrale Ecole des Arts et Métiers of Paris, in the same way
as the provincial schools of art in England have their paternity
in the school of art at Kensington.

An identity of views seems to have actuated the founders
of both institutions.

The necessity for this establishment is thus asserted,
" L'industrie (I use this expressive word, though not English),
" makes vast strides daily ; its methods are continually pro-
" gressing by means of incessant changes ; that progress may
" really be made prudence and intelligence are requisite—
" the prudence of experience, the intelligence of scientific
" applications."

There is now great contention and rivalry among nations,
and victory will belong to those who possess most intelligence,
knowledge, and energy.

" L'industrie," formerly unaffected by foreign rivalry, com-
peted only with producers of its own nation, and the contention was comparatively small. But now that free trade has
opened to the world one grand universal market, the contest
has become, in truth, a severe reality, and it demands the
utmost powers of the ablest man to gain the prize.

It is not only l'Industrie that has advanced ; every idea
has made progress. Protection has crumbled into night, and
the sun of free trade is already resplendent on the horizon ;
a new era manifests itself, and an immense field is offered to
the energy of new generations. Under this novel régime
l'industrie must put forth renewed efforts to maintain its
place, and support that immense competition which day by
day is becoming more and more established. Men of sense,
instructive, intelligent, and energetic, must be found or
created, and the rising generation must be provided with the
means of obtaining an education, say educations, of a special
order, adapted to the new condition of circumstances in which
it will be placed.

To supply such needs these central schools of art have
been created : uniting practice to science, they fulfil at once
the position of the school and the apprenticeship. In the
school the theory is developed, in the workshop the practice,
and in the visits to the different factories the experience of
manufacturing life is acquired.

Of course they are not intended for the mere labourer, but
for the upper class superintendent, the foreman, eventually to
become the partner in the firm, or the master engineer, in its
highest sense. The aim is to produce the mean between the
savant who devises the principles, and the workman capable
of comprehending and applying the discoveries of science.

This central school of Lyons seems to have adopted much the same course as that of Paris. Great stress is laid upon drawing freely and quickly, as well as accurately, from designs, and from the machine itself, and from memory, any object, however complicated, placed before the eye.

The pupils visit various factories in Lyons and the neighbourhood, and in the summer make excursions to observe any celebrated works in course of completion, as bridges, buildings, tunnelings, &c.

Amongst the excellent features of the establishment must be named the collection of models of machinery made by the advanced pupils, which is formed with a double intention—1st, as a collection of models for the use of the school; 2nd, to exhibit to the pupils the manner in which works of the factory should be executed, and the defects of those at present in use. It also teaches them manual labour. The models exhibited are very interesting. With all their labours, however, the directors do not pretend to make perfect men:
" They continually and forcibly remind their pupils that
" after quitting the school they have still a long apprentice-
" ship to serve, that of experience and actual labour. All
" commencements are difficult and laborious ; but by utilising
" the instruction they have received the future of the pupils
" is in their own power. It is for them to make known the
" knowledge and science they possess and to bring into
" favour more and more the name of the school, which has
" already shown its title by success and has bestowed upon
" them the means of gaining an honourable position in
" society."

Ecole
Théorique et
Pratique de
Tissage de
Mulhouse.

The Ecole Théorique et Pratique de Tissage Mécanique de Mulhouse is intended to form managers and overlookers for manufactories of weaving, and gives instruction at the same time both in the theory and practice of mechanical weaving.

It owes its origin to the introduction of free trade principles. The rivalry of other nations in their own market has made France comprehend that to maintain her position she must be forward to use every advantage, and among the chief is to be reckoned the bringing up of skilled upper class artisans occupying the position of intelligent and well instructed foremen. To train such men is the object of this institution. Before entrance they are subjected to examination, and must exhibit considerable general knowledge and information. The students most probably belong to the lower middle class. The price paid for instruction is 600f. (24*l*.) per annum.

The school is well provided with all the apparatus necessary for its objects. It possesses steam power and workshops, and a complete range of machinery for weaving has just been added.

These machines are constructed on every approved form, with the latest improvements, either English or French, and for every sort of weaving work; so that the student may be thoroughly instructed in all the best and most modern methods of fabrication.

The principles of action of each machine are thoroughly inculcated both in theory and by practice.

In the first years the pupil learns how to decompose and analyse all the different forms of stuffs, ordinary velvets, gauzes, &c., and studies principally the patterns suited to the local industry. The course of study finishes by lessons in drawing of patterns, of machines, of buildings for factories, of the best plans and construction; and in accounts, with the principles of commercial arithmetic and the chances of commercial success.

The whole of the student's acquirements are attested by examinations, to which a certificate of capacity follows if successful progress has been made.

Inventors are invited to send their inventions to the school, that the newest improvements may be seen and known.

There is also a school of spinning on the same model, and with the same advantages for learning the principles of the art—or, rather, art-trade.

The establishment of Le Creusot, occupying a vast territory, has formed an immense manufactory of iron and coal, situated between Autun and Chalon-sur-Saone. It was founded in 1769. It may be interesting to the English reader to know that one of the earliest engines of Watt was erected on these works; its old cylinder, bearing the date 1782, is preserved in one of the courts. The description of the situation of the works reminds of the country around Wolverhampton or Stoke-on-Trent; but the company possesses a much more extensive range than is found in either of these places, occupying 24 square leagues.

From the period of its establishment, in 1769, it suffered various vicissitudes and changes of direction and owners, and produced a great number of the larger works manufactured in iron in France. During the wars at the commencement of the century it was much employed for military service. Cannons, balls, and bombs were made there. Nor were its labours less onerous or successful for the more useful arts of peace, as the original gaspipes of Paris, the cupola of the Halle aux Blés, and the pumping machinery of Marly, bear witness. An English firm held possession from 1826 to 1834, and it fell into the hands of M. Schneider in 1836, the gentleman elected by the Emperor to sustain the very high and very important position of President of the Senate.

Since his accession the name of Creusot is to be found on very many of the largest iron-wrought erections of France and elsewhere, the bridge of Brest, that of Freiburg, the large steam-boats of the Rhone, and rails for many railroads; in fact, every production of a very first-class iron working establishment.

The number of workmen employed reaches 10,000. It is a curious fact that the hands equal in number the steam power, being the same as the number of horses. The establishment is exceedingly well conducted, and the greatest attention is paid, in every respect, to the wants and comforts of the workmen and their families. Houses are built for them and churches and schools maintained. It is to the latter that our attention must be directed. No boy is allowed to enter the workshops till fourteen years of age. No females are employed in any way or of any age. It is to be regretted that attempts to introduce into the district proper industrial work for women have not hitherto proved successful.

The schools. The influence of the works has been such as to improve most materially the population of the country round about; and the directors attribute this progress chiefly to the establishment of their schools, in which a high class of education has been afforded to the scholars with very great success.

Before the present establishment commenced its wise and liberal labours the population are described as neither strong in mind or body; but now better nourishment and dwellings have improved their faculties, and better schooling called out their intelligence, so that the present generation much excels its predecessors, and will be succeeded by a higher class still, when those now on its school benches shall rise up to occupy their places.

One great cause of this success is that the wages of the men rise in proportion to their power of executing their work, and the company arrange it so that the best fed and the best taught obtain the highest salaries, thus offering a decided prize for good conduct, good education, and good rearing. The number of children under fifteen years of age amounts to a third of the population.

No praise would be exaggerated which gives to Creusot the merit its schools deserve. Their expense is provided for by the firm, with the greatest liberality: they build the rooms, they provide the teachers, they direct the morals and the course of studies.

The director of the schools received his education at the University. It is unnecessary to speak of his complete aptitude for the conduct of such an establishment. There can be no doubt he has been well selected and is especially able.

The schools furnish the skilled and intelligent workman to the factory, whence they draw their support ; and both the schools and the factory gain much advantage from the interchange of mutual civilities. The rivalry between them is confined as to which shall most aid the other.

There are two principal schools, and a number of smaller ones connected with them; 4,065 children—2,259 boys and 1,845 girls —attend them ; and the very youngest are received, in addition, into dame schools—"garderies."

There are 12 professeurs (teachers) for the boys and 11 Sœurs de St. Joseph for the girls. Under the name of primary instruction is included a much more extensive programme. The school has nine classes. The inferior ones receive only the mere elements of knowledge ; in the upper ones the powers of the children are so enlarged that in the highest class they attain a very extended acquaintance with literature as well as science, exercises in style, history, cosmography, arithmetic, algebra, geometry (descriptive), mechanical physics, chemistry, and the elements of sculpture and drawing.

Here, then, are found all the elements of a real special education, which has this great advantage—it is entirely based on the applicability to certain useful requirements, and gives to these an immediate purpose.

The factory keeps lists, on which are inserted the names of those of their people who manifest a capability of becoming good clerks, of workmen who comprehend at a glance the drawings of a machine to be constructed, of foremen able to direct a Bunsen pile and to whom the phenomena of chemistry may be familiar. The director has also established courses of lessons in bookkeeping, drawing, physiology, and chemistry. Though it is true that these studies have enabled some few of their people to apply themselves to other spheres of labour than that of the factory work, yet the firm itself has benefited much by the number of excellent workmen and foremen who, having manifested special aptitudes for various branches of their own industries in school life, have afterwards entered into their employ.

The establishment at Mettray* is so well known by various publications in England that it is only necessary to point out that there is in the Exhibition building a model of the build-

Mettray.

---

* A report on these schools was made in 1845, I believe by a Mr. Hills.

Rev. M.
Mitchell
on
Libraries,
&c.
———

ings of that institution and several articles manufactured by its *détenus.* Mettray may be considered as the parent of all similar institutions for the reception of young people who have subjected themselves to penal law by theft, violence, or vagabondage. From the example set at Mettray industrial penal schools had their origin in most countries, as Redhill, &c. among ourselves. It was a grand invention at its com-

M. Demetz.

mencement, and M. Demetz is worthy of all honour for the establishing of an institution on such enlightened principles as commend themselves at once to the approbation of the religious, the philanthropic, and the philosophic. It was he who first imagined that untamed youth of headstrong and malevolent passions unrestrained might be better brought into order, reason, and propriety by mild and gentle opera- tions rather than by the 'exercise of mere brute force. He has also possessed, what is of even more influence and utility, the merit of establishing an institution conducted on the highest moral and civilising principles, which has been a success from the beginning, and which now for more than 30 years has continued to be most ably worked, without degene- rating in any degree; but, indeed, with every year increased and increasing usefulness. One of its chief charms to an English mind is the fact that its great achievements have been obtained in the soundest and severest manner, by simply adhering to the plan of carrying out the highest scheme of usefulness with calm, deliberate judgment, without enthu- siasm, or fanaticism, or excitement, simply from a sense of religious duty. It is impossible to point out with too high a sense of admiration the labours—personal labours — of this most excellent gentleman. The member of a learned profession, and very high in the ranks of that profession, he has for 30 years devoted himself unceasingly to the interests of the establishment; he has resided constantly amongst its dwellings, and his absences have been only when he felt it a duty to seek and to save the lost sheep of his fold or to bring others into its enclosure.

Mettray was founded principally to remove criminal male children under 16 years of age from the public prisons, and subject them to an ameliorated and reforming treatment. Its principles of action were those of the Gospel—" Do unto " your brother as you would be done unto." " Pity the " unfortunate and abandoned—restore them to reason and to " society. They are ignorant, teach them; they are vicious, " reform them; they are idle, give them a pleasure in work; " they love evil, give them a power of enjoying good."

Mettray was established in 1838, about six miles from Tours, by M. Demetz, in conjunction with Le Vicomte

Bretignières de Courteilles. These promoters considered that agricultural labour would afford the best employment for the young *détenus* (sentenced criminals). His idea is expressed by himself—" to improve the land by man, and man by the " land ; " and another of his maxims has become the legend of the establishment, " *Loyauté passe tout* " (Good faith is the key of society). We regret not to be able to enter into the plans by which success has been obtained. The establishment has become the type and model of all similar institutions in France.

Mettray has received more than 3,000 *détenus*. Of these, 2,245 are known to be dwelling with propriety, engaged in various trades and in naval and military service ; three have received the Legion of Honour ; the rest seem to be still in the colony. I suppose some may be (though it is not stated in the report) considered as relapses or dead. Touching stories are told of the inmates ; but the best proof of the value of the institution is the sense in which it is held by the people of France. " All the departments every year vote a " sum for its support."

Statues have been erected among peoples to men with less claim to honourable recognition than M. Demetz ; and, perhaps, in time to come, the tardy cities of enlightened Europe will raise in their public places monuments to his honour, as Genoa, after 300 years of neglect, has lately erected a trophy to Columbus's fame.

A peculiar establishment has been added to Mettray since 1850.

The law of France authorises parents to shut up for a limited period, as a means of correction, any child against whom they have grave subject of complaint. This seems founded on the old *lettre de cachet.* It seems that the young gentlemen of that country revolt not unfrequently against the strict discipline of the Lycées ; they are returned on their parents' hands ; no other Lycée will receive them. " I shall " expel you," says the director. " Bravo ! " says the boy ; " *vacances perpetuelles !*—nothing but holidays ! " And what on earth are his parents to do with such a lively specimen of precociously vicious humanity ? In England he does as he likes ; in France there is the prison. Now, the thought struck M. Demetz that he would found an institution to receive such peccant individuals, where they might, according to law and the will of the parents, be detained, if under 16, for a month ; if under 21, for six months. They are subject to almost penal discipline, which appears to be very strict, and includes solitary confinement. Once there, he has no longer a name. Two brothers have been in the establishment at one time without knowing it. He speaks only to the chaplain or the director: with his teacher he takes daily walks; he may write to his family. By aid of solitude and continual talking, the young recluse, at first obstinate, at length comes round; he repents; after some weeks the régime is softened, and ultimately he is restored to his friends, an altered, and perchance a sadder, man.

It is possible to express doubts as to the desirability of this penal enactment and this system of solitary confinement for crimes, which, after all, may only amount to what in England would be considered mere boyish petulance. However, it appears to have its admirers in France, to agree with their system of child government, and to be entirely in accordance with the letter and spirit of their laws. In England we should be jealous of authority thus placed in the parents' hands. What use might a step-father make of such power? What use a vicious father to get his son out of the way? We see one father has already had two sons in the establishment at the same time. Were the sons alone to blame? What was the father's conduct? How had he brought up those youths? These and other questions will arise to the English mind. It is useless to push such inquiries further. It is not likely that a "maison paternelle" will ever be founded in Britain. M. Demetz, however, deserves the highest praise for devising a plan of humanity suited to the laws and feelings of his own nation, so different to ours.

Among the objects in the Exhibition that will be regarded with greatest interest, not on account of its artistic merits or the beauty and excellence of its mechanisms (which are great), nor of our sympathy with its origin, but for itself, for its high yet shudder-causing utility, is the block of buildings, distinguished by a flag with red cross on a white ground, devoted to the Société de Secours aux Blessés Militaires.

This admirable institution received the sanction of the Emperor on June 23, 1866. Its object is to assist in providing comforts for the sick and wounded on the field of battle, in the ambulances, and in the hospitals. It is purely voluntary and supported by subscriptions, donations, and legacies. In time of peace these are funded so as to form a bank on which to draw if any lamentable occasion should arise to demand the exercise of its kindly offices.

Though the head department is in Paris, the society is extending itself through the provinces, and promises to be well supported by a people to whom the horrors of war are not personally unknown, and among whom is no family but may some day or other in its members demand and need its benevolent assistance.

The principles on which it is founded are recognized by every great State of Europe, with one exception ; and similar societies are in action.

The society has provided an exhibition of intense interest, including ambulances of improved construction, surgical instruments, medicine chests, hospital beds, tents ; in fact every conceivable necessity that may be required for the wounded soldier. One of these, a paper bag of water, which cools by evaporation, may be very valuable, and is certainly curious. But the mere mechanical is not the only means by which its members hope to be useful if, unhappily, wars should arise. They are busy in organising a society of members who should accompany the armies to the field and act, in conjunction with the authorities, in their pious and evangelical work. At present they are obliged to confine themselves to the members of a religious society, the brotherhood of St. Jean de Dieu, a corporation who pass their lives in attendance on lunatics, old men, and sick children ; and whose devotion to their work is above all praise.

It is believed, should the occasion arrive, that they will be joined by large numbers of laity, whose religious zeal or generous impulses may lead them to give personal aid to suffering humanity, and who will not scruple, from sense of religion and duty, to hazard the dangers of the battle-field and its almost still more terrible accompaniments. There is also a yet more ultimate and secret intention of the society : they hope to be the means of so turning men's thoughts to the horrors of war as to make wars less possible on earth, and render to all nations the truth of the Gospel proclamation, " On earth peace, good-will toward men."

PRUSSIA.

The association of working men at Berlin is worthy a notice. It is an establishment similar to our own mechanics' institutions. In 1864 the society built a hall on a piece of land bought for 24,000 thalers (3,500*l*), and the establishment cost 44,000 thalers (6,400*l*.) additional. It is the first establishment in Germany destined exclusively to the instruction of the working class. There are 3,000 members, who must be 17 years, at least, of age. They pay three silbergroschen (10*d*. a month). Of the members nine-tenths belong to the working class. By the apprentice usages of the country certain years of the apprenticeship are passed in travelling. This institution is open to these wanderers ; they equal 10,000 per annum ; and it is considered that 60,000 workmen have used the institution during the last seven years, the society having been really formed in 1843, but re-constructed in 1859. The arrangements seem very complete, and include lectures on all subjects of science, with soirées, concerts, and balls. A large hall and garden receive on these occasions 2,000 guests, among whom are women and children. There is a library of 3,500 volumes, much used by the members, especially those works which relate to commerce and trade.

SAXONY.

The following exposition of the state of education in Saxony will not be without interest to English educators, more especially when the success attending it may most un-deniably be recorded in the following terms :—" We dare, " without presumption, and in perfect harmony with truth, " affirm that our institutions in the main have entirely " answered all reasonable expectations. That not only have " the arts of reading and writing become diffused amongst " the whole nation, but a very elevated state of religious, " moral, and actual instruction pervades all ranks of the " population."

In Saxony the origin of elementary education of the poor dates from the Reformation. Still, it was only in 1835 that it commenced its present form. Before that period no system had been developed and spread through the king-dom.

Under the title of schools of elementary instruction is included all schools in which the children obliged to attend them receive, for eight consecutive years (from six to 14 years of age), a systematic education, which finishes at their confirmation.

All these schools in their principles set themselves the same task. To them is confided the first methodical develop-ment of the human faculties, by means of instruction and teaching; and they only fulfil their duty when they have established in their scholars all the elements of knowledge and science, and brought out those capacities which constitute as well the education of man in general as of each one's particular vocation.

In addition to the ordinary instruction of English working-class schools, the elements of universal and natural history and geography are introduced.

A distinction, important to observe, is made in the instruc-tion given in mere village schools and that afforded by the schools of large towns ; for these latter a higher class of study is required, extending to literature (general), drawing, and geometry.

In the kingdom of Saxony the smallest village, even the most remote cottage, is included in a school district.

The attendance at school is obligatory on every child from six to 14 years of age ; and if the children neglect to go to school, the State punishes the parent or the guardian (next of kin ?) by a fine or even short imprisonment.

" The State," says the report, has a perfect right to require an entire obedience to this law, because it will not be able to maintain the position for which it was itself established (viz., the good order of the people), if its citizens have not received a certain amount of knowledge and education.

So fully convinced of this view are the people of Saxony that there is no difficulty in (I might even say necessity for) enforcing this law. The people rather demand its requirements ; and the most satisfactory proof of the goodness of the schools and of the wisdom of severity in carrying out the law, is derived from the fact of the rarity of any necessity for bringing its provisions into action.

The present generation, having itself enjoyed the fruits of this good instruction, has by degrees acquired a conviction that no greater benefit can be conferred upon their children than faithfully and conscientiously to provide for their education ; and, far from abstracting from them the obligatory attendance, the poorest parents often pay for extra instruction.

All parents, rich and poor, are under the same law of education : but the richer classes send their children to schools of superior instruction, or else have them taught at home by capable teachers, who are certificated.

Every household contributes its portion to the support of the public schools of the district. The State pays nothing, except in certain very poverty-stricken places.

The contribution of each child is in simple schools, 2½ sous a week ; in the superior schools the fee rises to 5f. 10 sous a month.

The salary of the teachers is fixed and variable ; the lowest is not under 562½f. (say 25*l*.), the highest, 1,350f. (say 54*l*.).

This is the sum required by the State ; but, of course, this lowest figure is by no means the rule.

What has contributed most to educational advancement in Saxony is that the population are almost all of the same religion ; there being only 60,000 Catholics in a population of 2,343,994.

This population includes 400,229 children of school age— viz., 199,446 boys, 200,783 girls.

Schools are opened on Sundays for poor people's children, for boys at work and apprentices ; I conclude above 14 years of age.

Side notes: REV. M. MITCHELL ON LIBRARIES, &c. — Education compulsory. Reasons why the State should insist on education.

Rev. M.
Mitchell
on
Libraries,
&c.

Ecoles
Réales.

It is not necessary to enter upon the teaching of the higher order of schools and colleges.

The Ecoles Réales form the commercial and mechanical branch of instruction for those intended for commercial or engineering life, and the college for those of professions. In the former, mathematical science ; in the latter, Greek and Latin, form the bases of instruction, which seems to extend over a period of nine years. One peculiarity of Saxon education is to be found in its gymnastic establishments, for which masters are trained who pass an examination.

The Saxon Government is the first in Germany that by legal enactment has regulated the education of masters in gymnastics and the extent to which this branch should be carried in elementary schools. Teachers of gymnastics are formed in the gymnase at Dresden.

The Saxon educational portion of the Exhibition is well worth attention. A very excellent and large model of the gymnastic school at Dresden is one of its most prominent exhibits. The number and variety of gymnastic apparatus are very great and complete.

Much of the educational apparatus exhibited is very extraordinary on account of its cheapness. Thus, No. 82 is a complete apparatus for teaching physical science, at a price of 26f. 25c., or about a guinea. It contains 29 objects.

The applications for teaching of M. Glootz, of Dresden, also are very good ; and for those who desire to know how Greek and Latin are taught in Saxony, and with what success, their curiosity may be satisfied with compositions in both languages, from Zwickau, Grimma, and Meissen.

WÜRTEMBERG.

The exhibition, or rather exhibitions, made by Würtemberg in regard to education, especially as connected with the fine and industrial arts, are among the most excellent in the building. In galerie 11 are shown the most exquisite models, in plaster and wood, of architecture, of carpentry, and all that comes under the name of artistic industry. They will amply reward the most attentive consideration of every one who believes that the progress of manufacture depends much upon art knowledge in the workman. Not only are the forms themselves excellent, but the execution of each object is all that can be desired ; and there is no other country which pretends to anything like their completeness and success. The second portion is equally worthy of observation, consisting of exhibits of the use made of this material for instruction, as shown in the works of the students of the various communal schools of art in the kingdom. No less than 45 of these schools have sent specimens of the works of their students, and many of them are most deserving of praise for the complete artistic feeling which pervades the character of the drawings. These are hung in the gallery of the annexe in the park, behind the Bavarian picture gallery. They well repay a visit, and explain whence it comes that art in so many ways manifests itself in all the very interesting productions of that small but enlightened State.

The development of these communal schools for workmen in Würtemberg demands consideration. In schools of technical art not only should the student be called upon to acquire the theory, but, if possible, what is even more important, each young artisan should have opened out to him, in addition to the elementary instruction given in the primary schools, those methods by which he can appropriate to himself the sum of his scientific studies; of that knowledge, both scientific and technical, so necessary—so indispensable—in an age when rivalries of trade and refined public taste make such large demands on improved production.

In Würtemberg the whole people seem to have come to one opinion on this matter, and that from a very early date. In 1818 " a series of lectures on art and mechanical science " was added to the programme of the then ordinary Sunday schools. These were enforced and created with the object of preserving the knowledge acquired previously in the day schools of the people, and establishing in the Sunday schools of large towns special classes for apprentices, where drawing should be taught. These attempts, however, seem to have produced but small results ; they were isolated, and wanting in unity. But in 1848 the Council Royal of Science, and that for Commerce and Industry, established a commission, in order to advance " des écoles professionnelles "—technical or trade schools. This commission appears to have worked, not authoritatively, but persuasively, and perhaps chiefly by the power it had of offering to the various communes (say parishes) a subvention from the State as large as the half of their expenses, on condition that the school should be organized with the object of carrying out the scheme adopted by the Royal commission.

Two fundamental principles were required by the commission—1, that the schools should be free to all ; 2, that a certain part of the expenses should be paid by the commune, because, as the report says, it is incontestably established that whatever a man gives something for he esteems more highly than what he gets for nothing ; and the result has borne out the force of this conclusion.

Origin of.

REV. M.
MITCHELL
ON
LIBRARIES,
&C.
—

The commission was amply aided by the Government and by the Chambers of Parliament, and large funds were supplied for all the necessities of the service. Models, drawings, drawing and plastic materials, were by no means grudgingly provided. Normal schools were created for the instruction of teachers, of which that at Stuttgart was the chief; and at the present day there exist working class schools in numerous parishes where, on Sundays and evenings, courses of lectures on industry and trade are given, and also where drawing schools are open daily, either with or without the assistance of the teacher. At Stuttgart, Ulm, Reutlingen, Heilbronn, four schools exist, with a total of 2,500 pupils, of whom 130 are females, in two schools at Stuttgart and Reutlingen.

These schools are styled " Ecoles Ouvrières Communales." Other towns possess like institutions. Schools that seem not to belong to so high a class are scattered over the whole country. The total of schools is given at 101; of pupils at 8,000.

Such is the provision made in this small kingdom for the instruction of its people in art. It is to this system it owes its very high rank among the artistic nations of Europe, and which gives its manufactures an impulse of great force, creating an exceptional demand for its products. We may believe, also, that the steady, sober, quiet, enjoyable, sensible life of its people has received from this source an addition of real happiness of much more value than words or wealth express; and amidst the conflicts of the period, amidst all the late political divisions, excitements, and disturbances of Germany, the population of Würtemberg has been eminent among those people who have exhibited most quiet, most satisfaction, and the greatest absence from internal and domestic strife. Würtemberg is reported to be mother and chief fosterer of all the educational progress of Germany.

BAVARIA.

Academy of
Nuremberg.

The school of art at Nuremberg was founded under the name of " The Academy of Nuremberg, in 1662." In 1852 M. Kreling, of Munich, was appointed director.

The working principles of the institute are based on the capacity of the students. A young man of talent, who devotes himself to the career of an artist, obtains here the means of making himself acquainted with all the branches of the fine arts. The less endowed student, who prefers attaching himself to a special branch of the arts of industry or architecture, receives an instruction solid and conformable to his future plans.

The school joins the science to the practice of art, and has furnished many beautiful works to various churches and towns. The pulpit of St. Sebald may be mentioned as one; also bronzes, altars, candelabra, and crucifixes. It applies its resources also to painting on glass, and, in fact, to every species of artistic construction. Many proofs of its success will be found in the Exhibition.

The terms of admission to the school are : —*a.* The candidate must be 16 years of age; *b.* must have attended with successful results a preparatory school of drawing and modelling; *c*, must give actual proof of talent in these arts; *d.* and submit to a satisfactory examination. He is then admitted for six months, and, finally, as a pupil of the school.

There are altogether 12 professors and masters. The buildings seem well adapted for the purpose; and, among other requisites, include a bronze foundry and a large art library. The school is supported by the State. The commune (town) repairs the buildings; and scholarships have been founded by the city of Nuremberg and by private legacies.

AUSTRIA.

The art-institutions of Austria are similar to those of Germany in general. The specimens from their school of weaving at Brunn seem peculiarly excellent. They exhibit some magnificent collections of models in wood, very cheap; also some large drawings for a whole class to copy are good. It would of course be impossible to hope for a demand in England for these materials, as the expense of carriage would depreciate their value as to cheapness. The models of M. Bauer, of Pick, are very good; also those of M. Theodore Böhm, of Reichenberg. The Imperial School at Vienna (52 and 53) shows some plaster modelling which may be usefully compared with that of Lambeth School of Art.

The establishments included in class 89 (57, 58, 59, and 60) show the progress of art in Viennese schools, and have received high commendation. They are supported by the Chamber of Commerce at Vienna.

In class 90 (4), a museum for schools has high merit; also some small models of articles used in teaching for infant schools; also some models in plaster of insects (foraminifers), of M. Charles Gerold, of Vienna; also models of natural history, by M. Fric.

ITALY.

It is gratifying to observe that the renewed Kingdom of Italy, amongst other progresses, rapidly advances in the education of its people. Normal schools and schools of art and drawing have been established, and the documents of the Minister of Education at Florence are highly valuable for the information they afford. The Institute Manin at Venice deserves very high mention, class 89 (49); also the Technique Institution of Florence (45). There is also a society (Association Italienne pour l'Education du Peuple) answering to our great societies. Indeed, the progress of education among the poor in Italy seems to excite by its success the jealousy of the upper classes, who have united to procure for their own children the advantages afforded to the classes below them, and have formed a society at Milan for that purpose.

EGYPT.

From Egypt there are calendars, Arab and Turkish; books for schools, and also works executed by the scholars, interesting for themselves; but few of our visitors will be able to decipher their contents. It is a mistake to suppose that Mohammedans are uninstructed. All read and write; all repeat the Koran; and it is a condition of their religion, I hear, that every Mohammedan writes out during his life a copy of that book of the Prophet.

SPAIN.

The following sketch of the state of public instruction in Spain will be interesting, as it concerns a people whose institutions are so little known in England. It is from the pen of M. Carderera, the Spanish juror, to whose kindness I am much indebted. He is an inspector-general of schools, and chevalier of several orders.

The instruction of the people (instruction *primaire*) is conducted in infant schools, elementary schools, superior schools, and adult schools. Any certificated person may keep a school. There is a school for boys in every village, and one for girls in every village of 500 persons; and for every 2,000 persons additional there is another school both for boys and girls. The teachers are well recompensed.

For the secondary or higher instruction there is an institute in each province maintained by the province, also private schools. The instruction is given in two branches, classical and commercial, industrial or agricultural. The highest class of instruction includes philosophy, literature, sciences, law, theology, and medicine. There are ten schools in the university for these subjects. In the University of Madrid all the branches are studied; in the universities of other towns, only three or four.

The second course comprehends architecture, the fine arts, mines, engineering (*pons et chaussées*), agriculture. The chief schools are at Madrid.

There are also normal schools for the formation of teachers.

The following are the statistics:—

Public boys' schools	-	-	-	13,238
Free boys' schools	-	-	-	1,643
Public girls' schools	-	-	-	6,117
Free girls' schools	-	-	-	1,770
Mixed schools	-	-	-	2,094
Infant schools	-	-	-	573
Adult schools	-	-	-	1,665
	Total	-	-	27,100

The number of pupils is, in

Public schools, boys	-	-	763,022
Private schools, boys	-	-	87,869
Public schools, girls	-	-	424,112
Private schools, girls	-	-	94,074
	Total -	-	1,369,077

The expenses of these schools are thus stated:—

At the charge of the communes (parishes)	-	-	17,178,359 f.
At the charge of the provinces	-	-	1,547,245 f.
At the charge of the State -	-	-	245,916 f.
Endowments	-	-	409,620 f.
Payments of scholars	-	-	2,350,905 f.
	Total	-	21,732,045 f.

Education of the working-class schools in Spain is conducted, as respects teaching, on the model of the British and Foreign School Society, and their infant schools on that of the Home and Colonial.

I took great pains in going through a series of their Bible pictures for infant schools, and there was nothing that in any way would offend the most Protestant eye. They were, in fact, exactly of the same character as our own.

The schools are entirely (as I understood) Catholic, none other being (as may well be conceived) sanctioned.

The above statements will prove that education is in a much more advanced state in Spain than is commonly believed in England.[*]

---

[*] Having visited schools in Madrid, Seville, and Valentia, I am able to state from personal observation that the schools of the country equal the average of our own. There are few infant schools here as good as that at Valentia.

GREAT BRITAIN AND IRELAND.

The exhibits of class 90, in the British department, cannot be said to have equalled either the dignity of the nation or the importance of the subject. I speak of the *private* exhibits —those of the Kensington Museum are too well known and too conspicuous to need any comment in this place. Nor would it afford any information to detail the arrangements of any of our educational establishments. The reports of our bluebooks are sufficient. The religious societies and the Pure Literature Society show considerable collections of books. These afford, however, only scanty specimens of works for which the demand, on account as well of religion as of language, cannot obtain a great circulation in France. Our educational booksellers do not seem to have considered the advantage of exhibiting equal to the cost, and have not made, consequently, a large show. No novelty is exposed ; there is, consequently, nothing particular to observe.

South Kensington School of Art.

The drawings and modellings of South Kensington—not numerous in comparison to what could have been shown— attract attention ; and the methods of teaching in that establishment have been highly appreciated by the jury of foreign artists. They consider, however, that the figure drawing is not equal to the rest, and should be more cultivated. It has been explained to them that there are difficulties in this branch in consequence of the general distaste of our people for figure subjects. A gold medal has been awarded to the establishment, notwithstanding this defect.

Lambeth School of Art.

The exhibition of the Lambeth School of Art appears to be very good ; and there is no doubt that had a large selection from the works executed by the students of all our schools of art been exhibited, as in the Würtemberg division, we should have obtained a higher place in the opinion of our neighbours. We are, however, justified in stating that immense progress has been made in the last ten years.

British catalogue.

I must refer to the English catalogue of the British section, price 10*d.* in four languages. Its price is extraordinary. Among other desiderata in education is a book on nomenclature. This publication goes a long way towards furnishing this want ; relating as it does to all trades and manufactures, it gives the name of most objects of art and science, and that in the four languages. It may be considered a very good educational book, and in that light its usefulness will extend much beyond the year of the Exhibition. It might be introduced most profitably especially into all commercial and scientific schools, not to omit those of the highest class also. Perhaps a compendium might better answer the purpose.

M. Cronmire (class 89, No. 1) exhibits some very excellent as well as cheap mathematical instruments. The collection of M. Damon (class 89, No. 3) deserves attentive consideration; so also does M. Wright's (16).

M. Stanford's maps have obtained a medal.

The Home and Colonial Society also exhibits its books and models.

CANADA.

The cases exhibited by Canada are very interesting, containing documents concerning the educational condition of that very important country, which appears to be making great progress.

SANDWICH ISLES.

Among not the least interesting of the Government exhibitions is that of the Sandwich Isles. The advancement made by that people in schools, literature, and printing is really marvellous. The character of the Queen seems to have impressed itself on the people and their institutions; and, if there be no jewelled crown and sceptre to manifest its regal wealth, there is that exhibited of much more importance to the well-being and happiness of the nation, the results of an extensive and real religious, moral, and intellectual instruction. The visitor will observe the Bible, and other religious books, and works on arts and science, produced in a tongue not indeed "understanded" of his own people, but equally efficacious for good to that small and isolated nation. Though he may not be able to read the language, yet he will perceive its significancy; he will mark the progress of civilization, not, as of old, by the gallows, but by the Divine word, and believe in the presence of a life and love inspired by Gospel truth and moral virtue.

I have, unfortunately, not been able to include reports of Prussia or Belgium in this notice, a matter to me of much regret, softened, however, by knowing that Belgium adopts a system similar to that of France, and Prussia to that of the rest of Germany, so that *mutatis mutandis*, what is spoken of the one country may be equally applied to the other.

To any reader of these pages it will have occurred that all nations desire, as I started by affirming, progress; that most nations have devoted very large funds to education, both the higher and the lower and the artistic; that they have all obtained, for purposes of education, the assistance of the ablest men, whom each Government has not only created, but also provided with ample emoluments, and rewarded with noble

REV. M.
MITCHELL
ON
LIBRARIES,
&c.
honours.   Such is the report as respects foreign nations. None are ignorant as to what extent such observations apply to ourselves.   But if there be any who imagine that England can remain behind, can fold its arms quietly and look on without taking steps to emulate the progress of other people, and yet retain a high position at the head of nations, such are entirely mistaken.   The present Exhibition proves the fact. Once the chiefs, we are now scarce the equals of our rivals. To their superior common class education intelligent foreigners attribute this result, as well as to the pains taken in forming overlookers and foremen; and, in answer to objections that have been made, each Continental State unites in one common voice to declare that moral progress and virtue have gone hand in hand with intellectual, artistic, and scientific advancement.

M. Dufresne.
In regard to the whole report on the class, I cannot improve upon the language of M. Dufresne, a most accomplished and able artist, named among the French members of the jury, all of whom, I have great satisfaction in stating, showed the utmost liberality and fairness in their decisions, and the greatest politeness in their manner, wishes, and bearings towards their colleagues from foreign countries.

" We have," says he, in a report made to the jury, " been altogether much struck, as well with the praiseworthy successes obtained by each nation as with the universal desire to pay increased care to studies in all times useful, but now indispensable for modern society, at a period when all classes, craving knowledge and advancement, desire not only to profit by certain artistic vocations, but to bestow on every branch of life those acquirements which demand science and industry to produce.

" Undoubtedly, in the midst of this general excitement, the peculiar character of each nation is manifested in its peculiar fashion.   The English, for example, with a pure mathematical habit, seek that special perfection which may be observed in all their productions.   Patient and laborious Germany rests on details and on partial effects.   She does not despise difficulties, but exhibits, in 1867, amidst the children of her schools, the same order of ideas as animated her old masters of the 14th century.   While we (the French), pupils of Primaticcio, address ourselves to an elegant facility, we avoid the display of labour, too often well satisfied, even too soon sometimes, if we find the whole a happy effort, or that it manifests the artistic spirit.   Yet, after all, with every qualification, our national errors, our partialities, we yet are able to affirm, with joyful satisfaction, that there exists a noble elevation and a spirited emulation amongst the greater number of our peoples. Miserable is that country which, after this Exhibition, cannot comprehend the necessity of progress.

"But the desire to advance," he continues, "is not sufficient. Having given credit and praise to goodwill, we must next, in the spirit of useful criticism and sincerity, expose the peril which, originating in France, is now extending through all countries. We mean the danger of encouraging youth to seek only agreeable and bounded results in the place of directing them towards a serious apprenticeship in the art of correct drawing. The elements of art will ever be the true, the simple, and the beautiful. The inspirations of talent awaken in objects the soul of art. We cannot hope that on all will be bestowed a privilege that really belongs to few. Still, what is necessary at least for all can be accomplished. The boy of the workshop, the artisan, the foreman, the manufacturer, the commercial profession, can learn the simple, naïve, and true proportions of any model presented without being enrolled in the ranks of the artist corps. All ought to know enough of art to appreciate its excellencies, but few should be induced to follow it as a profession. Nor should the artisan be encouraged in the idea that to copy for a year from prints or drawings will make him a Raphael or a Michael Angelo. The teachings will sufficiently have performed their purpose if the pupil can sketch with rapidity the parts of a locomotive, comprehend the divine beauty of an insect or a flower, and can reproduce these glories in cotton, or wool, or silk."

I cannot better conclude than by repeating the remark of M. Dufresne * :—" Miserable is that nation which, after this " Exhibition, comprehends not the necessity of progress."

The information and statistics of this Report have been obtained from documents furnished by the several Governments and exhibitors.

---

* He received the gold medal for a most valuable invention in gilding silver by which the health of the workmen will be much benefited. He also exhibited a magnificent cup of chased silver, which rivals work of Cellini.

REPORT on FURNITURE, CLOTHING, and FOOD, from all Mr. R. H. SODEN SMITH ON FURNITURE, &c.
Sources, remarkable for USEFUL QUALITIES combined
with CHEAPNESS.—(Class 91.)—By R. H. SODEN SMITH,
Esq.

CLASS 91 is defined as including Furniture, Clothing, and Scope and importance of Class 91.
Food of all kinds, distinguished by the qualities of utility
combined with cheapness. It is, therefore, an epitome of
the important groups 3, 4, and 7—namely, furniture, clothing
and personal ornament, and food—and includes thirty-three
whole classes, and occasionally objects from some others; but
it is distinguished from these, and rendered in some degree
special, by the price being required to be stated with every
object, as a point for consideration in judging of its merit.

The importance of the articles forming class 91 is too
obvious to require much comment. The degree of their
abundance and perfection supplies a test of the advance in
civilisation of any country; the home-life of the bulk of the
population can be judged of by their use; and, if a comparatively comfortable home-life be secured, by food, clothing,
and furniture, at reasonable price, it is needless to repeat
here the trite conclusions—which are not the less important
for their triteness—as to the moral effect of such advantages
upon the humbler classes of any population.

These objects, therefore, of small domestic economy, apt
enough to be overlooked or despised in a universal exhibition, have, notwithstanding their little external attraction,
an importance of which the ordinary visitor may not be
aware, and of which it is not out of place to remind him.
They possess, it is true, little external attraction; they are
wanting in beauty of form or in excellence of colour, and yet
they surround the daily life of the mass of our people, almost
insensibly influencing the eye and the mind. It is, moreover,
notable that the absence of art-beauty in these homely objects
is most conspicuous among nations claiming to be the highest
according to the present scale of civilisation. The people
whom we are content to regard as semi-civilised--Oriental
nations, tribes of Northern Africa, races in the distant parts
of the Russian Empire—show an understanding of colour,
at least, which renders their otherwise rude household goods
models for the skilful European to study and strive to imitate. Art is not thus instinctive among Western nations.
The objects that minister to the daily needs and conveni-
ences of common life are for the most part wholly wanting

MR. R. H.
SODEN
SMITH
ON FURNI-
TURE, &c.
___
Want of art-
knowledge.

—and it is a lamentable want—in every quality that can give pleasure to the eye.

The entire household furniture, carpets, fittings, articles of daily use, complete clothing for young and old, may be selected from the contents of class 91, and yet not one object found which ministers in the smallest degree to that art-instinct which is gratified by the commonest productions of Oriental workmanship; neither colour nor form is truly understood by any of those who have contributed their quota to the heterogeneous series which forms this class. Utility is the professed aim of everything exhibited; and, while it may be admitted that this object is often ingeniously attained, it is to be regretted that in its necessary attainment the workman never even deviates into good taste or strays as it were by accident into the slightest appreciation of beauty. Where any exception can be made to this censure it will be found hereafter studiously noted. A French writer, indeed, observes, as one of his conclusions from the consideration of the whole contents of the class, that cheapness has not been obtained, as far as France is concerned, at the expense of good taste. It would be satisfactory could this conclusion be accepted; but not only as regards France, but also with respect to all other countries represented, the writer has been compelled to arrive at one entirely the opposite.

Objects on
which art
might be
shown.

In the objects composing this class, whether furniture, objects of domestic use, or clothing, there is room for taste to display itself, notwithstanding the essential requirement of cheapness, either in general outline, as in pottery; in colour, as in carpets, mats, and clothing; or even in raised surface ornament, as in objects moulded or cast. Among Oriental nations what may be called an instinct of art-feeling guides their work conspicuously in colour, and to a lesser degree in the other sources of beauty. It is not so among the most civilised Western nations—not so in France, any more than elsewhere. The common combinations of colour in the cheap objects exhibited are as false and painful as notes out of tune in music; and the surface ornament is meretricious in character and inappropriate in application. Where traditions of Orientalism still exist, as in Spain, Portugal, and Sicily, art lingers upon household objects—such as the pottery, matting, and parts of clothing. Where manufacture has wholly triumphed in rapidity, certainty, and cheapness of production, the results are usually astonishing examples of the power of making common and really useful objects hideous. In one manu-

facture, at length—namely, in pottery—a step beyond this
is beginning to be gained : in addition to the triumph of
manufacturing skill, which produces a body and a glaze
excellent for everyday use form is occasionally considered,
and even colour and decoration that can be commended
begin sometimes to filter downwards to the home furniture
in stone- and delft-ware of the humble dwellings. This is a
pleasant augury for the future. The slightest infiltration
of art-feeling is a gain ; and we may, perhaps, look forward
to a time when household furniture will be cheap and yet
cease to be an eye-sore, and when the costume of ordinary
life will no longer be absurd in form—take a swallow-tailed
evening coat, for example—as well as wanting in every
quality that can combine usefulness with beauty or grace.

In the following observations on the objects exhibited,
the order in which the various countries are mentioned, and
the numerical references appended to exhibitors' names, are
in accordance with the French catalogue.

FRANCE.

France is more fully represented in class 91 than any
other nation, upwards of 500 exhibitors being enumerated,
and the variety of objects shown being so great that a bare
enumeration of them would occupy much space. It was to
be expected that France on her own ground, would largely
display objects of domestic use ; but it is to be observed
that while in the British division of the catalogue a marked
poverty and deficiency under class 91 is observable, this
deficiency is rather apparent than real, the class being in
fact absorbed in other groups, where, under pottery, glass,
hardware, and textiles, especially woollen goods, examples are
to be found superior in quality at their price to those of
perhaps any other country. The British goods of cheap
price have not been placed by their producers in class 91,
but are shown in their respective groups, where the fact of
their low price, for which in some cases they have been
chiefly exhibited, is of no avail, and does not receive notice.
On the other hand, selections have been sufficiently made on
the French side from the contents of groups 3, 4, and 7,
containing furniture, clothing, and food to form an extensive and important display of objects to which attention can
be directed on the score of cheapness. As regards furniture
moreover the park and detached building round the Exhibition are chiefly supplied by the French exhibitors in class
91, who have thus had a practical opportunity of making
their productions known.

It has been remarked that the French objects brought together by more than 500 exhibitors are very various; they range, in fact, from metal bedsteads and garden-seats, through every article of male or female clothing and of personal use, to "articles de religion,"—musical instruments, and thence to preserved vegetables, meat and wine.

Garden
furniture.

This heterogeneous assemblage may, however, be broadly divided for convenience of reference, into certain groups; and the first will include furniture and objects of household use. Of what may be called garden furniture, chairs of painted iron, of good design are shown by Letourneur (2), Mutet (11), and others. These are known to all visitors as being the seats chiefly used in the central garden and other parts of the exhibition grounds and building. The seat is formed of iron ribbons curved a little upwards, and thus having sufficient spring to make the seat easy and comfortable. The cane chairs shown by Mutet, and also used for visitors and in the cafés, will be mentioned presently. Wooden garden chairs, the frame of trestle form, the seat and back made of laths with $\frac{1}{4}$ in. between each, are shown by Auge, Auxerre; these, painted green, are priced 2s. each. The same exhibitor has light garden open palings, in rough sawn oak, at $4\frac{3}{4}d$. per square metre ($39\frac{1}{2}$ in.); planed ditto at $6d$.; painted at $8\frac{1}{2}d$.; a flower-stand, painted, nearly 5 ft. long, of four stages, 5s.

Household
furniture.

Of household iron furniture, Massé, Paris (1), exhibits a spring mattress, constructed to turn over, so as to be put aside in a small space when not in use. It is made for hospitals and boarding schools; but is inferior as a cheap object of its kind to that shown in Belgium, and alluded to below (Belg., 1720). Bray, Paris (6), has a steel cot of fairly good pattern and workmanship.

Of wooden furniture shown, the chairs by Lefebure, of Versailles (13), are worthy of notice. They are framed in wood, artificially curved, the back and back legs being of one piece, the seat frame formed of another curve with a straight brace in front. The woods used are principally ash, beech, and walnut. The prices, varnished, stained, or otherwise finished, are 6s. 4d., 8s., and 9s. 6d. each. Furniture and other objects made of curved wood have been manufactured for nearly twenty years at Vienna, and these chairs are imitations of the Viennese work, but less perfect than the original. The invention originated with a carpenter at Boppart, on the Rhine; and for years he spent all his earnings in endeavouring to perfect his process. He attained his object, migrated to Vienna, and, more fortunate than many inventors, succeeded in creating a great establish ment, whose workshops there and in Moravia and Hungary now turn out 700 chairs daily, and half Europe is acquainted with the results of his invention. In the Austrian section are shown some curious examples of this wood curving: double spiral springs of six coils formed of one piece of beech, and arm-chairs, with framework of most ingenious curves; tires of wheels also are thus made in one piece. The present specimens from Versailles possess some, but not all, the advantages of his invention.

Cheap unpainted furniture is shown by Dieudonné and Co., Paris (9), of beech, oak, and deal; kitchen tables and chairs of deal, framed in beech. A chest of drawers of this manufacture, about 3 ft. high by 4 ft. wide, containing four drawers, costs 16*s.*; a dresser, with cupboard and drawers below, about 5 ft. by 4 ft., costs 19*s.* These are roughly made, and inferior to the work of similar material and general character exhibited in the Canada section and noticed below.

J. Viollet, Paris (12), also shows cheap chairs and other furniture. Hat and coat pegs of good make, in oak and deer's horn, are exhibited by Morisot, Paris (10). Chairs, arm-seats for three persons, baskets, work- and other tables, made of rattan-cane, are shown by Mutet, Paris (11). They are strong from the toughness and elasticity of their material; are easy as seats, free from the chill and rust of iron, and light to carry; but the work is rough. A chair costs 5*s.* 8*d.*; a round table, 1*l.* Chairs of this manufacture are employed for the use of visitors in various parts of the exhibition building—a good test of their strength.

Niderer-Bresson, Paris (14), exhibits household furniture, with various coloured covers of plush, velvet, or reps. These sofas, arm-chairs, &c., are not to be commended though cheap. They belong to a style of furnishing frequent in France, but which had better be disused than extended.

Miroy, Paris (19), shows, among many exhibitors of similar articles, chimney-clocks, candelabra, candlesticks, lustres, and other ornamental objects in gilt metal, bronze, and its imitations. These, and such articles of decorative furniture, are a very important branch of manufacture in Paris, and are cheaply produced; it is officially stated that they form the main trade of no less than 30 quarters of the city, from the Quartier St. Denis to the Faubourg St. Antoine; and it is certain that for many such objects Paris is the market which supplies a great part of the world—the carrying traffic being, however, chiefly in English hands. They have a certain air about them which captivates the half-educated eye, and which passes for good taste; but they are really, for the most part, beneath criticism on the score of art. They may, however, lay claim to considerable ingenuity and to some prettiness; and it is satisfactory to remark that an advance has been made in some directions in the style of these cheap objects, better designs having been imitated or adapted from ancient models or from the costly works of distinguished artists—thus candlesticks of zinc bronzed, the designs for which are partly Greco-Roman and sometimes not inelegant, are to be bought at a very cheap rate. Bisson, Paris (42), exhibits mouldings and various room and shop fittings, glazed cases, bronzed, gilt, silvered, and oxydised decorations; to all these the remarks above made as to the ordinary character of such showy objects are fully applicable; they belong to a pretentious and often tawdry style, which seeks to bring art down to its own level rather than make the effort to lift itself to the level of art.

The second group of objects may be taken as those of personal use.

Blondel-Duval (73), exhibit spoons and forks of buffalo horn, at 16s. 8d. per dozen. Nail and tooth brushes are shown by several exhibitors, but not in general of satis- factory quality; those of Boulenger (88) may, however, be noticed. Mathez, Vosges (198), exhibits spoons and various objects of domestic use of tinned iron; but all these, and white iron goods in general in this division, are inferior, price for price, to those produced in England.

Buttons, in horn and bone, and spoons of bone, are shown by various exhibitors; but not of quality or price that com- petes with other countries.

Bachond-Caillat a Nantua, Ain (69), exhibits turned work of boxwood, similar to that supplied to the London market from Northamptonshire. Powder boxes are priced 7s. per dozen. He also shows chessmen, games of loto, &c.; ninepins, these of boxwood, 6 in. high, are 2l. 11s. 6d. per gross of sets.

Odent-Cauchois (86) shows metre and half metre gradu- ated rules, in ivory, buffalo, horn, and boxwood; half metre rules, in boxwood, are priced 2s. 6d. per dozen. Metre rules less finished, the same price. Rules, squares, and other drawing appliances are shown by Larive (72), Oise; these are cheap. Crosnier-Fleury (82) and Odent (82) exhibit fans, which in point of price can, perhaps, be best compared with those supplied to the European market from Japan; but the subjects upon them want the skill in colour and also the quaint humour which the Oriental artists throw into their sketches; the French fans can be sold in retail at 2*d.* and 2½*d.*

Feathers and feather brushes exhibited by Loddé, Paris (64), and those shown by Thuiller, Paris (185), are well prepared: the soft feather brushes of Paris manufacture are superior for their price to any to be got at present in England. The points of the feathers are not harshly cut, so that delicate lacquered and varnished objects can be safely dusted with them. They are also well got up and dyed, and the smaller sorts are thus made, if not ornamental, at least not unsightly, in a sitting-room. The trade in these is very considerable in Paris, and they are now exported in some quantity.

Lanterns, candle-shades, and lamps are exhibited; they are of lacquered tin; a dark lantern, at 3*s.* 2*d.*, of gilt metal and brass; a small brass lantern with bull's-eye, neatly made and very portable, for walking at night, is priced 2*s.* 9*d.* Tin and lacquered ware is also shown by Sapy, Haut Rhin (27); but these, in comparison with English hardware goods, do not call for remark.

Of pottery and the cheaper kinds of ceramic manufacture, Dureault, Motte, and Co., Rhone (151), exhibit glazed earthenware printed in colours, plates at 2*s.* per dozen, and other articles in proportion. Gosse, Bayeux (151), shows hard porcelain, test-tubes, retorts, &c., which is stated to be of a quality that has been severely tested. In the annexe to the south-east of the park are larger collections under this head. Stoneware for ordinary use, beer and water jars, ink-bottles, tobacco-pots, match-pots or boxes, &c., are shown by Bosset, Ciry, Saone et Loire (507); also liqueur vessels enamelled within, and other enamelled stoneware. The imitation of the texture and the applied ornament of the old Cologne Grès is successful in some of the cheap tobacco-pots. Boulanger exhibits, from the considerable manufactory at Choisy le Roi, Seine, a collection chiefly of semi-porcelain, marked "granit." This is for the most part of good body, and well glazed. Dinner, soup, and dessert plates, printed in two colours, are priced 2*s.* per dozen; cheese plates, 1*s.* 9½*d.*; dessert, with various subjects "de genre," printed in brown, 2*s.* 10*d.*, with monogram, 2*s.* 2*d.*; printed with well-designed pattern, covering the surface, of arabesques, trophies, &c., in lilac or blue, 4*s.*; dinner plates, ditto, 4*s.* 9*d.* Guerin, Gren-sur-Loire, shows a considerable collection and variety of "opaque porcelain," answering to our delft or glazed earthenware, but with a style and character very well marked. Some of the patterns on such ware may be regarded as tra-

Pottery.

ditional in France since the end of the 16th, and some since the beginning of the 18th centuries; others are reproductions from the fine glazed earthenware of Rouen, Nevers, Moustiers, &c., and often very successful; the glaze, contrasted with original examples, is thin and poor in comparison, wanting the creamy quality which brings out the colours on some old Rouen and Marseilles specimens; but for objects of use or ornament in which an effort is made to combine cheapness with effective colour and decoration, the manufacture of M. Guerin is to be commended.

It is not out of place to remark here that under the head pottery, in Class 91, there is no competition on the part of England, no selection having been made by our manufacturers of their cheaper goods; therefore, in commending the French examples a comparison is not intended. The pottery for household purposes produced by Doulton, of Lambeth, for example, is superior in quality of material, in style, and in its most excellent glaze to anything shown at similar prices by any other country; while, as regards the small objects of daily domestic use, there are hawked about the streets of London pieces of cheap pottery altogether better than anything shown in the whole Exhibition under Class 91. A teapot, holding a pint, made with a skill seemingly unknown to the cheap manufacture of France, the dark brown glaze fit to bear heat, and the lid closely-fitted and with a deep ledge, may be bought at a street stand in London for $5\frac{1}{2}d$.; its wholesale price in Staffordshire is small indeed.

Clothing. Under the head of clothing the number of French exhibitors is considerable, especially of articles ready made; in these the Paris trade, as must be the case in every great city, is very extensive; and some of the establishments whose advertisements on a gigantic scale cover the spaces in Paris left by the Bureau des Démolitions have further taken advantage of the Exhibition to announce themselves.

The clothes of tweeds and other woollen materials exhibited by Jacob-Levy and Simon, Paris (367), are of good substance at their price, generally well cut and made up. A short tourist coat of Tweed is priced 1*l.* 4*s.*; a light grey tweed shooting-coat, 1*l.* 10*s.*, and other articles in proportion. Devillard and Devillette, Paris (366), are principal exhibitors in the class of children's ready-made clothes. Piotet, Paris (368), exhibits shirts of check, &c., blouses, and various calico and linen clothing of fair quality and low price. Cheap felt hats for the poorer classes are shown by Jouany, Bourganeuf, Creuse (398); light grey, at 1*l.* 1*s.* 8*d.* per doz.; darker, and somewhat inferior in quality, at

MR. R. H.
SODEN
SMITH
ON FURNI-
TURE, &c.

17*s.* 6*d.* Caps for boys, képis, such as are worn by young cadets, and generally by French school-boys, are shown by several manufacturers ; they are, for the most part, of good material and remarkably well got up for their price, the large demand making them cheap. Herold, Paris (405), shows caps in dark cloth, neatly laced with imitation gold or silver cord, at 2*s.* 6*d.* and 2*s.* 2*d.* ; others of inferior cloth and with less ornament at 1*s.* ; some with gold-lace band, cording, and pattern over the peak in front, at 1*s.* 5*d.* Haas, Paris (407), also exhibits cheap caps. Straw-plaited work from various parts of the south of France, the great seat in the country of the manufactory, is shown by several exhibitors, and taking, of course, price into consideration, is of respectable quality. Rey and Galan (Department, Tarn and Garonne) show straw hats of various styles of plait. Beehive-crowned hats of black and white plait, straw band, finished with straw edging, are priced 3*s.* 2*d.* per dozen. Leborgne and Co., Grenoble (426), exhibit straw hats and trimmings of plait of very good quality, and also at low prices.

Cloth fez caps are shown by Dujoncquoy, Seine and Oise (237), of fairly good cloth, and of excellent colour. Boots, shoes, and slippers have many exhibitors, and in general the form and style is better than a similar cheap class of work would show in England ; this advantage might be expected to appear even in the most ordinary foreign work, as the French and many German boot—and shoemakers greatly surpass most of our own in adapting their boots to the form of the foot, and in making them neat, and at the same time comfortable. The difference in respect of neatness between the boots and shoes of the middle classes in London and Paris is very notable ; on the other hand, French work is apt to be less solid, and, respecting the important point of the probable durability of the materials in the specimens exhibited, no opinion can be expressed. Chollet, Seine and Oise (416), exhibits strong shoes, riding-boots, workmens' strong boots ; the last are of stout brown leather, but it would scarcely seem waterproof. These are priced 9*s.* 4*d.* This is stated to be the retail price ; if so, it is very cheap. Canvas shoes and slippers, somewhat similar to, but not so well finished as our gymnasium shoes, are much used in France and Switzerland, and are convenient in warm dry weather, and very cheap. Latour, Paris (413), exhibits them, of rather rough work certainly, but at 1*s.* 8*d.* per pair ; the better qualities at 2*s.* 6*d.* to 3*s.* 6*d.* Hempen-soled slippers, resembling the sandals frequent in Spain, mentioned below in the exhibition of Spanish objects, are

Mr. R. H.
Soden
Smith.
on Furni-
ture, &c.
much used in France, especially in the Pyrenean provinces,
made with canvas uppers; these, of good quality, women's
size, are shown by Salles, Lower Pyrenees (413), priced 7*d.*
per pair.

India-rubber waterproof clothing, wrappers, overcoats and
leggings, of good material and make, is shown by Engrand
and Co., Seine (319), and by Torrilhon, Verdier and Co.,
Paris (320). Duché and Co., Paris, the large manufacturers
of shawls of Cashmere patterns, who exhibit under class 32
(16), show a class of goods here cheaper in style and material.
These can only be judged of as regards quality and price by
examination and comparison with other specimens; but
when thus compared they will be found to be cheap, and
they so much excel ordinary productions of low price that
they merit having attention called to them.

Food.

The last of the groups into which we have broadly divided
class 91 is food; and the collection exhibited by France is of
considerable importance and variety.* Chocolate of which
the preparation is very extensive in Paris, and the consumption and exportation large, is shown by many manufacturers.
That exhibited by Ibled and Co., Paris (452), and prepared
with the aid of hydraulic pressure, is of good quality.
Ménier, Paris, shows chocolate prepared in a variety of forms,
also with much skill and success. It is from this manufacturer that many houses in London are supplied. A considerable variety of preserved vegetables are shown by twelve
principal exhibitors; but their preparations require the test
of experience to discriminate between them. Such vegetables are, however, much more employed in Continental
cookery than in English, and with considerable success. In
Holland and Belgium, as well as in France, dinners, during
winter, and especially the preparation of soup at that season
are much aided by these comparatively inexpensive kinds
of food. Asparagus, celery, portions of artichoke, are shown
seemingly well preserved, also carrots, peas, kidney-beans,
cauliflower, &c. Besides these, which are secured for the
most part in bottles, many exhibitors have tin cases of
preserved meat and vegetables, fruits, pickles, vinegar;
liqueurs and wines are also shown. Guillaut, Paris (437),
exhibits cakes of gingerbread similar to those for which
Amsterdam is noted. These are sold, according to quality,
at 5½*d.* to 7½*d.* per kilogramme.

---

* It may be noted that the position of this collection is such that it may be
easily overlooked, being wholly out of its order—if any order can be said to be
even attempted, much less adhered to. The collection is shown in a separate
small court, on a line with the cafés, and is entered from without the building.
Another important section of class 91 is in a remote " annexe," on the extreme
south-east of the park.

BELGIUM.

MR. R. H.
SODEN
SMITH
ON FURNI-
TURE, &c.
___
Belgium.

The objects shown are not numerous. They consist chiefly of textiles, and iron and wooden furniture. It would seem that the collection in class 91 suffers in the Belgian division, as it does on the English side of the Exhibition, from the circumstance of articles which might fairly have come within the scope of the class being shown in their special groups, without consideration of the question of their cheap production.

Lemaieur, Brussels (4), exhibits shawls, wrappers, and various woollen goods, tolerably exact reproductions of Scotch style and pattern, of good quality at their price ; for example, a tartan shawl, not the cheapest make, about 5ft. 6 in. square, is priced 6s. 6d.

Ruelens (1720 in Belgian catalogue) exhibits an iron spring bedstead, about 3ft. 6 in. by 6 ft., efficiently constructed with ribbon instead of coil springs, thus gaining the advantage of a spring mattress. This is cheap (1l. 4s.) Compare in construction with those noted under France (Massé, No. 1).

Messrs. Cambier, De Blauw, and Verheyden exhibit chairs of cherrywood and beech. Of these the best at their price are the folding cane-seated and backed chairs of Cambier (1), in varnished beech, at 4s. 2d. The same maker produces a varnished cherrywood chair, cane-seated, at 3s. 2d., and a beechwood ditto at 2s. 6d.

BADEN.

Dr. H. Meidinger, Carlsruhe, exhibits a sitting-room stove, constructed of dark tiles of a good chocolate-brown colour. It would not readily show discolouration by smoke or heat, and is so far well adapted to its purpose. The general plan of the stove is good, but it is not skilfully put together, and the glaze of the tiles is not of first-rate quality.

AUSTRIA.

The objects exhibited by Austria in class 91 are numerous and of very various character. Among those calling for observation are the following :—Elsinger and Son, of Vienna (No. 4), exhibit waterproof clothing and travelling objects ; the former are light and seem to have a surface sufficiently tough and flexible to wear well. Driving capes and coats, leggings and gaiters, are shown ; of the former a thin black waterproof coat, buttoned, and with loose sleeves, costs 12s. ; a white, of better quality and finish, 15s.; gaiters 2s. 6d. ; haversacks of the same material. They also exhibit a water-

MR. R. H.
SODEN
SMITH
ON FURNI-
TURE, &c.
proof tissue for hospitals, at 1s. 8d. per metre (39½in.) of a very tough and durable texture. This is a valuable and cheap material for its purpose.

Unterwalder, of Vienna (27), exhibits tarpaulins of strong but rough texture ; no information respecting their price has been furnished.

Wooden
blinds.
Attention is especially to be directed to the preparation of wood for matches and for window-blinds, screens, &c., the specimens shown for these purposes by Austria being superior to any exhibited by other countries; the wood is straight-grained deal, and, by means of planes made for the purpose on the principle of moulding-planes, it is cut into rods of ⅛ in. or less, in diameter and 3 ft. or 4ft. long. From these rods the small round Viennese match-boxes, with which we are familiar in England, are filled; the long pieces are made into sun-blinds and screens of excellent construction, which are light, strong, and roll into small compass. For these the demand is great, the inexhaustible supply of wood which the Austrian fir-forests yield affording cheap material.

Matches.
The process of the match manufacture which at present enables Austria to supply, in great measure, the English market, might, it would seem, be introduced with advantage into towns like Gloucester, where the large importation of wood supplies material and where the manufacture of matches is already established, but by processes less economical of labour. Schuberth, of Ottakring, near Vienna (23), is the principal exhibitor of this prepared wood, and the blinds, &c., made from it. Franz Reif also exhibits wood prepared for matches, frames for seives ; thin deal veneers, for match and other boxes; sabots, and wooden spoons.

Porcelain-headed nails of various colours, for furniture and for fastening down carpets, are shown by No. 23, above mentioned.

Among domestic utensils are to be noted the wooden staved and turned work shown by Neumayer, of Vienna (18); barrels, tubs, churns, bread-platters, &c. The staved and hooped work is good ; barrels, for example, composed of various woods ornamentally arranged and well fitted. Their prices may be judged from the following : barrel with move-able cover, chiefly oak, but composed like a Scotch quaigh, of several woods, about 1 ft. by 9 in. at its greatest diameter, 7s. 2d. ; barrel-churn, of oak, brass hooped, with fittings, about 15 in. by 12 in. 9s. 6d.

A useful beefsteak beater is shown by Simon Marth, of Vienna (14); a wooden clothes-horse, by Weiss and Son, Vienna, similar in plan to that mentioned under Canada, is priced 5s.

Some of the cast-iron household objects shown in class 40 (19) come also within class 91, as cheap utensils of domestic use; iron pots and skillets, enamelled within; a pot, well enamelled, 14 in. deep by 10 in. diameter, is priced 4s. 2d., and so on, in proportion to weight and size; a skillet, 7 in. diameter, 2½ in. deep, enamel-lined, 10d.

Beschorner and Co., Vienna (2), and J. Fr. Mayr (15), exhibit sarcophagi and coffins in metal and marble. Beschorner exhibits cast-iron sarcophagi, bronzed, silvered, and brown, lacquered, with gilt handles, plates, and ornaments, varying in price, according to size and finish, from 10s. 6d. to 36l.

SPAIN.

Of the few objects shown by Spain in class 91 the following deserve notice :— *Spain.*

Manuel Mas and Son (1), from Crevillente, in the province of Alicante, exhibit matting of grass and rush, which forms an exception in one respect to most objects shown in the class. It is exceptionally good in point of taste, the specimens being for the most part woven in diapers of various colours, the diapers well designed, and the colours generally suitable and harmoniously combined. A fine Turkey red, yellow, and purple are employed, the colour of the grass being itself of a good yellowish tone. Some of the diapers are minute and very skilfully woven on a hemp warp. The coarser matting is plaited. One of these, rich in colour, of red, yellow, and purple, about 6 ft. by 3 ft. 6 in., of very strong material, but rather rude work, is priced 6s. 6d. *Matting.*

Sandals of strong material and low price are shown by N. Peranton (2). These—in Spanish, *alpargatas*—have soles about half an inch thick, of twisted hemp, an edge of strong web, and black tape bands. For the army they are produced at less than 19s. per dozen. A better quality are 2s. 2d. per pair. (See the slippers noticed under France, No. 413) *Sandals.*

Similar sandals are shown by Miguel Casayus (4), from Huesca, and also another kind (*alborgas*) woven of tough bent grass, with toe and heel piece of the same material. These are sometimes gaily coloured by wools—scarlet, purple, &c.,—woven with the grass fibres, and are also manufactured very cheaply.

Caps worn by the peasants and others are shown by the Sociedad Economica de los Amigos del Pais (Economic Society of friends of the Country) : these are from Murcia. Catalonia also sends scarlet and purple long caps of cloth similar to those worn by Italian peasants at Spezia and elsewhere on the coast. The scarlet dye is fine and the cloth *Caps.*

fairly good. These cost only from 1s. 7d. to 2s. Some textiles are shown, but do not call for observation.

PORTUGAL.

Portugal.
Pottery.

In class 91 Portugal exhibits various Pottery, and among the specimens shown are some which, while they can be commended for the qualities of fitness and cheapness, that specially bring them within scope of class 91, deserve also to be noticed for satisfactory colour and forms of good outline. The texture of the porous pottery is good, and well fitted for the purpose ; some of the other kinds want strength and solidity. A green glaze used, on many pieces, is admirable in colour, and varies in tone sufficiently to escape the dead monotony and flatness often remarkable in English and French glazes. Several pieces are made in direct imitation of old English ware, some marked with the Davenport anchor. They are inferior in texture to but better in colour than their prototypes. The principal exhibitors are the Commission of Poyares and others, from Coimbra. Eugenia Vasconcelles (9), from Lisbon, exhibits some vessels of cheap character notable for good form.

ITALY.

Italy.
Chairs.

Chairs and specimens of straw and willow plaiting are the objects of exhibition most to be noticed from Italy. Of the former, those shown by J. Canepa (17), from Chiavari, Genoa, and by L. Descalzi (18), are to be commended. Most of their specimens come fairly into class 14 of furniture, but some for plain household use are included in class 91. They show well-made light chairs of beech, maple, &c., with woven white willow seats, varnished wood, at 3s. 4d., and Straw-plait. stained at 3s. 8d. Straw-plait is shown by J. F. Bo (25), from Sestri—hats of cheap work and material, chiefly for the peasant class. V. Bertolani (27), from Modena, exhibits willow-plait, for hat-trimmings, of even work and well-prepared material.

CANADA.

Canada.

Class 91 is represented in Canada by objects of considerable importance, though the number of exhibitors is small. One of the valuable industries of the country is the home-manufacture during the long winter, of woollen stuffs, cloths, shawls, blankets, &c.; these employ the females of the families and the young women generally in the farmers' households, and the results of this home-work as shown in the Exhibition are most satisfactory.

Mdme. Bouchard, from St. Valier (1), exhibits various stuffs made with considerable skill, of excellent material, and apparently of the most durable character. In classes 28 and 30 she also exhibits strong unbleached linen of home manufacture at 1s. per yard, and dark check, a stout material for plain dresses, at 1s. per yard. Marcel Fortin (11) shows stout woollen cloth of dark dye, 3s. per yard; good grey material, fit for shooting-suits, 3s. 6d. Mrs. Chandler (12) and James Busted show woollen socks and stockings of good quality, also of home manufacture. The conditions of the production of these objects at a period of the year when the severity of the climate causes a cessation of much ordinary female industry, and when a practical and profitable resource is of double importance, give their manufacture a greater social value than its extent would otherwise entitle it to claim; moreover, their excellent quality for purposes of domestic use and their cheapness, considering this quality, claim notice and commendation.

Messrs. Jacques and Hay (2) and Owen M'Garvey, Montreal (3), exhibit household furniture, perfectly plain in character, commendable for its substantial make and cheapness. The work is thoroughly honest, unpainted, or varnished, having the surface finished up with glass paper; each article delivered in pieces for putting together. Oak and hickory are the woods chiefly used, the lighter parts, where no stain occurs, being of white pine; almost the whole is machine-made. A chair of hickory costs 1s. 3d.; an armchair, 2s.; a chest of drawers, about 3ft. 6in. high, framed of oak, with hickory mouldings and white pine drawers, costs 15s.; locks and neat polished handles are forwarded for fitting on, and these are extra. This furniture is almost entirely made for exportation, and the West Indian islands are the chief market.

The portable folding clothes-horses—four moveable arms radiating from a centre—as well as the louvre shutters for windows and meat-cupboards, exhibited by George Hager and Co., Montreal, and made at their factory, Shearers Mills, Lachine Canal, Montreal, come within class 91, as examples of convenience and economy: these are all machine-made, of hickory and white pine, and are manufactured chiefly for exportation.

In the preceding report incidental allusions only have been made to articles exhibited by Great Britain. In point of fact, our own country cannot be said to be represented at all in class 91, the objects, as has been already observed, that would have fairly come within the class on the score of their cheap production being distributed under their several heads

[Side notes:] MR. R. H. SODEN SMITH ON FURNITURE, &c. — Woollen and linen goods. — Furniture. — Great Britain not represented.

in other groups, and no selection having been made by their producers to illustrate the very class which would have explained the condition and quality of their manufacture. Thus, the country which supplies the greater part of the world with cheap manufactured goods is unrepresented in an exhibition of the very articles of her principal commerce. In some instances, indeed, this failure seems to have been accidental. Amongst the woollen goods sent by Messrs. Firth, of Heckmondwike, Yorkshire, were some intended for class 91, as examples of cheap manufacture ; but they are shown in class 30, No. 29, where their quality of cheapness is not necessarily noticed. This has been the case with others, also. There remain, therefore, but a few objects, to be found by diligent search in the British section ; and it has not been thought so necessary to draw the attention of the visitor to them as to others, even similar in general character, shown by foreign countries. Among aids to do-mestic economy and convenience, it is, however, right to mention that the well-known knife-cleaning machines of Geo. Kent, High Holborn, are exhibited. The asylum at Redhill, Surrey, has sent proofs of the industry of its unfor-tunate inmates ; and the Society for Promoting Female Education in the East shows needlework, &c. Silver and Co., London, exhibit ready-made clothing and various objects of household use, at very low prices.

Conclusion

In conclusion, without recapitulating the few observations made at the commencement of this report, some emphasis may be added to them by noting the following points which forced themselves on the writer's attention while studying the mass of various articles which constitute this very com-prehensive, and socially most important class :

1st. A great advance has been made by some continental nations, notably by France and Belgium, in competing with Great Britain in the supplying of cheap goods and objects of daily use : the textiles of Belgium, some of them in direct imitation of our Scotch woollen goods, are an example ; so also are some of the water-proof clothing, and the pottery and porcelain produced in France.

2nd. Continental nations still completely retain some minor branches of industry which could be advantageously pursued by Great Britain, and largely share in other manu-factures ; many of the "articles de Paris" may be instanced ; also hat, glove, and silk manufactures.

3rd. The relative success of foreign competitors has been obtained by improvement in machinery, in processes of manufacture, in more ready supply of raw material, in additional facilities for transport and exportation, not by the development of other and higher sources of success to which allusion will presently be made.

These observations touch more especially matters affecting Great Britain, but the following are applicable more or less to all countries exhibiting:

4th. The effects produced upon the objects composing class 91 by the conviction to which their manufacturers have more and more yielded that success in trade can scarcely be attained except by the supply of articles at small profits to large numbers of purchasers.

> *a.* The consequent necessity of rapid and vast production with the necessary intervention of much machine-work between the original brain-labour that conceived the object and the ultimate result.
>
> *b.* The increase in production in the direction of inferior and cheap goods rather than in those of higher quality; centres of manufacture formerly notable for a high class of products are now in many cases given up almost wholly to the trade in cheap and inferior goods.

5th. The great room there is for improvement beyond what has hitherto been achieved in the production of almost all articles various as they are, that come within the scope of class 91, not only in design but in adaptation to their purposes, in material, and in manufacture. It is scarcely possible to conceive anything more false in taste, more absurd in the application of what is miscalled ornament than the majority of the objects displayed in class 91; nevertheless, in many cases the application to these articles of a very little true art would instantly raise their mercantile value. Roubiliac's drawings and Flaxman's designs gave money value to Wedgwood's pottery even at the time when it was produced, and Wedgwood well understood this. As far as the requirements of cheap manufacture go, it would be almost as easy to produce carpets, rugs, and mats at least inoffensive to the eye as to weave things that are hideous; an oriental workman using his inheritance of art-practice goes right as it were by instinct; at this side of the world art-education is needed, and no comment on that want could be so cogent as a visit to class 91 in this Exhibition.

6th. The probable social effects of the great difference still existing between the cost of production and the retail price of an article to the poorer class of purchasers; a difference which suggests to these classes the economy of associations among themselves, such as are already at work in some localities, for the production and supply of articles of daily consumption.

Finally, it is obvious that if Great Britain is to continue competing successfully with her continental rivals in the supply of articles which surround the daily life of millions and which represent a trade encompassing the whole globe, her manufacturers must bring to bear on their business higher qualities than are commonly deemed necessary for money making; qualifications, some of which at least must necessarily be sought beyond their own body—inventive capacity, knowledge and practice of art, wide acquaintance with new materials, and scientific skill to make them available.

No other than brain labour and that of sterling quality will enable supremacy in manufacture to be retained, and that brain labour becomes more and more difficult to depend on as superficial systems of hurried education, with some special examination always in view, come into use for those who ought to be trained to power of thought not merely to hasty acquisition of ill-assorted facts.

REPORT on DWELLINGS CHARACTERISED by CHEAPNESS MR. CHAD COMBINED with the CONDITIONS NECESSARY for DWELLINGS. HEALTH and COMFORT.—(CLASS 93.)—By EDWIN CHADWICK, ESQ., C.B., Correspondent of the Institut.

IT may now be taken as proved to' all who have a com- Extent of petent knowledge of sanitary science that fully one-half of premature the diseases which afflict the wage classes in the towns, and mortality in many rural districts of Great Britain, and, more or less by improved so, those in the Continental cities, are occasioned by local dwellings. causes in or about their dwellings, together with the misuse of their dwellings by overcrowding. This has been demonstrated in various instances in towns. Indeed, from particulars furnished to me by the late Sir Charles Phipps in relation to the death rate prevalent amongst the cottagers on Her Majesty's estate at Osborne, where attention has been directed to their sanitary condition, it was manifest that if the like attention were paid to the sanitary condition of the dwellings of the wage classes throughout the United Kingdom, their general death rate would be about one-half what it now is, even in the rural districts.

Considering the vast extent of evil which is proved to be preventible by improved sanitary constructions, it must be confessed with regret that the Exhibition presents evidence of only incidental and an utterly incommensurate amount of attention to the great subject; and that the model dwellings erected within the precincts of the great building, with one exception, display no advance in principles, and no important improvement in construction, and, in one most important point, a falling off from those which the careful judgment of H.R.H. the Prince Consort adopted and displayed in the model dwellings which he caused to be erected in connexion with the International Exhibition of 1851. Nevertheless, an extended attention to this important subject has followed that first public exhibition of a model dwelling, and important efforts of special interest to those who appreciate it are presented in this Exhibition. France, which had no model dwellings in connexion with its Exhibition of 1856, has now six models constructed; Prussia has one, and Austria one. England has only plans and models, of no novelty or special merit, that are not familiarly known, and may be passed by for further improvement.

3.

The leading Continental example of model dwellings within the Exhibition is one, a block of four, a type of the new houses of the wage classes of a new town, or cité ouvrière, constructed in connexion with the manufacturers of Mulhouse.

The foremost minds of France, of the Academy of Moral and Political Science of the Institut, had their attention directed to the manifestations of misery and disorder concurrently with the spread of manufactures in its chief cities. The late Dr. Villerme, of the Institut, visited and examined the condition of the working classes in the manufacturing towns, and drew a frightful picture of the drunkenness, misery, and physical and moral disorder in which he found the wage classes of the new manufactures heaped together in old or temporary habitations. The Academy deputed another of its distinguished members, M. Reybaud, to continue and extend these investigations; and he has prepared able reports on the progress of the cotton, woollen, and silk manufactures. M. Jules Simon, also of the Institut, has devoted himself to the task of visiting and examining the condition of the wage classes, and stated his results in two masterly works, "The Workwomen" and "The Workmen." In my own view, if I may venture to say so, my honoured colleagues of the Institut have even yet fallen short in their estimate of the demoralising influences of bad physical conditions, or the means of their removal. A comprehensive review of the economical and social results of the efforts made up to this time, which may be commended to all who would study the subject, is contained in a work, "Les Institutions Ouvrières de Mulhouse et des Environs, par Eugène Veron." In this last work will be found interesting narratives of long fights maintained by benevolent and enlightened persons against misery and ignorance, in which he shows how inferior were the results of all measures of cure and alleviation by charities, and how superior were the results of well directed exertions in the way of prevention, under the leadership of M. Jean Dolfus, an eminent manufacturer, the present Mayor of Mulhouse, who deemed the great point of attack on the progressive mass of evil to be in the amendment of the habitations. He has told me that his own thoughts took this direction from a view and study of H.R.H. the Prince Consort's model dwellings attached to the International Exhibition of 1851. M. Dolfus first got a plan of a house with four dwellings, made by M. Muller, a local architect, with modifications considered to be adapted to the people and the country, and had it built as a trial work. He then got up a society, under the title of the Société des

Cités Ouvrières," with a capital of 300,000f. ; and, out of 60 shares, took 35 himself.

His Majesty the Emperor has always been in advance of political parties in his special regard for the welfare of the wage classes, and his desire to improve their physical condition. In 1849 there was erected, under his direction, as President of the Republic, a cité ouvrière of Paris—that of the Rue Rochecourt. Shortly afterwards, by decrees of the date of Jan. 22 and March 1852, a sum of 10,000,000f. was allotted for the amelioration of the dwellings of the labourers in the great manufacturing cities, from which grant Mulhouse derived some aid. But of the cité ouvrière it must be said that although devised with a view to economy its construction was ill-advised and unfortunate ; for, with the aspect of a barrack, it had not the complete independence of each tenement which is maintained in the houses of Miss Burdett Coutts and Mr. Peabody, and in other recent constructions ; as also in the construction of " flats," or dwellings for the higher classes, such as those in Victoria Street and other places.

The ouvriers of Paris refused to be what they called " caserné," or " barracked." The result of this well intended effort has, I apprehend, been to retard progress; for, where it is necessary for the wage classes in manufacturing towns to be near their work—a necessity which is increasing with us—where land is consequently high priced, it follows as a collateral necessity to construct what I have called " perpendicular streets," to save the heavy ground rents of horizontal streets, and also to do something on narrow space, where wide space is not obtainable at any price. There are moreover, in the massive constructions various economies and collective advantages obtainable beyond those which are to be got for small separate cottage constructions—e.g., common wash-houses and drying-sheds, baths, common store-rooms, &c.; and a better future—for improved water supply, improved drainage, warming, lighting, and ventilation—than is yet furnished for single tenements for the wage classes. Moreover, the report of the working of detached or semi-detached or widely spread suburban dwellings, with cheap railway transit, for the wage classes, is not entirely favourable. The wives find it dear to be at a distance from the town markets and the town shops as also from their work. The men make one complaint, which would not commonly be anticipated—that, after a hard day's work they feel the vibration of the common railway carriages, as they are now constructed, to be peculiarly disagreeable to them, if not injurious. They, many of them, say they feel

Q 2

MR. CHAD-
WICK ON
DWELLINGS.

after a few weeks' use of railway travelling, they have an increased degree of lassitude beyond what they had before, and are not so well up to their work as they were in their town residences.

At Mulhouse, the distance from the manufactory of the land available for the new company was not very great. "After due deliberation," says M. Veron, "the committee unanimously rejected the principle of the great barracks which had so ill succeeded in Paris and elsewhere. If these buildings have the advantage of economy and ground-rent and cheapness of construction, they have on the other side, in the agglomeration of the population, a crowd of inconveniences, the least of which is the repugnance of the working classes to this sort of dwellings."

Several modifications of the principle of detached dwellings were tried at Mulhouse; but that which, after some years of trial, has been found the most eligible, is the one exhibited in the garden of the Exhibition, on the principle of the Prince Consort's cottage of four houses under one roof, occupying, however, each a perfect quarter of a square, separated by a double wall, light and ventilation being received at the gable end as well as at the front. The ground occupied by each house is about 45 yards, and each has about 144 square yards of garden extending in front of the house and a part of the gable to the line of the wall of the next house.

The Mul-
house plan.

The following is a portion of the plan of a Mulhouse village (*see next page*).

External
ventilation
of dwellings.

The sanitary advantages of this arrangement of the dwellings, primitive as it is, as parts of a town, consist in the more free sweep of air through the town and better external ventilation of the dwellings, as well as the advantages of the garden, for children and the family in fine weather. But from various plans exhibited of blocks of dwellings of the wage classes it appears to me that further attention is required to be paid to this subject of external ventilation in the arrangement of buildings and of towns, which it may be well to notice for the sake of new colonies as well as new suburbs.

Some of the healthiest and strongest populations, at least in England, are those living in detached cottages on high elevations on granite, sandstone, or other primitive rocks, where, from the indifferent carpentry, or loose window fastenings, the cottages are constantly ventilated externally as well as internally on all sides, despite of themselves, where the ground about them is frequently storm washed, where the water they get is soft and pure, and where their food is ample though simple, of oatmeal, potatoes, meat, and unlimited

ROAD

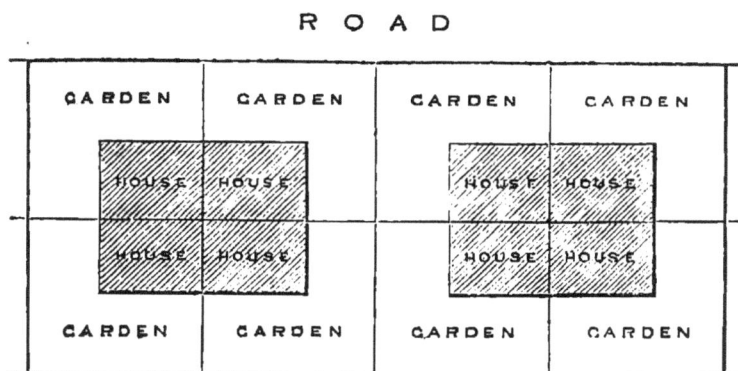

ROAD

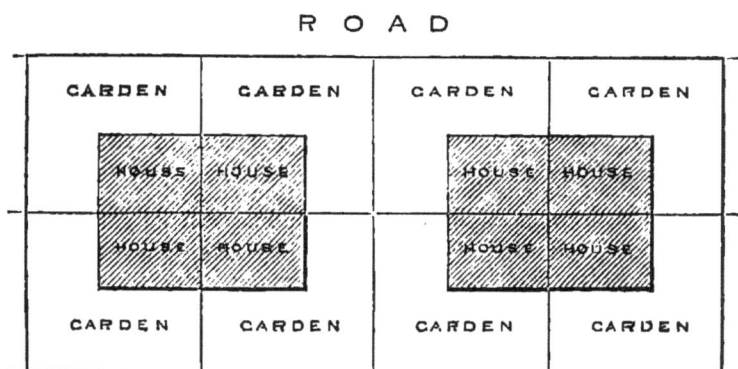

ROAD

supply of milk or butter-milk. A frequent arrangement of dwellings of the wage classes, as displayed in several plans adopted by the army sanitary commissioners of blocks of dwellings connected with manufactures is often in completely or nearly-closed squares, constituting reservoirs or wells of stagnant air, which becomes vitiated. In the arrangement of hospital huts, the subject of external ventilation is often well attended to, and their plans may be presented for consideration in suburban districts or in rural districts where the price of land is not a serious obstacle. Thus the common arrangements, even of detached dwellings, should be avoided on low ground, or on all but exposed situations. Thus on this usual arrangement, the winds blowing from the

directions A and B are the only winds which would sufficiently ventilate each hospital hut or dwelling. Any movement of the air from the points C and D will be arrested by
the end huts, and the effluvia from the huts would be carried
from one end to the other along the line ;—air moving from
all intermediate points would be more or less interrupted,
and free external ventilation interfered with.

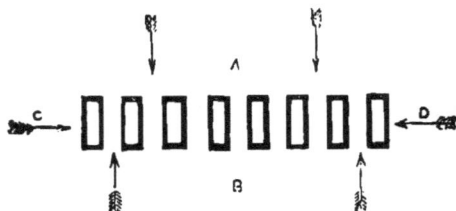

A modification of this arrangement has sometimes been
adopted which to a certain extent obviates these objections. It consists in arranging the hut in two lines
instead of one line with the huts more apart, and so placed
that a hut in one line is opposite to a space between two
huts in the opposite line. But each line will be subject to
the same condition that the wind can only blow beneficially
upon it, at right angles to its direction. If, however, the
huts or dwellings be arranged in echellon, the advantage
obtained in external ventilation becomes apparent.

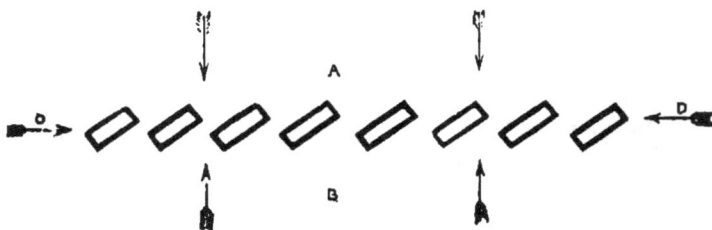

It will be seen that in whatsoever direction the wind
blows, it must sweep freely round the huts. When it is
practicable to obtain the full benefit of the prevailing winds
the sides A or B should face them. If the ground should
not admit of such a length of line the cottages may be
arranged in double echellon, the lines being kept at a

sufficient distance from each other, or the line may be bent thus:—

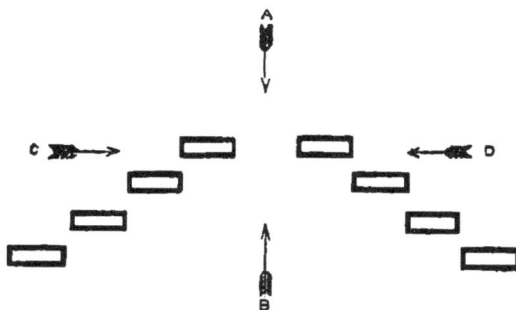

But it is possible to enclose a space within and yet to retain the advantages of full ventilation, as thus:—

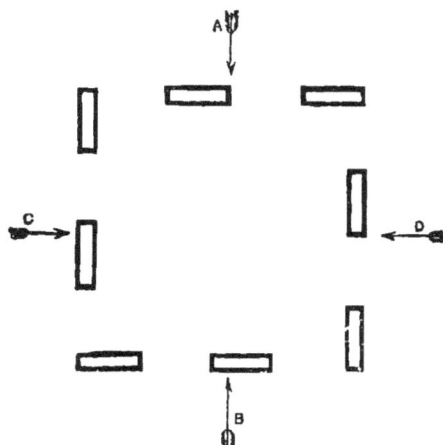

In the arrangement of close urban blocks of dwellings and in laying down new colonial sites, the plan of Sir Christopher Wren for the rebuilding of the city of London after the great fire may be advantageously studied for the introduction of diagonal and polygonal lines, which admit of a better sweep of air and external ventilation, as well as better lines for traffic, than the square closed block, plans on which urban districts are commonly arranged. In the improvement of Paris the diagonal principle of arrangement has been advantageously adopted. In all these arrangements care should be taken to keep the lines open to the suburbs, and not allow them to be crossed or made dead ends, by other dwellings. In the instances even of hospitals, as well as in private dwellings, I have seen too many instances, where the internal ventilation ended in pumping in an almost worse external air from closed streets or courts, in which the air was stagnant and vitiated by the want of external ventilation.

The following are sketch views and plans of one block of the Mulhouse dwellings.

SKETCH VIEW AND PLANS OF ONE BLOCK OF THE MULHAUSEN VILLAGE.

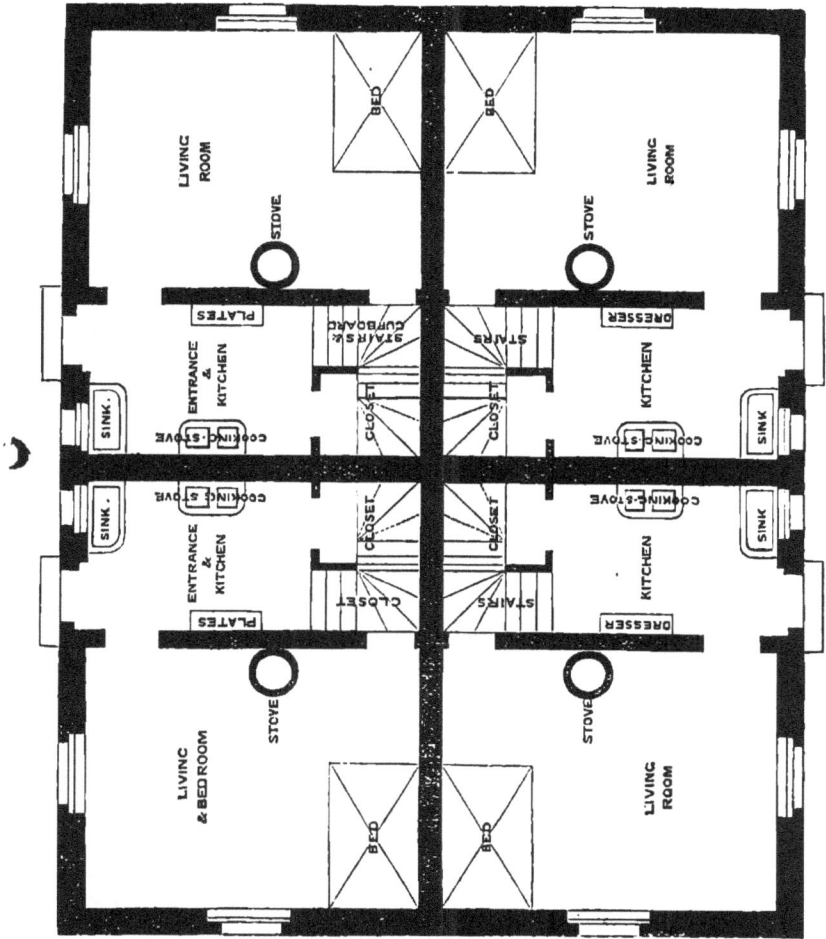

Ground Plan.

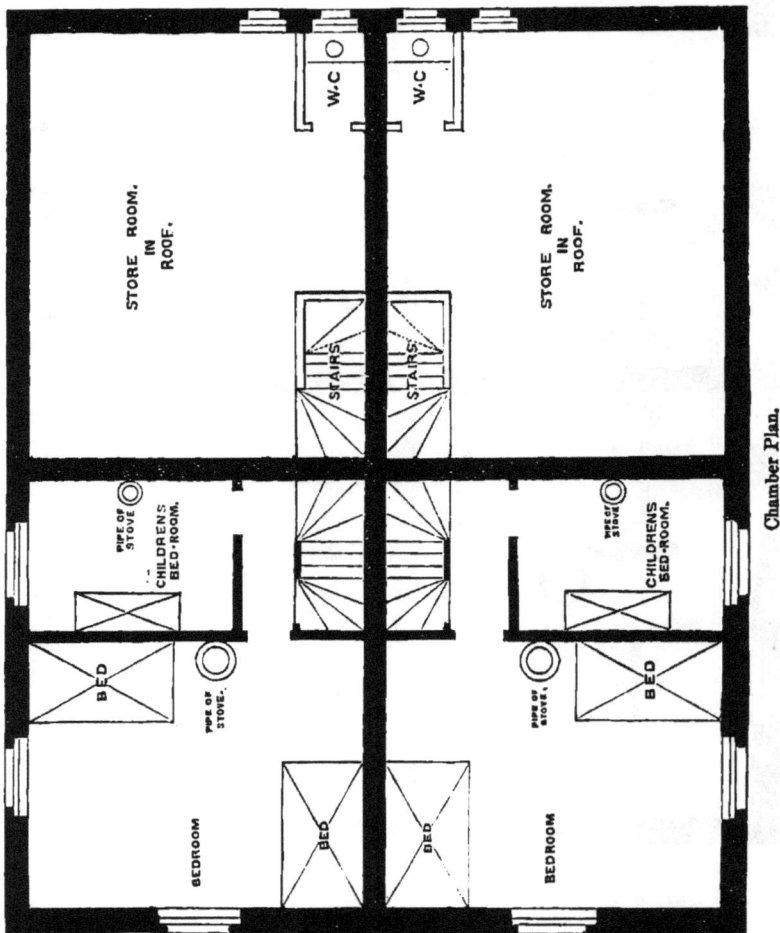

W.C. W.C.

STORE ROOM. IN ROOF.

STORE ROOM. IN ROOF.

STAIRS. STAIRS.

Chamber Plan.

PIPE OF STOVE.

CHILDRENS BED-ROOM.

PIPE OF STOVE.

CHILDRENS BED-ROOM.

BED

PIPE OF STOVE.

PIPE OF STOVE.

BED

BEDROOM

BED

BED

BEDROOM

It appears to me that the plan is good, and that several internal sanitary arrangements are very good in principle. I shall, however, reserve some observations on details of the construction of these dwellings until I am enabled to make them comparatively on the same points in the other dwellings to be noticed in connexion with the Exhibition.

The cost of each house complete is 3,000f., or 120*l.*, with the adjuncts of the garden, the kitchen, the cellar, and the loft. They are sold to the workmen, who pay for them, first, by an advance of 250f. or 300f., and then by annual

instalments of principal and interest, so as to become proprietors of their houses in fourteen or fifteen years. Out of
692 dwellings constructed by the company up to August
1865, 640 were sold, and the financial operations of the company were completely succesful. The example was followed
at Guebwiller, by the manufacturers of the distinguished
house of Bourcart, where 139 model houses have been
constructed of which 49 are attached to the manufactory of
the Messrs. Bourcart themselves, who do not sell, but let
them to their own workpeople. Another company has been
formed with success at Beaucourt; and the example of
these three places has, it is reported, given a great impulse
to the construction of improved dwellings in other manufacturing towns of France. As an advance upon almost single
chambered dwellings, the Beaucourt cottage, for the village
watchmaker, and the village tailor, with the work room and
living rooms combined, are deserving of notice as a distinct
species.

SKETCH VIEW AND PLANS OF THE BEAUCOURT COTTAGE.

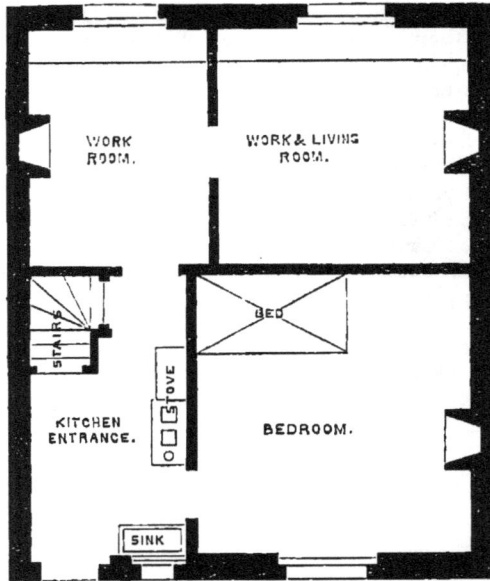

Ground Plan.

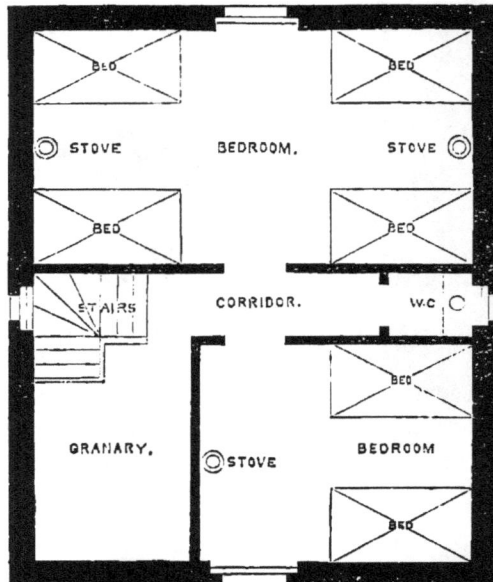

Chamber Plan.

Other sets of buildings, and the foundations, indeed, of new towns, are declared to have been originated in other Continental states by the influence of the successful example set by the Prince Consort at the Exhibition of 1851.

At the present time three distinct economical principles for the provision of improved dwellings for the wage classes are brought under consideration in relation to the chief examples in the Exhibition. 1st, that of ownership by the occupant; 2nd, that of the occupation of dwellings constructed and owned by the employer; 3rd, that of the common renting of the tenement for weekly or various periods. The 1st is chiefly the principle of those buildings actually constructed and contributed from France in the Exhibition, the 2nd the buildings constructed by Mr. Titus Salt, of Saltaire, near Bradford, of which plans are exhibited in the British department. I was sorry not to see in the Exhibition the plans of what is reported to be a highly-distinguished example of workmen's dwellings, with adjuncts, baths, &c., built by M. Godin Lemaire, of Guise, for the 600 workmen he employs, near St. Quentin, in the manufacture of kitchen ranges, grates, and stoves. Of the third principle, that of the ordinary renting, the chief examples offered in the Exhibition are from England; those of the metropolitan society for the improvement of labourers' dwellings, and those of Miss Burdett Coutts, Mr. Peabody's, and the Waterloo buildings. Each principle has its advantages for application under different conditions. The success of the proprietary principle (of which there are various legal administrative conditions for the study of imitators, open for examination in the buildings at the Exhibition) is reported upon by trustworthy observers as most conspicuous and decided for the wage classes, as well as the capitalist, at Mulhouse. The repeal of the pernicious law of parochial settlement in England, and the increasing scarcity of labour, are beginning to create a competition for good, steady, and respectable labourers and their families by the erection of comfortable dwellings by proprietors. And the question is beginning to be widely entertained as to the most eligible principle of construction. When intelligent capitalists and manufacturers take the matter up it may be anticipated, from examples already given, that a higher degree of comfort may be anticipated than is or can be attained by individuals of the wage classes. On the third principle of ordinary renting, it is to be observed in the interests of those classes that the investments of the most advanced in intelligence may often be more conveniently and economically made otherwise than in fixed habitations. A study of the chief products of the Exhibition will show that the future condition of manu-

[marginal notes:] Mr. Chadwick on Dwellings.

Economical principles of dwellings, construction, and holdings.

MR. CHAD-
WICK ON
DWELLINGS.

factures, as well as the present, will be a condition of great change in their location as well as in their subject-matter, —of change from province to province as well as from one part of a city to another. In these changes the wage classes must participate, of which I might adduce large examples. In poor-law administration I have been concerned in sales of small properties, chiefly cottage property, to the amount of nearly a million sterling, which, by such changes, or by destitution, or by death and want of competent succession to the property, have fallen to the local administrations. At Mulhouse, however, changes, by the death of the family, by the terrible conscription taking away one of its most productive members, or by the need of going elsewhere for employment, are recognized and provided for by the building society. A repurchase is made *à l'aimable,* and to the greatest extent in the interest of the purchaser, who is considered to have been a simple renter, to whom his monthly advances of purchase-money are returned. This liberal policy partakes of the wisdom of the whole management of the company, which may be commended to particular study, as set forth by Mons. Veron. Holdings under such a company, which are not unconditional even when the purchases are completed, are very distinct from perfectly individual proprietorships. As a rule, a poor man makes a poor landlord, and for his family a bad one; and it would be better for them to be under a rich one. The family of the poor man have to submit to discomforts from dilapidations, without the power of freeing themselves by any change from him. Moreover, I have never hitherto met with an instance of any structural improvement or advance in the dwellings of the wage class or peasant proprietary made by themselves. There is, however, one conspicuous and interesting example presented by the present Exhibition. In respect to the general economical policy of the wage classes, which is applicable to peasant proprietary of land as well as houses, when a man of this class can rent his land, as he commonly may in England at $3\frac{1}{4}$ or $3\frac{1}{2}$ per cent., or if he can rent his house at 5 per cent., it will be better for him to place his money in any insured investment for an equivalent or a better amount, as it will leave him free to change his market for his services or his savings. The peasant proprietor who holds his own lands at little more than 3 per cent., might, by purchasing manure or stock with his capital, get 10 per cent. or more.

The Emperor's plan.

His Majesty the Emperor, in his continued interest in the question of the improvement of the dwellings of the wage classes, about two years ago directed some new dwellings to be built, as is stated, on a plan of his own. They are erected in the Avenue de la Bourdonnaye, in the Champ de Mars, not far from the Exhibition building. They are on the following general plan :—

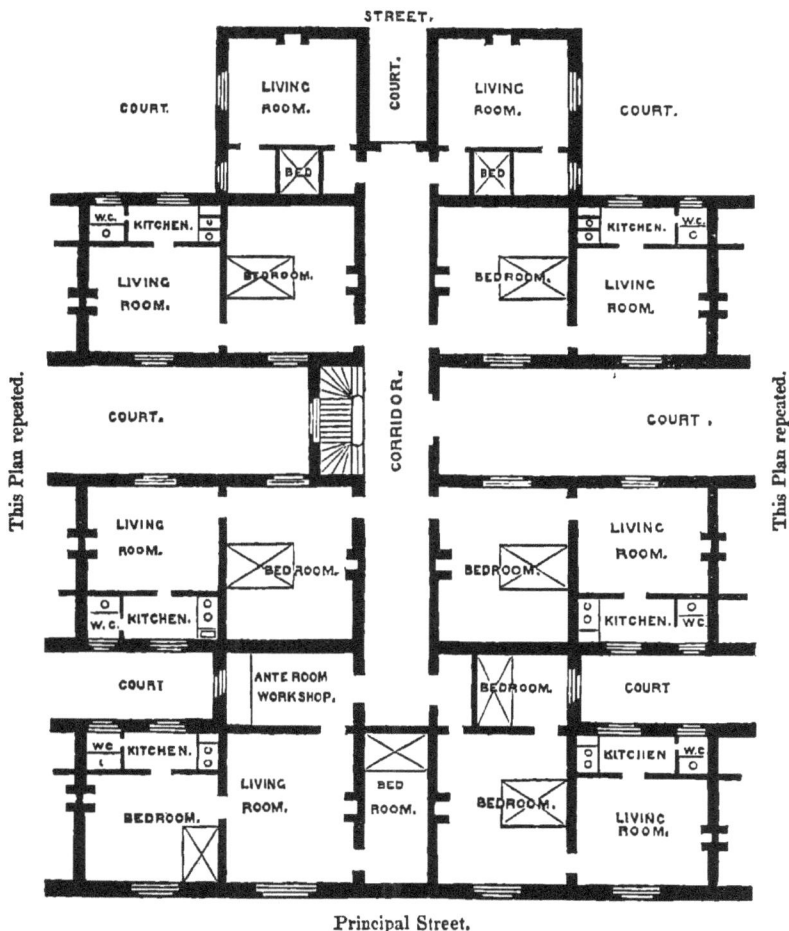

STREET.

COURT. | LIVING ROOM. | COURT. | LIVING ROOM. | COURT.

BED

W.C. | KITCHEN. | KITCHEN. | W.C.

LIVING ROOM. | BEDROOM. | BEDROOM. | LIVING ROOM.

COURT. | CORRIDOR. | COURT.

LIVING ROOM. | BEDROOM. | BEDROOM. | LIVING ROOM.

W.C. | KITCHEN. | KITCHEN. | W.C.

COURT | ANTE ROOM WORKSHOP. | BEDROOM. | COURT

W.C. | KITCHEN. | KITCHEN. | W.C.

BEDROOM. | LIVING ROOM. | BED ROOM. | BEDROOM. | LIVING ROOM.

Principal Street.

SKETCH PLAN OF THE EMPEROR'S HOUSES IN EXHIBITION.

This plan was the result of his individual attention, and he maintained it against some objections offered to it, in a block of 41 more dwellings for the wages class (in the Avenue Dumesnil, near the Bois de Vincennes), but with a very important change in the principle of the wall construction, to be hereafter described.

The following is the elevation of these dwellings :—

I went over the occupied buildings with some of the international jury, and I requested that the experience and
feelings of the occupying housewives might be consulted as
to the dwellings; and they were consulted separately, when
they were found to be in unanimous and passionate disagree-
ment with His Majesty's arrangement of the rooms. They
complained, that he had so arranged the rooms, that they
had always to go through the bedroom to the kitchen, where
they have their principal occupation. Perhaps the mistake
arose from following the common English arrangement, which
is to place the *scullery* in the rear of the house, the cooking
being done by the English housewife in the front living-room,
at the common fire.

The associated workmen of Paris, whilst they bowed
reverently to his judgment in the great arrangement of the
position of States, yet ventured to assert their own in the
position of their cuisine, and of the rooms in which they were
to live, and declared that they could themselves make improvements in them—as they would show if they only had the
money. Whereupon the Emperor benignly said they should
have the money to show what best suited them, and granted
them an allowance of 26,000f. to make their own trials, and
the first result is the model dwelling of the workmen of
Paris, which is constructed close by that of Mulhouse, within
the Exhibition. We give the elevation of their building,

which they conspicuously proclaim is designed and con- structed by themselves—*sans architecte et sans entrepre-* *neur :*—

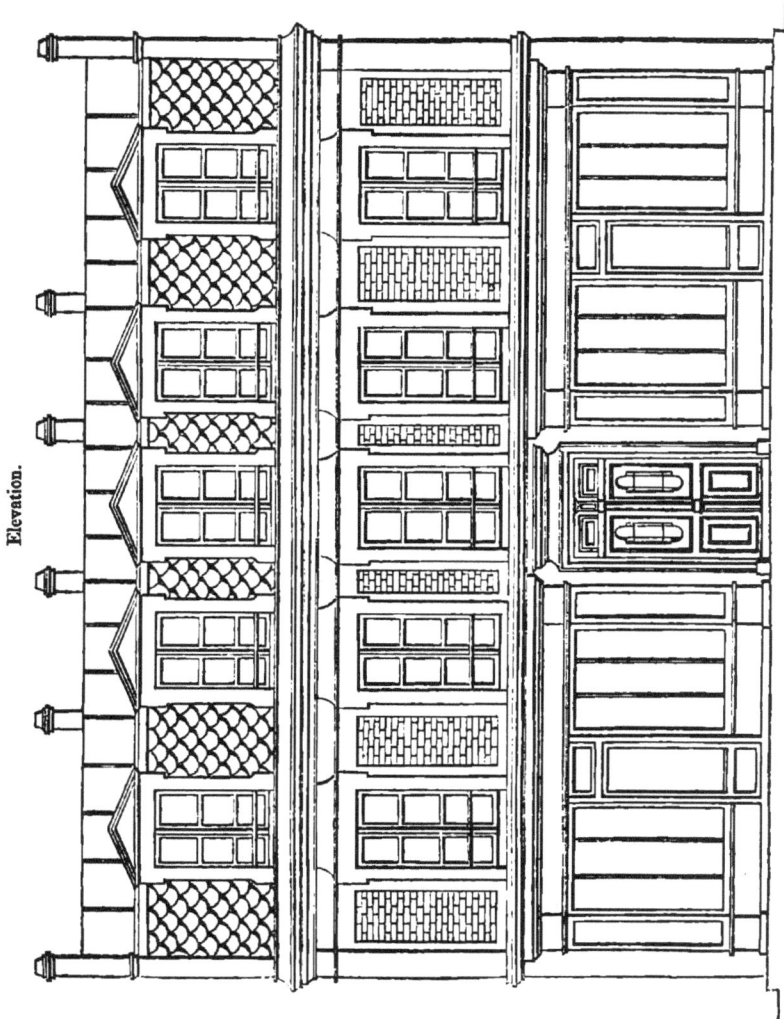

Elevation.

Section.

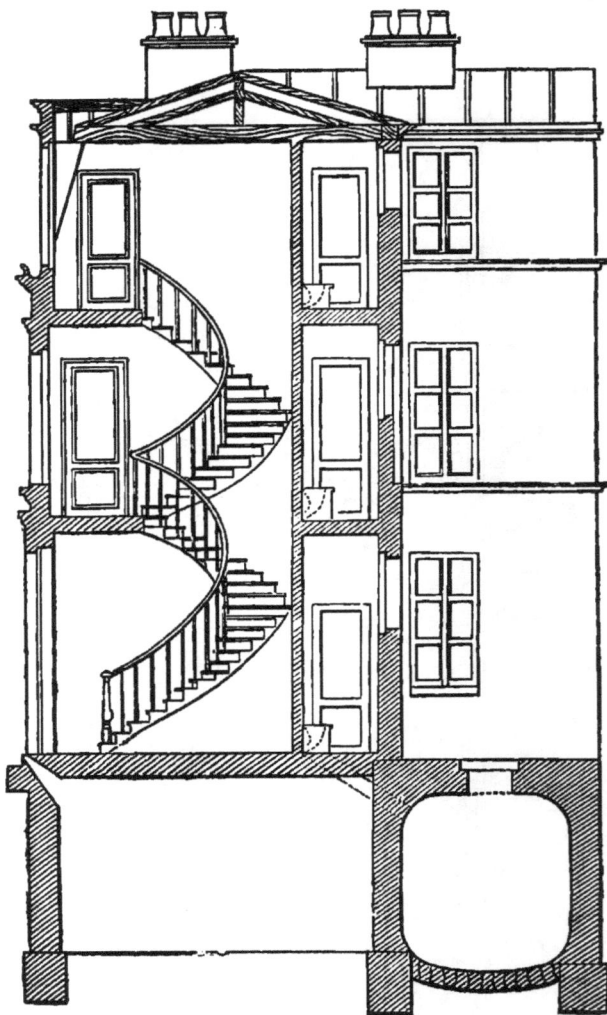

The following is their plan, in which it may be observed
that they reverse the arrangement made by His Majesty, and place the cuisine in front of their dwelling.

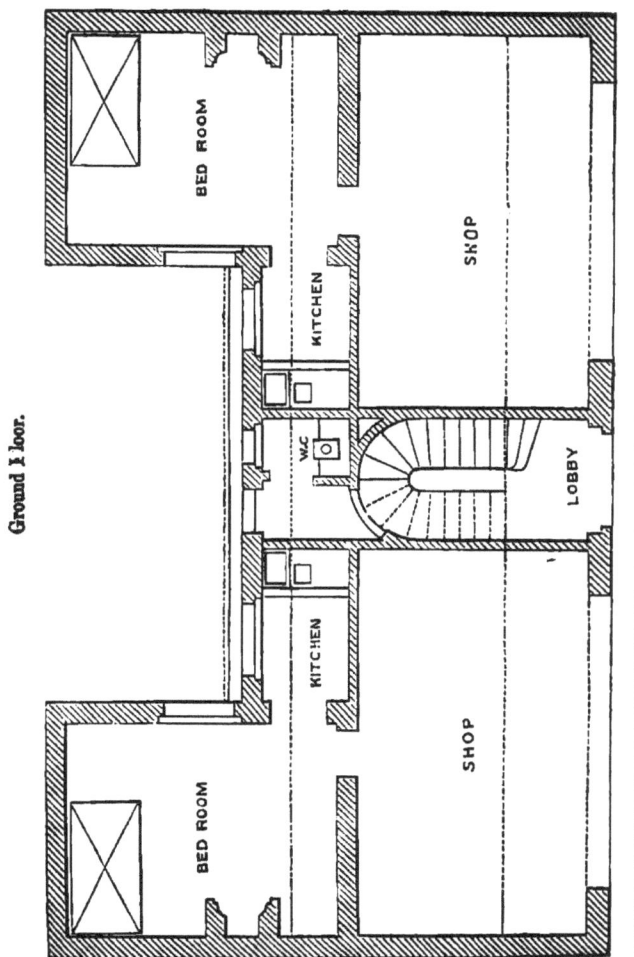

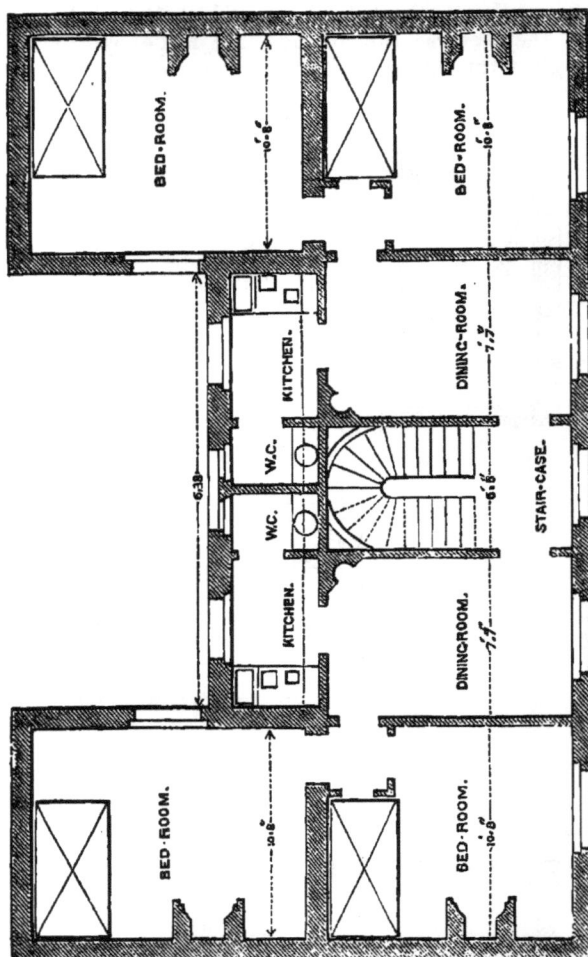

First Floor.

On the whole this house, on examination, it will be agreed is, under the circumstances, a decided success. Some ventilation, though I deem it imperfect, is provided for the living and the sleeping rooms; but the window space is large. They have preserved an open ornamental grating for the front door, and the stair space is large; but with that front door aperture it will serve for aeration and contribute to make the whole house one which will be of good, or comparatively superior, aeration. The elevation is cheerful and in good taste, and the papering and internal decoration (without saying that Mr. Owen Jones could not improve it) are superior to any real workman's efforts that I have seen in their dwellings in England. Allowing that the occupants of model dwellings in Paris, as well as with us, are mostly of the foremost of the wage classes, it was observed, in visiting a new set of model dwellings erected by Mdme. Jouffroy Renault, at the Rue de Cailloux, and others, that the style of the decoration, the large mirrors, and the taste of the pictures, as well as of much of the furniture, is greatly in advance of those in dwellings of the same class in England. Of its superior *batterie de cuisine* I shall make separate mention.

The workmen in refusing, as I have stated, to be, as they expressed it, " caserné," had been influenced by a feeling of repugnance to being dissociated from the middle or other classes of society. I have observed similar feelings manifested in England, and I must submit that they are right. A cité ouvrière exclusively—a dead level of society—is not good for them. Their wives prefer to have high instead of exclusively low neighbours, and to see, and have their children see, what is going on about and above them. This feeling is also widely prevalent in England. The cottager's wife would prefer being near the Hall, or the Mansion, or the Parsonage, or to people of high rather than those of low degree. Cottagers' wives and children, occupying cottages in wastes or byeways, always lose in cleanliness, tidiness, and in other respects, by being out of the observation of " my lady," or of the clergyman's wife, or of the squire, or of the clergyman. Go where you will the occupiers of cottages in out-of-the-way places are of inferior social condition. It was observable that the wage class of Paris took up a position of advantage over the shopkeeper. It will be observed that the lower part of the dwelling of the ouvriers of Paris is laid out as shops. I gathered that this arrangement was of a policy entertained by the wage classes to associate themselves with the middle classes, or the shopkeepers ; and to do this as associated owners or as landlords, and in that position to obtain in reduction of their own charges as rent somewhat out of the shopkeepers' profits. This would be to reverse the conditions which prevail in some parts of London and other certain districts, where the smaller and poorer shopkeepers reduce their own charges by letting out (reserving to themselves only a back room as a living-room) the upper parts of their houses in lodgings to artizans.

Of the model dwellings in the Exhibition, as a type of numbers in actual occupation, one of the next is that of

Japy Frères and Co., of Beaucourt, in the Upper Rhine. The firm of that name, who, it is stated, employ several thousand people in the manufacture of watches and of jewellery, following the example set by M. Dolfus and the manufacturers of Mulhouse, started an association for the construction of improved dwellings for their workpeople, and especially for their journeymen watchmakers. Their model dwelling is one on a distinct plan from that of Mulhouse, in being self-contained, and as containing a workshop.

Social ad-
vantages of
detached
dwellings. Conceding the economical advantages of the four-tenemented houses at Mulhouse over the house rows or the street, I should yet advise to proprietors in rural districts the construction of completely detached dwellings as having considerable social advantage. For, the lower we descend in the social scale, the less is the self-restraint, the greater the passion and violence, and the greater the need of a certain extent of separation. In blocks of four contiguous houses, one morose owner, one shrew or " common scold," or one set of ill-conditioned children, from whom there is no power of escape, may render the habitation and the ownership of the other three almost valueless. I do not know how this may be or how it is provided against at Mulhouse. But experience in penal administration shows that too close aggregations of ill-trained people frequently work badly in England, and how important is the power of ejection and freedom of change of occupancy. A magistrate's clerk of great experience in the City of London once observed to me that in rebuilding a city the architect should for social reasons be prevented making close courts or alleys with common pumps. When the rooms in close places overlooked the opposite rooms, the female occupiers were apt to put about offensive tales and criticisms on what went on in each other's rooms, which ended in fierce quarrels and assaults. One or two common pumps almost kept two low attorneys, the sequence being this :—A little girl going to fetch water was thrust aside by a big girl, and being saucy was beaten by the big girl ;—then the mother of the little girl came out and straightway beat the big girl;—then the mother of the big girl came out and straightway attacked the mother of the little girl ;—then the husbands came forth to do battle for their wives and children, and then, usually with the Irish, sides were taken by the other occupiers of the court, and then there was a " battle royal"; then came prosecutions for assault before the magistrates, and work for the attorneys. One owner of a close square of buildings told me that he found it necessary to make two entrances to it, so that

people in feud might avoid meeting each other. Precautions Mr. Chad-wick on Dwellings.
are necessary to prevent 'people coming too close to each
other, and jostling each other, for if they jostle each other
they hate each other. I regret to say that according to
my observation, in our own country, the great Christian
precept "love thy neighbour as thyself," has yet to be
made completely prevalent amongst people of high, as
well as of low degree. As a minor illustration of too close
contiguity, a proprietor stated to me that he found that he
had made a great mistake in building cottages in rows with
the doors contiguous to each other, as he observed the women
in constant idle gossip with each other. This will be observed in streets with one side of the street with contiguous
doors and the other with separate doors. Even in middle-
class houses, the semi-detached, by which the speculative
builder saves a wall and a yard of space between the two
houses, are found to be productive of discomfort in other
ways than the noise through the walls, of which hereafter;
and higher rents are given for dwellings with the same
internal space, but completely detached.

I pass by the single-chambered habitations, of which there
are several types in the Exhibition; and also notice several
of the remaining dwellings in the Exhibition as being cottages ornés, as little resembling the dwellings in question as
opera shepherds do the veritable shepherds of the fields.

There are sanitary as well as economical questions of Public ar-rangements determining the internal sanitary conditions of dwellings.
construction connected with each type of dwellings, and
questions of collateral and external public arrangement by
which their external arrangements and conditions are modified. These questions—the wall question, the window
question, the grate or the warming and cooking question,
the chimney question, the ventilation question, the water-
supply question, the house or cottage drainage question, as
applicable to the dwellings of the wage classes—may each
be best considered separately with the appliances for each
displayed in the Exhibition.

The Cottage-Wall Question.

Those who visit the common crowded dwellings of the The wall question.
wage class in our towns, even when they are unoccupied,
are aware that the walls have a peculiar depressing, musty,
or foetid smell. On visits after severe epidemic attacks,
in some of these dwellings a peculiarly offensive smell
has been perceived, and on inquiry what that could pos-

MR. CHAD-
WICK ON
DWELLINGS.

Foul walls.

sibly be from, the answer has been that it was the "dead man's smell," the dead body had been too long kept near the wall in a state of decomposition, before it could be removed for interment, and the fœtor inhered to the wall. In the course of the service, under the Public Health Act, when the occupiers were nearly all struck with fever, we have, in some cases, ordered all to be removed and the walls and ceilings to be limewashed. But it has occurred that the performance of this service has been obstructed or neglected with respect to particular houses, and in those uncleansed houses, and those alone, and with fresh occupants, the fever has broken out again, thus demonstrating the condition of the "leprous house" and the efficiency of the work of purification.* Walls lathed, plastered, and papered are even worse for such tenements. The laths rot, the size of the paper decomposes, and the paper itself harbours vermin. The condition of some houses of this construction is horrible. To admit of the cleansing of the walls by lime-washing in Miss Burdett Coutts's, in Mr. Peabody's, and in other

---

* The following extract exemplifies the cases that were of common occurrence under the Public Health Act:—"Shepherd's Court consists of about six "houses. It was notorious that fever had prevailed to a great extent in this "court; in the house in question several cases of fever had occurred in "succession. The house is small; contains four rooms, two on the ground "floor and two above; each of these rooms was let out to a separate family. "On the present occasion, in one of the rooms on the ground-floor there were "four persons ill of fever; in the other room, on the same floor, there were "at the same time three persons ill of fever, and in one of the upper rooms "there were also at the same time three persons ill of fever; in the fourth "room no one was ill at that time. It appeared that different families had in "succession occupied these rooms, and become affected with fever. On the "occasion in question all the sick were removed as soon as possible by the "interference of the parish officers. An order was made by the Board of "Guardians to take the case before the magistrates at Worship Street. The "magistrates at first refused to interfere, but the medical officer stated that "several cases of fever had occurred in succession in this particular house; "that one set of people had gone in, become ill with fever, and were re-"moved; that this had occurred several times, and that it was positively "known this house had been affected with fever for upwards of six weeks "before the present application was made. On hearing this the magistrate "sent for the owner of the house, and remonstrated with him for allowing "different sets of people to occupy the rooms without previously cleansing "and whitewashing them; telling him that he was committing a serious "offence in allowing the nuisance to continue. The magistrate further "gave the house in charge to the medical officer, authorizing him to see "all the rooms properly fumigated and otherwise thoroughly cleansed, and "said that if any persons entered the house before the medical officer said "that the place was fit to be inhabited, they would send an officer to turn "them out, or place an officer at the door to prevent their entrance. The "landlord became frightened, and allowed the house to be whitewashed, "fumigated, and thoroughly cleansed. Since this was done the rooms "had been occupied by a fresh set of people, but no case of fever has "occurred."

model dwellings, the walls have not been plastered or paperel.* In some instances the sanitary orders arc that the walls shall be limewashed twice, and in other instances as often as four washings a year are deemed necessary. The occupiers greatly dislike these bare brick walls. In new hospitals the evil is in a great measure prevented by

---

* French hygienists are strong in their denunciations of the mephitisme as also the damp of habitations. They state that the deleterious emanations from the body, discharged by respiration, and even by the sweat, even in perfect health, attach themselves to walls as well as clothes, "et plus parti- " culièrement aux pierres des murailles, à celles surtout qui sont de nature " poreuse ; la elles sont condensées et frais par l'humidité de la transpiration. " Les ventilateurs qui renouvellent l'air sont presque sans effet par rapport " au *mephitisme* des murs. Les vapeurs desinfectantes lavent bien l'atmo- " sphere des souillures dont elle est impregnée, mais l'infection des murs " échappe en général leur action." There have hitherto been no satisfactory analyses of this mephitisme, but " Quoi qu'il en soit de ces explications " il est certain qu'il existe suivant l'energique et pittoresque expression de " Moïse, *lepra domorum*, une lèpre des maisons, une lèpre des murs, qui, si " elle ne va pas jusqu'à les ronger, n'en est pas moins funeste, au point de vue " de la salubrité. Le méphitisme des murs résulté de l'accumulation de " l'infiltration, des miasmes à la surface, et dans les interstices des pierres " du mortier du plâtre, etc. etc. Il s'y forme, pour ainsi dire, des nids de " miasme, qui sont des foyers d'infection, et qui agissent comme un poison " spécial sur la crasse du sang. Une fois qu'ils ont pris droit de domicile, " pour ainsi dire, ils persistent avec une opiniâtreté vraiment fabuleuse. Nous " citerons des exemples à l'appui. Sous le ministère de Lamoignon de " Malesherbes, le donjon de Vincennes, cessa d'être prison d'Etat. Plusieurs " années après leur mise en liberté d'anciens détenus retourneront visiter " les lieux qui les avaient renfermés ; ils furent frappés d'y appercevoir " absolument la même odeur que celle qui regnait dans leur captivité. Un " médecin, Sainte-Marie, donnoit des soins à une personne atteinte d'une " affection gangréneuse à laquelle elle succomba. Deux ans après, étant re- " tourné dans la même place visiter un autre malade, il retrouva la même " odeur gangréneuse, l'odeur *sui generis.* Il y a quelques années, à Lyon, " dans une des salles de la Charité, sevissait une épidemie de fièvre puer- " pérale très menstrien. Quinze ou dix-huit femmes recemment accouchées " succombèrent dans l'espace de quelques jours ; l'administration s'en émut, " on évacua la salle, et on mit des ouvriers pour la nettoyer. A mesure " qu'ils détachaient le plâtre des murs et du plafond, c'était une odeur des plus " fétides qui se répandoit. Nous avons entendu le Docteur Polinière, admi- " nistrateur des hospices, raconter que l'infection était si grande qu'elle " l'emportait même sur celle d'un amphithéâtre de dissection. Une fois la " salle appropriée l'epidémie s'arrêta. D'après ce que nous venons de dire, " les inductions sont faciles à tirer ; il faut, nous le répétons, pour détruire les " miasmes qui causent le méphitisme des murs et des plafonds dans les " hôpitaux, les chambres particulières, les alcoves de détacher à certaines " époques les veilles couchés de mortier et de plâtre, changer même les pierres " vermoulues, suivant la recommendation du legislateur Lébrun. Ces me- " sures seront très importantes à prendre ; on le comprend dans une pièce, " on aura séjourné longtemps un malade affecté de phthisie, de dissenterie, de " cancer, de gangrene, ou de toute autres maladies chroniques infectantes." " Dans les grandes villes, et surtout dans les anciennes quartiers, le méphi- " tisme est endemique, chacun peut le reconnaitre." ("Devey, Hygiène de " Famille," p. 401). In this work of cleansing the hospital walls in England, where the work has been delayed, in several instances every workman engaged in it has been made ill.

facing the interior wall with some hard and smooth surface, generally of the best non-absorbent and washable cement. As a principle, all interior cottage walls should be made washable. Besides the evil arising from absorbency of the animalised gases by walls of the common construction, there is another great source of evil attaching to walls of the common brick and the common soft stone construction—the Damp walls. absorbency and retentiveness of water or damp. In England, the common bricks absorb as much as a pint or a pound of water. Supposing the external walls of an ordinary cottage to be one brick thick, and to consist of 12,000 bricks, they will be capable of holding 1,500 gallons, or $6\frac{1}{2}$ tons of water when saturated. To evaporate this amount of water would require nearly a ton of coal, well applied. The softer and more workable stones are of various degrees of absorbency, and are often more retentive of moisture than Extent of common brick. Professor Ansted states that the facility damp in with which sandstone absorbs water is illustrated by the as in bricks. quantity it contains both in its ordinary state and when saturated. He states that even granite always contains a certain per-centage of water, and in the dry state is rarely without a pint and a half in every cubic foot. Sandstone, however, even that deemed fit for building purposes, may contain half a gallon per cubic foot, and loose sand at least two gallons. When water presents itself in any part of such material it readily diffuses itself by the power of capillary attraction, by which, it is observed on some walls in Paris, it ascends 32 feet from the foundations. Walls of such absorbent constructions are subject to rising wet by capillary attraction, as well as to the driving wet of rain or storm. To guard against the driving wet on the coast expensive external coverings, " weather slate," are used. But these do not stay the interior rising wet. This wet, having to be evaporated, lowers temperature. Damp walls or houses cause rheumatism, lower strength, and expose the system to other passing causes of disease.

In London it is admitted that houses, even of the better class, cannot safely be inhabited in less than nine months. Indeed, registrars of deaths are aware that an extra death rate is, after all, usually attendant on their first occupation. The majority of bent figures in our villages are due to the infliction of rheumatism from damp.

An experienced traveller in England laid down a rule to avoid bedrooms with northern aspects, which, having less sun upon them, were, when unoccupied, the most damp, and if the bed touched the wall there was the most danger of a damp bed. To keep out the damp an extra quantity

of fuel is necessary; the evil is the greater with the poor
who are often obliged to leave their rooms without the fires
which the more wealthy are enabled to have kept up.

In Paris, notwithstanding its particularly dry subsoil and
its drier climate, the sanitary, or insanitary, evils of the
common architect's constructions appear to be even greater
than in London. I was assured by a Parisian builder of
considerable experience that it was unsafe to occupy any
new house in Paris in less than a year after its construction, and that there were houses in Paris which would
never be dry " in their lives," and would always afflict their
occupants. In going over the new model dwellings constructed for the Emperor we observed marks of damp upon
some of the walls, though they had been erected nearly
two years. The concierge who showed them to us was
suffering from a grievous rheumatic affection; and I was
informed that the occupants had had much illness amongst
them from having occupied the houses " too soon."

Complaints, I found, were made in another set of the
model dwellings, to which the jury had proposed to accord
a medal, of the inferior quality of the tile pavement of the
rooms. And certainly the common tile or brick floorings—
especially absorbent tiles and tiles which conduct heat
rapidly, as some of them do—are detrimental to strength.
A cook, who suited her master, an eminent manufacturer,
gave him notice to quit, as she found that she could not
work so well, or without detriment to health, on the brick
or tile floor of his kitchen as she had done in a kitchen with
a wooden floor. He found that a number of his female
workers made the like complaints of the bad influence of
common tile floors. He could not be persuaded of these
different results; and, to try them, he had a wooden floor
laid down in part over a tile floor, so as to enable him
to walk up and down for a length of time, with one leg
on the tile and the other on the wood, when he found that
the leg on the tile floor sooner became cold and tired;
and he was convinced. He had a wooden floor laid down in
his manufactory, and his benevolence was rewarded, and his
expenditure repaid by more steady, longer, and better work
from his people. If the tile, however, be of good quality,
dense, and non-conducting, or if the floor be hollow and
warmed, which would be practicable in large buildings, the
conditions are altered in favour of tile floors.

In one set of model cottages, to which a prize had been
awarded (for advances on other points), complaint was made
to me by the housewife of another set of inconveniences to

which the common absorbent and permeable wall constructions are exposed, and that is, that, although they are comparatively thick, they are permeable in a high degree to
sound, as well as to damp and the mephitic gases. The
housewife stated that as they lay in their bed they could
hear through the wall what was said in the bed room of the
next house. In consequence of this annoyance they paid
an extra rent for an end house, in which the inconvenience
would be confined to one side. These sorts of constructions,
generate angry passions and inflict much misery, as a person
of feeble health and susceptible nerves of another condition
of society might appreciate by taking up his abode in such
a dwelling.

In view of the first class of evils of insanitary condition,
those of absorbence of damp and miasma, it occurred to me
some years ago that an improved brick would be the pre-

Hollow
brick drier
than solid
brick. ventative, if it were made hard and non-absorbent. But
this it could not, with many clays, if it were made thick or
solid. To get the London clays or other clay to dry without cracking they are mixed with breeze or cinders, by which
they are made spongy. It appeared to me that the drain-tile
making machine, which produced cylindrical forms so rapidly
and cheaply, might turn out equally well rectangular forms
or hollow bricks, which, having less clay in them, would
absorb less moisture, and might, indeed, be burnt hard and
made impermeable. The first machine-made hollow brick
ever made, as far as I am aware, was made at my instance
by my friend, Lord Fortescue, with his tile machine, and
used in 1847 for the construction of some of his new cottages. Lord Shaftesbury also had some made and used,
undoubtedly with the advantages contemplated of increased
dryness and warmth. Subsequently I submitted the plans
of cottages with hollow impermeable brick walls to his
Royal Highness Prince Albert, who considered and approved
the principle of the impermeable and washable wall, and
applied it for his model cottages in forms varied from those I
had suggested, but with glazed, impermeable, and washable
interior wall-faces.

It is this important and established sanitary principle of
construction which appears to have been overlooked, and
that there is a falling off displayed in all the model
dwellings. None of them have a washable wall. All in
due time will have a musty smell, and be infested with
vermin, which, I am informed, is frightfully the case with
the houses of the wage classes in Paris. It is the fact,
however, that in several of the wall constructions in the
Exhibition there is an advanced application of hollow brick;

instead of lath and plaster dividing walls they have improved hollow-brick walls, which are economical, less sonorous than the old walling, and answer very well; but their facing is of porous plaster, papered. In the annexe of class 65, of materials of architecture, will be found examples of hollow brick in common use for walling beyond any that have yet got into common use in England, though not in advance of scattered examples to be found there. The further improvement which the French bricks require is in the qualities of greater density, greater non-absorbency, which it is found may be imparted to them by an improved machinery at an inconsiderable extra expense. If the sanitary knowledge were wide and the appreciation of the importance of the sanitary qualities and the demand were extensive, smooth and coloured brick or tile surfaces might be produced on large scales at rates that would render them available, at prices no greater than papered or coloured walling. The best specimen of a sanitary wall-surface, as I deem it, will be found in class 24 of the Prussian department of the Exhibition, in the white pottery, large exterior surfaces covering stoves, manufactured by T. C. F. Feilner, of Berlin. In them the joints are almost imperceptible. I am assured by Mr. Scrivener, the engineer of the potteries, that by machinery, if there were a sufficient demand, ornamental terra-cotta or impermeable tile surfaces may be produced at a charge below that of unhewn stone for architectural constructions.

I have stated that the best sanitary construction of a house, apart from any question of cost, would be on the principle of the Crystal Palace, only with thick slabs of opaque glass, and with double walls, inclosing (like double windows) a still air, which would be the best means of meeting external variations of heat and cold and preventing the evils of the interior absorption of moisture or of miasma. These impermeable walls should, however, be accompanied by improved means of ventilation, of which hereafter.

The chief and the important novelty in construction in the Exhibition is in the model dwelling of the co-operative society of Paris, made by Mons. Stanislas Ferrand, the architect, to some extent on the principle I have stated.

He constructs his walls of hollow brick, and makes the wall double, thus:—The thickness of the double wall is 5 in., which, of course, would be insufficient for bearing purposes. But the wall is held together, and the bearing power is obtained, on what I have termed the Crystal Palace principle, by iron columns, beams, and cross-trees.

MR. CHAD-WICK ON DWELLINGS.

Cost of pottery as compared with stone.

Double hollow brick wall.

The following plans and cross sections display the principles of his constructions, which appear to me to be
deserving of attentive study :—

PLAN OF FRONT WALL.

| VOID | VOID | SPACE FILLED WITH AIR FROM CELLAR | VOID |

Scale, 0ᵐ·028 =
1 metre.

SECTION AT A.B. ON FRONT WALL.

PERSPECTIVE SECTION OF A WALL.

VACUUM

CONNECTING BRICK

EXTERIOR-FACE

INTERIOR-FACE PLASTERED

VACUUM

Scale, 0ᵐ·14=1 metre.

FLUE

Scale, 0ᵐ·14=1 metre.

Scale, 0ᵐ·028=
1 metre.

CELLAR.

Scale, 0ᵐ·14=1 metre.

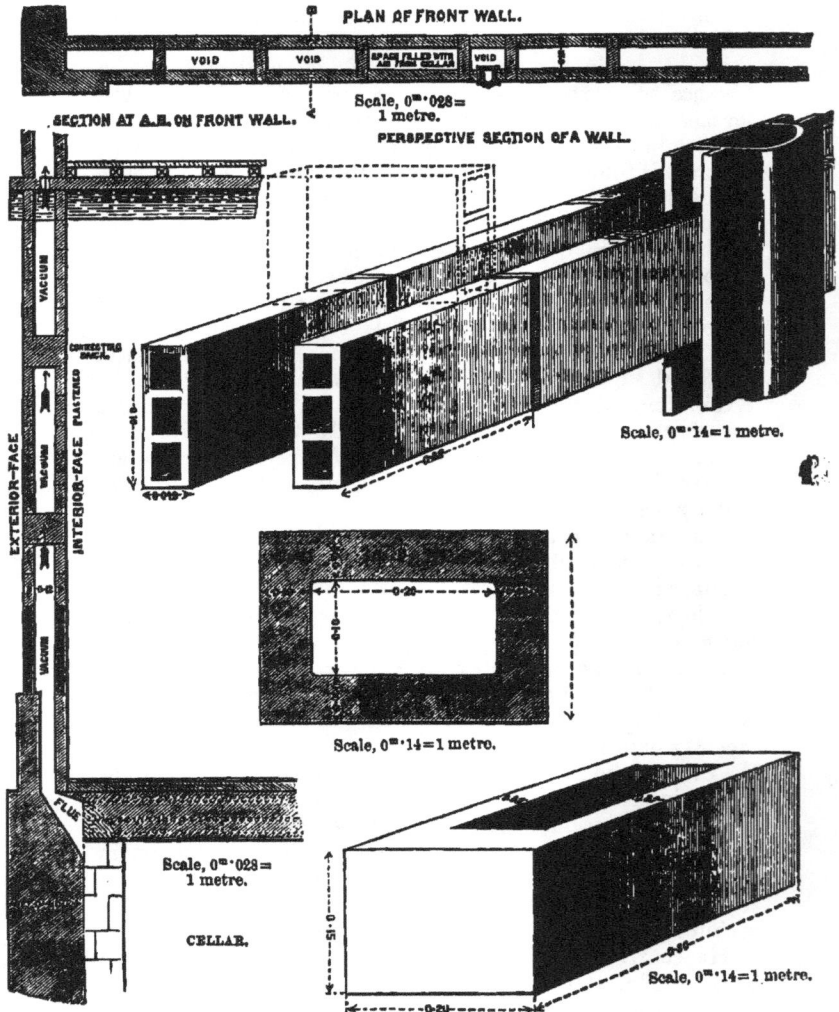

A. Ordinary brick 0m. 22c. × 0m. 15c. × 0m, 045c.   Price per 1,000 in Paris, 70 francs.
B. Bricks, Ferrand's system, forming the thickness of the wall, 0m. 30c, × 0m. 20c, × 0m. 15c.
Price per 1,000, 100 francs.

The following is the cross section, which further displays the principle of construction :—

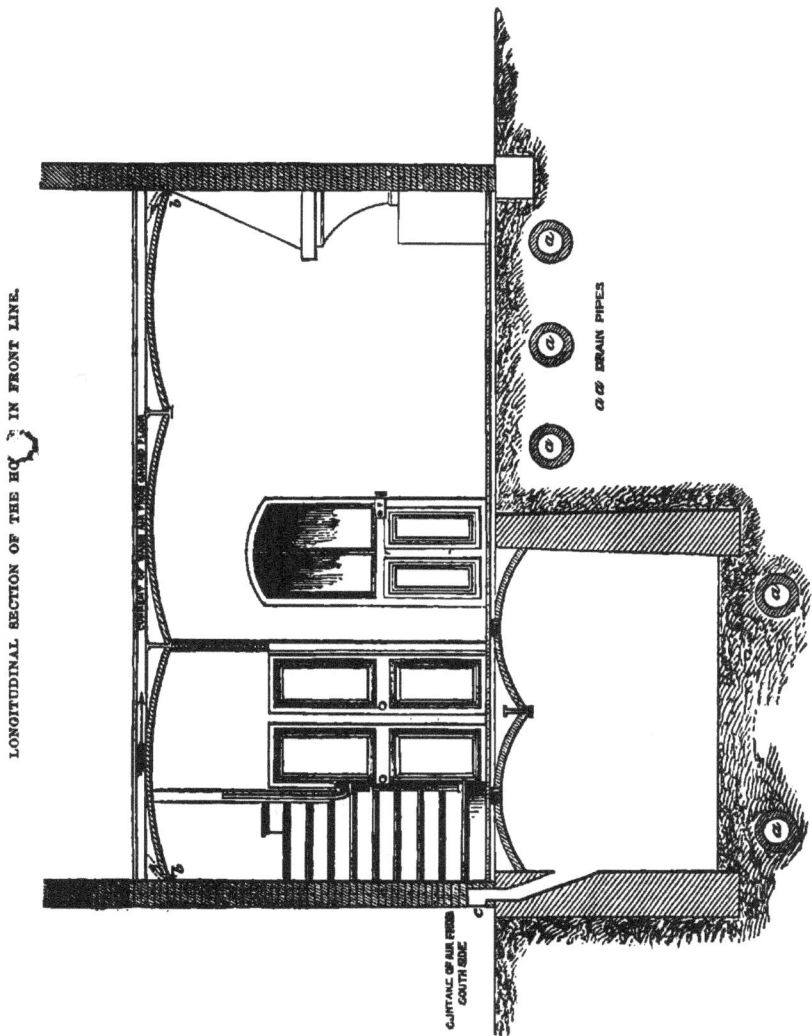

LONGITUDINAL SECTION OF THE HOUSE IN FRONT LINE.

ENTRANCE OF AIR FROM SOUTH SIDE.

aa DRAIN PIPES

bb. Valves establishing communication of hot air under the flooring of the first floor.

The following is the elevation, with the plans of the cellar, and lower and upper floor :—

ELEVATION.

Scale, 0ᵐ·013 to 1 metre (or, about 2″ to 1 foot).

BASEMENT

GROUND

CELLAR

CESSPOOL

3.

S

GROUND FLOOR.

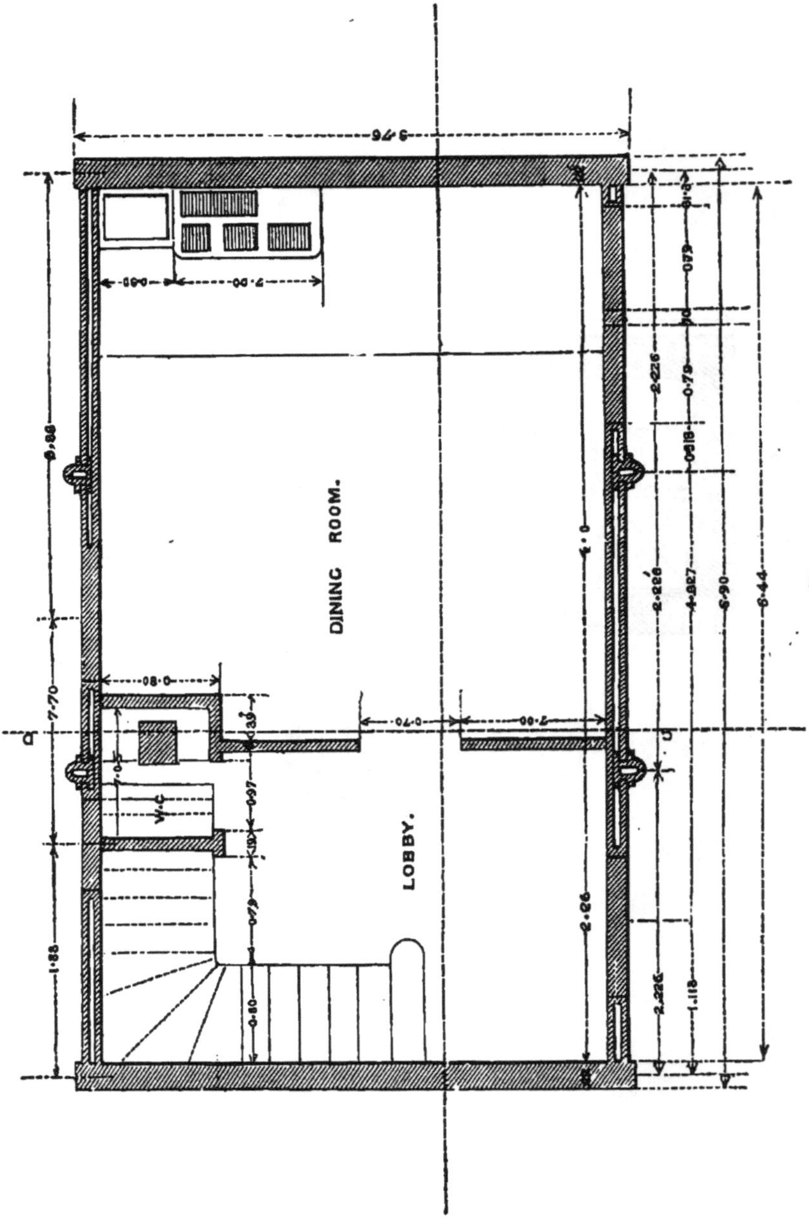

FIRST FLOOR.

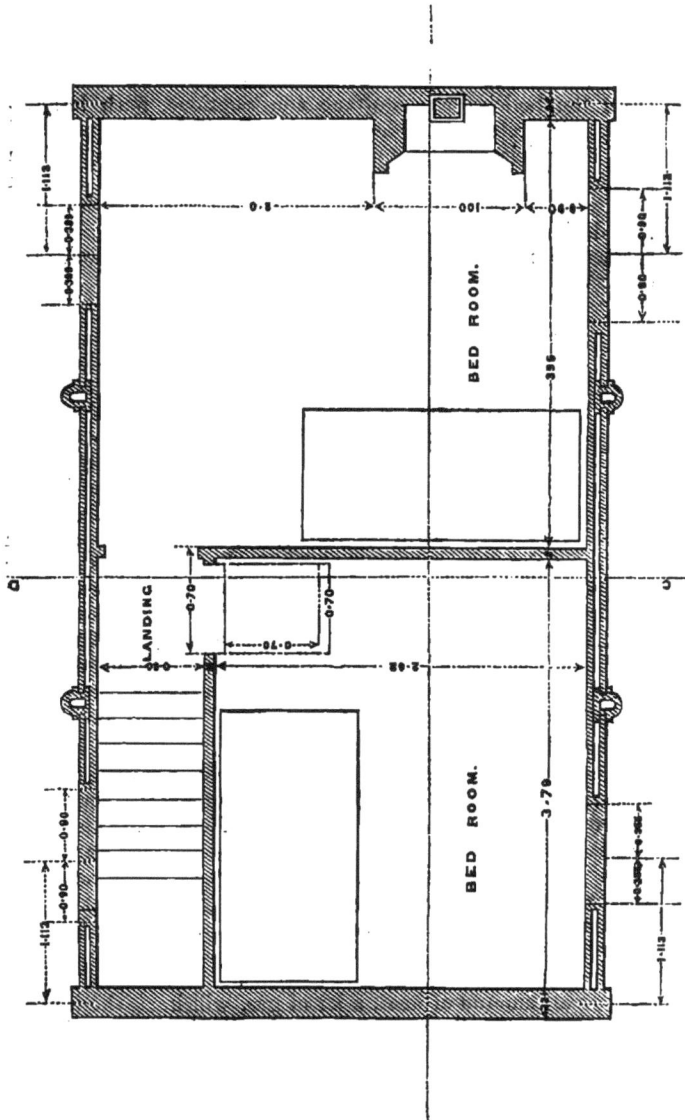

He claims for this construction the advantages of walls which are thin, and which therefore save space, and yet are warmer, resist changes of temperature better, and are better non-conductors of sound than the common brick or stone bearing-walls, and that at a lower cost.

Of the hollow-brick cottage constructions, with hollow-brick flat roofs as well as walls, in England, it is reported that, as anticipated, they are warmer in winter and cooler in summer than the common constructions; whilst of ancient hollow floors that are warmed by hot air underneath them, it is declared that the warmth derived from their extended surface is more comfortable than that derived from any other mode of house-warming.

Of the superior quality of the wall itself, of its advantage as a non-conductor of heat and of sound, of its economy of space, and of the general advantage of this iron-tied construction, there can be no doubt. If it were of our common brick construction, the expense of a dwelling of the same size, constructed in the cheapest manner, would not be less than 150*l.* I have an estimate from Mr. Samuel Sharp, the architect to whom I am indebted for assistance in the drawings and the technical points of this report, that on a large scale the improved iron-tied double wall detached dwelling might be constructed in England for about 110*l.* ; that is to say, if the construction were on a large scale, and as a manufacture. Moreover, the substitution of the 5-inch wall for the common brick 14-inch cottage wall would ensure a gain of 710 cubic feet of space, which, as such space is now allotted in cottages, would serve as breathing space for two people.

The principle of this construction is to obtain an equable temperature by the couch of air between the two hollow walls. It may be observed in the plan that the space between the walls opens into the cave beneath. The space there it is assumed is usually kept unoccupied, and that the air there is of the medium underground temperature,— cooler in the extreme heat of summer, and warmer in the extreme cold of winter than the outer air. By openings in the upper rooms, the interior wall space may have a circulation of air to serve for ventilation. But in still air a very small amount of heat, a jet of gas, will keep the interior wall space and the floor (if the hollow brick construction be extended to the floor), agreeably warm in winter.

The principle of the hollow wall construction has been tried in the construction of hospital huts in the tropics, and is reported to work well. The following is a cross section of one of them as given in the report of the Army Sanitary Commissioners.

Cross Section showing ventilation under the floor, and up the side and roof.
a Holding-down bolts.

The huts have been constructed of ordinary scantling, and it is reported of them that their temperature during very hot weather has not been higher than the air outside in the shade, and that during a rigorous winter they were sufficiently warm; whilst the air within was always pure, even during hot weather. This experience is entirely confirmatory of the independent theory of Mons. Ferrand, which is of very great importance for application in India and the tropics generally.

Though the principle of hollow wall construction was new to us it was well known to the Romans, as is shown in Vitruvius, and was in extensive use amongst them, as shown by their remains. Wheresoever damp was to be arrested, they had recourse to hollow tile walls. Their principle of warming hollow floors would be of great value for block buildings occupied by the poor, and also for school rooms. Warmth applied from such a medium to the feet is most economically applied to the body, and it induces throwing open windows, and a freer ventilation by the people.

The hollow brick iron-tied roofs that have been recently
introduced into this country are proved to be cool in summer
and warm in winter, and at the same time of a cheaper
construction than the common pitched timber and slate
roofs, the experience of which is the reverse, the slates
being sometimes so hot in summer that it is found necessary
to whiten them, whilst they are excessively cold in winter.

Of the double hollow wall it is to be observed that the
outer wall serves in a superior manner the purpose of
" weather slating."

Inconvenience was apprehended from the quality of expansion and contraction of the iron supports and ties with
variations of temperature, but although there are various
methods of meeting it, M. Ferrand assured me that hitherto
no inconvenience has really been experienced from it, at all
events in these smaller houses.

Instead of facing the wall with soft plaster and paper,
a non-absorbent and washable surface might be used.
M. Ferrand's attention having been directed to that desideratum, he has invented a new wall surface, the specimens
of which I saw were almost as white as alabaster, and
washable.   He expected that such a surface might be
obtained at about a shilling a yard.

With this fine impermeable wall surface the whole construction would be one of very great improvement in sanitary quality, as I was glad to be assured, without any
increase of expense, or even with a reduction of expense, as
compared with our common brick constructions.

On the whole, Mr. Ferrand's model is eminently worthy
of consideration as being an advance in the principle of
construction, and as affording the best promise of any in
the Exhibition in connexion with the sanitary improvement
of the dwellings of the general population.

Some years ago Mr. Semper, the architect of Dresden,
entered into the consideration of the wall question, and
prepared a plan of construction of tiles with lock joints
instead of hollow bricks.   These tiles were to be used in
pannels between iron supports.   The advantages promised
from this tile construction were, that the tiles would pack
closer in kilns, and might be made and transported more
cheaply ; that a finer species of tile might be used for the
inner wall surface, and of different colours.   The promise
for ornamental constructions was very high indeed; but the
difficulty was then, as it is now with terra cotta, to get
perfect exactitude in form of joints as well as surface
without enormous additional expense.   Subsequently a

means of obtaining the desideratum, perfect exactitude of form in the construction of earthenware pipes for house drains and sewers.   At my suggestion of the desideratum Messrs. Burton constructed a machine which applied great mechanical pressure to the pipes whilst the clay was only so partially dried as not to have entirely lost its plasticity. This second pressure corrected the twist given to the pipes in drying, and produced very complete accuracy of form, and increased very considerably the strength and imper-meability of the stoneware.   The principle of the second pressure by the machine was proved to be equally applicable and successful with rectangular forms, with hollow brick, and also with tiles, and that at an inconsiderable expense, for bricks of the common size not more than 1*s.* 6*d.* or 2*s.* per 1,000.   But at the time there was no trade demand for exactitude in form, and the important improvement has yet to be brought into use.   Neither tiles nor hollow bricks are confined to the square or usual form, and they may be made in sexagons or in polygons; the interior and exterior tiles, not necessarily glazed, may be of different colours; and if the manufacture be on a large scale, the price may compete with the common stone and brick.   The exactitude of form so much prized by architects may be more readily obtained with tiles than with hollow brick. Houses of the impermeable tile construction may be put up with great rapidity and used for occupation immediately.

Besides the sanitary improvement of the impermeable and washable interior glazed brick wall of the model cottage of 1851, there are other long-tried and proved improve-ments in construction in England, which nevertheless have not got into extended use.   There are various practical reasons for this.   In the first place, they are little known to private individuals, and the common builders only attend to general demands; and any improvements requiring new forms which need care or study in alterations and adaptations for which there is no general demand can only be executed at increased expense to the first individual who adopts them. The common builder rarely feels any interest in changes, and is usually prejudiced against them, as requiring a change of habits in construction.

Besides these trade obstacles to amendment, there have been experienced serious obstacles from the trades unions to improved constructions of hollow brick.   If the hollow brick be made of the usual size, the gain is chiefly in the quality of the brick, and there is little advantage in the price of the manufacture.   But there is much gain if the cubic contents be enlarged; and a plan and estimate of a cottage, which I directed to be prepared for the Prince Consort, was submitted to the late Mr. Thomas Cubitt, the eminent builder and contractor, with walls of hollow brick, each of the size of twelve of the common bricks, and the 9-inch wall set in cement, costing 3s. the superficial yard, against 4s. 6d. and 5s. for the common brick wall set in mortar; the whole cottage, with improved qualities and washable walls costing 25 per cent. less than the common brick construction. The contractor admitted the correctness of the estimates, but he declined to adopt the new construction, and gave to me his

reasons, to this effect:—" If I adopt that new and large " form of brick, which requires the use of both hands to set " it, my men will strike, and I shall have all the labour of " overcoming resistance; and when I have done it, and " shown how much more cheaply the construction may be " made, others will follow me, and I shall have no profit and " nothing but trouble and vexation for my labour. I will " not, therefore, undertake it." In other instances of the introduction, not of hollow brick of new sizes, but of machine-made brick of the common size, but consolidated and improved by pressure, the trades unions, at the instance of the brickmakers, have combined to prevent them; and thus one section of the wage classes have been blindly led to oppose most important improvements in the dwellings and the health and comfort of the whole of the wage classes.

There is, however, one important material, of which extended adaptations from all parts of Europe are displayed in the Exhibition—namely, Portland cements, in various forms of concretes, that appears to present great and earlier facility of individual use, with the least amount of skilled labour.

My attention was particularly directed by the late lamented Captain Fowke to concretes, as a means of advance in quality as well as economy in labouring-class dwellings. He used much of it in constructions connected with the South Kensington Museum. An inferior specimen of it is presented in a small entrance-lodge there. It is proved that with a proportion of from one-fifth to one-eighth of Portland cement to sand, gravel, or small stones, a wall may be made one-third stronger than common brickwork; or with concrete a wall may be made of equal strength with one-third the thickness of common-place brickwork, and of equal thickness, at about one-half the price. The common brick absorbs about 20 per cent. of water. The concrete wall does not absorb one-quarter that quantity, and takes about a fourth the usual time in drying, and when made of the harder stone, and properly mixed, it may be said to be impermeable to wet. In the French Exhibition of building materials there is a very interesting collection of specimens of concrete from Vicat's cement (which is nearly the same as Portland), with table tops for wine taverns, of polished stone, held together, like mosaic work, by the cement; as well as stone for foot and road pavement, and blocks for walls. In the North German department, from the manufactory at Bonn, there are large tiles made of Portland cement, with coloured concrete facings, worth examining, as also some very good sculptured casts and objects of external decoration. But the chief development of the application of cement to concrete constructions is made by M. Coignet, who by machinery crushes stone into as fine a sand and powder as he can get it, and mixes the materials of lime and cement, and by pressure produces specimens of enormous strength; when powdered granite or porphyry is used, of strength approaching to that of the original stone. In the annexe near the pond, in the direction of the Pont de Jena, there is a school-house constructed by him, with statues of granite, porphyry, and other objects, specimens of the material. These various specimens go to prove that, if objects with the qualities of hard stone are required with repetitions of design, it will be more economical to break the stone into pieces and recast it in moulds with cement than to carve it. One of the most important specimens is the flat concrete roof and its wide span, proving the possibility of making the ceilings and roofs of houses as with one large slab of stone. The principle of construction established by these concretes is, that everything is made as it were a monolith. A church at Vesinet, near Paris, is made of the Beton Coignet, and the steeple may be said to be a monolith. In inferior constructions this is of importance, as cisterns and large water-tanks are made of it, as in one piece, without the insecurity of numerous mere common mortar-joints. The proportions of the common beton, or concrete, were: of river-sand, of good quality, 5 cubic metres; hydraulic lime, slaked in powder, 1 cubic metre; heavy Paris cement (considered equal to Portland cement), 250 kilogrammes. I went over a house which had been built of the Coignet's concrete, more than twelve years ago, and it appeared to have stood frost and weather satisfactorily, and some chimney flues of concrete appeared to stand heat and soot very well. In 1848 I got some trial works made for the use of concrete for public drainage and sewerage work. I do not know what cement was used, but as cements were at that time less understood, probably the wrong sort was used, for the report was unfavourable. Subsequently large quantities of Portland cement have been used for the Thames Embankment ; and Mr. John Grant, the engineer in charge of the works on the south side of the river, has made very extensive trials, stated in an interesting paper to be found in the *Transactions of the Institute of Engineers of London,* which establish the great strength of the material as about one-third greater than the commonplace brick of which cottages are constructed.   The chief engineers of the city of Paris informed me that they have used large quantities of the Beton Coignet for sewers, for which, on account of its monolithic principle and evenness of surface, it is very advantageous ; and that they were using it in the construction of bridges, and are well satisfied with it.   I did not ascertain the various costs of production, but the price charged for this more finely manipulated concrete is less than for stone, though I did not perceive that in the class of dwellings in question it would have any material advantage in price over common brick ; in sanitary qualities, however, it would have very great advantage indeed.   It was averred that houses constructed of it, instead of being unsafe to occupy within a year, would be very safe to occupy within little more than a month.

Concrete constructions of the Emperor's new model dwellings.
But the Emperor has, on the advice of Mr. W. E. Newton, the English engineer, adopted for the 40 new dwellings of which I have already given the form, a concrete construction which will remedy almost entirely the common default of the damp walls of the first set of buildings erected by him, and give him the advantage over all the model dwellings in the Exhibition in economy and quality of wall construction except as to quality in the double hollow walls of the co-operative association.

The new wall construction is of Portland cement, one-eighth of cement to the gravel, sand, and stones to be got from the stratum of the foundations, and may be made without bricklayers or masons, and with common labour.   Various forms of concrete walls—the cob walls and floors in Devonshire— are of old date ; but there has been inconvenience in their construction, sometimes from deep troughs of the height of the story being necessary, but for the Emperor's new dwellings there was used a movable case, invented by Mr. Joseph Tall, with which the walls may be constructed very quickly to any height with considerable gain in time.   The extent of the gain over old methods is, however, disputed, and it is alleged, that by a method of making cob walls in use in Devonshire and Cornwall, about as good work may be produced by less expensive means. With one-eighth of Portland cement the cost of this construction in England, where there is fine sand or good gravel near the spot, is generally about one-half the price of brickwork; and as in small dwellings with much division-walling, more than half or nearly two-thirds of the entire cost of construction is in brickwork, this economy of half upon two-thirds is a very important gain, constituting often a turning-point of commercial advantage. Where improved model dwellings now yield $5\frac{1}{2}$ per cent., as the average of the later buildings in the metropolis do, there is a great convenience of the concrete walling for distant places in this respect, that, inasmuch as the cement is only about one-eighth the weight of the mass of brickwork, there is only about one-eighth the cost of carriage, where brick is not to be had on the spot, and where there is loose stone, sand, and gravel, or clay that may be burned, and where there is common unskilled labour available. By putting in cylinders of zinc, and lining them with cement as the walls are carried up, and when completed taking them out, round and smooth chimneys, and water-spouts, and ventilation and warming flues may be formed readily, cheaply, and exactly. In respect to air-flues and spouting, the concrete construction appears to have the advantage over any of the other constructions that I found in the Exhibition, and to be readily available for much sanitary improvement. The concrete renders skirting-boards—those great harbours for vermin—unnecessary, and it runs all round the door and the window-frames, and therefore no filleting round them is required. The ceilings and roofs are made with concrete, for which Colonel Scott has invented a very economical iron framing. Of this concrete construction of ceilings and roofs, as well as of walls and stairs, there is little but the doors and window-frames to burn, and they may be said to be fireproof.

The colour of the concrete wall of Portland cement is that of the darker stucco colour of houses in London, or of brown paper; which, however passable it may be for exterior surfaces, leaves improvement necessary in lightness and cheerfulness, even if the inner surface of the concrete wall be smooth. Colonel Scott, who succeeded Captain Fowke at the South Kensington Museum, and who has conducted extensive experiments on cements (stated in the *Transactions of the Royal Engineers*), and is deemed a leading authority on the subject, has invented one cement, which appears to be the desideratum for cheap wall-facing.

It is a species of artificial gypsum, of a light warm colour, or of a light lime colour. When properly laid on it is stated to be as good as parian facings. It is hard, impermeable to wet, and it is, above all, washable. It has already been introduced for the lining of hospital wards, as possessing the requisite qualities. The expense of a facing with this cement, if properly used, is about two-thirds the expense of the ordinary three-coat work. Mr. B. Nicoll, of London, has adopted a new facing of magnesium, which admits of various cheerful colours, is non-absorbent and washable, and of very high promise at a low rate of charge.

On the question of comparative economy of the concrete walling and the brick walling, it is assumed that the two walls are of equal thickness; but in the plans of model dwellings originally presented to the Prince Consort a construction was proposed on the panel or buttress principle, to economise material as well as space, the bearing power being supplied by the buttresses; and this may be given by 9-in. walling, with concrete, or in appropriate forms of hollow brick; and 4-in. or 5-in. walling of the right materials may serve for the necessary protection against the weather. 4½-in. walls of properly made hard hollow brick are proved to be better protection against weather in times of frost than 9-in. or 14-in. common brick or soft stone.

In the English exhibition of materials there is a new species of walling, invented by Mr. B. Nicoll, which presents very great advantage in non-absorbency of moisture, in non-conduction of heat, in having a washable internal facing, in saving space as against common brickwork, and being available at a much lower price. Over a framework of strong cross wires, of about an eighth of an inch thick, there is woven by a powerful machine a mass of straw or fibrous matter, which is saturated with a solution that renders it fireproof. It is then subjected to a very powerful pressure. A coating of light Scott's cement mixed with parian cement is then put upon it for inside facing, and of Portland cement for the outside facing. The surfaces are impermeable to moisture, smooth and washable with water, so as to save the expense of repeated lime-washings. It is formed into slabs in iron frames, which are put together and closely and securely fastened with bolts. The slabs are from 1½ in. to 4 in. thick. These slabs serve as superior panelling for dividing walls and partitions. Where space is of importance it has the advantage, perhaps, over concrete walling, in enabling a wall to be made of not more than 1½ in. or 2 in. in thickness, and yet its quality greatly deadens sound. It has also great advantages for weather-proof roofing superior to slate or tile—though not, as I conceive, superior to well-made hollow brick (when it can be got), tied together with iron ties and covered with layers of asphalte and cement. In the Prince Consort's model the principle of the flat roof was adopted, but none of the model dwellings in the Exhibition have attained to that principle.

Where ground space is dear, as it is with the dwellings of the labouring classes in town, there is good reason for utilising the roof space. It serves as an additional drying-ground. In dry weather it may be used for the children to play on. One example has been set in London, where, in a densely crowded neighbourhood, there being no playground for a boy's school, they have made one for them on the flat roof. If anyone will look over the cité ouvrière of Mulhouse it will be seen what a large amount of roof space is lost; and yet the cost of the weather-tight flat roof of concrete or hollow brick is nearly a third less in England than the timber, slate, or tile roof. Its greatest convenience or use, however, would be for self-contained dwellings; on them the father of the family may sit in fine weather, and have better air and an extended prospect, and enjoy himself in the Oriental fashion.

In respect to the economy of these improved constructions, I have had trustworthy assurances that fully 24 per cent. of saving is obtainable, either on the hollow-brick principle, on the simple concrete principle, or on the Nicoll wall principle of construction. Mr. Samuel Sharp has made a very close estimate of a four-tenemented dwelling, on the principle of construction of the Prince Consort's model dwelling. At the present prices in England such a dwelling could not be constructed of brick for less than four hundred pounds, or a hundred pounds each separate dwelling. On the concrete principle of construction, with Nicoll dividing walls, it might be constructed for three hundred pounds, or seventy-five pounds each dwelling, minus the cost of land. Apart, however, from the superiority in quality, the improved dwellings would have a gain of cubic space. The cost of the chief dwellings and the space in them is as follows:—

	Total cubic space.	Cost per cubic foot.
The Mulhouse dwellings - -	9,625	3
The Workmen of Paris ditto -	5,950	$5\frac{1}{2}$
The Co-operatives of Paris ditto -	7,480	4
Model dwellings (concrete) with washable interior walls, on the Prince Consort's principle of flat roofs - -	4,800	3

Mr. Sharp has prepared the following plan of a single storied cottage, which he estimates can be manufactured in numbers complete, for 60*l*. each, with grates, sinks, closets, and drains, all included.

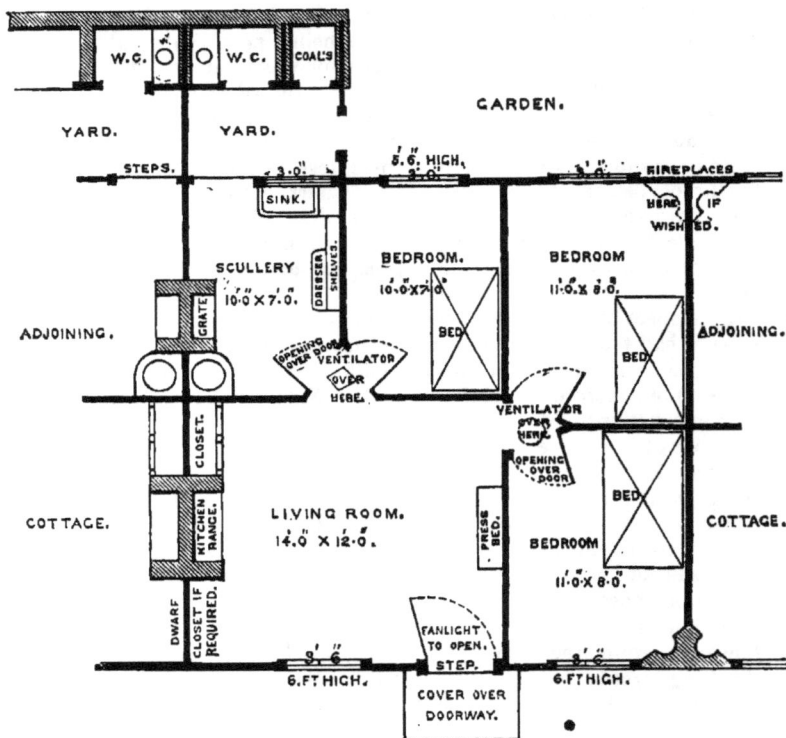

SKETCH PLAN FOR A ONE STOREY COTTAGE BUILT AND COVERED WITH NICOLLS' SLABS.

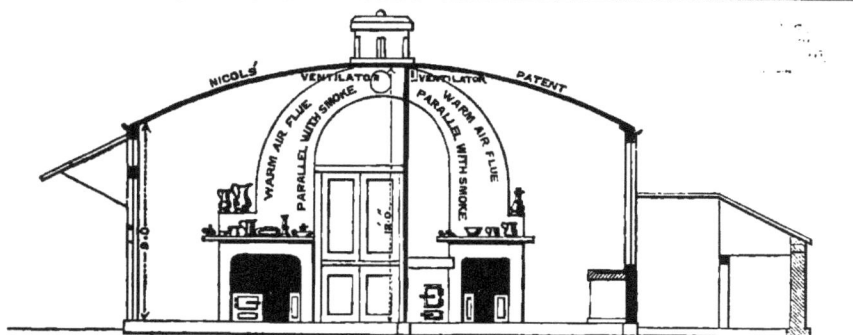

SKETCH SECTION OF A COTTAGE COVERED WITH NICOLLS' SLABS.

Saving of space over 9' outside and 4½' inside walls, 66 square feet floor space, 726 cubic feet air do.

Contains sitting or living room	-	-	- 14' 0" × 12' 0"
,,	2 bed-rooms	-	-	- 11' 0" × 8' 0"
,,	1 ,,	-	-	- 10' 0" × 7' 0"
,,	Scullery, with sink, range, and copper.		
,,	Yard, with W.C. and coals.		

SCALE OF 10   5   0   10   20 FEET

Parallel with the chimney flue is a ventilating flue, acting by the heat of the chimney, and made in concrete. The flooring is of wood laid in bitumen. A cottage of this construction has been erected near Wandsworth, and has stood one winter in a manner to offer the presumption that it will stand well for many winters. But it is expected that there will be other constructions of the kind shortly open to examination, from which a judgment will be formed of the great qualities they are warranted by Mr. Nicoll to attain,—namely, that they shall be damp proof, and have washable interior surfaces, that they shall be warm and vermin proof, and fire proof.

The Cottage Window Question.

I need not state the sanitary importance of the utmost sunlight in climates like our own for this class of dwellings. It has been a frequent question put in Scotland, "Why do " you make those cottage windows so small now that the win- " dow tax is removed?" The answer is, "because if we " make them large in our severe climate the rooms will be " so cold in winter." It is commonly overlooked in respect to this class of dwelling how rapidly thin window glass radiates heat. I have had my attention directed to that on the question of warming union houses. As a rule, under the old constructions, about one-third of the warming power was, in cold weather, radiated through thin windows; but a

Waste of heat, by thin glass windows.

double window with the stratum of air between, make the
window space about equal to the common wall space in non-
conducting power, and of very thick plate glass, approximate
in proportion to its thickness to the double window. By
one experiment in winter time it was found that the difference of radiation (the thermometer being at 30 deg.)
between a thin window and one of thick plate glass is about
8 deg. To bring this home to the case of the labouring-class
dwellings. If a man pays a shilling a week, as he generally
does in London, for his coal for warming his one room in
winter, one third, or fourpence of it, would be wasted through
the thin window. Now this waste of heating power would
compensate for getting a thick glass window or a double one.
All the model dwelling windows in the Exhibition were of
thin window-glass; some of them unnecessarily small panes,
the woodwork of which would go far to provide thick glass
and larger panes. The Austrian model dwellings, however,
had a good double window, 6 ft. by 3½ ft., which I was
told might be made for about 30f. Saving heat, as it would
do, for a large proportion of the year, this window certainly
would be economical. Windows made flush with the wall
gain light as well as space. The Mulhouse and the model
dwellings are defective in their window construction. There
has been as yet no introduction into cottages of cheap forms
of thick ground glass, which, without interrupting light, performed the service of curtains to the lower panes. Very thick
glass is safer from breakage than thin glass; and therefore
may be safely used in large panes, even for cottages. In some
houses of a higher condition, in the north of England, plate
glass is used of near ½ in. in thickness. It is so difficult to
cut through, and requires a work of so much noise, that it
is thought to render the use of outside shutters unnecessary;
and only curtains are used to keep out light.

In the Mulhouse and other model cottages in the Exhibition I thought the outside shutters, particularly for the
upper rooms, might be dispensed with, and the expense com-
muted into thicker glass, which had also the advantage in
crowded neighbourhoods of adding to comfort by keeping
out sound. Altogether this window question is one which
calls for attention as a means of relief from the alternative
of shutting out light to keep in heat in our colder climate,
and for economy and health in the dwellings of the labouring
classes.

THE COTTAGE-WARMING AND COOKING QUESTION.

In the condition stated of the cottager one-third of the
heat of whose fire escapes through the thin window-glass in
cold weather, the greater proportion or seven-eighths of the re-

mainder goes away up the chimney, unapplied, in all weathers.
If the chimney be large, on the old plan, to enable it to be
swept by climbing boys, and it has been left to cool, and get
wet by rain, the ascending air is cooled, the smoke is not properly carried away, and the heavier coal gases of the inferior
coals pervade the room. Entering inferior dwellings in our
large towns, a stranger is commonly assailed by the cesspool
smell, and the wall smell, compounded with smoke and the
chimney smell. Now, the arrangements of some of the
cuisines at the model dwellings at the Exhibition, especially
the cuisine of the ouvriérs de Paris and that of the Mulhouse, are particularly deserving the attention of English
visitors for their fireplaces.

MR. CHAD-
WICK ON
DWELLINGS.

"The smoky
house"
smell.

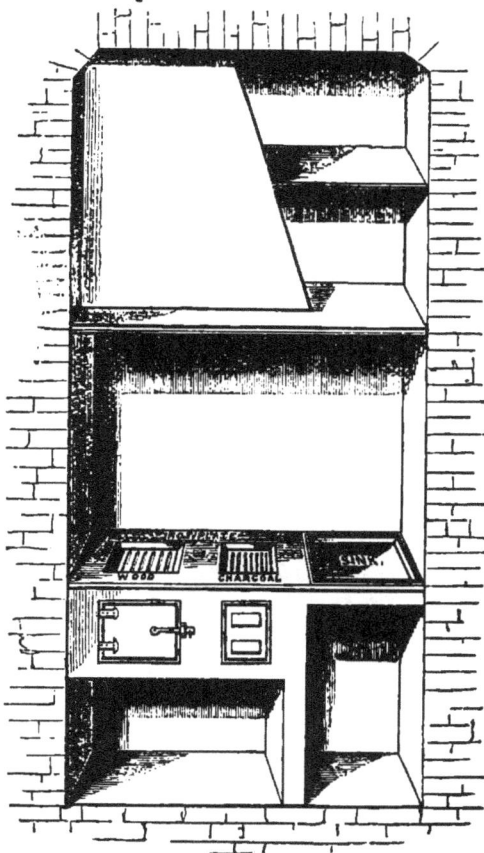

VIEW OF COOKING STOVE, SINK, HOOD, SHELVES, &c. IN KITCHEN.

MR. CHAD-
WICK ON
DWELLINGS. The foregoing is a view of the arrangement without the
neat well chosen pots and pans, which are placed on the
shelves or suspended on the wall. To the left is a hood for
collecting and carrying away the fumes from the cooking
apparatus.

The housewife of the Mulhouse cottage claimed for her
cuisine the preference on account of the greater room it
afforded her for larger operations, including clothes washing,
and it was admitted to be an arrangement of merit. The
Parisian workman's cuisine had the advantage of a cheap
gas apparatus, supplementary, or at times in substitution of
the coal-fire. The Mulhouse cuisine had the advantage of
one ingenious contrivance for economizing chimney heat, by
a copper vessel placed round the stove-pipe and filled with
water, which was kept hot by the ascending heat, the sink
being kept apart in larger space.

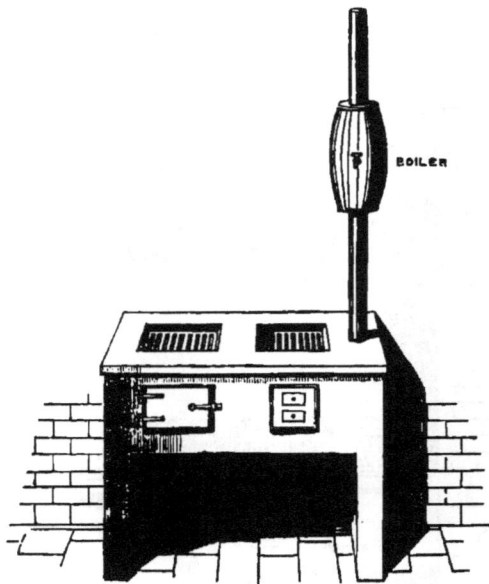

STOVE IN THE KITCHEN. MULHAUSEN COTTAGE.

But the one from Mulhouse is a marked example of
economy of the heat ascending the chimney. Surrounding
the stove flue is placed a brass vessel, which is filled with
water by hand, and is furnished with a tap. It is kept
heated for use by the ascending chimney heat. The like
economy of chimney heat I found displayed on a large scale

in the Hôpital de la Riboisier, where a worm surrounds the
interior of a large chimney, and is filled with water. It was
stated they got 60 per cent. of the chimney heat by this
contrivance. The water thus heated is led off to water cases
to warm other parts of the building.

This cottage-heating and cooking question forms a large
part of the towns' smoke question. The economies of fuel
practised in France, on account of the dearness of fuel,
makes the chief difference between the atmosphere of Paris
and London. Let any Englishman compare the two, and
imagine in how short a time those bright white-fronted
houses of Paris would be as soot-begrimed as St. Paul's if
they were under a London smoke; yet I have ascertained
that by the economy of fuel in large edifices warming is
often as cheap in Paris, with coal at more than double the
price, as it is in London. The contract price for warming
the Madeleine, with 60,000 metres of space, is 14f. per
diem. The contract price of keeping up the heat of a
hospital to 61 deg. Fahrenheit, night and day, and giving
2,000 cubic feet of air per hour to each bed, at a cost of 1*d*.
per diem for the 24 hours in the La Riboisier hospital, and
the contractor acknowledged to me that one-half the price
was the reward of his service of attention. At this rate of
charge for warming and ventilating a block of model dwellings, like the Peabody dwellings, would be, for the 12 hours,
about 4½*d*. per room per week.

The waste of fuel and of smoke in the great number of
dwellings involves an excess of washing and the wear and
tear of linen. English ladies resident in Paris declare how
much longer linen is kept clean there than in London—
perhaps double the time; and I have estimated that the
washing bill of our metropolis is at least 5,000,000*l*. per
annum. In appreciation of the importance of the subject
the British Commission proposed a committee and a testing
house for testing the heating and cooking powers of different
forms of grates, kitchen ranges, and boilers, as also the
illuminating powers of different gas-burners and modes of
lighting, and the testing-house has been brought into operation in the British annexe by Captain Webber, R.E.. with
the aid of a committee of two military officers for military
cooking, and two naval officers for the naval cooking, and
two civilians, of whom I have the honour to be one, for the
civil service. The researches of the Army Sanitary Commissioners had shown the possibility of large reductions of
the consumption of fuel. As exemplifying progress in this
respect, I may mention that the coals required for cooking
for 1,000 men were more than 22 cwt. a day in the ordinary

Mr. Chad-
wick on
Dwellings. boilers. By an improvement introduced by Captain
Grant, R.A., the cooking was reduced to 5½ cwt. or 10½ oz.
per man per diem, with a daily allowance of 3 lb. of wood for
lighting the fires. But there is now on trial a new cooking
range on a new principle, invented by Capt. Warren, R.N.,
to be seen at the testing-house, which cooks the day's rations
for 100 men with only 24 lb. of coal. There is also at
the testing-house a locomotive oven, which requires only
¾ lb. of coal to bake better a 4 lb. loaf than is done with
2 lb. of coal by the common baker's oven. The powers of
several domestic ranges have been put under trial with
advantageous results, as will be seen in Captain Webber's
report. But, considering the great importance of the subject, I submit that the trials may be advantageously extended
as to kitchen ranges, and also to the warming powers of
various forms of chamber fire-grates, with different adaptations, of diameters and lengths of smoke flues, as to which
the information varies widely.

The ouvriers of Paris have, however, made one advance
of considerable importance in the introduction of gas for
intermittent uses. We found the workman in charge cooking
his breakfast over a very small and convenient gas-stand
attached to the cuisine, which he would probably accomplish
for less than a halfpenny's worth of gas, and a saving of half-
an-hour of time over lighting and getting up a coal fire, even
with an apparatus invented by Captain Donelly, R.E., of a
peculiar form of gas burner which lights fires and saves wood.

The extension of the use of gas for domestic purposes
would operate proportionately to the reduction of the great
smoke nuisance of the towns; and it is to be hoped that the
trials commenced at the testing-house of the Exhibition may
serve to determine at what point gas becomes more economical than coal.

Test point of
the economy
of gas for
cooking and
heating. The late Mr. Glegg stated that the turning point of
economy in the use of gas for heating and cooking purposes
was when gas was at about 4s. the 1,000 cubic feet. The
prime cost of its manufacture on a large scale in London, is
stated to be about 1s. 9d. the 1,000 cubic feet; but it
would be of great public advantage to have the point of
economy between coal and gas settled by a very special
examination and public experiments.

It is one point of sanitary importance with respect to the
introduction of gas into dwelling houses that each burner
ought to have a distinct channel for the removal of the
products of combustion. The facilities of making flues in
the concrete constructions will afford means of doing this,
and of making each channel an additional means of ventila-

tion. The cowl over the cuisine of both the Mulhouse and
the dwellings of the workmen is deserving of attention as a
means of keeping the air of the rooms comparatively pure.

In some of the model cottages special attention appears
to be paid to the size of the chimneys for the removal of
smoke. In the Emperor's new cottages a new principle is
adopted. Count Rumford's plan was to narrow the entrance
of the flue. In the Emperor's cottages the dimensions of
the flues are 10 by 8, and at the exit only four inches, which
it is declared works well.

At Dresden, Mr. Semper, the architect, found that circular
chimneys of little more than five inches serve well for coal
fires for the great majority of buildings for which the large
parallelograms are commonly in use. By the better adaptation of size and form, with a better draught of air and better
combustion, less coal is consumed as well as less soot deposited. Moreover, by the better draught, much of the heavier
and offensive and pernicious gases from the decomposition of
coals, more particularly the inferior coals such as are used
by the poorer classes, which escape and pervade the living-
rooms, when the draught is sluggish or the chimney smokes,
is not cleared away. For the larger sized houses flues of
$8\frac{1}{2}$ in. are there used; and flues of $11\frac{1}{2}$ in. are found to
answer for kitchen ranges and very large establishments.
The power of adjusting the size of the chimneys so as to
remove the heavier coal gases is one of considerable importance to the cottage dwelling.

In the Exhibition there is a plan of a M. Leon De Sanges
applicable apparently to blocks of labourers' buildings, such
as those of Mr. Peabody or of Miss Burdett Coutts, which
appears to merit attention. He concentrates all the chimney
flues of one house into a smoke chamber at the top; from
this chamber there is only one exit. The heat accumulated
in the chamber is utilised for heating water for the supply
of the lower part of the house. In one I saw it was used for
warming a drying closet. At first considerable difficulty
was found in the working of the plan until the exit pipe was
made of the same sectional area as the collective flues.
Mr. de Sanges next found it necessary, for the prevention of
down draughts from the chimneys of the fireplaces not
in use, to carry a distinct air flue to each fireplace, for its
separate supply of outer air. With these amendments,
which first checked its application, I was assured, in respect
to one house in particular to which the system had been
applied, that it worked completely satisfactorily. The advantages claimed for it were :—

    1. Ensuring an equal and constant draught of each
       chimney ;

2. Preventing the disturbing effect of high winds;
3. Suppressing chimney tops;
4. Diminishing the frequency and expense of chimney cleaning;
5. Giving a means, through the smoke chimney, of stopping a particular chimney in the case of fire;
6. Giving heat to a water tank for baths.

M. De Sanges stated that the heat of a smoke chamber in a first-class house was nearly up to the boiling point of water. In large blocks of workmen's, as well as other dwellings, in which there might be several smoke chambers for the collection of the chimney heat, the economy of a perfected plan may be expected to be considerable. But the most important purpose, as it appeared to me, to which it would be applicable would be in supplying a means of ventilation. According to the report of General Morin, the best motive power for the removal of vitiated air, easily, regularly, and economically, is by means of a hot-water tank surrounding the iron cylinders forming the ends of vitiated air flues, and keeping up a current by the expansion of the air by the surrounding heat. I witnessed myself the proof of the great regularity of its action in the Hospital La Riboisier. It appears to me that the same principle is applicable on a smaller scale to private dwellings, and that a hot-water tank for the purpose might be circled or kept heated by the hot air of the smoke chamber, so as to carry on the ventilation of sleeping rooms through the night, which will not be accomplished by the important ventilating chimney which I shall subsequently describe. This may be the more necessary where the chimney draught from each room is diminished by a separate supply of air to the fireplace.

One architectural advantage of the plan in towns would be getting rid of ugly chimney stacks, and substituting a construction which, without much extra expense, would be susceptible of art ornamentation.

The next page contains one of M. De Sanges' plans, exemplifying his arrangement.

The architect declares that the expense of this chamber is not greater than that of the unsightly stacks of chimney pots which it abolishes.

In the exhibition there is one plan, by Mr. Muller, by which, it is stated, he has overcome difficulties in concentrating the chimney flues at successive stages into one main front flue, so as to avoid the occupation of space in carrying up each flue separately to the top of the building. The same architect has also a most compact laundry, deserving of attention from its arrangement and for the compactness of all the apparatus, as applicable to common washing houses.

VARIOUS EXAMPLES OF THE APPLICATION OF THE SYSTEM OF M. LEON DE SANGES, ARCHITECT.

Scale, 0ᵐ·0105 = 1 metre.

SECTION OF A ROOF WITH SMOKE-CHAMBER ABOVE FALSE FLOOR.

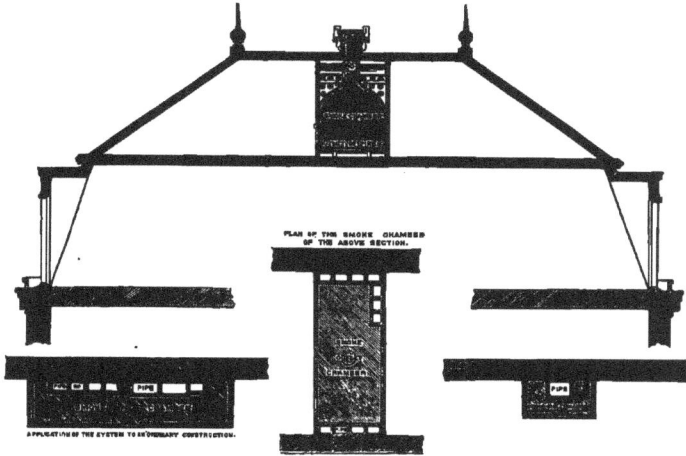

PLAN OF THE SMOKE CHAMBER OF THE ABOVE SECTION.

APPLICATION OF THE SYSTEM TO AN ORDINARY CONSTRUCTION.

APPLICATION OF THE SYSTEM TO A CHIMNEY WITH THE ADVANTAGE OF DRAUGHT, SWEEPING, AND SUPPRESSION OF THE PASSAGE OF WORKMEN TO THE ROOF.

A. Warm water.   B. Spiral hot-air tube.   C. Ventilator.   D. Door.   E. Smoke outlet.

He has one principle of great importance—of saving friction
of linen in washing, by pumping the soapsuds from the bottom
of the vessel in which the clothes are washed, and passing it
through the linen without rubbing. I had the testimony of
the lady of a private establishment where the principle was
applied, that the saving of clothes by it was very great—a
saving of importance, when it is considered that clothes are
far more worn by the washing in the common methods than
by their wear.

The living-room of the Mulhouse dwelling is warmed by
a tall cylindrical iron stove, the flue of which is so adjusted
as to create a ventilating current of heated air from that to
the upper rooms. In respect to warming by the common
close stove by large iron surfaces, there is a sanitary objection
which does not attach to warming by earthenware surfaces.
The iron surface, as it is commonly expressed, "burns the
air," and creates disagreeable conditions which are appre·
ciated by the lungs and the nose, but which chemists have not
yet analysed. There are in the exhibition various forms of
earthenware-covered stoves, and some open fireplaces adapted
for labouring as well as other dwellings. Some of the forms
will be seen in the Austrian department, as also in those of
Sweden and Norway, as well as some in class 24, to which
I have already adverted, in the Prussian department, though
those are stoves of a higher class. Americans, accustomed
at home to warming in winter by iron heated surfaces,
declare how much more agreeable, how superior, the air is
in Sweden and Norway in the rooms warmed through earth-
ware surfaces. On the other hand, I have heard Swiss who
are accustomed to house warming from pottery stoves declare
that they find, when they go into some parts of Germany,
the house warming by the iron close stoves extremely disagreeable and often unbearable. The effect on health is very
important, and an Austrian or Swedish earthenware stove of
the economical types in the Exhibition might well be substituted for the iron one used in the Mulhouse dwelling.

The iron surfaces of the French economical kitchen
ranges, and of some of our own, is an objection to their use,
especially by ladies, that would be removed by covering
them with a tile surface, which need not be of an expensive
quality, and would, from its non-conducting power, be at
the same time economical of heat. There is in the test-
house one example of an English warming stove so covered,
though with tiles of an ornamental and expensive description,
which would not be necessary for cottage use. Chemists
have hitherto failed to account for this effect of warming by
heated iron surfaces, but General Morin assures me he has

MR. CHAD-   detected the cause, and an explanation of it from him may
WICK ON
DWELLINGS. be shortly expected.

THE COTTAGE VENTILATION QUESTION.

The nose   All the French model dwellings, except those of the co-
test of sani-
tary condi- operatives of Paris, follow the English model cottages in
tions.   providing openings for ventilation, but do not advance upon
them. In my view, most of the means used are entirely insufficient. I proposed to the international jury that they should
apply what I call the " nose test," which is far better than
any at present known chemical tests, to the various methods
of ventilation of dwellings, and that they should do it in this
way—by going in early morning, before the inmates had
risen, and, permission being obtained, put their noses into
the sleeping room. But I failed in persuading them to
adopt my proposal. Physicians who are called upon to visit
the sick at all hours have painful experience of the foul state
of the atmosphere in which the poor commonly have but
imperfectly refreshing sleep.

In suggesting some plans of cottage constructions of
hollow brick, I proposed a tubular chimney made by a
tile machine, on this section, which was given in the plan
of a cottage submitted to His Royal Highness the Prince
Consort.

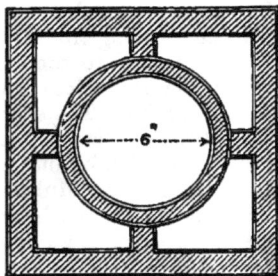

It appeared to me that the angles of the smoke flue
might be utilised as air flues, which might be used for the
removal of vitiated air by the action of the heat of the
smoke flue, for ventilation. The action of the smoke flue
will be the more regular, from the interior being confined to
its proper service, and from its having the least admixture
of cold air. The same principle was subsequently adopted
for earthenware tile chimneys by Messrs. Doulton, of Lambeth,
but with a variation in construction displayed in the following
section; and it is reported that it acts satisfactorily. It has

been proposed to use the external action of the chimney heat, in various modes, for the removal of vitiated air, but we have now introduced a most important, tried, and proved method of utilising the chimney heat for the introduction of fresh air and for warming houses.

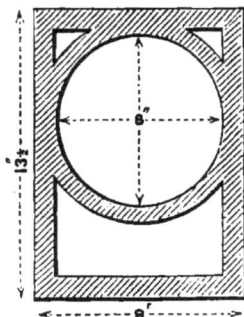

Amongst the fire-grates exhibited in the testing house was one invented by Captain Douglas Galton, R.E., C.B., who has connected with it a principle of warming and ventilation, which, as developed by some trial works and experiments appears to me to be one of the most important sanitary inventions of our time.

In plans for warming and ventilating soldiers' barracks, Captain Galton struck out the principle of adapting the chimney heat of the smoke flue for bringing in a supply of fresh warmed air, by carrying, parallel to the smoke flue, a fresh air flue, which leads the fresh outer close to the smoke flue, the heat of which expands the fresh air, and causes it to rise in current, which is discharged near the ceiling of the room, across which it spreads. It then descends and mixes with the colder and heavier air beneath, and it is carried with the current into the open fire-place and is thence discharged as vitiated air through the smoke flue. The smoke flue surrounded by a fresh air flue constitutes a pump,—pumping into the room warmed fresh air, in quantities proportioned to the warming power of the smoke flue, and the adjusted size and length of the fresh air flue.

Captain Galton's first experiments were with a fresh air flue carried parallel to the smoke flue and warmed by it. I had met with an example, in principle very near this, and had given a plan of it in my report of 1842, yet I confess I overlooked it. General Morin saw and appreciated the importance of the principle, and made a number of careful experiments with it, with the fresh air flue surrounding the smoke flue, and has obtained important results with it. The principle of the invention is displayed in the following section.

CHIMNEY VENTILATOR.

Fig. 1.

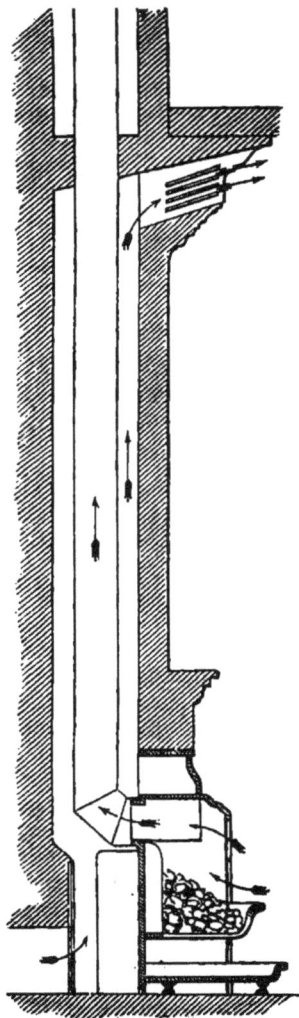

The following are the elevations and plan of Captain Galton's grates, attached to the flue. But the General states to me that the greater number of cast-iron fire-places, on existing systems intended for coal and coke, can be easily and economically fitted with the arrangements described, though Captain Galton's fire-place has the advantage of throwing into a room more of radiant heat with a given quantity of coal.

Fig. 2.

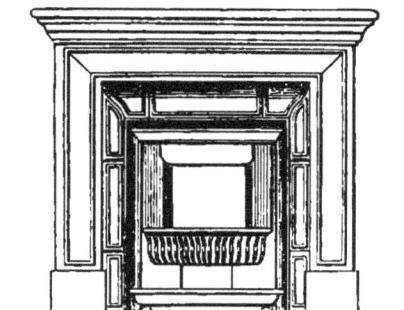

Fig. 3.

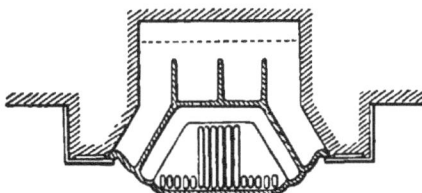

The General has determined that the air of the room will by this fresh air pump properly adjusted change the air of the room at least three times an hour, and in respect to the warming, whilst under the common arrangements only one-eighth of the chimney heat was gained, by warming the fresh air with the ventilating chimney at least one-third of the heat is gained. Another effect produced by the invention is the maintenance of an equable temperature in all parts of a room, and the prevention of draughts. The soldiers in the barrack rooms where the principle has been supplied, state that they are now better warmed, and that they are not now roasted in front whilst they are frozen behind, as they were with the old grates. It prevents smoky chimneys by the ample supply of fresh air created in the room, and by the draught created in the neck of the chimney, especially those of the peculiar form of grate invented by Captain Galton.

Dr. Parkes, of Netley Hospital, the author of the Manual on Hygiène has caused experiments to be made which show that at the rate at which the air passes through the fresh air flue, and the short time of its contact with the heated surface of the smoke flue, it is carried into the room without being " burned " or " dried," or its hygrometic condition being materially altered.

The invention supplies are important desideratum for the ventilation of dwellings in flats, such as most of those occupied by the wage classes in our crowded towns. The rooms on these flats are usually ventilated from the common staircases, which I will call an aerial common sewer, carrying with it vitiated air from the lower floor, and from the rooms of each stage opening into it. Now by the invention* each room would derive its supply of fresh warmed air, and its ventilation from without and independently of every other part of the premises.

General Morin has been so good as to give me the following table of the results of his experiments as to the sizes of smoke and air flues adapted to different sized rooms.

Cubic contents of room to be heated.	Probable dimensions of room.	Volume of air impelled and admitted per hour.	Section of smoke pipe.	Area of passage of chimney top.	Total section of passage for admitting fresh air.
cubic ft.	feet and inches.	cubic ft.	sq. in.	sq. in.	sq. in.
3,600	20 × 15 × 12	17,658	77·5	38·7	217·0
4,320	24 × 15 × 12	21,189	93·0	46·5	260·4
5,376	28 × 16 × 12	26,487	116·2	58·9	325·5
6,480	30 × 18 × 12	31,784	139·5	69·7	390·6
7,840	32 × 17 6 × 14	38,847	170·5	85·2	477·4
9,180	36 × 17 × 15	45,910	201·5	100·7	564·2
10,560	33 × 20 × 16	52,974	232·5	116·2	651·0

It is to be hoped that the important principle will soon be seen in extensive and varied application, which may be facilitated by a work which General Morin has in preparation, containing the results of all his important experiments on warming and ventilation.

I did not find in the foreign part of the Exhibition any instance of the application of the syphon principle in ventilation. At the head of the staircase of the dwellings of the

---

* It is to be observed that neither Captain Galton's grate nor the chimney are patented.

ouvriers of Paris such an apparatus as that of Muir's ventilators may be commended, especially in the larger blocks of dwellings, to remove the vitiated air accumulated as in inverted receivers in the upper apartments. In the tall houses let off in flats in Edinburgh and in other towns, it was common that attacks of cholera were chiefly on the occupiers of the basement floors, and on those in the attics, leaving the dwellers in the intermediate tenements untouched—that is to say, the attacks were chiefly in the ratio of the vitiation of the air. As marking the backward state of sanitary science in house construction, it is to be observed that in a large proportion of instances in the new and largest first-class houses in Paris the servants' sleeping-rooms are mere unventilated cells, called "coffins," in which the inmates are crowded together in a manner equally destructive to health and to morality.

The power of warming hollow walls, on the principle taken up by the architect of the Co-operative Society, and also the power of warming hollow floors, are means of promise to induce people to keep open the doors and windows of their living-rooms for the most free aeration in summer time, when fires are not used. The experiments and observations of General Morin, to be found in the transactions of the *Conservatoire des Arts et Métiers,* but which he promises to publish separately, appear to me to make important advances to definite principles of ventilation in their application to large public edifices, that are as applicable if not to detached cottages and urban block buildings, occupied by the wage classes, when due attention is paid to them, as they are proved to be to our prisons. It is an advance that some of these block buildings are now let sometimes with water and gas laid on, as part of the rent; but a further advance may be made in such block buildings in letting rooms warmed and ventilated, and in the heats of summer cooled as well as ventilated, from pure air sources, night as well as day, with hot water laid on, and that, too, with an economy of the existing charges. Seeing indeed what has been done by sanitary engineering for the best hospitals and the best prisons, it is surprising that no application has yet been made of the ascertained principles to new and grand hotels, and even to the cabins of large ships. The leading principles of ventilation which it appears to me General Morin has determined, are—1st, the superiority of the principle of ventilation by suction, by the method of the hot-water tank acting in the vitiated air flues, over the existing method of ventilation, by driving fresh air into rooms by steam power. 2nd, the principle that the vitiated air should be taken out as closely as possible from the sources of vitiation; in hospitals near each bed. 3rd, that for the avoidance of the inconvenience of draughts, that fresh air should be brought in from a distance, to the place of supply. These principles may now be applied to the removal of air in exactly fixed quantities and temperatures; and 4thly, that the heat in entrance halls, passages, &c., should be kept up to the same heat as the inner chambers. But in the practical adaptations of clearly ascertained principles there is a great deal to be studied, and there are trial works to be made, to overcome the difficulties which yet beset the important subject. Meanwhile, attention should be given to the prevention of overcrowding, or to the massing of the people too closely together, of the effect of which we have had samples in prisons and other public institutions. Thus in the Dartmoor prison for military prisoners, which is situate in one of the healthiest sites in England, on granite at a great height. When it was greatly overcrowded the inmates were horribly ravaged by typhus;—when the numbers were reduced to a certain extent, typhus disappeared, but phthisis remained;—when the numbers were still further reduced phthisis too almost entirely disappeared, and there prevailed a state of health befitting the site;—the case exemplifying a principle in my observation, that different doses of aerial impurity have different classes of diseases attendant upon them. Dr. H. Hunt, who is a good observer, seeing the sequence at the Dartmoor prison, has prescribed to patients with incipient phthisis to take residence there; to have no second person in the living room, and always as much as possible to keep the doors and windows open; and this treatment has been eminently successful. Good ventilation might have mitigated the overcrowding, and produced the beneficial effect of the last stage in the second stage. Missionaries (in the South Sea Islands) in ignorance of sanitary laws, have induced their flocks, who had been accustomed to sleep in huts with the tops open to the air, to betake themselves to live in closed houses like Christians, and have certainly brought upon them European diseases, which they never had before. Natives who were ill returned to their open huts and got rid of the new disease.

THE COTTAGE WATER SUPPLY QUESTION.

All the foreign model dwellings are intended to be supplied with water by hand, brought from wells or from public fountains; none are presumed to have pipe water supply.

It appears to be matter of surprise that in Paris, with unity of administration, and with such undoubtedly able administrators, the interests of water-carriers should be allowed to prevail, and an improved and superior pipe water-supply should not have been obtained.

In some of the model dwellings, those of Mdme. Jouffray Reynault, I found that the inmates paid a sous a day, or $3\frac{1}{2}d.$ per week, for what we should consider a scanty supply brought to them by water-carriers. Where a city is supplied with a constant supply of more than 20 gallons per head, or a supply practically unlimited, and which is carried up to the highest tenements as a public service, it ought to be at a penny a week or at a rate which makes it dear to the poorest person to go from the top of the house to a yard to fetch it, although it may be had thence for nothing. In such cases as those of the isolated blocks or cottages, such as in the instances of the Emperor's new cottages or dwellings, the Mulhouse dwellings, or in cases where pipe-water or well-water supplies are bad, it is a mistake not to make provision for the reception, in underground tanks, of the rain-water from the roofs, as that water, when properly preserved, is of great value for washing, for cooking, and for making tea, for which last purpose it serves to procure about one-third more and better extract than common hard or mineral waters. Soft drinking water adds to the solubility of all food, and as an aid to digestion, was prescribed successfully by the late Dr. Prout, to dyspeptic people; and where natural soft water was not to be had he prescribed distilled water, though it is very flat from being decerated. I have known dyspeptic people to get well simply by a change from a hard to a good soft water.* When rain water is caught in the common method it is, however, kept stagnant, in open butts or receptacles, often near cesspools, or near the dung-heaps of outhouses, the foul air from which it rapidly absorbs, toge-

Marginal notes: MR. CHADWICK ON DWELLINGS.
Cottage economy artificial water supplies.
Advantages of soft water supplies.

---

* What Miss Nightingale says of water for the service of the sick in hospitals is applicable to a great extent for the use of those who are not sick. "The water must be soft; people think very little of this. They think "mainly of hard water as chapping the hands, not as being a promoter of "drunkenness, uncleanliness, and indigestion. It is very little observed that "water dressings, every day more used by surgeons, have absolutely the op-"posite effect, viz., poisoning the sore, when made with very hard water, to "what they have, viz., cleansing and healing the sore, when the water is soft. "When water is hard, it is worth while to have distilled water for every "water dressing. For all washing of the sick it is worth while to collect rain "water or condense steam from a boiler, or to boil water, which will often "remove from one-half to three-fourths of the hardness. Soap and hard "water actually dirty your patient's skin. The oil in the soap, the exudations "from the skin, and the lime in the water unite to form a kind of varnish "upon the skin, which comes off in the above-mentioned black flakes when "rubbed."

MR. CHAD-
WICK ON
DWELLINGS.

ther with floating spores, of vegetation and animalcules, and it becomes often more unwholesome than hard or mineral water similarly exposed. Pure soft water is, I believe, of so much value, that in the chalk districts or in other districts where it is not to be got, it is worth while to prepare roofs expressly to catch it, and underground tanks to preserve it pure. In Britain it is estimated that the average quantity of rain water which falls on a square yard of surface in a

Quantity of
rain water
available
for house
supplies.

year is 126 gallons. Three yards would give rather more than a gallon a day; or a surface of 100 yards would give 12,600 gallons, or 34 gallons per diem, or about 6½ gallons per head to an average family of five. If this were insufficient for the purpose of the household, it would be worth while reserving it for drinking and for washing the person, and the more special uses. The collection of the rain water is one important use of a flat roof, properly prepared by an inpermeable surface of hard tile or other material to which access may be had for cleansing it from soot or bird's dung before any coming rainfall, of which the first should be allowed to run to waste. A deep underground covered tank,—for which concrete faced with impermeable earthenware tiles, are the best materials—should be prepared to receive it, and keep it cool, and out of the way of any floating cause of impurity. The best trainers of racing horses in England are very careful to do all this for their horses, and even to have water carried with them for the use of the horses at races. I was glad to hear the intelligent foreman engaged in the construction of the Emperor's model cottages, near Vincennes, point out the absence of any proper provision for collecting and storing rain-water, as a serious defect in them. He had constructed receptacles for the purpose in various parts of France, and he bore testimony to the high order of their utility to the poor. In densely populated districts such provisions are scarcely practicable, and under good public administration, collective arrangements may be made with greater efficiency as well as vastly greater economy. The estimate of one engineer, Mr. Bateman, for bringing an ample supply of soft water from the Welsh mountains, beyond the Severn, to the Metropolis, is a charge of about 6s. per head per annum of the population, including even compensations for existing

Cost of soft
water sup-
plies from
long dis-
tances.

works. Our estimate at the Board of Health was much less than that even for bringing fresh water from Wales. But we found that upwards of forty-six millions of gallons of soft perennial spring water of a superior quality, pure, free from the taint of peat, and well aerated, or double the then actual consumption of the metropolis, might be had, by proper administrative consolidations, within the existing charges. Yet, as a matter of sanitary economy, a charge of 1½d. per week per head of the population, for an ample supply of pure soft water, would be a great saving. Nevertheless, it is to be borne in mind, that the best water may be made bad by the method of distribution. If water, instead of being delivered by constant supply from the steam pump direct into every room, cool, fresh, and well aerated, be detained, as is the practice of some engineers, and spread out into large open reservoirs, where it is deaerated, and vegetation is rapidly engendered, attended by animalcules, and impurities contracted which no after filtration effectually removes; or if it be delivered direct only intermittently, so as to be stored only in open butts, to be kept in them, near cesspools or in cesspool-tainted atmospheres; or even it if be delivered direct, by stand pipes in the courts and alleys, occupied by the wage classes, and has but to be carried up to their close, crowded, cesspool-tainted warm rooms, and kept standing there in pails and mugs, it is rapidly decerated and absorbs the foul air of the place, becomes flat, often tepid, and positively nauseous;—water delivered under such conditions, it fails to stay the appetency for strong drinks, and fails of sanitary results, as proved where new and improved supplies of soft water have been obtained, and where it has failed to arrest increasing death rates, as in the large and flagrant results of Glasgow, Liverpool, and Manchester, where from neglect or incompetency to attend to the sanitary conditions influencing the dwellings of the wage classes there is with the greatest local prosperity, and the highest amount of wages, the heaviest mortality.

It is an important principle, which should be acted upon, that ample supplies of water, conveniently placed at hand, must precede the formation of habits of personal cleanliness, by regular head-to-foot ablutions. By such ablutions the people are armed, as it were, against epidemics and passing causes of disease. Moreover, their food goes farther. Four members of a family that are regularly washed will be kept in as good a condition on the same amount of food as five that are unwashed. Even pigs that are regularly washed and kept with clean skins put on one-fourth more flesh with the same quantity and sort of food that is eaten by pigs that are unwashed. In well-managed prisons, where the cells are well supplied with water, where the prisoners are made to have head-to-foot ablutions, where there is good ventilation kept up, and where wall smells are prevented, and drain smells excluded;—although there is a watercloset in each cell —in these dwellings, although the diet is much lower (ex-

Marginal notes:
MR. CHADWICK ON DWELLINGS.

Deterioration of good water by bad modes of delivery.

Economy of head to foot daily ablutions.

3. U

MR. CHAD-
WICK ON
DWELLINGS.
cept that there is good milk as part of the vegetable
dietary), epidemic attacks, and almost all spontaneous acute
disease is abolished;—typhus, or the gaol fever, is now unknown there; and there is less than one-third of the sickness and death-rates prevalent amongst the general outside
populations.

One obstacle to the extension of the minor distribution of
water into houses and rooms, so important for cleanliness
and health in cottages, is that it is often, in the present
condition of the common apparatus, an extension of waste.

Wasteful
modes of
delivering
water.
In the metropolis and many cities and towns, fully three-
fifths of the water is pumped in waste, partly from the
defects of intermittent supplies and neglected ball-cocks and
overflows of cisterns in the house, and numerous pipes
letting the water run away, in the notion of clearing bad
drains and bad sewers of deposit. As a check to this waste
lower rates should be charged on houses proved, on inspection, to have self-closing taps or meters or other waste
preventers. Another obstacle to the improved internal
distribution of cottage supplies is the practical difficulty of
carrying water-pipes inside the thin walls, or of attaching
them to the soft lath and plaster walls, or to the soft surface of walls such as those of the model dwellings in the
Exhibition.

I did not see in the Exhibition any examples of a very
important invention presented to us 15 years ago, at the
General Board of Health, by Mr. Philip Holland (one of
our then inspectors, now inspector of the health department
of the Home Office), by which these obstacles were provided

Economical
mode of dis-
tributing
water in
dwelling
rooms.
against. He used very small pipes of glass or of gutta-
percha, of a size, or with a very small bore, not larger than
that of a tobacco pipe. Small lead piping, tinned or protected inside, as has been done by an enamel, against the
action of the water, would also serve. The small-bore
water-pipe enters a vessel of earthenware, or of the cheapest
glass, which is closed at top, and it enters by a three-way
tap. The water passes through the pipe very slowly, a
mere ooze, compressing the air until its tension equals the
pressure of the water when no more enters. With the
pressure of about 100 ft. the air is compressed to one-fourth
its usual bulk, a gallon bottle contains three quarts of water
and one of air, the pressure of which forces out the water,
when the tap is turned, as fast as it would do if the supply-
pipe were of the size of the tap, getting gradually slower as
the closed bottle is emptied, and then ceasing altogether,
as the three-way tap prevents the water flowing in and out
of the vessel at the same time. For a wash-stand a gallon

vessel will suffice, even for a complete personal ablution (with a sponge or a wet towel). For a scullery or cuisine, such as those in the model dwellings, one of three or four gallons is enough. The following are sections of the three-way tap, open and closed, together with a view of the vessel.

A THREE-WAY TAP.

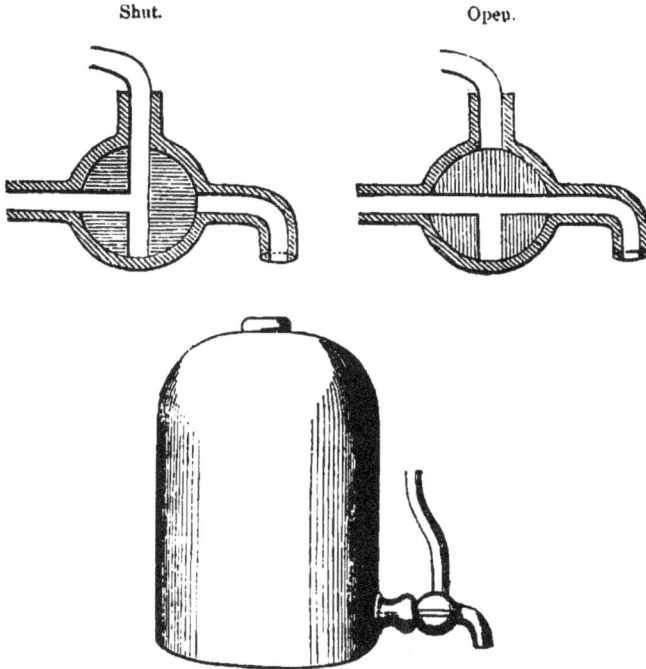

Shut.   Open.

VESSEL FOR CONTAINING WATER AND COMPRESSED AIR.

The vessels are refilled, and are intended to be refilled, only very slowly, after each charge is drawn, as the slowness prevents waste. The consumer must wait until the fresh supply is obtained. In the case of breakage apartments are not flooded, as in the event of the breakage of a pipe of the common bore ; and vast aggregate wastes are thus preventible The small piping may be carried along the cornice of rooms, where it is little more seen than bell wires. Where exposed to frost it may be inclosed in a pipe made of bitumen and paper, which is a good non-conductor.

By the saving from the substitution of the very small pipes for the large pipes now commonly used, this simple apparatus is much less costly than common cisterns. The cost of supplying every room of a dwelling with water need not be greater than that of supplying one cistern only. The saving of the trouble of fetching and carrying up water into rooms on this system of constant supply is considerable, besides the advantage of avoiding the risk of receiving the impurities to which all water kept stagnant in open cisterns—commonly placed so as to absorb the deleterious gases of cesspools or refuse heaps of close habitations—is exposed, for on this system the water is never exposed to such foul air. By the evaporation of a wet cloth thrown over the vessel in hot weather, the water may be kept cool and well aerated for drinking—a great advantage for health and temperance. In special cases, for sick rooms, receptacles may be provided to be easily charged with carbonic acid or oxygenated gas, which would be absorbed under constant pressure.

This distributory apparatus is peculiarly eligible in cases where there is in the neighbourhood of any *cité ouvrière*, village, or town, a peculiarly good spring or supply of water well fitted for drinking or for culinary purposes, leaving any other less pure supply that serves for other ordinary purposes to be distributed in the ordinary way. On this system of supply, the mains may, with pressure, be relatively as small as the minor or capillary distribution pipes. Whilst there is proper grief and severe denunciations of the waste of means by the wage classes in the cabaret or the beershop, it is overlooked that at present, in most towns, their common alternative is of water usually discoloured and repulsive to look at, flat or nauseous to the taste, and utterly unfitted for drinking. The first step in improvement is to secure by administrative means such water for *their* tables as would be admissible in water bottles for *ours.*

Some waters act upon metal pipes more powerfully than others, and on lead pipes very injuriously. Vitruvius states that the Romans distributed water in earthenware pipes at
100 ft. of pressure. Some years ago I got some trial works made of the strength of stoneware pipes, subjected to a second mechanical pressure, when it was found that they bore pressure equal to a head of more than 1,200 ft. of water. Our engineers who tried them failed, however, in several instances; but in the French annexe of Class 65 there are to be seen specimens of red earthenware glazed pipes for the distribution of water, with testimony of success in a number of towns, under various high pressures. The failures of the trial works in England appear to have been with the common

spiggot-and-faucit joints. The success under the practice of Messrs. Constant Zeller appears to have been with joints, wide and strong rings of Portland cement covered by rings of earthenware, thus :—

The objection to the use of earthenware for water distribution on a large scale, and for the interior of houses, that it won't stand it, is that it does stand it. Mulhouse and a number of other cities in the north of France, several in Switzerland and Germany are supplied with water in earthenware pipes laid down by Messrs. Constant Zeller. The greatest pressure at which they have been called upon to lay down earthenware pipes is 60 metres. But it did not strike me, that their red earthenware glazed pipes though obviously well made, were so strong, as we had some vitreous stoneware pipes made in England, some of which stood a pressure of as much as 500lbs. the square inch, or upwards of 1,000 feet of altitude. At some of the points of the most severe pressure it appears that the Messrs. Zeller put in short lengths of lead pipe to withstand the hydraulic shock, which is otherwise duly provided for by water cushions. The highest pressure they have got particular earthenware pipes to stand appears to be 34 atmospheres.* Here, however, is an established and proved practice of laying down earthenware pipes, and their working at upwards of 120 feet of pressure, at more than a hundred places, towns and villages in France. The advantages of the earthenware pipes over the metal are, greater

Mr. Chadwick on Dwellings.

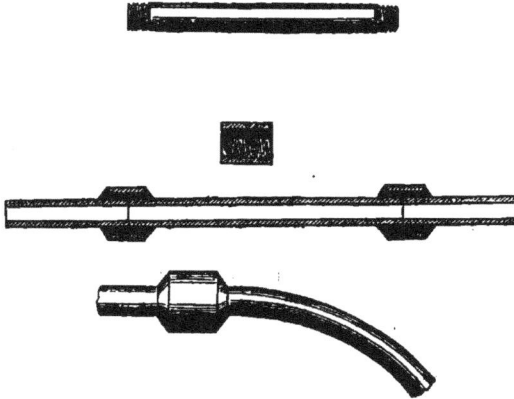

Advantages of earthenware pipe distribution.

---

* Vide tabular results, p. 190, Appendix to Minutes of Information of the General Board of Health, on the removal of soil matter and the sewerage, and cleansing of the sites of towns, p. 152.

purity, indefinite durability, and it is alleged that they are less subject to derangement, more easily repaired, and less expensive to keep up, and are laid down at half the first cost of metal pipes. One result of this is, that by means of these pipes a pipe-water distribution has been effected in villages where the price of iron pipes would have been prohibitory.

There were in the Exhibition various pipes made of paper and bitumen for the distribution of water, whether tried or not for any length of time under constant pressure I could not ascertain. But I am informed that pipes of beton or concrete, with a large proportion of very strong Portland cement, have been used under moderate pressures, with success. The late Count Gasparin, the most scientific agriculturist of Europe, informed me that, being unable to get either iron or earthenware pipes at his estate near Avignon for the distribution of liquefied manure, his brother made pipes of concrete or beton, by the following method, which
may be worth knowing :—He distended a flexible hose of the suitable length with water, and laid it on a level bed of concrete in a trench. He then covered the distended pipe with concrete, and when it was set let out the water from the pipe, which had been so covered as to protect it from the adhesion of the concrete, pulled it out, and proceeded to refil it with water, and to form another length of beton piping in the same way. With these pipes the Count made fountains for his gardens.

THE COTTAGE OR DWELLING-HOUSE DRAINAGE AND CLEANSING QUESTION.

The sanitary principle of constructive arrangement to be striven for is that all animal and vegetable refuse matter shall be constantly removed from within, or from about, or from beneath or near habitations, from beneath the sites of houses, of streets, or of towns, before it enters into advanced, which are the noxious, stages of decomposition. For this purpose there is no method so cheap or so efficient as by the reception and immediate removal of excreta in suspension in water. There is no mode of arresting decomposition and saving and applying it to manure so efficiently and cheaply as in water. All the French model dwellings now adopt the English water-closet as the means of effecting this object, though I did not consider they were quite so good as those
in the model dwellings of the Prince Consort. The cost of maintaining such an arrangement within a house in good working order ought not to exceed one penny per week. Experience in England has shown that the syphon closet is

the best under all ordinary conditions, when a proper supply and scour of water and trap is applied to it. The closets on the principle of the flap-trap are all objectionable, as being more expensive, and as usually keeping an accumulation of soil underneath or about them, though out of sight. Little attention appeared to be paid to the economy of water for the service, which varied from half a gallon to two gallons or more. A proper and complete apparatus of the syphon type should be connected with a self-cleansing house drain (properly trapped to prevent the regurgitation of any products of decomposition arising from accident), and the interior house drain must be connected with the self-cleansing sewer, both of which may now best be made of a proper and smoother concrete, free from the interruptions of joints, has now been done in some instances in Paris with the Beton Coignet, and I am informed it has also been done successfully with one form of concrete at Zurich and at other places on the Continent. The advantages of a skilful application of these new modes of construction to house as well as to town drainage will be considerable in economy, as well as in efficiency, in getting better adaptations of lines and gradations than are given by the common manufacture of tubular drain pipes, which were the first gain upon the rude rough brick or rough stone house drains.

MR. CHAD-
WICK ON
DWELLINGS.

Concrete
house drains
and sewers.

The extended use of the water-closet is, however, opposed on the ground of the waste of manure. But manure is best preserved by its immediate reception in cold water, which arrests decomposition, which is detected by the nose in the escape of noxious emanations, and prevents waste ; and in the liquefied form the manure ought to be removed and deposited, within the day of its production, on fallow land, and deposited there not in mechanical suspension, but in chemical combination.

Economy of
manure by
reception in
water.

The first stink of fœcal matter is to be taken as a warning for removal, or worse will follow the products of decomposition which are of a different nature. It is a result of considerable observation that, in ordinary weather in England, the incipient decomposition of sewage begins about the end of the first day, and advances until there is very full decomposition, usually about the fourth day. But it ought and may, by proper arrangements, be all put, within the first day, in chemical combination with the soil, in which condition it is the most securely preserved for production.

Some plans are presented for using prepared earth in prepared closets for the reception of the manure. But even if on these plans the earth were manipulated with the care they require, which with cottagers they rarely are, and if

The earth
closet pan.

they were effectual, they are objectionable on the score of
expense, in the labour of preparing the earth, in bringing
it to the house, and in the removal of the increased bulk,
for a closet, if used by six persons, it is stated will require
about 2 cwt. of earth per week to be prepared and applied,
or more than 2½ tons per annum, or for a population of
10,000 persons about 13 tons a day. The expense as set
down for the lowest class house is greater than that of
putting down a soil pan, whilst the annual working expenses
appear to be double for the removal of urine and fæces
alone, but the mistake is made of regarding such matter as
constituting the only sewerage, whereas they form only an
inconsiderable proportion of the sewerage proper, in some
cases less than a two hundredth part of what is comprised in it,
the foul and the waste water, kitchen slops, soap suds, &c.,
for the removal of which house drains and sewers must be
provided. On examples of the use of the dry conservancy
system in public institutions, as in some of the prisons in India,
where labour is under control and employment wanted, and
where the places are near from which earth is to be taken and
whence it is to be returned after saturation, it is proposed
to apply the system to large towns, where labour must be
paid for, and where the places where earth is to be got and
returned is distant. In an able report Captain Tulloch, of
the Royal Engineers, has demonstrated that a system of
" dry " conservancy worked out for Madras would be six
times more expensive than a system of self-cleansing sewers.
Instead of taking the earth to the manure, it is the
cheapest to take the manure to the earth, and to prepare
the earth *in situ* for its reception. In the instances of
detached cottages in rural districts unconnected with any
general water supply, or with any systematised means
for the removal of the waste water, a simple glazed
earthen vessel under a seat in the outhouse, or a common
tin pail with water, or better, with the house slops and
soapsuds also in it, is a more ready and better provision.
Assuming that a garden is attached to the dwelling, the
cottager should be taught to keep a portion of it trenched
two spits deep, and to deposit regularly every day the
liquefied manure in as much of the trench as it will immediately absorb. The day's deposit should be covered at
once, to " save the manure " from loss by evaporation and
decomposition ; and a far larger portion of soil may thus be
more readily and completely fertilised than by any manipulation of solid manures. The trench should be in the direction of the roots of trees or of growing crops. In the
Swedish annexe, and also in the Danish annexe, there are

well contrived pails with seats, and with interior divisions
to receive and keep separately the urine and the more solid
fœcal matter. This may do very well where there is special
agricultural or horticultural preparation for the treatment
of the manures, separately and immediately. But this is
rarely the case. Moreover, it is the result of much observation that the miscellaneous manures—liquefied—soapsuds,
and the other house refuse, which can be removed in suspension, and the very miscellaneous manures of most towns,
act better for most vegetables than any single manure. In
the case of *cités ouvrières*, or detached houses, where they
may be no sufficient means for the regular application of
the manure near the houses, or it may be beyond individual
attention, it should, as a commencement, be made the subject of a distinct regular service by the collection and the
daily removal of the refuse in proper water carts or tanks.

I shall not be supposed to countenance the system of the
movable cabinets "inodores," so-called, which are being
abandoned in the Continental cities. The great sanitary
object, and the minor agricultural object to be kept in view
is to have all matters removed before they enter into advanced
stages of decomposition. This system of the *fosses inodores*
attempts to retain such refuse after it has entered into those
stages, and to confine the products, which it never does,
until a late removal. All fixed cisterns or fosses of stagnant
refuse are magazines of poison. It is matter of surprise
that, with such unity of power and with such very distinguished administrative ability as there is in Paris, the
system of fixed fosses should be allowed so long to remain,
to the deterioration of its superior atmosphere to an extent
that, in the summer time, often makes the houses in the
best quarters uninhabitable, and that, too, at a cost to con-
tracting companies for intermittent and offensive cleansing
that, if capitalised and duly applied, would suffice for the
complete removal of the evil.

In respect to the question of the application of excreta
as manure, which is made to govern the internal household
arrangements for its removal, I had, in the course of the
International Exhibition of 1856, and as one of the international jury on hygiène, the honour of an audience with
the Emperor, at which I directed his attention to the subject of the application of sewage to agricultural production.
I submitted to him the expediency of having trial works
made upon the question by his own officers for the public
information. He was pleased to give directions to that
effect; and the trials of the productive power of sewage or
of liquefied manure were made, chiefly under the direction

of Professor Moll, of the Conservatoire des Arts et Métiers, one of the most able scientific agriculturists of Europe, aided by Mons. Mille, the Engineer-in-chief to the municipality of Paris. I may say that the trials they conducted were becoming their positions, and were the most comprehensive, with different forms of culture, and the best and most complete public trials that have been anywhere con-

ducted. The results of later and extended trial works on a farm may be seen stated and the principles expounded in the " Annales du Conservatoire Impérial des Arts et Métiers," by M. Moll, in a paper entitled " L'Assainissement des Villes, par la fertilisation des Campagnes." It must be said, however, that all the trials were conducted with sewage from the fosses, which is old and putrid, instead of with sewage which is fresh; for sewage which is fresh and unwasted by decomposition would be difficult to obtain in Paris, or anywhere else—except in a district which is drained by tubular self-cleansing drains and sewers. It marks the little progress made in the diffusion of sanitary science that it should be yet commonly conceived that sewage is all of one quality only, that found in all towns; that there is yet little conception of the difference there is between sewage which is old and putrid and sewage which

is new and fresh; that it should be known that sewage which is old has one third less fertilising power, and at the same time requires above a third more of deodorising or disinfecting agents than sewage which is fresh. Though sewage should be put to more profitable use than feeding fish, it may be proper to mention, as a point of progress since the last Exhibition, that it is now found that where sewage is conveyed through systems of self-cleansing tubular house-drains and sewers direct from the house to the river, instead of killing fish it feeds them. Anglers find their best sport, and catch the largest fish at the mouths of sewers which discharge sewage that is fresh. At the last Exhibition the attention of the Emperor was directed to the example of the distribution of sewage by pipes and jets at Rugby. Since then Mr. James Blackburn, the agricultural engineer, has demonstrated in the distribution of the manure of the camp at Aldershott, that by enlarging the size of the pipes, and a better application of engine power, sewage may be distributed at about half the expenses at Rugby, or within a half-penny per ton. It is further demonstrated that sewage may now be utilised on one third the area than commonly considered to be requisite for the purpose. On experience of the application of the less putrid sewage of Aldershott camp, Mr. Blackburn concurs in the general statement, that with active garden cultivation, the land being well trenched, and the liquefied manure being applied in appropriate doses, the sewage of a family of five persons may be utilised on an eighth or a tenth of an acre of land; so that the day's sewage may be utilised on a plot of land four feet square, or even on a yard square if worked two feet deep. On such trials and estimates, the sewage of the million of inhabitants of Paris proper may, by high cultivation, be utilised in 20,000 acres, or on an area of $5\frac{1}{2}$ miles by 6 miles, or the sewage of the three millions of inhabitants of London on 60,000 acres, or an area of ten square miles.

In the Exhibition and the annexe there is a display of varied manufactures of hose pipe and of distributing apparatus which marks the extension of the system. In a paper upon it, printed in 1852, I proposed the distribution of liquefied manure by movable carriers with *lateral* apertures. This has not yet got into practice in England; but it has been adopted in France, and it may be seen applied for the distribution of water in the Bois de Boulogne.

In the report on the water supply of the metropolis (1850) the results of some trial works were given, with woodcut illustrations, showing that, by means of flexible hose pipe, on rollers, paved surfaces might be kept washed as clean as a paved courtyard, and the roadway watered at an expense not exceeding a halfpenny per head per week of the population—a means of a great economy of washing and the wear and tear of clothes, as well as of personal and household cleanliness. The conditions of the trading water companies and of our local administrations have not been sufficiently advanced for the adoption of the plan in England; but it may be seen at work in the chief thoroughfares of Paris, in watering the roads and keeping down the dust, to the great relief and comfort of the occupiers of houses as well as of passengers.

With an ample vote of money and a given style, it is very easy to assemble a staff of architects competent to construct a palace or any great first-class edifice; but it is one of the problems of the day to construct, with the necessary rigid economies and with the proper sanitary qualities, a cottage or pattern dwelling for the many—the poor. Here in Paris we have the example of the greatest power animated by beneficent intentions, having at its command the highest architectural art and science, which has superbly rebuilt cities with the most splendid of modern edifices, and has yet left the habitations of the many with walls absorbing damp and

[marginal notes:] Mr. Chadwick on Dwellings. Extent of land requisite for the utilisation of sewage. Cost of washing the fronts of dwellings.

MR. CHAD-
WICK ON
DWELLINGS.

mephitism, and in a condition to continue to be fever nests and to harbour the Egyptian plague of vermin. What I humbly submit to power, to avert this state of things, is that the extension of the existing improvements, and their advancement in economy as well as in other desirable qualities, would be greatly aided by authentic public trial works of different materials available for construction, not merely as to strength and bearing power, but in impermeability to moisture, and washability, and their powers as non-conductors of heat and

Course of
improve-
ment.

sound. Neither individual proprietors nor common builders have the time or the means to determine these questions; nor are they to be expected to move in them at their own individual expense for the common gain. Advances in economy, with improvements in quality, can only be promoted extensively by applications of capital, on the scale of a manufacture of such dwellings with the advantages of large quantities, or of repetitions of large numbers by machinery. Some parts—woodwork, doors, windows, and flooring—are now produced by machinery, but separately, and the subdivision of labour only entails at present, it is stated, a multiplication of the separate trade profits. What appears to be now wanted for economy is complete manufactures under one head. And, on the manufacturing principle of repetitions, the cost of good first moulds, when spread over large numbers, will be inconsiderable; and some relief from the common repulsive forms may be expected to be given by a chaste and appropriate interior (and washable) as well as exterior art decoration, for which there are symptoms of a rising perception and desire on the part of the wage classes. The objection of a common contractor or a common builder to the introduction of any improvement in detail—to the introduction of an improved cooking range, or an improved window, for example, or to any sort of ornamentation—is, usually, that it cannot be introduced except at a certain price—namely, at his retail trade price of 20, 30, or 40 per cent. of profit on the cost of

Associated
non-trading
effort neces-
sary.

production—making up a charge which is prohibitory. It is important to observe that the majority of the examples of extensive improvements represented in the Exhibition are examples achieved by associated individuals or companies, such as that of Mulhouse, under highly-intelligent and zealous direction. Such associated effort,—or the individual efforts of intelligent large owners,—must be looked to for the best improvement under such direction as will not accept existing habits and practice of construction as fixed and unchangeable conditions (as most associated building companies in England have hitherto done), and as will set aside obstructive interests, and will be content with whole- sale profits, such as 10 per cent. upon materials obtained first hand, or manufactured expressly on a large scale.

On the whole, viewing collectively the various models and collateral appliances presented for examination in the present Exhibition, there will be found in it the means of very important advances in the improvement of the dwellings of the great mass of the people—in the means of relieving them from the cesspool smell, or the bad drain or sewer emanations and smell; from the foul wall smell and from the wall vermin; from the damp wall; from the smoke nuisance; from a great proportion of the waste of fuel and the loss of heat; from stagnant and vitiated air; from the deterioration of good water supplies; from much of the exclusion from sunlight, and it is proved that by new appliances their dwellings may be made cooler in summer and warmer in winter; and that too, not only without any increase but with a very material reduction of direct expense. I say of direct expense, because, when the losses from excessive sickness, premature disability, and premature mortality are taken into account, a great proportion of the common dwellings of the wage classes, though they may be cheap to construct, are indirectly and eventually dear to use. By dwellings with the improvements specified, the rates for insurances against sickness, disability, and mortality would be reduced nearly one half. With clean, light, bright, warm, comfortable, and healthful dwellings; with the habits of personal cleanliness, sobriety, and frugality,—to which such conditions would conduce,—new and improved populations would arise. To one accustomed to inspect town schools in the lower districts, the comparative condition, external as well as internal, of the dwellings may, to a considerable extent be inferred by the comparative aspect and condition of the children. Already, in neighbourhoods where partial sanitary improvements have been made for a few years, school teachers mark an improvement in the condition and quality of the children received from them, who are less squalid, less ugly and less vicious, and more apt for instruction. It is now generally admitted, by all who have attended to the subject, that moral and social advancement is dependent on physical improvement, and that on the sanitary improvement of dwellings.

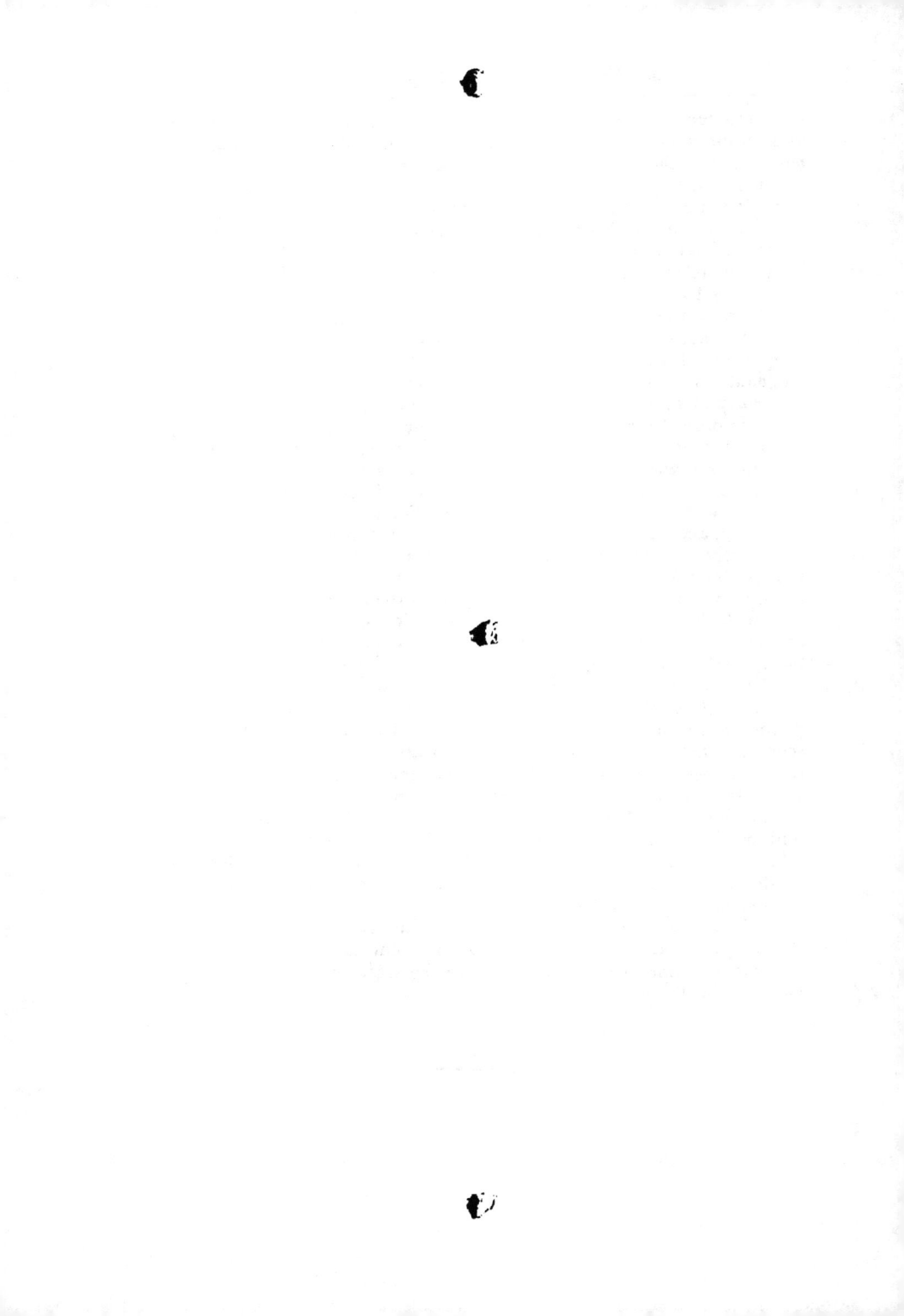

REPORT on ARTICLES of all Kinds manufactured by Skilled Workmen—(Class 94.)—By BLANCHARD JERROLD, Esq.

MR. JERROLD ON ARTICLES MADE BY SKILLED WORKMEN.

THE tenth group is a new feature in exhibitions of industry. We are officially told that it comprehends " the " whole series of objects exhibited with the special view of " furnishing the rural and urban populations with the means " of improving their physical and moral condition." I pass by the classes which comprehend popular education, cheap food, clothing, lodging, and household management, and com to— *(margin: Novelty of the tenth group.)*

Class 94. Articles of all kinds manufactured by skilled workmen.

Class 95. Instruments and modes of work peculiar to skilled workmen.

The former class is represented in the catalogue by 486 French exhibitors, 18 Prussian, 3 Hessian, 10 Austrian, 7 Greek, and 1 British colonial.

The latter class consists exclusively of French exhibitors, who are thirty-two in number.

The exhibitors who are described in the catalogue as appearing in Class 94 do not, in many cases, belong to it. Strictly speaking, half the exhibition might be brought within this class, if its range were admitted to be that which some exhibitors have given it; and, indeed, which the authorities appear, in some instances, to have adopted. The main object of this class was to show the work of artisans who labour on their own account, either alone or with the assistance of their families, or with one apprentice —for a trade or for domestic consumption. The purpose to be served was excellent. M. Jules Simon, Audiganne, and other French writers have dwelt of late years on the destruction of the family by machinery, which has drawn father, mother, and children from the fireside to be brigaded in different mills and factories. According to M. Jules Simon, in those districts where machinery has supplanted entirely home labour, there has followed an increase of drunkenness and immorality. *(margin: Main object of Class 94.)*

The first impression that is made by an examination of the court of skilled workmen, situated in the French section, at its junction with the Algerian section, is, that the tendency of every trade, save and except those which may be generally described as the minor trades of the *Articles Paris*, is towards large workshops. Indeed, it is difficult, as this Exhibition *(margin: France.)*

MR.
JERROLD
ON
ARTICLES
MADE BY
SKILLED
WORKMEN.
—
proves, to find enough skilled workmen working on their own
account, or working apart with the help of their family or an
apprentice for their trade, to make an important show.

The skilled works which are ranged under Class 94, in the
French section, consist of bronzes, art-work in metal, ivory-
turning, wood carving and carpenter's work, toys, mechanical
and scientific engineering, and other models, including an
ingenious calculating-machine by L. Chemar, and a small
variety of clever inventions. The most notable skilled industries of Paris represented in the court are bronze and works
in wood. There is some excellent brass and steel work.
J. Mathieu exhibits some accurate, delicate, and gracefully-
designed ivory-turning. There are a few *tours de force*—as
A. Panon's dwarf fiddle, weighing 25 centigrammes, an
instrument that might be useful in Liliput. There are, moreover, some exhibits that are mere monuments of patience,
as Mdme. Douil's woolwork, which pictorially describes the
marriage of the Emperor and Empress. M. Chriten's cross
of honour, carved in a single agate, is a highly skilful bit of
labour. The two industries, I repeat, which make the important features of Class 94, in the French section, are the
Works in
bronze.
bronze and the wood work. The works in bronze which are
exhibited in the main central case are nearly all well known
and already rewarded trophies of the Paris bronze-workers'
highest skill. Barye's fine group, inspired—as many sculptors have been—by the struggle of the Lapithæ and the
Centaurs, cast in bronze by Boyer; Poux's works, which have
gained the highest prizes at the competitive exhibitions of
the bronze manufactures; Gonon's rough cast of a bird's-
nest, and his finished bronze, are excellent samples of the
vigour, the finish, and, at the same time the delicacy which
characterise the work of the foremost bronze modellers and
casters of Paris.

Woodwork.
In woodwork there are one or two of those great models
of fine timber-work which the carpenters and cabinetmakers
of France have delighted to carry in their processions for
centuries, and which have caused so many lively contests of
skill since the old freemasonry of labour split into two fac-
tions—the Gavots and the Devoirants—under the towers of
Orleans Cathedral, four centuries ago. Over these trophies
many savage quarrels have happened. The two latest
monuments of skill, which are in the skilled-labour court,
are exhibited by the journeymen of the Devoir and the
journeymen Passants. They are fine examples of the skill
and knowledge of the leading carpenters of Paris. That of
the Devoirants—a temple, dedicated to Solomon—was completed in the present year. The intention of the framers of

Class 94 was undoubtedly to illustrate the skill obtained by independent workmen, or workmen taking contracts from manufacturers and working apart with their families, or with apprentices, or with the help of one or two men. I repeat that the bronze-workers and the workers in wood, the carpenters and cabinetmakers, furnish the most important illustrations of the effects of the small-workshop system as opposed to the factory system. The Paris Chamber of Commerce, in the first report issued under their authority on the industries of Paris, having divided the group of industries, which include every kind of art-furniture, paperhangings, bronzes, and cabinet-work into thirty-two sections, placed the bronze trade at the head of them. These thirty-two sections, it will be seen, comprehend all the notable art-industries for which Paris is famous. The bronze-workers of Paris still command the markets of the world, if not always because their works are artistically superior to ours, because we cannot produce them at anything like the Paris price. The system of labour by which the Paris bronzes are produced is that of dealing through overseers with skilled mechanics, who employ one or more journeymen or apprentices. It is this system which prevails in the leading trades of Paris, but is very slowly giving way to collective labour in great factories, like that of M. Barbédienne, the celebrated bronze manufacturer and worker of the Collas patent, and M. Boy, the great imitation bronze manufacturer in the Marais. In order to justly appreciate the value of the works exhibited under this class, is is necessary to get some experience of the *grand atelier* system, as opposed to the *petit*. Examples of the work sent forth by independent skilled workmen are to be found, indeed, scattered over the first three groups of the Exhibition, and more particularly in Classes 8, 10, 12, 17, 20, 26, 34, 35, and 39. Then there are some few articles of skilled manufacture which belong to the fifth and sixth groups—carpenters' work, for instance. Agriculture, again, presents, in groups 7, 8, and 9, examples of home or independent labour. It has not, however, been found practicable to bring this vast variety of products from every nook and corner of the Exhibition into a great court of independent skilled labour. Nor indeed would any very useful purpose have been served by such an assemblage, unless the authorities had been prepared to institute at the same time a searching inquiry into the relative results of the rival systems of great and home workshops in every country. As it is, Class 94 affords an opportunity of comparing the *grand atelier* system with the *petit atelier* system of Paris. The insignificent exhibits of Prussia, Austria,

Bronze industry of Paris.

Home and factory systems

Compared.

3.　　　　　　　　　　　X

MR.
JERROLD
ON
ARTICLES
MADE BY
SKILLED
WORKMEN.

Hesse, and Greece can give us no idea of the value
of the home system of manufacture in any of these
countries.   J. Carvellas sends a bracelet cut in apricot
kernels, from Zante ; and at hand are a crook and bagpipes
of home manufacture.   There is some fair morocco-work and
amber cigar tubes, and brushes from Austria.   The collecve
exhibition of industrial articles from the Industrial Society,
of Hermanstadt, in Transylvania, does not properly belong
to Class 94.   The brown cloth for the national costume by
M. Basak is a good home-spun fabric ; but, in order to test
its value as a cheap material for the costumer, and as affording fair remuneration to the producer (and in this light only
-does it belong to Class 94), it would be necessary to make a
serious inquiry, such as I have indicated, into the relative
merits of the great factory and home factory systems as they
appear in Austria.

*Petit
atelier*, or
home
system.

The *petit atelier*, or, as I will call it, the home system, as
opposed to the factory system, in Paris, appears advantageously in the bronze trade, as contrasted with the trades of
the workers in wood.   The home system has a tendency to
degenerate into what we understand by, and deplore as, the
sweating system.   If the home system could be kept within
the bounds those social economists would strictly assign it
who set a high value upon the promotion of the domestic
virtues among the working population in a State, it would
be, I think, beyond all question, the best system for the
workman and his family.   But competition, widened by free
trade, has sharpened the wit of manufacturers, and driven

Subdivision
of labour
and sweat-
ing system.

them in quest of the cheapest modes of production.   They
have, inevitably, recourse to every possible subdivision of
labour.   The son of the great art workman, who could execute perfectly every part of the most elaborate cabinet,
becomes the mechanical fashioner of a chair-leg.   This subdivision of labour necessitates the close congregation of the
labourers.   The sweater is making havoc among the cabinetmakers of Paris, who are the descendants of André Boulc
and Riesner.   Great quantities of manufactures are cheaply
produced ; but, I take the Paris cabinetmakers' own statement, the skilled art workman is disappearing.   In this
trade the home system has merged into the sweating system.
A skilled workman gets materials from a patron, and employs
a clumsy journeyman or two and apprentices at something
like starvation wages.   In nearly every Paris trade the
sweater has made his appearance, and he operates most
disastrously for the workman when he finds him at home.
The complaints of such skilled art workmen as the engravers
for textile fabrics and paper-hangings are to the effect that

the men who trade in designs—who stand between them and the manufacturers who want designs—are continually driving down their already scanty wages. In the case of the bronze workers, men of extraordinary skill command, as in any other trade, exceptionally high wages. But I found, on close inquiry, a short time ago, that the wages of 80 per cent. of the bronze workers of Paris did not exceed 3s. 7d. per diem, and that only 5 per cent. exceeded 5s.

The skilled workmen who employ one or more men and take rough castings from manufacturers are, I apprehend, in the last category, and pay the lowest wages in the trade. A glance at M. Boy's imitation or zinc-bronze factory, in the Rue Saint Louis, and at the *grand atelier* system as herein developed, will afford a favourable contrast between the home and factory systems as they regard the bronze trade. In this establishment there is a minute subdivision of labour that indubitably tends to the growth of an inferior race of workmen. One man can only lay on the vert antique; another passes his days at a little fire soldering zinc arms to zinc trunks. Each man, of course, acquires marvellous dexterity and rapidity. The race is for cheap production, and time is a main element of cheapness in this imitation work, for the material makes a great part of the price. It is stated, however, that these comparatively mechanical workers in imitation bronze earn, taking the good with the indifferent workman, an average of 7f. a day. This is an employer's statement, which, I am bound to observe, is contradicted by the delegates who represented the Paris bronze trade in the Exhibition of 1862. On the one hand, the workmen point to the dull season; on the other, the masters blame the men, who will only work, even in the brisk season, four or five days in the week. M. Open (who exhibits a spirited and finished bronze representing two birds fighting, and who calls himself an independent workman, employing others) has stated to me that the average wage of his employed men is 6f. a day, and that the work he undertakes is of the finest quality.

In the Paris carpenters' trade there are great and bitter dissensions. This trade is divided broadly into two classes— the menuisier, who may be described as the maker of small articles; and the charpentier, who is a builder in timber—a house carpenter. There are sub-divisions of the menuisiers and the charpentiers; but into these it is not necessary to enter. In all branches of this trade we find the home or small workshop system in force, and it appears to have been degraded to a very aggravated form of the *marchandage* or middle-man system. The disputes between the skilled and

MR.
JERROLD
ON
ARTICLES
MADE BY
SKILLED
WORKMEN.
—
Wood-
carvers.

crafty carpenters who take petty sub-contracts and fulfil them by paying bad wages to clumsy country journeymen and apprentices are incessant.   The ever-increasing use of iron in building operations has aggravated the hardships which the sub-contract system has produced among the Paris carpenters.   The woodcarvers of Paris, who chiefly work in shops, and therefore exhibit little or nothing in Class 94, are an independent, highly-paid race—that is, those among them who can produce any of that delicate work in wood for which Paris is famous, and besides which the Swiss carving is coarse and unnatural.   The carvers may be parted into those who work on chestnut and the close and fine grain of the pear-tree and the mechanical carvers in coarser woods. The highest rate of pay is about 6*s.* for a day's work of eight hours, while 3*s.* 4*d.* is the lowest.   The men who are em-ployed in the vast cheap carved furniture trade, and are on a level with M. Boy's piecemeal workmen, complain of the *marchandage* system which is now carried on in the little workshops, and which, in point of fact, Class 94 represents. The clever sculptor in wood, when he has once managed to rent a shed and a back yard, takes a quantity of contract work from a firm, and performs it by getting low-priced inferior workmen in his pay. The most cunning plan appears to be to employ a shopful of apprentices, and to teach each one only the art of fashioning one ornament.

A. de Sorbet, Rounay, and Company, of the Faubourg St. Antoine, exhibit in this class a little not remarkably good cabinet-work.   The firm describe themselves as a Société Ouvrière, and in their prospectus distinctly state that they have opened workshops where all their goods are manu-factured.   They add that the workmen share in the profits of the business, an intimation that gives some interest to their exhibit; but since their cabinet-work is produced in a factory it ceases to belong to Class 94.   Many exhibitors who are printed under this class, both in the English and French official catalogues, entirely repudiate any connection with it.   Many printed under Class 94 actually appear in Class 91.   There are in the list of exhibitors under this class many well-known Paris and provincial firms who do not exhibit under it, and would, indeed, appear ridiculous in it.   For instance, Messrs. Mazaroz-Riballier and Co., upholsterers, repudiate the least connection with either Classes 94 or 95. Among skilled workmen working on their own account I find the Count de Boissimon, who exhibits (but not in Class 94 at all) " artistic, household, and earthen and other ware; fire-brick, flooring, and other tiles." Indeed, the greater part of the list consists of names of great whole-

Errors in
the cata-
logue of
Class 94.

sale and retail Paris houses, who appear in all kinds of groups and classes save group 10, and Classes 94 and 95. The list is swollen with a number of collected exhibitions, as those of the Chamber of Commerce of Elbœuf, the towns of Sédan, Saint-Quentin, Rouen, Mulhouse (the charities and provident societies of which are worth the personal study of every student of social science), Troyes, Rheims, Vienne, (Isère), Mazamet, Limoges, Tourcoing, Lodère, Bedarieux, Lisieux, Lille, Cholet, &c. But, I must repeat, not any of these exhibits are in class 94, except in the catalogue. Undoubtedly the French skilled workmen show " increased finish " in the execution of works of art in bronze ; variety and " judicious selection of models, in the manufacture of fancy " articles, the improvement of certain musical instruments, " of new tools, apparatus or implements for certain manu- " factures, ingenious applications of electricity ; and, lastly, " interesting inventions, in accordance with the programme " of the Imperial Commission, relating to the physical and " moral condition of the working classes." But these improvements, inventions, instruments, and articles have been already treated of by the reporters on the classes under which they are respectively exhibited.

The bronze trade represents in a more striking manner than any other trade the two rival systems of art-industry in Paris. Machinery has had no influence on the trade of late years. The Collas machine, for the mechanical production of reductions, is the only mechanical worker that has raised the ire of the bronze-workers. If, then, they have suffered reductions of wages of late years, it is not because a mechanical force has been brought into competition with human skill and strength. M. Open, who exhibits as an independent workman employing fellow-workmen, and is a bronze chiseller of mark himself, returns the average wages of the men he employs at 6f. per diem. So that we do not find at present that men working in small shops earn more than men working in great factories like Barbédienne's or Boy's. The preparations among the bronze-workers for this Exhibition, however, presented an incident in which the small atelier shows an advantage over the factory. The factory directors (I need not mention names), as usual, were behindhand with the works they intended to exhibit, and consequently had to insist upon over-work. Their work- men struck for higher wages and obtained them, but not until after the manufacturers had been put to great inconvenience. While there was a strike in the great workshops the little workshops remained busy.

M. Poux, whose works are perhaps the finest examples of

Bronze trade machinery.

Strikes.

M. Poux.

finished bronze exhibited in this class, is a good example of the highest skilled workman who is an employer of labour also. He is famous among chasers for the marvellous skill with which he renders the texture of the human flesh. The examples of his skill which are in this court are remarkable chiefly for the perfection of " le chairage." He is the art workman who is employed by leading bronze manufacturers, like Lerolle and Barbédienne, whenever highly delicate anatomical modelling and chasing are required. Such work-men have become rare in Paris, for this reason, that directly a bronze worker or chaser makes a reputation he drops the chisel and takes to the more remunerative art of modelling. So general is this course that it has become an accepted dictum that only the dull and defective remain bronze-chasers. " Bête comme un ciseleur " is a French proverb. M. Poux, however, has stuck to his chisel, and has set up a small workshop, where he employs from eight to 20 work-men.

According to him, chasers employed in the great factories earned, on an average, between 4f. and 5f. a day, before the recent strike; whereas they now earn between 6f. and 7f. for a day's work of ten hours. Most skilled men in this trade can work, if they please, at home. During the busy season many prefer to work under their own roof; but during the dead season they return to the workshops of the great manufacturer, who can generally find employment for them, on preparatory works for the next season. M. Poux adds that he is never without work. There is a great desire among the leading skilled bronze workers of Paris to try their fortunes in England, created by the renown of M. Vechte and others. The masters of little workshops main-tain that independent art workmen and those who are employed by masters who are themselves workmen, produce the best bronzes. They are not tied down by hard factory rules; they are not the slaves of a bell. They are free to work when inclination prompts them; and therefore they work with something like inspiration—at least, with earnest-ness.

Included in this class are some interesting models and ingenious contrivances—little monuments of workmen's patience and intelligence. They illustrate no system of labour. They are hobbies of earnest and exceptionally patient and intelligent working men. M. Barat exhibits the model of a locomotive. He is not a working engineer; he was, during 18 years, a railway employé, and is now co-manager with his wife of a shirtmaking business. This highly finished, compact, and well-adjusted model occupied the leisure hours, chiefly stolen from the night, of 12 years.

M. Barat exhibited the movement of a similar engine in 1855, and received the compliments of Mr. Crampton. The model locomotive now on view may be at any time examined by engineers. M. Margotin exhibits two inventions by M. G. Monot—viz., his universal horarium and his chronometrical planisphere. The horarium—it may be a watch, or a chronometer, or a clock—indicates at a glance the hour in every part of the world. By this invention, M. Margotin explains, everybody may carry in his pocket the actual hour in any latitude. He takes a sentimental view of the planisphere, saying, " Those who have an absent dear one, may " tell by it at any moment when he or she is rising or going " to bed." The presse-papier is also an ingenious and elegant novelty. M. Philarète Chasles advised M. Margotin to make these clocks cheap, so as to be able to sell them at schools. Their educational value is no doubt appreciated in Class 88, where they are also exhibited. M. Margotin's chronometrical planisphere, which tells the position of the moon and stars in relation to the earth, is exceedingly simple and ingenious, and has been received by the Academy of Sciences. I may add that the single clocks can be made for 1*l*. An interesting fact about M. Margotin is that, as a workman, he was led to the study of astronomy by a translation of James Ferguson's works, which he found in the Imperial library.

M. Battaille exhibits in this class a beautifully finished model of a country-house, on which he has spent the leisure hours of 25 years. It is, indeed, a miniature palace. The brass and steel work of the balustrades and candelabra ; the marqueterie, the mosaic work, are all highly finished, and display wonderful taste in the selection of material. The imitation mosaic carpet in the salon is a rich bit of minute art-work. Every description of costly wood has been used. The model contains 13 rooms, and each room is a separate and charming study. It is covered by a roof composed of 6,000 little tiles carved in wood. It is a trophy of patience and of highly cultivated taste ; but, strictly speaking, it does not belong to Class 94.

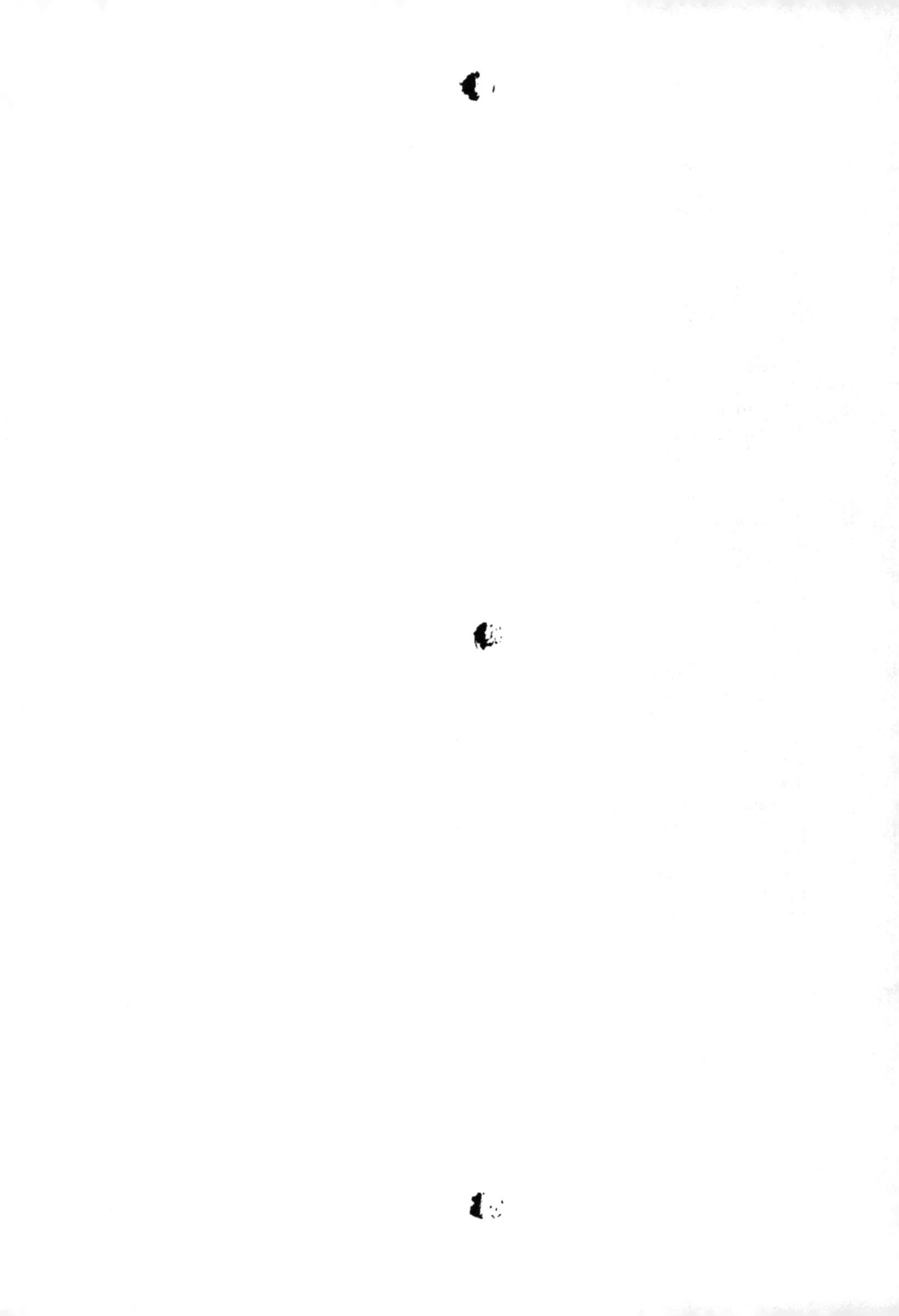

REPORT on INSTRUMENTS and MODES of WORK peculiar to SKILLED WORKMEN.—(Class 95.)—By BLANCHARD JERROLD, Esq.

MR. JERROLD ON INSTRU-MENTS, &C. OF SKILLED WORKMEN

IT was intended by the Imperial Commissioners that this class should comprehend : 1, the instruments and processes (enumerated in the sixth group) habitually employed by workmen acting on their own account, or specially adapted to the demand of industries carried on in the midst of a family or at home ; 2, the manual labours which exhibit, in the most remarkable manner, the taste, the dexterity, or the perseverance of the artizan ; 3, those industries which, from various causes, have best withstood to the present time the introduction of machinery. The object of forming this class was, we are further told, to bring to light those productions in which skill forms an essential ingredient, and which require a spontaneity and artistic sentiment of which man alone is capable. The exhibits of this class were to make known new and ingenious processes, and to prove highly advantageous to working-men, as offering them the opportunity of study and selection amidst " a well-arranged series " of productions and methods, and to awaken within them, " perhaps, capabilities of which they did not believe them-" selves possessed." This class was, moreover, to prove a revelation of processes that might be carried on at home or in small workshops. Many trades were necessarily excluded on account of their unsightliness or unwholesomeness, or, again, of their slow development. The exhibits actually grouped under this class are all French, and are thirty-two in number. Workmen and workwomen carry forward and complete many industrial processes, under the public eye, in that part of the French section of the great machinery gallery which borders on the Algerian section. Indeed, within the square set aside for Class 95, are some picturesque Arabs embroidering slippers, cutting corks; and in two exceedingly picturesque, well-disposed corners are Ali Ben Mohammed, of Algiers, embroidering purses and slippers, and two jewellers from Tlemcen working delicate silver fili-gree-work, with a few tools and a little charcoal fire. Native work—amusing and pleasant to the artist's eye, but not socially instructive to the workman and manufacturer—goes forward daily in the Egyptian Bazaar in the park. The Commissioners admit, in their prefatory notice to this class, that their idea has been only partially realized. They

Intended exhibits of the class.

Actual exhibits.

M R
JERROLD
ON INSTRU-
MENTS, &C.
OF
SKILLED
WORKMEN.
—
acknowledge that they could find only a few independent skilled workmen who could command the means so to instal themselves in the Exhibition as to present to the public an exact reproduction of the methods, processes, and tools of their home workshop.   They were compelled to call some manufacturers to the rescue who would agree to exhibit their manufacturing processes, and at the same time give to their workmen employed all the honours which the juries might deem the fair reward of their skill.   By this combination the following industries have been got together under Class 95 :—Engraving on metal, glass, mosaic work, glass-blowing, optical glasswork, composition and printing, furniture-carving, the manufacture of pocket-books, baskets, ivory and horn combs, hats, fans, feathers, flowers, and various small wares, enamelling, precious and hard stones, shells, shawl-designing, artistic beadwork, embroidery, lace and trimming making, diamond cutting and polishing, hairwork, and imitation jewellery.

There may be much that is striking to the uninitiated in these exhibits, which discover to them the skilful flower-maker fashioning roses and violets with her little pincers; the cameo-cutter at his minute work ; the workers of the commonest imitation jewellery, making trinkets by the bushel ; glass-blowing and engraving ; the pasting and contriving of porte-monnaies and pocket-books ; the laceworkers at their cushions, and M. Dupont's female compositors hand-
Absence of
novelty in
the exhibits.
ling the composing-stick ; and the manufacture of screw-boots and of felt hats.   But I cannot find any new tools that are employed in these exhibits, nor the revelation of any process that is not familiar to every follower of the trade in which it is employed.

Industries
carried on
in the
French
section.
The three or four specially interesting industries that are carried on under Class 95, in the French section, are the manufacture chiefly of felt hats by Haas, and the making of silk hats by the associated working hatmakers of Paris ; the lace manufacture by Lefebure ; the lens grinding and polishing of Lemaire ; the ivory-turning of the Maison Moreau ; the hair net-making of Girard-Thibault ; the fine and delicate gold embroidery executed by Dupuis and Co's workwomen ; the wood carvers ; the comb-cutting by machinery of E. Casella ; and M. Bernard's diamond-cutting.   There are some other pretty exhibitions of dainty work.   The glass-engraver at his delicate labour, the girls twisting columns of glass over a blowpipe into branches of flowers, the imitation-pearl blowing, and the rapid manufacture of common fans are amusing and instructive to the general visitor, as the manufacture of screwed boots unquestionably is.   But it is

impossible to maintain that the new felting machine, or the process which is carried on—much of it by machinery—by the workmen of M. Haas, is anything like home work, or labour which a skilled workman could carry on with the help of one or two paid associates. Nor is the manufacture of screw boots by machinery an industry which a skilled workman could compass with the help of a few apprentices, or in his family. Moreover, the manufacture of screw-boots, which necessitates complicated and expensive machinery, does not come fairly within Class 95. The Exhibition includes a revelation in bootmaking which has astonished and perplexed all the authorities in the trade from Mr. Sparkes Hall downwards. Among the English exhibits of boots is one by Mr. Glew. He shows at the bottom of his case some boots, the soles of which have been sewn on, and solidly and neatly sewn on too, by machinery. For years the bootmakers have been endeavouring to contrive a machine that would sew the sole to the upper leather. The difficulty has been solved at length; but nobody has been able, down to the present time, to get even a peep at the machine. It is not in the Exhibition. Its appearance would have created great curiosity and commotion in the boot trade; whereas the French exhibits of screw-boot making affords no new knowledge to the bootmaker. I cannot part from this subject without remarking that, after a minute examination of all the boot and shoe manufacturers in the Exhibition, leading authorities in the trade have agreed that the best handwork in the building is in the case of George Player, of George-street, Euston-road. Every boot and shoe in his exhibit is the work of his own hands; and he boasts that he is the only workman who ever received an international prize medal. He should have been included in Class 94, for he is a working-man who not only fairly and honestly presents for competitive examination the work of his own hands, but this work is admitted by competent authorities to be better than any shown by great manufacturers.

M. Lemaire's is an interesting exhibit; but it is that of an important manufacturer who employs about 150 workmen. M. Lemaire is the inventor of a new and most ingenious labour-saving machine for grinding and polishing lenses. This machine, which is at work in the French gallery, polishes seven glasses at the same time. The manual labour saved is immense, since one man can attend to ten of these steam-driven machines, which have now been in use about six months. There is very little home-work in this trade. The workman is paid by the piece, and his average wages

MR.
JERROLD
ON INSTRU-
MENTS, &c.
OF
SKILLED
WORKMEN.

are 5½ f. for a day of twelve hours. M. Lemaire's factory is specially interesting as showing the care of the employer for the employed. It includes a schoolmaster, who is ready to teach all who may desire to learn, and the roof of the factory has been arranged as a walk, or recreation ground, in the most ingenious manner.

The lace industry of France employs, it has been officially estimated, 240,000 women, of whom nearly 60,000 are to be found in Normandy alone. The point-lace workers of Alençon and Bayeux work in great ateliers. M. Lefébure, whose workwomen are in the French 95th class has opened special workshops at Bayeux, in order, he says, to break through the old prejudices of the isolated workwomen, and to get new effects of light and shade by an intelligent variation of the net that fills the flowers. A dress of this improved lace is exhibited in Class 33. One of the lacemakers who is seen at work, works all the Alençon points; but the rule is to have a different workwoman for each point, and there are twelve or fourteen varieties. Two or three years' apprenticeship is necessary to obtain fair skill in this work. The Alençon lacemaker earns from one to two shillings per day.

Black lace making is a much more important industry, and is the resource of the wives and daughters of agricultural labourers in Lower Normandy. This delicate and difficult industry has not been yet aided by machinery, even for the preparation of the cards. The card pricking is an operation that requires so much patience and regularity that many who begin to learn it are driven away from it by its tedium. M. Lefébure has educated girls to do this part of the work, which has hitherto been generally accomplished by men. The visitor will see at a glance, by watching the three women at this lacemaking, the use of the card. This industry is, as carried on in Lower Normandy, for instance, essentially a home one. At the age of five and six the little girls of the Norman villages begin to learn the art of lacemaking. When they grow up, and become mothers, the lacemaking occupies them profitably while the husband is at work in the fields. They can leave it at any moment, as in the harvest time, when they, too, work in the fields. It is difficult to get at the average earnings of a Norman peasant women by lacemaking, but an ordinary day's work may be safely said to produce a shilling to the workwoman.

Near the laceworkers are the makers of hair ornaments, who appear under the wing of Beaufour, Lemonnier, and Girard-Thibault. The former firm make hair ornaments mounted in gold, as jewellery; and the latter fashion hair-nets. M. Lemonnier's workmen and workwomen carry on their trade in his workshop. The trade is chiefly in the hands of women, whose wages vary between two and four francs per diem. The only men employed are special art-workmen in the trade, who earn from eight to ten francs a day.

The hair-net trade, represented by three workmen in the employ of M. Girard-Thibault, has increased enormously of late years. It is estimated that there are now 15,000 women and girls employed in it in France. Nets made by machinery are, of course, much cheaper than those made by hand. To the present time, the result of the introduction of machinery into this trade has been beneficial to the makers of nets by hand. The argument is that machine-made nets have created a taste for hair-nets. The cheap machine-made net is found to be frail and bad, and then the wearer casts it aside and buys the more durable, if dearer, hand-made net. Thus machinery has stimulated the employment of female manual labour in the provinces as well as in Paris. The country net or mitten maker earns about 10*d.* a day, and the Parisian workwoman can make 2*s.* A great export trade in hair-nets, mittens, &c., from France to England and to distant places—to Havannah, Chili, Brazil—has arisen of late years. The house to which the three workwomen in Class 95 belong employs more than fifteen hundred hands, and there are fifteen hair-net manufacturing houses in Paris.

Ivory-turning is carried on, as a rule, in great and not in little workshops. Steam is employed only in the very large factories. Most of the machinery is worked by the hand or by the foot. There are a few ivory-turners who work independently under their own roof. A firm that employs from twelve to fifteen ivory-turners, as the exhibiting house of M. Moreau, must have a large trade. The work which this house produces, and which is to be seen in progress, is the turning of billiard-balls and the carving of little ornamental objects. The wages for ordinary workmen are between 3*s.* 6*d.* and 5*s.* a day. Of course the highly-skilled artistic sculptors in ivory command, according to their talent, much higher wages.

The exhibit of the Working Hatmakers' Association is interesting as the result of a combination of 220 workmen, each of whom has, at least, a share of 100f. in the general undertaking. The association has a capital of 40,000f. As a rule, the society employs only from twenty to twenty-two of its members at a time. The rest labour in other work-shops, but all participate, each according to the amount of

Marginal notes:

Mr. JERROLD ON INSTRU-MENTS, &c. OF SKILLED WORKMEN.

Hair-nets.

Ivory turning.

Working Hatmakers' Association.

Mr.
JERROLD
ON INSTRU-
MENTS, &c.
OF
SKILLED
WORKMEN.
—

his shareholding, in the profits of the society. The introduction of machinery into hatmaking caused great commotion in 1855, but it has now been long accepted as a *fait
accompli*, and the workmen no longer complain that they
suffer by it. A Paris working hatmaker earns generally about
4*s.* a day.

Diamond
cutting and
polishing.

M. Bernard's diamond cutters and polishers are Dutchmen,
whom he has brought to Paris to endeavour to establish a
Parisian diamond-cutting trade. But this trade requires an
apprenticeship of twelve or thirteen years, and in Holland,
at least is poorly paid. M. Bernard, I believe, is helped in
his endeavour by a subsidy from the French Government.

Conclusion.

In conclusion, although the results sought by the Imperial
Commissioners in planning the tenth group have not been
realized, at least in Classes 94 and 95, these classes express
a generous and a lofty intention. They constitute a recognition of the workman's right to some share in the honours
of a universal exhibition of industry. I think a more immediate and practical good, however, might have been attained
by the arrangement of a complete exhibition of cheapness,
on the plan of that hastily got together by Prince Napoleon
in 1855, and also by a comprehensive and complete exhibition of the industry of female hands.

List of
works on
French
industry.

I append a list of works on French industry, and especially on Paris industry, that may be useful to those who
are seeking a thorough knowledge of work and wages in
France :—

The two inquiries into the state and customs of the industries of Paris instituted by the Paris Chamber of Commerce.

The annual general reports of the Assistance Publique,
edited by the chief administrator, M. Armand Husson.

" Annales du Travail." Rue Notre Dame des Victoires, 11.

" Notice sur l'Universelle, Société dans le but de propager
les Associations co-opératives et toutes les Institutions utiles
en général." Guillaumin et Cie., Rue Richelieu.

" Statistique de l'Industrie de la France." Par A. Moreau
de Jonnès. Guillaumin et Cie., Rue Richelieu, 17.

" L'Enquête du Dixième Groupe, Catalogue Analytique."
Dentu, Libraire.

" Les Populations Ouvrières." Par A. Audiganne.
Capelle, Rue Soufflet, 16.

" L'Annuaire de la Charité." Par E. Knoepflin. Dentu.

" Les Ouvriers de Paris." Par Pierre Vinçard. Gosselin,
Libraire.

MR.
JERROLD
ON INSTRU-
MENTS, &c.
OF
SKILLED
WORKMEN.

" Rapports des Délégués des Ouvriers Parisiens à l'Exposition de Londres en 1862.   Chabaud, Rue Dauphine, 34.

" L'Ouvrière."   Par Jules Simon.

" Les Institutions Ouvrières de Mulhouse et des Environs."   Par Eugène Véron.

" Le Travail."   Par Jules Simon.

" Statistique de la France."   Par Maurice Block.

" Consommations de Paris."   Par Armand Husson. Guillaumin, Rue Richelieu, 14.

" The Children of Lutetia ; or, Travels among the Working Poor of Paris."   By Blanchard Jerrold.